AUTONOMY

Life Cycle, Gender and Status among Himalayan Pastoralists

Aparna Rao

Berghahn Books
NEW YORK • OXFORD

First published in 1998 by
Berghahn Books

Library of Congress Cataloging-in-Publication Data
Rao, Aparna.
Autonomy : life cycle, gender, and status among Himalayan pastoralists / Aparna Rao.
p. cm.
Includes bibliographical references and index.
ISBN 1-57181-903-7 (alk. paper)
1. Bakrawallah (Indic people)--Psychology. 2. Bakrawallah (Indic people)-- Ethnic identity. 3. Bakrawallah (Indic people)--Social conditions. 4. Identity (Psychology)--India--Jammu and Kashmir. 5. Individuality--India--Jammu and Kashmir. 6. Muslims--India--Jammu and Kashmir. 7. Jammu and Kashmir (India)--Social conditions. I. Title.
DS432.B32R36 1997 97-15842
306'.089'914--dc21 CIP

British Library Cataloguing in Publication Data
A catalogue record for this book is available from the British Library.

Printed in the United States on acid-free paper.

For Ma – who has taught me to think autonomously, while feeling embedded

For Michael – who appreciates my acting as an autonomous partner

CONTENTS

Acknowledgements

The question of individuality confronted me early in my childhood. My parents were very much concerned with the assertion and affirmation of what they personally felt was right, and just. These views diverged at times across generations or along gender lines – and these were the moments at which the embeddedness of the individual became so important. Not in terms of "hierarchy", but in those of mutual love and respect. To take decisions without as far as possible hurting another's feelings, to be largely "in-dependent", and yet be there for one another, to think of the needs of others while trying to fulfil one's own desires – this was the stuff of daily "negotiation" between individual autonomy and embeddedness. Without this background, I believe, the field research for this book would not even have begun.

From the start numerous persons have contributed towards the making of this book. I have received help at various stages of research, data analysis and writing. To the very large number of Bakkarwal women and men in Jammu and Kashmir who appear in this book anonymously goes my deepest gratitude. I owe them the times of joy (and occasional frustration) found in a process of communication and learning, and thank them for permission to quote them.

This study would never have been what it is without the help, understanding and enthusiasm of Mr P. Padmanabha (then Registrar General of India), the late Dr N.G. Nag (Census, Delhi), and Mr H.L. Kalla (then at the Census Office, Srinagar). Dr

G.M. Wani (then Director, Sheep Husbandry Department, Srinagar) first introduced me to the Bakkarwal in the Kashmir Valley; his depth of knowledge concerning local concepts and practices of animal husbandry helped me broaden the scope of my own work. Dr R.P. Tandon (Sheep Husbandry Department, Kathua) took me along on many of his field trips and provided me with many insights. I shall always remember the hospitality of the Wani and Tandon families. My deep gratitude also goes to Dr K.C. Singh (Director, Sheep Husbandry Department, Jammu) for first introducing me to Bakkarwal families in the Jammu area, to Dr K.R. Sharma of the same department, to Dr S.K. Magotra (Reasi Sheep Breeding Farm) and to Dr Ticku of the Lal Ded Hospital, Srinagar, for help and advice in the early stages of fieldwork.

I am also deeply indebted to Mr Abdul Ghani Kucey, his brother Manzoor, and his mother Mrs Hajra for unforgettable moments of companionship and weeks of hospitality. Out of the "field", and yet in it in many ways, Mr Hakim Shaukat Ali, Mrs Zahida Mir, Mr and Mrs Mohammad Aslam, Prof. Arun Kumar Bose and Mrs Bose provided for hours of relaxation, conversation and comfort in Srinagar, Pahalgam and Jammu respectively. I am grateful for their attempts to provide me with a home away from home.

I am indebted to the German Research Council (DFG) for financing this study, and to Prof. Ulla Johansen (Institut für Völkerkunde, University of Cologne) for sponsoring it. I would like to acknowledge the affiliation I was granted for purposes of field research in Jammu and Kashmir by the Nehru Memorial Museum, Delhi, and the Department of Anthropology, Delhi University.

Andrea Mick was of invaluable help in the analysis of the quantitative data presented here; I would like to thank her for her resourcefulness and patience in dealing with piles of often very unorganised data. In hours of meticulous work my husband drew all the figures for this book; for this I would like to thank him, although he claims to have rather enjoyed the drudgery. To Goetz Leineweber's skills at the computer I owe the final preparation of the manuscript; without his assistance this book would certainly have taken even longer to go into print. Finally, a word of thanks to Shawn Kendrick for meticulous copy-editing and drawing my attention to a number of errors.

Several persons have spared time to read previous versions of one or more chapters of this book: Monika Böck, Thomas Helmig, T.N. Madan, Erwin Orywal, Pnina Werbner, my mother, and my husband on whom I inflicted all the chapters at one stage or another. Many of their valuable suggestions and incisive thoughts have contributed to this final version, and I am grateful to them all. Needless to add that in spite of all this "embeddedness", I alone am responsible for any factual errors, faulty logic, or lack of cogency in the various chapters that follow.

In my quest of individuals and dividuals, in the field and out of it, Michael Casimir and Amiya Rao have unfailingly walked the same road with me; together they have held me to myself.

A Note on Transcription

This study contains names and terms in the Bakkarwali, Urdu, Persian, Arabic, Panjabi, Hindi, Sanskrit, and Kashmiri languages. The abbreviations Ar., Hd., Pnj., Pers., Skt., and Ur. stand for Arabic, Hindi, Panjabi, Persian, Sanskrit, and Urdu respectively. The term "Bakkarwal" as well as all terms in Urdu, Persian, Arabic, Panjabi, Hindi, and Sanskrit have been transliterated, while all Bakkarwali and Kashmiri terms have been transcribed. I have tried to minimise complication and confusion, but a certain amount of inconsistency is inevitable especially as far as personal names are concerned.

In both transcribing and transliterating a macron indicates a long vowel and a dot below a consonant denotes a retroflex; all aspirated consonants are followed by an "h". The Devanagari and Arabic (or Urdu) characters have been transcribed and transliterated as shown below:

	TRANSCRIPTION		TRANSLITERATION	
	Devanagari	Arabic/Urdu		Arabic/Urdu
č	च	چ	ḥ	ح
čh	छ		<u>kh</u>	خ
h (rather than ḥ)		ح	ʿ	ع , ʿ
j (as in mijāj)	ज	ج		
k (rather than q)		ق		
ñ	ं , ँ			
s	स			
sh	श , ष			
z (as in zāt)	ज	ز		

List of Figures and Tables

Introduction

The question of individuality in non-European societies, and especially in those of South Asia is a much debated one. As part of this general discussion, many studies have appeared in recent years on South Asian concepts of "self" and "person". Almost all of these have, however, concentrated on ideologies, the question of practice being largely neglected. Using data collected in more than two years of field research among the Bakkarwal, Muslim nomadic pastoralists in Jammu and Kashmir (Fig. I.1), this book attempts to discuss the interplay between cultural ideals and context-specific social practice. I am fairly confident of not wrongly inventing the ubiquitous "other" when asserting that in Bakkarwal society the existence of individuals is recognised in both theory and practice, and that a certain demonstration of individuality – defined as the assertion of difference and even uniqueness on the part of one being in a given context – is appreciated, and is justified by the context-specific manipulation of ideology. I hasten to add that a clear distinction is made in this society, and correctly I believe, between individuality and individualism. Obeyesekere (1990b: 245–6) rightly points out that in much anthropological writing (cf. also Bhargava 1992) there has been

> a confusion of individualism with individuality/individual … "individualism" as a socioeconomic and historical condition can easily be confused with "individual", that is, with an individual's sense of himself as a separate being.

This confusion has been especially marked in studies of South Asian societies, and was perhaps inadvertently intensified by Dumont's chapter entitled "individualisme et holisme" (Dumont 1966: 22ff.). Although he is one of the few to define the term "individual" here, he does not distinguish between the philosophical connotations of the terms "individualiste", "l'individu" and "individualisme".

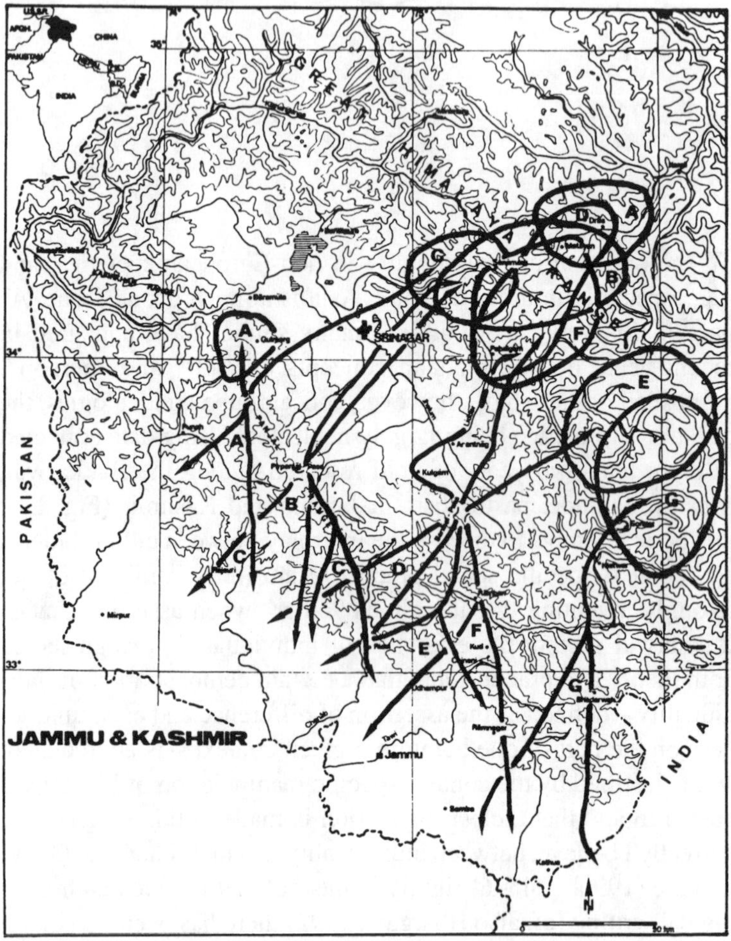

Figure I.1 Overview of the summer and winter areas of the Bakkarwal and of their principal routes of migration in the 1980s

The Spider in the Web

Commenting on Geertz' (1993: 5) almost aphoristic description of man as "… an animal suspended in webs of significance he himself has spun …", Obeyesekere (1990a: 285) wonders where the spider, the maker of these webs, is to be found. This question is especially pertinent to the debate on the concepts of the "individual". In the chapters that follow I shall endeavour to identify such web spinners, to enquire into their genesis, to discuss their growth, their life and death. But I shall also show that not all who (may seem to the anthropologist to) spin the webs are recognised as spiders, that not all spiders are allowed – by fellow spiders and by themselves – to live out their spiderhood. The web spun – analytically speaking by all the spiders together – is recognised as being spun by only a few, select spiders. And even these few often speak of themselves and of all other spiders as being "… absorbed in [their] surroundings" (Kakar 1978: 32) – inert objects, so to say, suspended in all-empowering webs. The women and men I speak of (in pseudonyms, except for some men of authority, past or present, too well known locally to be disguised), and who, I believe, speak (also in pseudonyms) through me in this book may indeed not try to trace (cf. Delaney 1991: 37) the meaning contained in the tangled mass of fine strands. The web as a whole is taken for granted, and its overall meaning would, I was often told, "be known to God alone"; but they do try to identify and trace single strands, to sort out parts of the web. By doing so they do not necessarily question, let alone challenge any part of the fine structure. They largely reproduce it by devolving, through habit and a conviction grown out of a subaltern ethos, accountability and agency on a chosen few – those deemed worthy of real spiderhood. After all, no two spiders are the same, though all may be part of the same web, just as "no five fingers of a hand are identical, though all go to make one working hand" (a proverb known in many versions in large parts of South Asia: e.g. Berland 1982). The interstices within the structure afford a still smaller number of these recognised, and even authorised, agents the possibility to weave new strands, to cross old ones – to bring in subtle changes. Depending on certain limits set by ideology but also by the real, material possibilities of choice, innovations are thus introduced by a few and tolerated and even accepted by others. Though "God Almighty is the ultimate cause of all", in daily discourse a basic theory of proximate causation leads to both personal fortunes and misfortunes being said to lie in one's own intrinsic nature. Yet, unlike, say, among the Newar of Nepal (Parish 1987: 13) or the Burmese (Spiro 1993), this does not lead to a clear-cut delegation of responsibility to every woman and man; thanks to the very specific nature each has, some are more accountable than others, and it is these who are endowed with agency. While some may never attain the status of an agent, those with the right inherent capacities do so with time. Indeed, no one is born as an agent. Just as the fingers of a hand, or – to use an informant's analogy – "the different branches of a growing tree change in shape and size over the years", so do the spiders, and with them their capacity to spin significance, to act out their eventual agency. In different phases of their lives people thus take certain decisions (or participate in processes of decision making) and make specific choices, which may or may not be identified as decisions and choices, depending on the extent to which their agency is recognised.

This book then, discusses the acknowledgement and denial of human agency, the culturally produced constraints it is subjected to, and the culturally constructed explanations of these constraints. Qualitative and quantitative data concerning the premises for, as well as the practice of, taking, formulating and implementing decisions over the life course are used to discuss and analyse agency, in terms of both cultural consensus and individual experience. This processual approach does not stop short at a one-to-one relation between formal decision making and agency. It explores the capacity of women and men "... to manipulate their ... environment" (Dyson and Moore 1983: 45), but goes beyond this to take into account the conceptualisation and formulation of local categories. It simultaneously dispenses with the "... radical [Cartesian] distinction between mind and body, [and the] ... parallel distinction [made by] contemporary anthropologists between mind and culture" (Obeyesekere 1990a: 285).

Agency – Whose, and How Much?

The *Oxford Paperback English Dictionary* defines the term *agency* as "the business ... of an agent; the means of action through which something is done". The term *agent* is in its turn defined thus: "a person who does something or instigates some activity...; one who acts on behalf of another ...; something that produces an effect or change." In the English language the concept of agency is thus linked to activity, rather than passivity, eventually to surrogacy and always to a certain dynamism. It is further linked to the much debated notion of the "person". Time and again in the history of anthropological discourse, terms denoting specific concepts prevalent in Western cultural contexts have been applied to other societies. In their original contexts the meanings and implications of these terms were, perhaps, fairly clear; transported elsewhere, these terms not seldom start off as misnomers and end up creating a "... somewhat baffling mist of uncertainty" (MacCormack 1976: 89). Not just "self", "person" and "individual", but also "agency" may well be such misnomers in certain cultural contexts.

There is no real equivalent in Bakkarwali for the English term *agency*, and the nearest one could get to the term *"agent"* would be *kārāḷo* – he who "does", "works", hence the actor. But this would be thoroughly misleading, since *kārāḷo* denotes the husband (cf. Ch. 5 for details). Besides, there are two words in Bakkarwali – *shakas* and *bandā* – which also denote "one who acts"; while the former is applied not only to humans, the latter is restricted to humans identifiable with specific roles – i.e. to those who act in obedience not only to God, but to their specific contexts and circumstances (cf. Chs. 1, 2 for details). The way out of the dilemma, I suggest, lies in the (I believe universal) logic behind the cultural construction of the English term *agency*.

All action presupposes either conscious or subconscious decision making and implementation (or more or less "instinctive" fixed motor patterns, which are of no concern to us here). As contemporary research in cognitive anthropology points out, every action is preceded by goal-orientated cognition wherein context-specific selection of the appropriate behaviour takes place. By conscious I mean an explicit process of reflection; by subconscious, one that is implicit and routinised, much in Bourdieu's sense of habitus. Taking decisions (incidentally, both the concept and terminology exist in Bakkarwali) universally presupposes the cognitive and material capacity to choose between at least a minimum of perceived alternatives; implementing these requires the material and cognitive framework within which to do so. If, therefore, we observe the making of choices, the taking of decisions and the translation of these into action, we can expect to get reasonably reliable information on the practice of agency, irrespective of cultural constructions. Since our observations must be context specific, we can also obtain data on who these agents are, why, for whom and on whose behalf they (are said to) act. In other words, we learn much about the roles and status of these observed agents.

As mentioned above, in Bakkarwal society not every observed agent is, however, permitted this culturally ascribed prerogative, just as not every observed decision taken and choice made is granted the status of a decision or a choice (cf. Chs. 3, 5 for details). The status of agent then, is culturally produced. Following the logic of cause and effect, every decision is considered in this society to be the basis for further decision making, and while correct decisions are said to enhance the state of being well, or well-being *(bal),* wrong decisions are held to destroy it. Well-being is defined in the *Concise Oxford Dictionary* as consisting of good health, happiness and prosperity. It is used here to gloss the Bakkarwali term *bal* (lit. vigour, strength), which, following a kind of Lakoffian (1987: 273ff.) "conceptual embodiment", serves as a body metaphor to connote a state of ordered plenty, attained through optimal physical, psychological, economic and social balance. Indeed, both physical feelings and emotions are generally expressed in bodily terms; for example *dildardi* denotes both sadness and stomach-ache, *sirdardi* means both headache and worry, while *khushi* is used to cover both happiness and good health. In this the Bakkarwal appear to conform to a widespread South Asian pattern, in which "physical symptoms" are associated with "a corresponding mental or emotional phenomenon" (Hoch 1966 in Kakar 1978: 33). The usual form of greeting in Bakkarwal society is "*bal e*?", which means not "how are you?", but "are you well, strong, healthy?" This culturally defined concept of well-being approximates fairly well with the idea of "subjective wellbeing" as defined, for example, by Diener 1984: 562 (cf. also Grob 1995; Myers and Diener 1996). Though based on the concept of good mental and physical health it diverges entirely on the other hand from Kakar's (1978: 33) interpretation of the term *svastha* (used in Hindi and other North Indian languages to denote "health"), which he traces etymologically to "… the root '*swa*' (I) and '*astha*' (stable) …", and which for him "… implies something which is resident, present or stable in the 'I'…". This "something" is "present or stable" "not in the body, not in the mind, not in the various organs or selves, but in the underlying *atman*". Unfortunately, Kakar does not elaborate on this. Nor does he say why he chooses to translate the term thus, since more ready glosses would be "self-present", "being in one's natural state", "being one self", or "being self-abiding" (Monier-Williams 1976: 1277) – in other words a "self" (*sva*) in a perfect state of well-being having/requiring no external help or interference.

However defined, well-being must in all cultural and social contexts be a desired aim, and ideally decisions taken must logically also aim at keeping as close as possible towards the context-specific, desirable optimum. Among the Bakkarwal the wise are said to be so precisely because, thanks to certain innate properties, they are capable of judging situations, optimising accordingly (or alternatively maximising under given constraints), and thereby negotiating ceaselessly. Those with little well-being are considered to be living manifestations of a chain of wrong decisions, just as those with great well-being are said to have proved that (by God's grace) they are capable of making the right choices. Hence, the former are judged unworthy of taking decisions, while the latter are said to have proved that they are capable of correct decision making. The former are thus often entrusted into the care of the latter; in other words, the latter are considered eligible to take decisions for themselves and for others in their charge. The freedom to choose is thus seen as a value (but this does not mean that those who are convinced of their inability to take the right decisions hanker after this freedom), and here I take issue with, for example, Apffel Marglin and Mishra (1992: 31) who write: "Freedom of choice as a value presupposes the unitary self, possessor of its body, locus of a natural resource. This in turn presupposes labour as a commodity freely available on the market." Among the Bakkarwal labour is (or at least was till very recently) by no means "a freely available commodity" (cf. Ch. 4, Rao 1995), and yet the freedom to choose is highly rated. I also take issue with Milner (1994: 133) when he writes that "Those who exercise domination … are also the ones best able to redistribute risk and deflect blame". Not so in Bakkarwal society (cf. Ch. 5), since blaming someone who is conceived of as intrinsically incapable of taking blame would be pointless.

Since choice is regarded as crucial, decisions are considered vital and can not be left to all and sundry. The decisions taken by every woman, man and child before acting cannot be observed; their actions can. Since their decisions cannot be recognised as such, the importance of their actions is belittled. Only decisions taken by men credited with much well-being are recognised as "decisions" *(phesla)*. Especially those actions which analytically must be categorised as decisions but are locally considered as pertaining to the purely domestic domain are disregarded as decisions – by both men and women. Of course, not just the Bakkarwal, but social scientists too have often been rather biased about which actions may be classified as decisions. Keddie and Beck, for example, while perhaps correctly stating (1978: 18ff.) that "… most Middle Eastern women lack … freedom of choice regarding basic life decisions", do not consider what degrees of choice are realistically available to a woman, or for that matter a man, in specific economic and political contexts. Nor do they differentiate between ideology and its eventually direct or indirect manipulation in private and public spaces.

Agency in Bakkarwal society thus needs to be understood from two perspectives – one (in rare contexts there may be more) constructed and produced locally, and one (the analytical) perceived and constructed by me, an anthropologist as observer. The former is privileged here, not only because it has statistical prevalence, but also insofar as it has rhetorical power to shape cultural models. It is, however, in the connection of the two perspectives that the ideology and practice of agency can be grasped.

As animal husbanders and breeders, the Bakkarwal are keen observers of the hereditary transmission of traits. Although God alone is all powerful, parentage, the quality of air and soil, and other features familiar from the work of Marriott and others among South Asian Hindus (and partly discussed in the following chapters) play no mean role, in their view, in influencing and even determining a person's material and cognitive capacities. This is, in short, the basic ideology behind the dominant view mentioned above. It is this ideology which governs the granting or denial of both agency and autonomy, a term to which I now turn.

"Autonomy" has been defined as "self-governance, independence" (*Oxford Paperback English Dictionary*). Another cognate term of interest here is *autarchy*, defined in the same source as "self-sufficiency" (especially in the economic sphere); its original Greek connotation may, however, be more relevant to our context: "... a state in which the sage desires nothing outside the immediate control of his will and reason" (Perrett 1989: 57). In other words, a state in which one is not desirous of any action beyond one's own control; a state in which the subject is nearly supreme, and agency approaches perfection. In recent years notable attempts have been made by anthropologists to relate the degree of autonomy to variables such as economic forms, degrees of hierarchy and types of social organisation. Thus, for example, Gardner (1991), in a cross-cultural comparison of thirty-seven foraging societies, comes up with the concept of the "individual autonomy syndrome", based on observations of decision making among these communities. In the pages that follow I too touch upon the relation between autonomy understood as "independence" – especially in observed decision making and/or implementation – an economy based on mobile animal husbandry, and the social organisation of an Islamic community. Most of the ten criteria Gardner lists (such as the principle of immediate return, or extreme equality between the sexes) are most certainly not met by the Bakkarwal. However, complete independence (entire lack of dependence on others) does not and obviously can not exist in any society; just as agency must always remain incomplete and the subject an imperfect one, so too "self-governance" can never be total.

What, however, is the "self" that is to govern – or be governed? "The self" is something that has long fascinated philosophers and social scientists, and still "... continues to hold center-stage position in psychology" (Banaji 1994: 297). The last twenty-five years have also seen a tremendous resurgence in anthropological interest in the topic (e.g. Fogelson 1979; Heelas and Lock 1981; Marsella, DeVos, and Hsu 1985; Crapanzano 1990). The roots of the concept of self are deeply embedded in human ontology (cf. also Hallowell 1955; James 1981). The world must per force be perceived in relation to oneself, for cognizance always takes the ego as its starting point (cf. Sacks 1987: 42). In every process of reflection, the importance of subjectivity is evident, since human perception and understanding of the world entail the intertwining of the perceiver and the perceived. The self as the perceiver (or part thereof) and the world (of which the self is a part) as perceived are thus inseparable from each other; hence, contrary to an argument put forward recently (Antony 1993), "… one's social relations are [essential] to the nature of one's thoughts". To reflect over something is to interact with the world; in other words, subjectivity is simultaneously constrained and constraining. Humans can use a combination of subjectivity and analogical reasoning to empathise and evaluate the similarities between their own and others' thoughts/emotions and actions, empathy being defined as "… the self-conscious awareness of the consciousness of the other" (Wispé 1968 in Vogel 1985: 377). The capacity to empathise is universal; how, when and with whom one empathises can be culturally formed (also see Ch. 7). The principle on which this is founded has in its turn been described by psychologists as follows:

> Worauf es ankommt, ist die psychische Abgrenzung eines Ichs, dem ich-eigene Erlebnisse zugeordnet werden können, vom Anderen als Träger der diesem zugehörigen Erlebnisse, wodurch eine Unterscheidung von Gefühlen mit "Ich-Charakter" gegenüber Gefühlen mit "Du-Charakter" möglich wird (Bischof-Köhler 1988 in Anzenberger 1991: 16)

Although such definitions and concepts are Western in origin, similar basic experiences ("Erlebnisse") exist in all cultures. Among the Bakkarwal these "experiences" are invariably said to be very basic ones: hunger, cold, shame, etc. Psychologists also hold that the basis for empathy lies in the existence of the concept of self (as perceived in the West), which from early childhood onwards gradually enables one to distinguish between him/herself and others. This concept of self is also generally thought of by psychologists to be composed of two components – personal and social identity – which refer to perceived similarities and differences at the individual and group levels (Banaji 1994: 310ff.). It is in the context of the perception of the interaction of self and non-self (who does not, necessarily, have to be viewed as the "other") that decision making and all processes of cognition take place. The degree of autonomy mirrored in the degrees of strategic freedom of action of a given man or woman is both dependent upon and constrained by the continuous interaction with others in a range of contexts. This interaction also leads to and is a precursor of what is generally known as self-introspection, which thus acts as a fuse to the prior self. Increasingly psychologists go further to suggest that the self must be viewed from a motivational perspective, which is closely related to the "... more basic tendency to seek pleasure and to avoid pain" (Banaji 1994: 299) – in other words to reach and maintain a certain level of well-being.

Given this ontological basis, we must, as anthropologists, now proceed to ask what *cultural* forms such concepts take in different societies. Yet, as we know from the abundant anthropological literature on the topic, the use of the term "self" and of the term "person" is ambiguous and highly problematic. As an example, two often cited studies are those of Hallowell (1959) and Shweder and Bourne (1984). Both deal with the question of the locus of subjective experience; but whereas the former refers to this locus as "self", the latter refer to it as "person". Between 1952, when Radcliffe-Brown wrote (pp. 193–4) that "... the failure to distinguish individual and person is ... a source of confusion in science", and 1980, when John Beattie noted (p. 313) that "confusion arises because we sometimes tend to use the terms 'self', 'person' and 'individual' as though they were interchangeable...", things hardly changed. In 1981 Strathern (p. 168) observed, "the terms 'person' and 'individual' are used in a number of ways, sometimes as synonyms, sometimes diacritically, sometimes in antithesis", and even today many authors do not care to define the ways in which they use these terms (cf. Desjarlais 1989; Hollan 1992; Spiro 1993: 114ff.). What exactly are we to make of the following statement regarding the Ilongot, for example

> ... the *individual man's* most intense "*sense of self*" is won when, casting off a victim's head, he establishes himself as an "angry" man – *autonomous because constrained by none.* (Rosaldo 1989: 226, emphasis added)

Or do Soharis, among whom women are, we learn, more "autonomous" than men, differentiate between a "... person's value in his own eyes ..." and "... a person's self-regard ..." (Wikan 1982: 163)? In this book I shall use the terms "self", "person" and "individual" in order to avoid cumbersome circumlocutions, but first I shall try to define the ways in which I use them. Such definitions do not in any way contradict the eventually protean ideology or practice concerning such concepts (e.g. Rosaldo 1986; Hollan 1992; Lifton 1993) – they only help us in understanding and explaining.

Self, Person, Individual

Self and Selfhood

The term "self" is used here to gloss the Bakkarwali term *shakas* which denotes a potentially autonomous being (understood as a relatively independent subject of action). This potential for autonomy can be traced to intrinsic and innate properties (*nafas*) that I sum up here under the term "selfhood". For the Bakkarwal these properties are universal, and all living or created beings, not just humans, are endowed with them in some measure, though certainly not equally. These properties, they believe, are largely influenced by biological factors (both environmental and familial) inherited over one or more generations, for example, during gestation, at birth, via mother's milk or other nourishment. Each self is based on a corresponding selfhood, and according to this understanding of the term, self does not denote a static property; it is, rather, a state of being that alters, following variation in the quantity (though not the quality) of selfhood – a change that generally takes place over the life span. This fluctuation and its implications will be traced in the following six chapters.

Person

Whereas the term "self" is used here to denote something that is achieved, the term "person" will be used to refer to a kind of holistic ascription. This is in keeping with Bakkarwal usage, whereby "person" is used to translate the Bakkarwali "*bandā*". This may sound familiar to those who with Mauss (1938) recall the idea of the persona and mask, but in Bakkarwal society such an approach would be misleading. Although, ideally, persons must fit certain roles, the precise fit depends on a person's innate temper or intrinsic nature *(mijāj),* and this in turn is related to a property which I gloss as "authenticity" *(akīkat)*; both these concepts are related to ideas about genuineness, about the inner core of a man or woman.

Since one can never successfully play a part which goes against this core, neither concept leaves much room for the metaphor of the theatre. A large measure of well-being is possible only when the fit between persons and their roles approaches perfection, and this is possible only when innate tempers and roles match one another. This again is conceivable only when selfhood and what I refer to as its corresponding personhood are properly proportioned. Innate temper depends on a variety of factors, such as sex, the family and the community one belongs to.

The ascription referred to above takes place in and through social interaction, and it is in and through "the nexus of social relations" (cf. Ingold 1990: 220) that a human child comes to be considered as a person. Yet again, then, the Bakkarwal do not separate the biological from the social, and thus the members of at least this society do not corroborate the distinction – suggested by Radcliffe-Brown (1977: 225) and taken up more recently by, for example, G.G. Harris (1989) – between the "Person", a "complex of social relationships", and the "Individual", a "biological organism". For the Bakkarwal there are no two Durkheimian (1976: 16) "beings" in every human, "an individual being which has its foundations in the organism … and a social being which represents … society". It is in the conjunction and interaction of the three related properties of selfhood, personhood and innate temper that every being is located. This status is partly intimately related to that of others, but is partly distinctive. In other words, individuation is at all times partial, but at certain moments or phases of the life span greater than at others, and for some always less than for others.

Individual

It is undebatable that "… the investigator who seeks ways of asking in rural India about equivalents of Western 'individuals'… risks imposing an alien ontology and an alien epistemology on those who attempt to answer" (Marriott 1989: 3). I did not ask about individuality, or try to find conceptual or terminological equivalents. Indeed, the impulse for this study came in many ways from some of the people themselves: from Makhni, the first wife of a wealthy husbander, who told me, "We are not just Bakkarwal with goats and sheep – we are also women – separate women …";

from Gamo, a poor hired shepherd, who commented, "Bakkarwal is our community, but I also have a heart, a mind ..."; from old Lakhio, who philosophised one day, "We are all humans (*bani ādam*, lit. sons of Adam), some are big, some are small ... but all are the same ... and yet each is different". As social scientists it must be our aim to search for universal equivalents – or at least compare phenomena which may appear equivalent (cf. Piatigorsky 1985 in Marriott 1989: 6). Thus a confrontation of two or more perspectives and models (one being the analytic, which itself is embedded in the folk models of Western science) is at least desirable, if not essential.

One of my informants once explained to me that just "as God made trees of many kinds, so also he made a variety of families; the branches of every single tree are different in size and shape – some break soon, others rot away, still others last many years. So also are the members of each family; some are more alike than others, but each has a specific 'ownness'...", which is partly due to his or her unique relationship with God. These thoughts could be expressed sociologically by repeating what Clyde Kluckhohn and Henry A. Murray (1948) once wrote: that every man is to a certain extent (a) like all other men; (b) like some other men; (c) like no other man. It is the concept informing this last aspect – the dissimilarity between persons – as well as its application that is of concern here; the other two aspects constitute the background to the discussion of the last.

Individuality – understood as the legitimate existence, and eventual assertion, of difference between two or more beings – thus has a base which is inherent, but the status itself must be culturally achieved. The "individual" is, no doubt, as Dumont notes (1970b: 135), "... a mental construct, not a physical phenomenon", but even this construct rests upon concrete physical and "social demarcation" (Morris 1978: 374) which must exist in all societies (see also Howard 1985). Now mental constructs can hardly be observed empirically. The observer has no direct access to "thought or will", even less to the "moral being" Dumont is concerned with; but he/she does have audiovisual access to action and to the actor – to the "subject of speech", to the "independent, autonomous" being. The eventual status of the "individual" may indeed be empirically ascertained only through the recording of discourse and the observation of actions impinging on the autonomy (independence, especially in decision making) of human beings. In other words, once again following Dumont (1970a: 9), the "individual" can be discerned only by locating *both* "the empirical agent, present in every society, in virtue of which he is the main raw material for any sociology" *and* "the rational being and normative subject…", since the former can not exist without the inherent logic of the latter. Hence I chose to concentrate on the empirical study of decision making, and through this on concepts and expressions of both autonomy and individuality. Since difference is relative and only partial, individuation must, following this definition, always be incomplete. Indeed, since agency is enabled only through and within society, there can be no individual without the social; but equally, without individuals one cannot speak of society at any level of organization. It seems to me that in the discussion of individuality several aspects – which may well be interrelated, but must nevertheless be kept distinct for purposes of analysis – are often confused as, for example, when La Fontaine (1992: 91–2) writes:

> Western thinking … gives unique moral worth and independent social identity to each living human; each is conceived of as, to some extent unique … The human being and the social actor are one and the same …

Identity is always relational, and hence can not be independent of everything; of what then, is it independent? Even uniqueness must by dint of logic be subject to certain limits. The intertwining of the individual and society can perhaps be best grasped if one considers the phenomenon of authoritarianism. It has been suggested by some (Dumont 1970a,b; Erikson 1975; Béteille 1991) that authoritarianism and individualism stand in opposition to each other, but this is only a matter of perspective. Authoritarianism is indeed the expression of one individual's more or less successful attempt at nearly absolute autonomy and surrogate decision making. It is a specific kind of assertion of the difference between one human and all others, through the expression of that human's will over and above all other individual wills – this assertion more often than not being veiled in terms of the greater good, or greater well-being, of a greater we-group, such as a state, an ethnic or religious group, or even an extended kin-group. To be authoritarian one must be an individual and have others over whom one can impose one's authority or power.

To discuss the phenomenon of individuality across cultures it is more meaningful, I suggest, to conceive of a human being and her/his relations and connections with other beings and things as positioned contextually anywhere along a continuum which stretches from the purely theoretical concept of the indivisible, entirely discrete being ("in-dividual") right up to that of an indefinitely fractionable man or woman ("di-vidual"). Between these two ends and all along this continuum we may find ideal cultural constructs, or typologies of fissive beings, divisable into two, three or more parts. Behaviour would then entail constant negotiation of one's position along this continuum, the dimensions of negotiation depending on the three factors of age, gender and socio-economic status – their precise significance being culturally determined. Every tolerated, if not accepted, departure from the ideal – and there must be at least a few – must also be culturally legitimated by specific views on human nature, the "self" or other aspects commonly analysed in anthropology under the rubrics of, for example, religion, ethnomedicine or ethnopsychology.

Before turning to the specific discussion of individuals and dividuals in South Asia, let me then first sum up. My basic premise is that a major goal of all humans is to strive towards the attainment and/or maintenance of as great a degree of well-being as possible, the components of well-being being culturally constituted. For this it is obvious that action is required and this in turn entails making choices and taking decisions. Several members of a group may participate in this decision making, but this very participation underlines the existence of separate beings – those who form the group – in other words, of individuals. The action(s) of each of these individuals may not be recognised as such, since the status of "individual" is culturally achieved, though his/her existence is a universal, empirical phenomenon. Further, depending on whether the action of a woman/man is recognised as such, she/he may or may not attain the status of an agent. The more one's action concords with one's person, i.e. with one's ascribed roles, the better the fit between these, and the greater the likelihood of one's agency being recognised. Agency can, however, never be perfect

– it can only approach such a state. The degree to which perfection is approached depends on the amount of selfhood one has, i.e. on the amount of culture-specific properties considered as innate and intrinsic which constitute the locally defined potential for autonomy. Since selfhood, which is also culturally conceived of, varies according to context and hence also over the life span, so also must one's self vary over time. The study of autonomy in any given society must thus take into account a variety of phenomena, such as ideologies (which include the concepts of self and person), socio-economic structures (which include roles and status), the nature and availability of choice and processes of decision making in different contexts.

THE INDIVIDUAL IN SOUTH ASIA

And no burdened soul shall bear the burden of another; and if a heavily laden one shall call for its load [to be carried] it shall not be carried for it at all, even though it be a kinsman

— Qor'an (XXV/18)

True happiness consists in self-reliance.

— Mānava Dharmashāstra IV: 160, 239
in Monier-Williams, *Hinduism*

One of the principal paradigms of the social sciences still applied, albeit with some opposition, states that whereas in "the West" people strive more or less successfully towards the ideal of complete individuation, in non-Western societies sociocentric, familial and community-based orientations dominate to such an extent that both the ideology and practice of individuation are unknown. Accordingly, in these societies identity is conceived of and expressed almost entirely in terms of relationships with others. A still more extreme form of this paradigm is that of the "communal society" in which "... relations of difference pertain between groups; relations of identification pertain within them. Intense interpersonal sentiment, which exists between two individuals, has no niche in this dichotomy" (Mageo 1991: 407). One may pause to wonder where, for example, the intensely interpersonal sentiments of honour and revenge, of love and faithfulness, of "guilt, alienation [and] betrayal ..." (Obeyesekere 1990a: 24) figure in this proposed scheme. Following this paradigm it is postulated that in

Western societies, on the other hand, men and women conceive of themselves as discrete beings, with relatively context-free, unrelational, unembedded identities (cf. Hollan 1992: 289–90 for a brief discussion of this cultural model). Whereas it is implicitly assumed that for "the Westerner" the practice of complete individuality is a reality and personal choice is unlimited – concepts particularly emphasised and exploited in a free market, capitalist society by advertising agencies which themselves di-vidualise their targets by projecting trends and fashions – for the "sociocentric organic" (Shweder and Bourne 1984: 193) South Asian, personal choice is said to be nearly non-existent, social roles being considered entirely dominant, both in theory and in practice.

Individuality in the South Asian context has, indeed, been denied time and again. In the colonial period "the natives" were classified into neat categories, and subsequently various administrative and legislative measures were undertaken, all designed to enhance the well-being of the objects of categorisation. In all these cases the individuality of women and men had to be denied. This denial has no doubt conformed largely to the locally dominant model, which serves to reproduce existing socio-political structures, and is probably also largely influenced by the labour structure of rural society and rural households, in which, as Wadley (1994: 59) notes, only "one straw from a broom cannot sweep … But when all are together, it can …". When Dumont (1970a: 1, 9; cf. also 1987) asserted that the presence of the individual as such is not recognised *within* the confines of Hindu society (and that an individual can exist only "hors-du-monde" – Dumont 1966: 336ff) he was thus merely echoing this dominant model (cf. Hollan 1992: 285ff.), in which caste identity – that "… ominous process of being levelled down into sameness" (Tagore 1925: 264) – can dictate even the colour and design of one's clothing and the shape of one's house. As Bharati (1985: 89 in Morris 1994: 70) writes, "When any of the Hindu traditions speak about what might look like the individual … it is … to denigrate it." No wonder then, that for many years subsequent students of South Asian societies left "the individuality of 'encompassed' persons … unexamined, and … largely ignored … the analytic problem posed by individuals in a group-oriented … society …." (Davis 1983: 50). How dominant models can stubbornly endure in "scientific" circles is clear from one of the latest publications on the subject of "individualism and collectivism", in which Indian society is designated unequivocally as typical for "vertical collectivism" (Singelis et al. 1995). Yet there are increasingly those who question this domination. Anthropological studies on the individual, self and person in South Asia have focused largely on Hindus in India, and many of the more recent writings are highlighted by a debate between the protagonists of what Mines (1988: 569) terms the "hierarchical-collectivist view" and those who, like Derné (1992: 41), stress that the treatment of "South Asian ethnopsychology" has largely tended to project the "Brahmanical, Sanskritic, male" perspective, which may well not be shared by non-Hindus, or generally by women, Dalits or other discriminated and disadvantaged groups of Indian society.

Like McHugh (1989), many social scientists increasingly emphasise the value in South Asia of "social embededdness and a recognition of an individual being who is embedded" (p. 77; this is very different from both Kakar's (1978: 32, emphasis added) "… individual, not separate but existing in all his myriad connections" and Roland's (1988: 224ff.) concept of the "we-self" – as opposed to an American "I-self" – which he perceives of as part and parcel of an intensely hierarchical society). The embeddedness McHugh speaks of goes beyond hierarchy, and was recognized as many as twenty years ago by a South Asian scholar himself who in his study of another, Islamic, region in South Asia advocated "neither the single application of individualist analysis nor an entirely holist one …", for "the individual must be defined as a social being" (Ahmed 1976: 139, 5). For Hindus and many Muslims this embeddedness is not just social, it is also physical and biologically conceived of. But just as not all Hindu and Jain renouncers "… leave [their] place in society" or "… renounce [their] existing role[s]" (Dumont 1970a: 185), either ideologically or in practice (e.g. Cort 1991; van der Veer 1987) to the extent Dumont feels they did, similarly embeddedness in itself does not, I suggest, turn non-renouncers into dividuals in all contexts. Nor again is the degree of embeddedness always constant (cf. also Ewing 1991). In a precursor to the "Hindu category of thought" debate, Marriott (1976: 111) stated:

> To exist, dividual persons absorb heterogenous material influences. They must also give out from themselves particles of their own coded

> substances – essences, residues, or other active influences – that may then reproduce in others something of the nature of the persons in whom they have originated. Persons engage in transfers of bodily substance-codes through parentage, through marriage … and other kinds of personal contacts.

The transmission of substances through various kinds of contact – spiritual as well as physical – is well documented for Hindu communities, but it is far from limited to these. Experiencing the world through the body/mind is part of all cognitive processes (Mauss 1938; Howard 1985; Lakoff 1987), and the practice of spiritual healing is based on this principle. The concept of spiritual kinship is yet another example of such structured processes; it is found throughout the Islamic world as well, not just in terms of biological-genealogical links or the master-pupil *(pīr-murīdi)* relationship, but also, for instance, through the transmission of *baraka* (cf. Chs. 1 and 2 and Rao 1990 for some examples of the transmission of special powers among the Bakkarwal).

The Bakkarwal are a culturally composite community (Rao 1988b) combining certain East Pashtun traditions with strong elements from the Panjab and further south. They are Muslims living in a mixed Muslim-Hindu environment; in other words they live in a society in which two seemingly contradictory ideologies exist: the egalitarian one of Islam and the hierarchical one of the Hindu order. The practice of the former may be considered under two aspects: that of the relationship every single human being entertains with God, both as a discrete human entity and as a member of the greater Islamic community; and that of the immediate we-group within which solidarity is said to be best represented by the concurrence of the aims, desires and well-being of all its members. The first aspect explicitly stresses both social equality and the concept of the spiritual-cum-social individual, for men are to be judged for their deeds as individuals, in isolation even from close relatives. The concept of social equality is often assumed to have first entered South Asia through European contact, but in fact it influenced many socio-religious movements throughout the area several centuries earlier, at least partly due to the impact of Islam. The second aspect, namely that of the we-group, is for the Middle Eastern model said to be the tribe (Ibn Khaldun's famous *'asabiya*), or in more urban contexts the family or district (e.g. Al-Khayyat 1990: 11; Berger 1964), and according to this, individualism is at its least when group cohesion and solidarity are at their maximum. Social and cultural practice often consists of a combination of these two aspects, and leads to context-specific selection of strategies that promote both individualism and group solidarity. Thus, for example Grima (1992: 73), writing of Pashtun men and women of Pakistan, notes that while there is a difference in the standards of behaviour expected of men and women in social contexts, on the whole "the 'individual' behavior is concerned with honor and ethics, while the 'group' behavior is concerned primarily with reciprocal relationships". This contextual choice perhaps appears at its clearest in what Gellner (paraphrased by Benthall 1991: 18) referred to as "competing patronage networks" (cf. Ch. 5 for a discussion of such networks among the Bakkarwal). What we have in the present context, however, is a South Asian variety of Islam, which, not surprisingly, accommodates numerous ideological currents and elements that serve to provide explanatory models for the practice of both individualism and group solidarity. Here a premium is placed on those who demonstrate that they are fit to be individuals by the very fact that they are, among others, able to knit and hold a group in cohesion. Here also, contrary to Dumont's premise, individualism entails equality only in the world hereafter (see also Béteille's 1986 critique of Dumont). In a more recent paper Dumont (1987: 669) suggests that individualism must not always entail equality, but in such cases equality "... will not attain the status of an overall valuation"; again my observations do not concord with this view, insofar as the Islamic ideology of equality has, for the Bakkarwal, an uncontested and overarching status valuation, even though it may, analytically speaking, often stand in blatant contradiction to social and cultural practice.

The Life-Course Perspective

Mattison Mines, one student (see also Khare 1984; Béteille 1987; Oxfeld 1992) of South Asian society to question the Dumontian perspective on individualism, has suggested (1988; see also 1992) that the relationship between holism and particularism, the proportion between discreteness and embeddedness, and the assertion of difference changes over the life span of men and women. My data corroborate this view, but I argue further that we need to identify the factors of gender and power as crucial to this relationship. Most studies of self and person have not even referred to the factors of gender and class, and indeed the anthropological discourses on person and gender "… have been developed in parallel" (Howell and Melhuus 1993: 47). In the chapters that follow I will show that the authorisation and legitimisation of human agency is closely linked to power relations couched in the idiom of community structures, but based on concepts and attributes of gender, economic status and age. The life-course is thus a crucial factor in the study of autonomy.

> The view of life as comprising a series of stages has a long history in the West. … Researchers in recent years have been … [using] an updated "Ages of Man" framework, variously called life stages, the life span, or the life age, course … when attention is paid to a particular stage … it is often viewed explicitly as bearing the fruits of preceding stages and sowing the seed for following ones …. (Schlegel and Barry III 1991: 2, 3)

The idea of stages or phases in life is, however, not confined to the West; similar ideas prevail in South Asia, and Bakkarwali language has different terms for these phases, which are naturally not entirely discrete. Within each of these phases every man, woman and child is seen to live a life which is unique in some ways, but similar in many ways to those of others of their age. This could present us with the problem of the normative individual as portrayed through "the typical life-course"; alternatively, one could be faced with the practical difficulties of describing individual life cycles and nevertheless end up with composite ones (cf. Erikson 1975: 113–68). One of my aims has been to observe not only differences between life phases, but also variations *within* each phase. This is because decision making varies within each of these phases, depending on a variety of factors, such as gender, economic status, kin-group, health. However unique a life led may be, certain social events always affect it to some degree, and especially in largely non-literate societies these events are important markers and constituents of time – "… une année n'est pas formée de jours, mais d'événements …" (Bonfiglioli 1988: 12). These events may be public ones affecting the entire community or many of its members; alternatively they may be personal ones affecting only a few, or just one person. As long as they were subjectively important enough, both of these types of events were found to be used to measure time, to remember the past, and to reproduce specific role patterns:

> Those events that are *purposively attended to* are crucial in the determination of time … individuals orient themselves according to the essential and private reality of their own temporal frames. (Hendricks and Peters 1986: 664–5)

For the Bakkarwal, and indeed for large parts of the population of Jammu and Kashmir, the period from about 1946 to 1955 was something of a watershed: the region got divided de facto between the newly formed states of India and Pakistan, the ensuing fighting created an atmosphere of great uncertainty and the new boundaries severely affected migration patterns (Rao 1992a). The land tenure system of the area changed; many new roads were built, again drastically influencing pasturage and migration routes; and the state departments of sheep husbandry, soil conservation and forests started playing a major role in the lives of all members of the community. The Indo-Pakistan wars of 1965 and 1971, often referred to by elderly Bakkarwal as World Wars I and II, again disrupted migration patterns and life generally, while the creation of welfare programmes in the 1970s, the legalisation of land encroachments in 1977 and the increasing import of animals on the hoof from beyond the region affected political and economic conditions within Bakkarwal society. Another crucial period will be from the mid/late 1980s through, probably, the 1990s, an era in which the nearly civil war–like situation in the region has affected every community and every individual in some manner or other (cf. Ch. 5 and Rao 1995; 1996). It is still unclear what impact their declaration as a *Scheduled Tribe* in 1991 by the Indian Government (thereby entitling them to certain social and economic benefits) will have on the group as a whole.

Even in purely personal events, the reckoning of time appears to follow certain patterns. In many societies

> … women and men "explain" and make sense of their past biography in rather different ways. Thus … their significant biographical "milestones"

> are often very different. … The "headlines" or "mileposts" used by women generally focus on personal relationships and family events.… (Burgoyne 1987: 34–5)

The Bakkarwal also have their own gender-specific ways of reckoning and marking time. Women tend to use the vital events of their own engagement, wedding, first pregnancy, birth of first child, etc., as markers; their visits between parental and marital homes help them remember other incidents. For men, time markers are the events of engagement, wedding, separation from father's flocks and/or setting up of own household. While none mentioned circumcision, probably because they were too young to remember the event clearly enough, many mentioned the first times they were out tending their fathers' flocks in winter nights, and hired shepherds always remembered their first contract periods. Some local units of time reckoning are common to both women and men; foremost among these are the times of biannual migration and the first Islamic ritual fast each kept, which also marks puberty in both boys and girls. People often mentioned events which happened "before" or "after" "my first fast", or even more accurately, "three months after my first fast", etc.

In studies of the life cycle, there are generally three types of time to be reckoned: life time, social time and historical time (cf. Fry 1980). "Life time" is based on the perception of a series of changes in the course of a life, as for example when I was told, "those days our pasture areas were in Gilgit, and not in Dras as they now are". It is thus the chronological measurement of a series of changes in life. "Social time" refers to time reckoned according to the various roles one has played in the course of one's life, as for example when a woman speaks of an event in relation to her first pregnancy. "Historical time" denotes the reckoning of time following specific, historically verifiable events, irrespective of whether or not the latter were of direct relevance to the life of the narrator. The current turmoil referred to above would be such a marker of historical time at a future date. The introduction of paper money or the installation of a new prince – neither of which directly affected them much – were mentioned by the very aged as markers of historical time, just as those slightly younger invariably mentioned the partition of the subcontinent (1947), while those still younger referred to the wars of 1965 and 1971 between India and Pakistan, which affected many a great deal. It is obvious that certain events fall into all three categories of time reckoning; more often, however, it was found necessary to juxtapose these three types of mensuration to be sure about the date of a particular event, or generally information about the past.

On meeting me for the first time women almost always asked me how old I was – a question common enough in South Asia. It was thus fairly easy for me to reply by asking them how old they thought I was. Their answers were invariably "[about] twenty [or] twenty-five"; not only were these answers an example of the phenomenon of "age heaping" discussed below, but they fell short of my age at the time by between ten to five years – something easily accountable by the privilege urban middle-class women like myself enjoy of looking younger than women exposed from an early age to hard physical labour. In any case I felt that this gave me an idea of how they estimated the biological ages of other people, and hence probably also their own. I then asked them how old they were. Additionally, I also applied the above-mentioned method of dating in relation to known events; relative age was also asked (i.e. "are you older or younger than X or Y"?) and then checked against other fairly certain temporal data. In their estimates of my biological age, as well as their own, Bakkarwal women conformed (cf. Fig. I.2) to widely reported patterns of digit preference, or age heaping, in which people tend to round off units and report ages ending with 0 or 5, while only relatively few mention ages ending in 1, 4, 6 or 9 (cf. Carrier and Hobcraft 1973: 2–5).

Here is an example of the kind of problems faced in determining biological age: a woman who was past fecundity and fertility in 1983 was taken as being above fifty years of age. This means she was born before 1933. But a woman giving her age as "fifty" could, in reality, be anywhere between forty-six and fifty-four years old, thanks to the phenomenon of digit preference. In other words, she could just as well have been born somewhere between 1929 and 1937. This again means that when she spoke of customs or events as they were "when I was young" she meant the period between about 1944 and 1962 – given that youth in this society is considered to be the phase between about sixteen and twenty-five years of age.

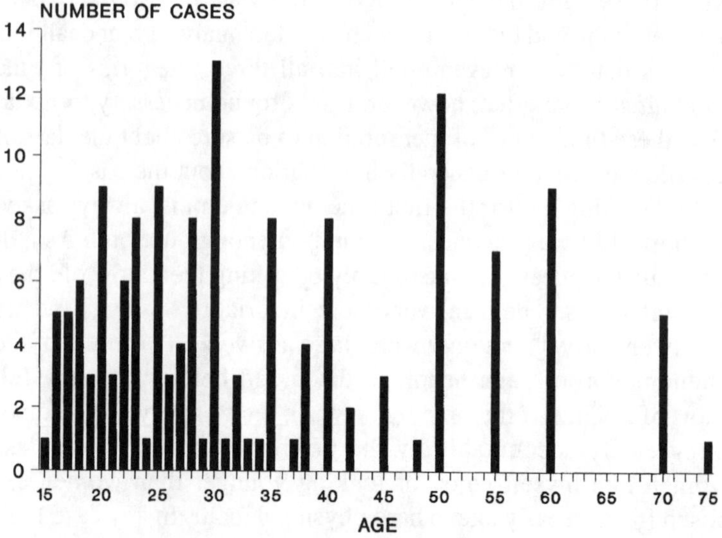

Figure I.2 Age reporting by Bakkarwal women and men. These show the phenomenon of "heaping".

For pragmatic reasons the various chapters of this book are arranged according to "the typical" life-course as conceived of in Bakkarwal society; it is hoped that this composition does not blend out individual variations. In the pages that follow the reader will also often come up against information on sample sizes and averages. This too is not meant to blur the individual into a mass of fellow beings; nor is it a reflection of a "fetishism of numbers" (Obeyesekere 1990a: 227). Ethnography can not dismiss with generalisations, but generalisations in their turn are meaningless, if not outright dangerous, unless we are given at least a rough idea of their relative extent.

A Comparative Approach

Both generalisations and individual case studies are no doubt of interest in themselves. They can in addition throw light on matters of broader concern if viewed in a comparative perspective. Such comparison can be both diachronic and synchronic, both thematic and regional (Schweizer 1978).

In the following chapters ethnographic material gathered in specific or numerous cases among the Bakkarwal have at times been compared with what I think are thematically or regionally comparable cases elsewhere in South Asia, which I regard as a cultural region, and even beyond. Comparison is obviously not an end in itself. As Muslims the Bakkarwal may be both comparable and contrastable with Hindus with whom they share certain concepts or practices; as pastoralists, they are worth comparing on specific points with other animal husbanders, be they in East Africa or in the Arabian desert. As women and men who mourn the loss of their children, they are further comparable with parents in other far-flung societies, if we are in search of the ways humans deal with bereavement and tragedy.

Fieldwork

The data presented in this book were collected over a period of a little over twenty-eight months of fieldwork, in addition to several weeks spent obtaining secondary data, mainly from local government and administrative offices. Much of the data gathered, especially on the economy and religion of the Bakkarwal, are still to be written up. None of the following chapters has been published earlier, but some material in Chapters 1 and 4 has been included elsewhere in an entirely different form (Casimir and Rao 1995; Rao 1988a; 1990; 1992a; 1995; forthcoming).

My first encounter with the Bakkarwal and my first visit to Kashmir took place in summer 1980. After a survey of roughly six weeks in various summer pasture areas, undertaken together with my husband, I returned to the pastures of the Lidder and Sind valleys in summer 1981 for another spell of about five weeks. After obtaining finance for research in 1982, I started participant observation in November that year in the Jammu-Jandrah area. From the beginning I told everyone concerned that I wanted to learn about the lifestyle of the Bakkarwal, and eventually planned to write a book; most people seemed to think it obvious that as an urban dweller from the plains I was interested in a lifestyle so different from my own, and while a few did ask my help in concrete situations later, no one ever questioned the basic "use" of my study.

Although to obtain primary access to the community I was introduced from the alien sphere to men of influence and their families, after the first few days I did not remain with these families, and most of my fieldwork was not done among this category. I stayed with and visited a whole spectrum of families and came and went as I pleased. I needed to ask no one's permission, but I sometimes heard that certain men of influence were displeased with my behaviour. Although I could visit and spend a couple of nights with various families right from the start, it took me till January 1983 to find the first family who was ready to "take the responsibility" of having me stay with them as part of their household. I stayed with this family till mid-April 1983, when the spring migration began. In the meantime I had got to know another, smaller, less wealthy family, and joined them for about two weeks during the migration towards the summer pastures. During this period I met yet other families, and joined one of them in their summer pastures in mid-June. After this, until September 1984, I continuously stayed with a variety of families in various parts of Jammu and Kashmir, but primarily in the upper reaches of the Liddar and Sind valleys in eastern Kashmir in summer, and in the areas of Basohli-Kathua, Jandrah and Reasi in winter – either in their tents/huts or in my own tent. I also visited related and unrelated families in northern and western Kashmir in summer and in the area of Rajouri and Poonch in winter, and stayed with them for short periods ranging from a couple of nights to ten days. I again visited some of the families I knew best in summer 1985 and 1986, and then again in winter 1987 and 1992, for a period of one month each time. Both in summer and in winter I was often joined for several weeks each year by my husband, who was studying diet, nutrition and the relationship between ecology and economy (Casimir 1991a).

On no occasion was I accompanied by an interpreter, and, despite fluency in Urdu and Hindi, I had in the beginning to struggle with problems of comprehension, especially since Bakkarwal women understand simple Urdu fairly well but speak only Bakkarwali, an Indo-European language closely related to Gujari and heavily influenced by various other languages spoken in India and Pakistan, including Panjabi and Marwari. From 1983 onwards I was, however, accompanied in the summer months by a young

Kashmiri Muslim, hailing from a high-altitude village, who owned a horse which I used as a pack animal. This man or his teenaged brother went along with the horse and helped me in innumerable practical ways; they were known to many Bakkarwal who passed through their village on migration. After setting me and my tent up they either went back home and came to visit me occasionally if I was in the Lidder valley, or else they stayed in the area and earned their living by hiring out their horse to others. At the end of each summer they fetched me and my baggage and brought me to their village where I always stayed a while before continuing with my work. I did not require or receive any such help in the winter area, where most Bakkarwal camps are within reasonably easy walking distance of bus routes.

As will be evident from the following pages, I have combined qualitative data with quantitative analyses wherever I felt that the latter would render the former more transparent. Many of the quantitative data have been presented from the female perspective, since as a woman I obviously had easier access to women. I was also of the opinion that since "… in Western society, … a strong sense of individual worth … [is] conceived of as [a] male virtue, the role of women [has been] grossly neglected" (Dyson-Hudson and Dyson-Hudson 1980: 16) in this sphere. Some of the quantitative data and all of the qualitative data – except those on life histories, migration patterns, and kinship and botanical terminology – were obtained through being present at (and increasingly participating in) conversations and through unstructured interviews. This had its drawbacks, especially in the first weeks in the field when my comprehension of Bakkarwali was rather limited. However, in this early phase, my systematic recording of quantitative data on household composition – "in order to get to know each family better", as I explained – also helped me a great deal in recapitulating the day's conversations and relating these to each person I got to know. From the start, songs and sometimes stories were taped directly, and as we got to know one another better I could also directly write down data on fertility careers and other demographic aspects. I did not face the problem, which for example Patel (1994) did among Hindus in rural Rajasthan, where women were often unwilling to talk about their deceased children. Much of the demographic data I collected were later compared with those recorded by the official Government Census officers. In many cases discrepancies were found between the two sets of data, and similar discrepancies have been noted for other neighbouring areas by, for example, Djurfeldt and Lindberg (1976: 46) and Patel (1994). Census enumeration is done on the basis of households and in the case of ever-married women on an individual basis. All these data are, indeed, guarded by a strict code of secrecy, and I have taken care not to reveal any personal details which I may have come across in these census schedules.

In spite of the gender hierarchy, there is no daily spatial sexual segregation among the Bakkarwal, and I had no difficulties in talking freely to both men and women, though sexual matters could never be broached openly with the former. Perhaps because the context was one of mobility and migration, I also had no problems in movement; Bakkarwal camps are small and dispersed, and even though Bakkarwal women themselves do not go visiting often, they are out of their homes almost as much as the men, herding, milking, fetching fodder, fuel and water, etc. In the summer area it is also common to see women from other communities of equal rank (pastoral Gujar, Kashmiri herders, or even high altitude Kashmiri villagers) pass by; the idea of a woman walking around on her own during the day was thus by no means an innovation. Since women do work singly unless they have close camp neighbours, it was also not considered unusual, after the first flush of informed curiosity passed, for me to sit on my own in the vicinity and write my notes and do my "work" – for this is how they categorized my activities. Contrary to certain anthropologists, the Bakkarwal I came to know had no doubt that the fieldwork among them which has culminated in this book, was "work" – why else should one be away from one's home and family for so long, for what other than professional reasons should I lead a migratory lifestyle? After all, they too led such a lifestyle because of their profession (*pēshā*). Besides, they knew that I received money (my grant) for my job, and was hence a person receiving a salary – something they were all familiar with and a few of the younger men even aspired to. Some also remained convinced that I would make a lot of money with the book I wrote about them. Looking back, it is interesting, however, that no one ever thought of bracketing me with tourists, those Western, and urban Indian, and Kashmiri men and women who came to enjoy the gorgeous landscape of the summer areas and ignored the local population.

The Ethnographer at Home

Although two geographers (Bisaria 1971 and Khatana 1976a,b; 1992; 1993) had worked among some of the Bakkarwal and allied communities, I was the first anthropologist to do so. For me it was also the first experience of doing fieldwork in South Asia; I was thus working in my own culture area. The question of the "native ethnographer" has been discussed by many, and there can be little doubt (cf. Narayan 1993; Kaare 1995; Rudolph 1997) that a clear-cut dichotomy between native and foreign is increasingly meaningless. As early as 1972 Mamdani had referred to the initial fears the Khanna study people had had in his restudy: "The study had misplaced fears of acting out of a cultural bias.… What plagued the study was not a *national* (Western vs. Indian) bias but a class bias" (pp. 48–50). During my study I was faced with frequent attempts at categorising me (correctly or incorrectly) in terms of class, religion, caste, etc., and as a result, I too was aware of correspondingly frequent negotiations of my identity. Surprising as this may sound, these negotiations appeared both familiar and strange – familiar, because the categories I was placed in were those I knew from "my own society", strange, because I did not personally feel I belonged in any of them. But this strangeness did not contribute to a feeling of alienation, perhaps because despite all the differences, it is incontestable that

> Sharing features of common culture and personality makes me sensitive not only to language nuances but also to cultural ones – problems of etiquette and tact, timing of questions, and sensitivity to areas that require delicate and careful probing. I fully recognize this common affinity and use it to understand my informants better … I am one with them yet not one of them … It helps the anthropologist to recognize implicit meanings and render them explicit for cultural analysis.… (Obeyesekere 1981: 11)

I would add that even without an initially good command of language the cultural undertones and nuances were reasonably clear to me from the start, and this is perhaps what being a "native ethnographer" is all about. This "common affinity" was apparently recognized by Bakkarwal women and men as well, for often enough they parried my questions and observations with: "but you know this – why do you ask?", "you must know this, you people do it as well", or "yes, you people don't do this, do you". In other words they too assumed that there existed perceived common ground in knowledge, if not in practice. Doing ethnography "at home" refers then to a context in which one's interlocutor expresses the feeling that you also know (or at least ought to know) an entire gamut of things on which there is great cultural consensus, not because you have learned it recently, but because you have in a way grown up with it. It is the feeling that in spite of all the differences you must share a great deal in the common pool of social and cultural knowledge – that the other is only an aspect of one's self.

The cultural differences perceived legitimised my doing fieldwork; the individual differences perceived greatly reduced my duties as "participant" observer, since in spite of being a kind of "man-woman" (something I refer to in Ch. 4), I was considered incapable (not strong enough, too clumsy, not sure-footed enough, etc.) to do the chores of either a normal woman or man in this society. My duties were thus confined to the care of (especially sick) lambs and kids in winter, packing for migration, feeding pups, washing clothes, slicing vegetables, lighting and watching over the fire in all seasons, and administering to sick children and adults whenever needed. My husband, though perceived as entirely alien culturally, was considered extremely fit to handle men's work, and during his stay in the field he certainly "participated" more than I did.

Tension and Contradiction

In Bakkarwal ideology there is no ultimate contradiction, no basic tension involved at the moral level between the assertion of the individual identity of a human being and his/her social commitments. Here "moral courage and lonely individualism" (Bellah et al. 1989: 144) are not paired, for there is no need to leave or renounce society to try to achieve the "moral good". A certain multiformity is made possible even in political organisation through the coexistence of principles and institutions of both a segmentary and hierarchical nature. There is equality before God and as a herder; there is hierarchy because of one's innate nature, which too, is God-given. Both relatedness and discreteness are God-given and in the final count dependent on Him, and must therefore coexist.

This study is an empirical approach to understanding local concepts underlying autonomy or the lack of it. Though based on data pertaining to one particular society, it hopefully extends our understanding of (individual) actors in social and economic processes at different levels of interaction within and beyond the specific community studied. While it may be futile to search for the value and meanings of autonomy across cultures too far apart, it may well make sense to try and approach the subject by examining the recognition and legitimacy granted to those involved directly or indirectly in processes of decision making, and by enquiring into the attributes ascribed to legitimised decision makers according to their gender, age and class.

I invite readers of this ethnography to try out the definitions and approaches I offer to study the practice of the assertion or negation of difference between separate women and men, the ideologies underlying this, and its consequences for their degree of autonomy in other areas of South Asia and beyond.

A Note on Style

All statements whose authors are not explicitly mentioned – such as the opening sentence of Chapter 1 – designate wide cultural consensus within Bakkarwal society, and are hence treated as factual statements, even though analytically speaking they may be subjective ones. The local terminology given corresponds to Bakkarwal usage; the etymology mentioned occasionally is intended to help the reader familiar with parts of South Asia to eventually compare concepts and connotations across regions.

Chapter 1

Coming into Being

Being Conceived

And of everything have we created pairs

— Qor'an (LI/49)

All creation *(aywān)* has a gender; only God is genderless (*be-jins*). Hence in all creative processes the basic chemistry involved is that of mixing male and female substances. The process of mixing male semen and female blood, the process through which human and animal life is reproduced, is explicitly compared by the Bakkarwal to two other creative processes, namely the creation of butter – which is part and parcel of their pastoral way of life – and the creation of agricultural crops. In all these processes the male element is said to work as a kind of catalyst (*darmiāni*, lit. mediator, intermediary). Among all mobile beings, be they animal *(jānwar),* human *(bani ādam)* or what one could call superhuman (such as fairies – *pari* – or *jin*), the fundamental process which takes place at conception is that male semen (*bīj*, lit. "seed"; cf. also Kashmiri: semen – Madan 1989a: 298) mixes with female blood *(rat or khūṇ).* The notion that semen and blood are the physical stuff a child is made of is common in large parts of the world, and Hindus in India have apparently always

> ... tended to view the processes of sexual intercourse and birth in terms of the interaction of various bodily fluids. Their notions about the precise nature of these fluids and the manner of their interaction have varied from time to time and from text to text ... (O'Flaherty 1980: 17)

In many areas in Iran also "each drop of semen is said to correspond to forty drops of blood" (Bromberger 1994: 192), and the Dhunds of northern Pakistan hold that semen is "concentrated blood" (Donnan 1988: 88). For the Bakkarwal each of these substances has a liquid part attributed to water, and a solid part which consists of seed – also known as *bīj* – which is basically red *(rattā).* The proportion between the liquid and solid parts in each substance varies between different types of creatures, as well as between individuals, and even for each individual at different stages of life. Not only do horses, for example, ejaculate more than goats and these more than sheep, but the semen of the first is the thickest. Elderly men and women, as well as sick persons, have little semen and blood, and the little they have is thin and watery. In healthy young men and women, on the other hand, both are plentiful and thick. The consistence of each substance is of relevance for its humoral quality – the more liquid it is the cooler it is. Water, which is responsible for the fluidity, is the diluting and hence the cooling agent, for the solid substances in both semen and blood are extremely "hot" *(tattā).* Indeed the solid element in semen is so hot that, though red in colour, it is almost invisible, blood-red being somewhat cooler. In healthy adult men and women the levels of semen and blood remain more or less constant; exceptions to this rule are the duration of the menses and old age, but more about these later. In animals these levels vary enormously throughout the year; in fact they vary so rapidly, that they wear them out (*thak jāyo*), with the result that the different phases of the life cycle run through so much faster among animals than they do among humans. Variation in these levels also takes place during illness, and although weakness can be explained by specially low levels of body fluids, especially in women, it is much more common to hear of excessively high levels. *Tangi* (<*tang* = narrow) represents the principle of pent up fluids struggling to break through, liberating the body from malaises of various kinds. Bakkarwal women also use the term extensively to explain menstrual and other pains. To prevent *tangi* and its concomitant troubles, these fluids must be released. Blood letting is one measure resorted to, and during parturition analogous measures of release are believed to help.

The variation in the levels of blood and semen in animals is one of the most important physiological differences between them and humans. It accounts for the fact that, whereas human females can on principle conceive at almost any time during the mature period of their lives, animals are seasonally restricted. An extreme example is the *Bārā Singā*, a stag (*Cervus elaphus hanglu*) who "they say, can mate only on the 10th of *pādro* (*ca.* 25th August); exactly nine months later, the female delivers, no one knows where." (In fact the rutting season lasts a couple of months, beginning in early October, gestation lasting about six months). Even more mysterious is the mating behaviour of the "silvery" common otter (*ud*, *Lutra lutra*), which leaves the waters of the Tar Sar and Mar Sar mountain lakes only once in her lifetime, to mate "in a place between the sky and the waters below the earth". Indeed in summer in Kashmir these otters do swim up the mountain streams to elevations of some 3,660 m (Prater 1971: 152). Less rigorous are sheep, who mate in the one-and-a-half months between mid-*kattā* and *mangar* (November to mid-December), giving birth in early *čait* (mid-March to mid-April). Formerly, goats too had such preferences, but since the early days of their coexistence with the Bakkarwal, and to provide the latter with milk *(duñd/tutio)* the year through, they have changed their ways. Now, said some, they "still prefer" to mate between mid-July and mid-August (in *sāoñ*, kidding then being in late December or early January *(pō);* others mentioned the months of August, September and October (*pādro* or *asu*), with kidding between mid-January and mid-March (in *mā* or *phagaṇ*). Indeed, late December to mid-February is the primary kidding period.

Restrictions placed on human sexual intercourse are of a religious nature and imposed by the *sharra*, and thus by God Himself. "Do everything except sexual intercourse", the Prophet Mohammad has been quoted as saying and the Qor'an (II/2) itself specifically prohibits intercourse during menstruation, and thus during the menses *(kapṛā)* and in the post-partum period *(lōs)* it is a sin *(guna)* to indulge in sex. At both these times the outflow of blood makes a woman polluted and polluting, and hence *makru* (<Ar. *makrūh,* i.e. disapproved of). Animals, unlike humans, have no knowledge of pollution, and hence these restrictions do not apply to them. The post-partum period has been divinely fixed at forty days, yet in keeping with the widely held view that females are inherently more polluting and hence more dangerous than males, the length of the period of sexual abstinence can vary according to the gender of the baby born. While for a baby boy it need be only three weeks, for a baby girl it must be full forty days; this difference also applies to restrictions on household chores, and while a woman who has borne a son may become commensal five days after delivery, a daughter's mother "should wait" at least twice as long. This gender-based difference in the length of the pollution period is also attested in general Semitic tradition (cf. 3. Moses 12, 1-5: forty days for a son and eighty days for a daughter), and for the Bakkarwal stems from the notion that "baby boys are cleaner (*sutro*) than girls", because "girls are from birth imperfect (*aibdār*, cf. Ur. *'ayb* = faulty, imperfect)". This kind of imperfection is something inherently female and unlike among Durrani Pashtuns, for example (Tapper 1991: 216), is not considered the result of "individual action". Thus sex determines at birth (at age 0) major aspects of one's inherent nature or innate temper (*mijāj*): it precludes even the attempt of a girl to try to reach certain social and moral standards, and restricts her capacity and ability to be responsible and accountable. This in turn has lasting consequences for her access to information, which, I suggest, is a prime factor in her being perceived (by others, and ideally also by herself) as incompetent to choose (*čunāñ*) and take decisions (*phesla*). The intrinsic imperfection of a woman's nature – she can not help being the way she is – limits drastically the degrees of freedom and autonomy to which she may even hope to aspire.

A Question of Transmission

In many parts of contemporary India, a child is held to take after its father in all major aspects (cf. Inden 1976: 95). Among the ancient Hindus the son was no doubt considered to be the "father himself born again" (Sutherland 1990: 87), and this is basically also in keeping with the Qor'anic "Your women are your tilth, so come into your tillage how you choose" (II/223). But the Qor'an has another verse too: "He it is who created you from the earth, then from a clot, then from congealed blood, then He brings you forth a child ..." (XL/ 67, 69). The "congealed blood" is the womb. But even the textual traditions of Hinduism are not as unequivocal about the roles of genitor and genetrix as has been generally suggested (cf. Khare 1970 and Sutherland 1990). Recent field studies (Gold 1989; Sax 1991: 18–26) further show that in the little, often oral, traditions the "female seed" plays a dominant role, and that in certain areas "... it is important that the qualities of the genitor and the genetrix are evenly matched" (Das 1976: 3; cf. also Enthoven 1914: 93).

Whether by analogy or homology, the theme of woman and her womb being the earth and the man and his semen representing the seed to be sown is widespread. The Bakkarwal conceive of semen as containing a juicy (*rasam*) element which seeps into the womb as do the sun's rays (*din ko dup/rasam*) into Mother Earth (*māi zamīn*), and an infertile woman and barren land are both known as *otar*. However, in Bakkarwal theory, although semen is held to be very strong indeed, the woman is no "mere field", but very much an active partner in the procreative process and has a very great influence on the child to be. Bakkarwal concepts also do not concord with those widely reported from many parts of northern, central and partly eastern India, following which "the blood of a female child ... can not be transmitted", and

> The child ... shares its blood with its father. A male child has the potential of being the transmitter of the same blood to the next generation; in other words, of continuing the blood line. ... A female has ... to join a man of another blood line and produce children for him ... The role of the mother is to augment what the womb has received, through her own blood which provides warmth (incubation) and nourishment ... (Dube 1986: 22)

Such views are also held by certain South Asian Muslims, among whom it is said that "blood comes through the male line" (Donnan 1988: 88; Jeffery 1979: 10). It has already been stated that among the Bakkarwal the blood an infant receives is considered entirely that of its mother, the father's semen acting only as a catalyst, bringing on conception. And yet this catalyst also has its role to play in determining a child's destiny. Despite the apparent contradiction, it is the semen which, for example, determines a baby's gender (the humorally hotter it is, the greater the likelihood of a son), and on this in turn partly depends, among other things, its inherent disposition or innate temper *(mijāj).* Gender, it is said, tends to repeat itself along the paternal line *(khāndānī),* and a marked preponderance of male or female children is a patrilineally transmitted hereditary phenomenon: "A family with many more boys, or many more girls will be this way over seven generations." Semen, whose specific qualities are transmitted from father to child (especially the son), is thus an important element in determining the basic qualities of a patrilineage.

The Milk-Blood Equation

While semen and blood are in many ways comparable, a third body fluid – milk – also plays a major role in relational models and practices of the Bakkarwal. In many South and West Asian societies milk and blood are equated (Sharif 1975: 84; Choksy 1989: 100; Beck 1991: 362) or paired (Unbescheid 1985), the former also sometimes being paired with semen. In Islam the kinship of milk (*rida'a*), like that of blood, restricts marriage between certain persons; by the same token it also functions, as blood does, to broaden bonds between individuals and groups and draw these all into one big family (Altorki 1980: 233–44; Eickelman 1984: 97–8). The Bakkarwal say that neither they nor their ancestors ever sold milk, and that their religion (*majhab*) forbids it. Indeed among many communities in South Asia (e.g. Westphal-Hellbusch and Westphal 1964: 66–7; Tiemann 1970: 482) selling milk is equivalent to selling one's mother, one's child, one's honour and one's patrilineage. Among the Bakkarwal milk and blood appear to be mutually convertible. This principle is illustrated by the wedding ritual of *leñdr denāñ* (cf. Ch. 3). *Leñdr* is a small sum of money (in the 1980s between about twenty and one hundred *rupees*), which the groom must gift either to his bride's biological mother, or to the woman who had nursed her (her *duñd māñ*), before he can actually take the bride with him. While presenting the money the groom is supposed to express his gratitude for the trouble the woman has taken in raising the young girl on her own milk. The concept of this milk being a gift is shared by Muslims elsewhere; Peters (1990: 197) refers to it among the Cyrenaican Bedu, and the Ghorbat of Afghanistan called this gift *shīr baha*. In the Bakkarwal weddings I observed the grooms remained shyly and respectfully silent, but the guests – especially the women – present chanted the following refrain: "*batri tār tēri pīṇi aī*", literally, "Your gift/debt of the vein was drunk." The "gift/debt of the vein" is blood-milk. The analogy between the two substances is symbolised by the term *batri* (cf. Hd.: *vritti*), which acts as a metaphor for the biological and emotional relationship between a mother and her own or foster child, and more generally in the context of all gynolateral relationships. As I shall explain later, through the "vein" a mother gifts her baby not only blood and milk, but various properties which go a long way in forming the child's character.

Converse to *batri*, we encounter *rag*, another term for vein, in contexts where biological relations between patri-kin are discussed. Whereas *batri* links a mother and her children through blood and blood-turned-milk, *rag* links a man to his children through blood-turned-semen. Both *rag* and *batri* link siblings, but *rag* specifically links brothers and male agnates – and hence those who build a *birādari* in the sense of a patrilineage (cf. Ch. 3). *Batri* links a man with his sister's children and hence it also links cross-cousins. *Batri* evokes collateral ties, whereas *rag* is associated with genealogical depth. *Batri* links specific human beings, whereas *rag* links families. A married daughter retains both her father's *rag* and her mother's *batri* – and hence also the qualities of both. But through her own *batri* she transmits mainly the properties of her maternal line, plus some properties of her father's *rag*, which she has absorbed; the primary transmission of her paternal *rag* thus stops with her – as does the blood line in Bengal (Fruzzetti et al. 1976). It is her brother who is responsible for the transmission of his paternal *rag*, though he too does transmit a few properties of his mother's *batri*. *Rag* links male agnates, but it is said that it also transmits feelings of competition (*barābari karāñ*, which also means to equalise); *batri* on the other hand is said to "bind" and transmit positive emotions, such as love. Hence it is explained that while a man is competitive towards his agnates, he has greater trust in his mother's family, whereas for a woman all these relations are those of love and care. In disputes between a woman's father and her husband, she is also expected to side intuitively with her father. These ideas could be compared to Middle Eastern concepts of segmentation following which although all men of the lineage are brothers, yet every ego is pitted against "some of my brothers, me and some of my brothers against some of my cousins" and so on. Among the Bakkarwal it is said that a man without brothers is nothing (cf. Ch. 5), and indeed brothers do not often fight each other openly; those who do often turn out to have different mothers (*matēr*) and not to be true *(saččo)* brothers. Life stories reveal that a common father who is no more acts as less of a barrier to fraternal disharmony than even a deceased common mother. Here, as for the Moghal Emperor Akbar "... the river of milk ..." (Malleson 1980: 177 in Khatib-Chahidi 1992: 110) seems hard to cross.

Rag, like the Pashtun concept of *siāli* (e.g. Edwards 1990: 70) connotes equality and fraternal solidarity, but also competition. In no way does it connote the "sameness" of brothers which Inden and Nicholas (1977: 13) postulate for Hindu society. Indeed it may be worth asking whether this ideological "sameness" is reflected in Bengali Hindu practice, where difference in age, for example, is such a potent social factor, and where competition for resources so often leads to the breakup of fraternal joint family households. Be this as it may, at the ideological level Hindu brothers "share the same body" when they share a father; among the Bakkarwal they share the same blood when they share both *rag* and *batri*. Thus ultimately, though the patrilineage (*zāt*) is explicitly connected with *rag*, *rang* (which is *zāt*-specific) is linked to both *rag* and *batri*. Unlike the Dhunds of northern Pakistan (Donnan 1988: 127, 130) among whom *rang* (blood) binds the patrilineage, here *rang* is a composite of *rag* and *batri*, of male and female blood and hence symbolises the identity of a *zāt* with its ideal of endogamy. Table 1.1 sets out the opposition between *rag* and *batri* as compared to male vs. female procreative oppositions elsewhere in South Asia (cf. Salzman 1992: 11 for similar concepts in Iranian Baluchistan).

Table 1.1 The opposition in Bakkarwal ideology between *rag* and *batri* as compared to male versus female procreative oppositions in other South Asian societies

PROCREATIVE OPPOSITIONS		**ETHNIC GROUP**	**SOURCE**
rag *vs*	*batri*	Bakkarwal	This Study
head blood (same clan)	skirt blood (affines)	Nunari (Pakistan)	Kurin and Morrow (1985 : 238)
back blood bone	abdomen skin	Baluch (Iran)	Salzman (1992: 10–12)
brain bone (father)	blood flesh (mother)	Bangladeshi (Bangladesh)	Blanchet (1987: 70)
bone	blood	Central Nepal	Lecomte-Tilouine (1993)
bone (patriline)	milk (matriline)	Lohorung Rai (Nepal)	Hardman (forthcoming)
bone	flesh, blood milk	Khumbo (NE-Nepal)	Diemberger (1993: 91)
bone (enduring lineage)	flesh (transient)	various populations (Central Asia)	Humphrey (1992: 177)

Authenticity and the Moral Order

At birth all animate creatures enter the world as beings (*shakas*). "*Koe shakas tho*" – it was some being – is a commonly heard phrase which may refer to some human, either unidentified or unimportant, or to a ghost, *jin* or fairy. When an unknown visitor appears at a Bakkarwal camp, apart from the even more vague *koe* (someone), he or she may be referred to as *shakas*. This is the case when the visitor is just a passer-by, for example, a tourist in the mountains. Unlike the term *bandā*, which I shall discuss in Chapter 2, and which is specific, situational and social, *shakas* is general, neutral and unrelational (Rao 1990). It thus also implies a certain ambiguity and uncertainty; on the other hand it represents the living being with a will *(marji)* and a consciousness of him/herself, and here we find a concordance with the meaning of the Arabic and Urdu term *shakhs*, from which it derives, and which is variously glossed in English as "individual", "self", "person" and "identity". The concept of *shakas* also approximates fairly well to certain concepts translated as "self" in a great deal of anthropological literature.

Not explicitly covered by the term *shakas* are animals, including those owned by the Bakkarwal. A goat is not really a *shakas*, although it does possess numerous properties and qualities also attributed to the latter. Goats, sheep, horses, dogs, cows, bears, etc. are all known as *jānwar*; there are basically two types of animals, although there are many subcategories: wild animals (*jangli jānwar*) and simply *jānwar*. It was not possible for me to ascertain the analytical differences made by the Bakkarwal between domestic animals, wild animals, humans and superhumans, but what did emerge out of numerous conversations was that one of the most important differences lies in what I shall translate as the innate temper of each of these species. The concept in question is that of *mijāj*, which, paraphrasing Madan (1989b: 118) from a different context, flows from one's social and biological position. One of the most important differences between humans and animals lies in the *mijāj* of each species. This innate temper briefly referred to earlier, and said to be transmitted largely by the genitor's semen, is based on the Bakkarwal notion of authenticity (*akīkat <Pers./Ur. ḥaqīqat* = essence, true nature), which must be understood in a broader cultural context where it is believed that every "genus of living beings shares from the moment of its generation its defining qualities …" (Marriott and Inden 1972: 7 in Wadley 1975: 55). These defining qualities are transmitted through interaction over generations among a host of items such as water, atmosphere, soil, beings of all kinds. *Akīkat* implies essentiality, the concept of a basic core formed by substances derived through blood, ultimately of course due to God's will. Hence, the Bakkarwal feel that an adult should not, after a certain age – after reaching what one could call maturity – change his/her ways. Intimately connected to the concept of *akīkat* are notions of genuineness, reliability, predictability of both disposition and action – and hence accountability. As a corollary a false, unreliable person (*be-wafā*) is a person who is liable to change (*tabdili*), and is hence metaphorically forever in the phase of puberty and early adulthood (*jawāni*, see Ch. 2). But most adults

are considered to have an authenticity, an innate genuineness, and it is this, for example, which hinders a basic change of tradition and culture; it is due to this that "in a foreign land one always remains a stranger". Or again, "in spite of all your comforts, we can not stay in your towns. If we stay two days in a town, we neither feel hungry, nor can we piss. We feel unwell". *Akīkat* can however be changed by external agents; it is vulnerable to attack by supernatural forces, such as the *jin*, whose aim may be to destroy the existing core to make a new one of their own liking. Since these agents can not reach *akīkat* directly, they resort to attacking bodily substances, entering the body through these and thence manipulating *akīkat* – leading to what is then observable in extreme forms of physical deviance. Figure 1.1 sets out the relationship of *akīkat* with certain other key Bakkarwal concepts, which are glossed for want of more suitable alternatives by terms commonly encountered in anthropological literature (cf. also Introduction).

Figure 1.1 The relationship of *akīkat* with certain other key Bakkarwal concepts

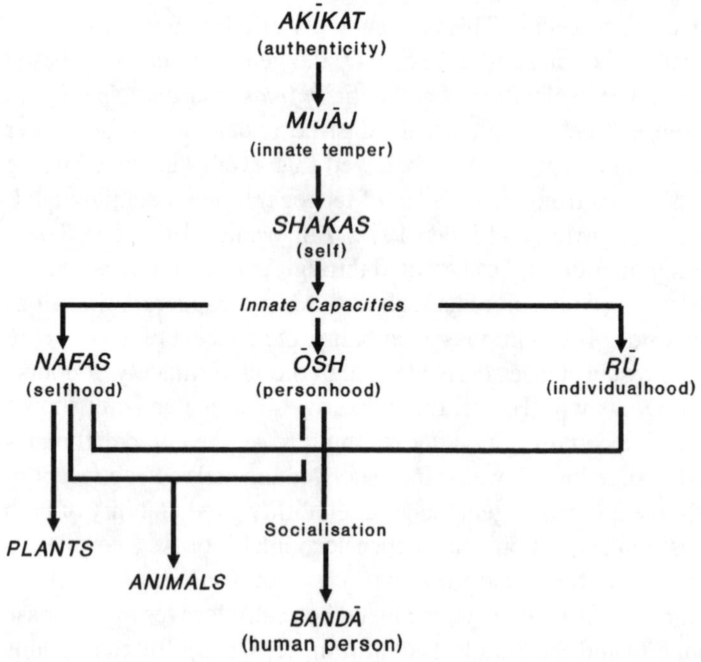

The most important of these related concepts is that of *mijāj*, which too is considered basically unchangeable – you are born with one and you die with it. It is considered subservient to the following conditions:

1. on whether one is human, animal or superhuman, or a plant. Thus not only the appearance, but also the basic traits of, for instance, a goat, a man, a fairy and a flower are so different from one another.
2. within each of these categories – on one's community (*kaum*);
3. within each *kaum* on one's family (*zāt*) if one is human, on one's breed or pedigree (*nasal/zāt*) if one is animal, on one's type (*tabka*) if one is superhuman, on one's species (*kisam/zāt*) as a plant;
4. finally, on one's "own-ness" – *apan apan* is how the Bakkarwal express it. This ownness – or is it uniqueness – is explained on the one hand by each human being's unique relationship with God, and on the other hand by referring to the fact mentioned earlier that no five fingers of a hand, no two branches of a tree, are identical.

Hence variation in temper (*alag alag mijāj*) exists not only between groups, however big or small, but also between members of the same small family; hence no two goats, men or fairies are of the same temper. This is why before being milked every single nanny goat must be caught hold of and held individually – "each has its own *mijāj*, and one must work accordingly". Whereas no change is possible at the first two levels of, for example, humanness or community, a certain temporary manipulation is conceivable at the last two levels of individual temperament and family or breed. Whereas normal mortals can not manipulate their humanness and become say, superhuman, nor can one change the community one is born into, a slow (*ṭhanḍā*, lit. "cold") horse can be made racy (*tēj*, lit. "fast", "sharp", "hot") by mixing "mustard oil or clarified butter and some spices you get in the bazaar". Similarly superhumans can alter their own physical appearance, at least temporarily, as is evident from the following incident narrated to me by old Jima:

> Once a *ban-buḍa* [lit. "old man of the woods", a superhuman creature] caught hold of a Kashmiri woman. He looked like a handsome, strong young man. She fell in love with him and he often stole up to her room and they made love. The neighbours had watched them and thought they were an immoral couple. So, one night, when the *ban-buḍa* had already climbed up the ladder to her room, they informed the police. They came and surrounded the house, and when the *ban-buḍa* tried to leave, they caught him and chained him to their jeep. Now he looked like one of those lovely white-faced, big monkeys you find in Kashmir. They beat him up and he admitted to being a *ban-buḍa*.

Here the *ban-buḍa* retained his own *mijāj*, even while appearing first as a man and then as a monkey – all he changed was outward form. Now *ban-buḍa* (and *ban-buḍi*, their female counterparts) are beings of a specific kind who, while continuing to be permanent members of that species, can at times make themselves invisible, or take on the form, the physical appearance (*shakal o surat*) of another genus or species. A human being can never make herself/himself invisible, but various, often maleficent supernatural creatures *(balā)* can; they are then visible only to religious specialists. The *ban-buḍi* who regularly visited *Bāji* A.Z.'s wife and her mother to beg for food and clothing could also make herself invisible to normal mortals. She could be seen by none except these two women who possessed special faculties.

Mijāj is a property ascribed by God through blood, the former because He is the ultimate arbiter and decides on goathood just as much as He does on humanity, the latter because it is through this link of specific types of blood that basically all goats are similar, just as all humans largely share very basic traits. It is again through this link of blood that people of one family have greater similarities than people of different families. Although no two men or women are of identical temper, the degrees of difference are least between siblings of the same gender, and much greater between the children of different parents. This logic applies to all those related by *rang* – hence both to consanguines and to affines in a society in which cousin marriage is frequent (Ch. 3). Figure 1.2 illustrates these concepts. It shows that there is minimal difference between those who share the same *rag*, *batri* and gender; the difference increases between both persons of the opposite gender and those of the same gender but with no *batri* in common.

Figure 1.2 The gender-specific transmission of *rag* and *batri*

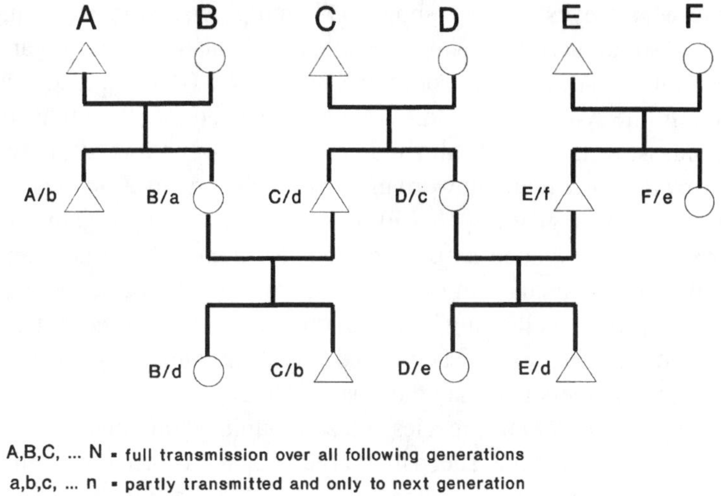

Since *mijāj* and the concept of authenticity are interwoven, and since the latter is intrinsic and implies essentiality and purity, it is also clear that great care must be taken when mixing different kinds of *mijāj*. Some *mijāj* mix better than others, just as in Bengal some types of blood mix well and others do not (cf. Fruzzetti and Östör 1982: 35). The tempers of a goat and a man are very different indeed, but some may at times harmonise, while others may not. The same holds true for a rider and his/her horse or mule – this is why they have to be broken in before being ridden regularly. Indeed the concept of harmony stretches so far that medicine prescribed by veterinary surgeons for goat diseases may be administered by the goat owner to humans in his family – sometimes with disastrous results, mainly perhaps because the dosage of modern pharmacopoeia can not yet be handled correctly. The occasional sale of an economically viable goat or a horse is explained by the fact that their owner did not hit it off with them, because their *mijāj* did not harmonise. This lack of harmony brought chaos or death to the herds or led to riding accidents. Similarly, there are cases in which the *mijāj* of husbands and wives did not harmonise, bringing them and their entire families much unhappiness and preventing, or even destroying, the tenuous state of *bal oṇa*, which I gloss as "well-being", and towards which all strive. Someone who is *bal* (cf. Hd.: *bal* = strength, power), may be described as someone whose eyes or face "shows *bā*", and glows; as in most cultures, so too here a glowing face or eyes are also signs of joy and happiness. *Bā*, derived from the Sanskrit *bhā* (glow, splendour), was in the Avestan "… almost always associated with notions of richness, well-being, health and beauty" (Mawet 1980: 290). The term *bal* is an important word in Bakkarwali conversation; it is the basic form of greeting (*bal e*) and expresses a whole gamut of positive states, such as physical power, mental happiness and material well-being – in other words, what psychologists refer to as "subjective well-being" (cf. Introduction). Together these states lead to harmony, to well-being, and to endanger this is by ignoring intrinsic tempers is, to say the least, foolhardy.

Mijāj varies among species and communities too; thus whereas those of goats are hot, sheep have cold tempers. Hence goats' milk is "hot", whereas that of sheep is "cold". Now, a little of a "hot" stuff satiates more than an equal quantity of a "cold" stuff. This is why, among others, the Bakkarwal almost never milk their sheep, only their goats; unlike a kid, "the lambs need all the milk. If we took some of it they would fall sick …". Another example cited by women informants, who during migration camp each year quite close to some Kashmiri villages, was the change in physical appearance of nubile girls among the Bakkarwal and the Kashmiri respectively: "Among us they say that the breasts (*čuča*) of a girl grow only after she has first slept with a man, but among the Kashmiri they grow even before marriage." Similarly, the age at menarche which is known (or supposed) to vary between populations, is related among other things to *mijāj*, not only at the level of the individual girl, but also to her social group, her community. At the individual level *mijāj* is decisive in whether a person fairs well or not after having a surgical operation. Also the actual number of days that a particular woman is "really impure" (*makru*) – in other words bleeds – after delivery may not be forty days; "usually it is much less, but then it all depends on her *mijāj*".

A person's blood (*rang*) is directly influenced by her/his parents, but indirectly also through places and their properties. It is through blood that, for example, grain – which as a plant also has a *mijāj*, depending on the properties of soil, water, air, altitude, etc. where it grew and by the innate temper of the community which grew it – influences humans who eat it over generations, absorbing it in their bodies, and hence in their blood. Similarly, though these themes are not elaborated upon by the Bakkarwal as they are in Hindu (e.g. Davis 1976; Zimmermann 1987) and Muslim (e.g. Hermansen 1988: 5ff.) texts, and though the concept of locationism may not be as sophisticated as in some other South Asian societies (Sax 1991; Vasavi 1994; Daniel 1984), here too places are thought to effect *mijāj* through the kinds of water that flow through them, the properties of their crops, the quality of their air, etc. All these properties are absorbed, but do not influence *mijāj* here and now; rather they are stored in the body and transmitted over generations through blood, in one of its many forms. Families living over generations in the same or contiguous areas and using adjoining pastures are thus likely to have *mijāj* which are reasonably similar; this is all the more so when they are actually related by blood.

The relationship between humans and their environment is often explained by metaphors drawing upon similar relations in the plant and animal worlds. In both worlds, the ideal principle is that of measure and proportion. Today these proportions have been largely altered by the interaction between humans and their environment, and it is this change which has led to an increase in general heat, and hence to the growth of vice and wickedness in the whole world. The heat is primarily caused by the excessive use of salt *(lūṇ),* by the excessive number of people. Thus many informants explained the phenomena of miscarriages and still births among humans and animals by comparing these with the excessive presence of chemical fertiliser *(khād)* as opposed to dung *(miñguṇ)* in the soil. Among humans excessive semen in the womb caused by intercourse in a late stage of pregnancy was said to be at the root of the evil (cf. Diemberger 1993: 108 for a similar metaphor of semen as manure among the Khumbo). The excessive semen or fertiliser, plus the increased use of sea salt *(samundar ko lūṇ)* rather than the traditional red rock salt *(guma lūṇ)* for the animals' salt licks "burns up" the soil of the lush mountain pastures, leading first to the growth of poisonous plants and ultimately to their barrenness. Among both humans and animals "since the new salt came in, things have changed". Among goats and sheep, not only does it start off by creating a kind of skin disease *(khārish),* but "of fifty animals about twenty miscarry". Among women, formerly "there was almost always a gap of three to four years between pregnancies … Now we all eat this new salt which is so hot and our girls get pregnant all the time and ultimately so many miscarriages take place". As among North Indian Rajputs (Kolenda 1984: 102), among the Bakkarwal too salt and semen are symbolically equated. The new salt plays the same dehydrant role as does excessive semen in the womb and too much sun in the earth (cf. Fig. 1.3). All are humorally speaking hot and are potentially capable of creating poison and death rather than life.

Figure 1.3 The potentially destructive role of salt, fertiliser, sun and semen, all of which can generate excessive heat and cause infertility and death

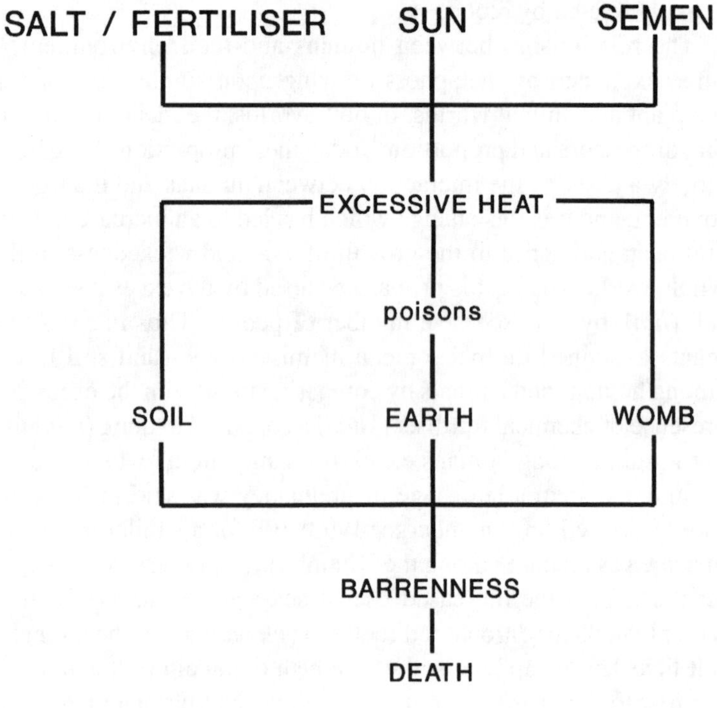

But all these negative trends follow a vertical gradient, and in the plains the situation is much worse than it is in the mountains. For the Bakkarwal, as for many other South Asian mountain communities, altitude is a wide-ranging metaphor, whose basic principle is, the higher the purer, and hence the more desirable (Parkes 1987; Stellrecht 1992; Diemberger 1993: 108). It is not altitude *per se* that matters so much, nor perhaps the single attributes of altitude, but all attributes taken together; it would not be wrong to speak of an overall syndrome of verticality. Figure 1.4 summarises some of these basic concepts.

Figure 1.4 The basic connotations of high altitude

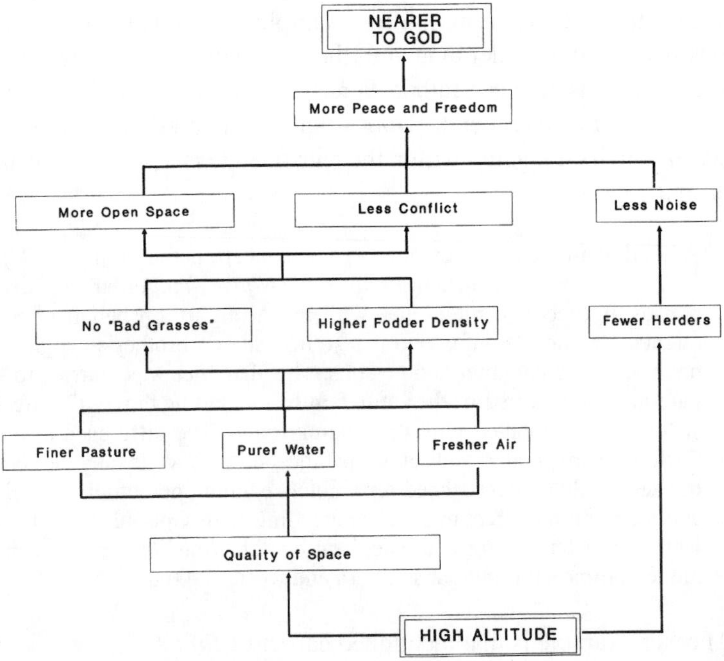

A family with high altitude pastures over generations thus has the following properties: it is not used to conflicts and hence is more peaceful and less quarrelsome; since the grass is better and abundant, its animals are healthier and more numerous; not only is the water but also the milk taken from these animals purer, and hence healthier. In addition, since the herds are more numerous, family members do not have to look for additional sources of subsistence, and can live off their pure, traditional occupation as herders. All this purity is naturally handed down through blood over generations. The contrary is true of those families who have been at low altitudes over generations. Incidentally, for a variety of economic and political reasons the wealthier a family, the higher its pastures (Rao 1992a).

The basic capacity to perform one's hereditary profession *(pēshā)* – whether that of herdsman or religious specialist – is also transmitted (cf. Malhotra and Trivedi 1981: 359 for similar opinions in Rajasthan) by *mijāj* via *rag*; the competence to perform it well is transmitted via *batri*. Only the notion of biological transactionalism widespread in northern India can explain that in spite of eventually better training, for example "A Bakkarwal will always be a better herder than you [the anthropologist], because his father and his father's father were herders too". This logic extends to all those related by *rang* – hence also to affines in a society in which endogamy within the patrilineage is a preferred form of marriage.

> A good example of the practice of this concept is the family of *Bāji* I.K., a religious specialist and a *pīr* of the *Naqshbandi* order, who dispenses amulets and intervenes with the Almighty on behalf of his clients. He and his wife, who is also his father's brother's daughter, have only one daughter and no sons. This daughter was married to a paternal relative. In time the entire family – including the *Bāji*'s wife's sister – were imputed with the healing touch. The difference in the dealings were gender- and status-specific, and thus while only the *Bāji* himself could be approached for amulets banning potentially maleficent superhuman creatures and interceding with God, all the others were competent to, for example, heal by "blowing" (*phūn̄k*), a technique common throughout southern and western Asia.

Another example is that mentioned earlier of *Bāji* A.Z.'s wife and her mother, who had access to special powers by virtue of being related through blood and/or marriage to a *pīr*. This spiritual transactionalism is, however, also the basis of the transmission of *baraka* in all Muslim societies.

Indeed, the concept of *mijāj* is perhaps situated at the nexus between the biological and the spiritual, because for the Bakkarwal these two are not, I suggest, two distinct domains. The notion is perhaps comparable to that of *svabhāva* (own nature) as mentioned in Sanskrit texts. On this premise, one could paraphrase Ramanujan's (1989: 46) delightful review of Hindu particularism, and suggest that each category of *mijāj* has its own laws, "… not to be universalized". The notion of *mijāj* serves to explain difference and diversity; every creature is in one way unique, but in another way it shares much with others – the amount in common depending largely on parentage. The concept is also used to explain why certain creatures and things do not eventually conform to expectations – these in their turn being couched in terms of authenticity and conceived of as something like what we tend to refer to as the average, the usual, but also the typical, the stereotype. Behaviour which is at variance with such expectations is explained in terms of long-term environmental influences which are seen as the result of human or superhuman agency. Finally, *mijāj* lays the foundation for the possibility of autonomy; as we shall shortly see it is simultaneously its major constraining factor. To conclude then, the notions of both authenticity and innate temper serve as the basic elements in constituting a world view which aims at establishing extreme coherence. What may be construed as incoherence is explained away by the context-specific manipulations of these same basic elements – till, hopefully, coherence is once again established. This coherence, I submit, is essential to the Bakkarwal concept of well-being, which will now be discussed.

Being and Well-being

Whether human, superhuman or animal, common to all beings is the fact that each possesses three interrelated properties, all derived from *rang*, and hence from parentage. These are *nafas*, *rū* and the capacity for receiving *ōsh*. While all three properties are, in the final count, God-given, *nafas* and the capacity for receiving *ōsh* are also largely determined by parentage. Unlike *rū*, which remains even after death, *nafas* and *ōsh* are destructible and liquid (Fig. 1.5), and "dry up" on death. *Nafas* (cf. Ar. *nafs*) is transmitted by the mother's blood (in Urdu *nafs* means blood also), and strengthened by her blood and milk. It manifests itself throughout life in various ways. Breath (also known as *nafas*) is its constant

Figure 1.5 Fluctuations over the life-course in the amounts of *nafas*, *ōsh* and *rū*, three basic properties that all beings are endowed with

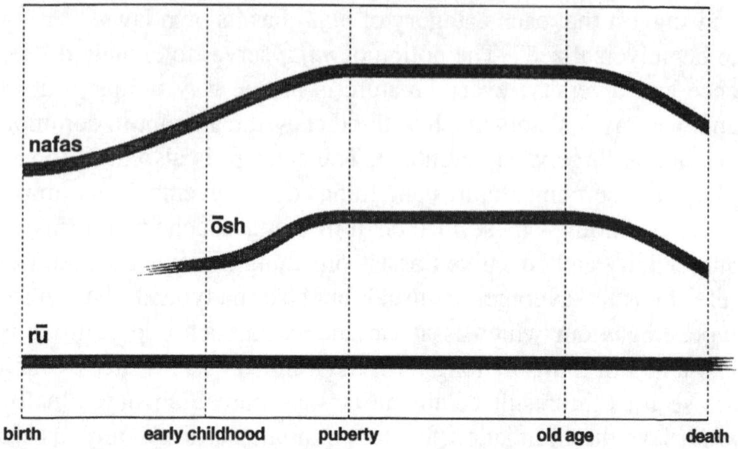

manifestation, alterable only through death, whereas physical strength (*jismāni tākat*) and certain character traits and behaviour patterns are, in principle, temporary and alterable manifestations. Breath is no doubt transmitted through blood, but it is also connected to air (*awā*), which when breathed in over generations transmits its specific properties and hence determines *mijāj*. Thus, a family living in a particular place and breathing in its specific air over generations not only has a specific *mijāj*, but its male members transmit this *mijāj* through their *rag* to their offspring, who also receive very specific ingredients for their *nafas* from their mothers' *batri*. The basic minimum *nafas* which an individual will carry with him/her through life is attained by a human child between the ages of about four and seven. In other beings it is attained much earlier. A sickly infant is said to have a weak *nafas*, while a healthy one is considered to have plenty of it. *Nafas* thus lays the basis for well-being in terms of physical strength. Mothers who mentioned babies who had died at birth (*jaman māñ*) or shortly after explained that their *nafas* was just too weak. The amount of *nafas* a being is born with depends primarily on the amount its mother has. *Nafas* is essentially "masculine" by nature and is classified as "hot" in the humoral system. Nevertheless it is transmitted to a baby not by its father through his semen, but entirely along the maternal line by its mother, partly through her blood, and partly through her milk. Hence, if a woman is deemed to have a good deal of *nafas*, it is assumed that her child will also have a fair dose of it. This is perhaps at the base of what transhumant Gujars of northern Kashmir told Pandit (1990: 110): "An immoral mother will always give birth to an immoral daughter." Beyond Kashmir, in other Islamic contexts similar beliefs regarding maternal transmission hold, and Al-Khayyat (1990: 22) reports the Iraqi proverb "... *al bint tala al-umha*, which means, 'The daughter takes after her mother morally'. In other words, the purity of the daughter reflects that of her mother". Similarly, among Mamasani pastoral nomads of southern Persia it is said that a "... son looks like his mother's brother, and a daughter looks like her mother's sister", since a mother influences her children through her milk in every way "... from physical features to character and later, personality" (Shahshahani 1986: 88). But this concept is echoed by Kashmiri Hindus too:

> It is commonly held that the substances of a wayward mother have a dominant and lasting influence on the daughter. This is expressed in the Kashmiri proverb: "if the mother and mother's sister are bad characters, what hope is there for the daughter (*maji masi yi ase kuri kus kasi*)". (Misri 1991: 242)

Among Kashmiri Hindus *nafas* represents a negative aspect of human physical compulsions; hence, for example, the expression *nafasay čhus* conveys commiseration for someone who has little choice but to resort to things unworthy of him/herself in order simply to survive (Madan: pers. comm. 1991). The potential negativeness of all that is conveyed by the mother through her blood and milk is strikingly evident in another example taken from the Hindu context of Bengal, where the term *prabritti* denotes not only inclination but also desire and a negative propensity – and this brings us back to the Bakkarwal term *batri*, the mother's vein.

Most negative characteristics imputed to a man or woman are explicitly traced to his or her *nafas*. Character is thus largely influenced by mother's blood and milk. Too much *nafas* in a woman leads her to be strong-headed, wilful and immoral, thence to disability and disease. In extreme cases she may even end up as a witch (*ḍākini*), somewhat like Khumbo women, who, if they "go bad", can turn into demonesses (Diemberger 1993: 99). In a man *nafas* may well lead to wealth and power, but if excessive, it also leads to his becoming cruel (*ḍaḍḍā*), and this again ultimately to sorrow and ruin for himself and hence ultimately for many others as well. So, when a man involved in a dispute is not prepared to accept the decision of the majority and compromise, because his *nafas* compels him (*jabrān ōṇa*) not to, he can ultimately become a danger to his community; he can then be delivered up to forces external to the group, such as the police. The two following examples illustrate typical situations in which excess of *nafas* was cited as being at the root of the problems.

T is a well-connected Bakkarwal. For the past several years he has been involved in a dispute with B concerning the marriage of his daughter to B's son. It is generally said that B paid money as bridewealth (*duniya*). After accepting the money and promising his daughter's hand, T married her off, allegedly for more money, to someone else. While T and his friends claim, among other things, that B never fulfilled his entire bridewealth commitment, B and his group claim that T's *nafas* has grown to such proportions that now he is selling his daughter for a living (*ūṇ nafas usko muč baṛh čale; ūṇ bēṭki na bēč khāṇ lag giyo e*).

P is around seventy years and crippled; she is also very poor and a widow. But she is full of verve – and she is the only Bakkarwal woman I know of who smokes. P's story was narrated to me by herself and by several other men and women; it is the gist of the latter which are of relevance here: When P was young, she was very beautiful; her first husband was poor and sickly … "it is not easy to live with a woman who has so much *nafas*" (*jis jaṇāṇi ko muč nafas oe, usko kul basāñ āsāṇ nai*). Anyway, the "poor fellow" died. Then she married a second time – a rich widower. And then she started behaving really strangely. "As long as she was poor her *nafas* was a lot (*muč*), but now, with wealth, it went out of bounds (*bē-ad*)." She began to do whatever she wanted and quarrelled with everyone – "she even started smoking", and "she abstained (*parēj na rakhio*) from nothing (especially sexual abstinence was implied, cf. Chs. 5, 6)". Eventually her second husband also died because of her; then she grew ill and lost all her animals.

The moral of P's story, as of so many others, is that an excess of *nafas* leads to an excess of fancifulness, and this in turn leads ultimately to ruin: "*muč nafas te muč shoñk āgiyo; muč shoñk te ōsh dabbe āyo, te barbād o giyo*". On the other hand, the basic consciousness of *shakas*, indeed the capacity for it, is both provided and embodied by *nafas*. The abstract Urdu/Persian noun *shakhsiyat* is not used by the Bakkarwal, and Bakkarwali usage also diverges from standard Qor'anic and classical Arabic usage in which, as Davies (1988: 83) succinctly expresses it: "The word *nafs* has many connotations: soul, spirit, mind, animate being, living entity, human being, person, self, mankind, life essence, humankind, vital principle." This variation appears to be in keeping with broader Semitic usage (cf. Wolff 1974: 24–48). Tapper (1991: 209) and Anderson (1985) suggest "emotion" and "passion" as additional translations of the term as used by Pashtuns in Afghanistan, its complement being *aql*; passion for the Bakkarwal, however, is only one expression of *nafas*.

If I retain the term "self" as a gloss for *shakas*, *nafas*, which provides and embodies the capacity for it, may be glossed by "selfhood". *Nafas* enables one to distinguish not only between humans and animals, between the dead and the living, but also between oneself *(apaṇ)* and the other *(pare),* between *man* (I), *tam* (you) and other similar categories in language (cf. Forchheimer 1953 for a review and discussion of such categories). It is the basis of self-awareness which, according to medieval Islamic concepts, is the "starting-point" of a child's "intellectual development", and is first observable when a forty-day-old infant first smiles (Gil'adi 1992: 23). This selfhood is not, as Cohen (1977) has suggested, "achieved"; it is innate. Yet, for the Bakkarwal the *shakas*, in which the idea of "I" (perhaps even of the "Private Self" – Lienhardt 1985) is implicit, is not static. The fluctuation in the amount of *nafas* in a *shakas* is the cause of the change in the latter over time and in specific situations. Sociologically speaking, one could interpret this as follows: In different roles we have different selves, but due to innate temper, the core remains constant. In other words, the kind of *shakas* one is is the result of factors that are both innate and achieved in negotiation and interaction with other *shakas*.

"God has ordered us", said Baggo, "not to be egocentric (*nafasai*), and to think and care for others before thinking of oneself." The theme of *nafase-nafasai*, of selfishness and self-centredness – the Bakkarwal do not to my knowledge distinguish between egoism and egocentrism – and the competition and hardship resulting therefrom, is indeed a fairly common one among elderly Bakkarwal complaining of present-day miseries both private and public. Self-centredness, they argue, must be destructive, for then *nafas* takes over entirely; from this follow necessarily irreligiosity and faithlessness *(bēdīnī),* with the ultimate result that God's commands are not heeded. To prevent egocentrism one must reach a kind of homeostasis between *nafas* on the one hand and a property called *ōsh*, on the other. As already mentioned, animate beings are born with the capacity to receive *ōsh* (cf. Ur./Pers. *hosh* = awareness, mind, understanding, care, consciousness, alertness), the capacity for personhood. This capacity is activated after birth (Fig. 1.5), in the first years of life, in humans later than in animals, and in superhumans, some said, earlier than in animals. But though human children are late-starters, they usually end up with much more *ōsh* than do animals, among whom horses and dogs in particular are credited with a great deal of it. In fact, while guiding a horse through steep or slippery terrain, for example, on migration, *ōsh* is the term used to indicate to the horse that it should be extra careful – for "horses do understand a lot". Goats have more *ōsh* than sheep and some goats are specially gifted; these, say the Bakkarwal, lead the flock.

Ōsh comes to a human child increasingly from the age of seven or eight years (Gil'adi 1992: 23 mentions seven as the age at which children in medieval Islam were said to start "to distinguish between good and evil") – to girls often a little earlier than to boys. However, generally boys are said to end up having more of it than girls. *Ōsh* is closely related to "God's own light" *(Nūr Allāh or Khudā ki lō)* and manifests itself through the capacity for reflection, reason and comprehension (*dyānat*), the capacity for sympathy and empathy (*amdardi*), and through intelligence (*čālāki*), bravery (*baāduri*) and other similar, positively rated characteristics. Someone who is without *ōsh* (*bē-ōsh*) may be either unconscious or indiscriminating; in this Bakkarwali conforms to usage in other North Indian languages, where the term denotes the sense of discernment and/or consciousness. In Kashmiri, for example, the expression *hōsh as* (lit.: *hōsh* is coming) can apply both to a child who is beginning to discriminate as well as to a person regaining consciousness after fainting (Madan: pers. comm. 1991). Among the Bakkarwal it is *ōsh*, which like *nafas* is masculine, but "cold", which enables an older child not to quarrel over a piece of dried molasses with a younger sibling – it is his capacity for reason which helps him overcome his desire for self-gratification. It is *ōsh* which enables a woman to continue to live with her husband, although she may be unhappy with him and in love with someone else – it is the capacity for comprehension which helps her overcome her wish for self-fulfilment. It is *ōsh* again which enables a wealthy man to help and support the poor – it is his capacity for sympathy which helps him overcome his desire for self-enrichment. It is *ōsh* which enables a shepherd to tend his flocks well, day and night – it is his intuitive understanding and bravery which help him overcome his laziness and fear. It is hence from the age at which a child first begins to have *ōsh* and demonstrate intelligence that he is gradually entrusted with herd animals for a short while each day; he can now take small decisions – for him these are the first steps towards the herder's autonomy. To eventually start sending a child to school also makes sense only when he/she has enough *ōsh*, for "knowledge (*ilum*) can not be obtained without *ōsh*".

As we shall see in Chapter 2, the Bakkarwal distinguish between different types of knowledge; however, since the basic capacity to understand is God-given, there is no potential conflict between human efforts towards, say, acquiring knowledge through secular means and revealed knowledge through the Qor'an. The concept of *ōsh* being a gift of God's own light ("*khudā to apni lō ditti e*") is a variation on a theme familiar in Islamic mysticism (cf. Gairdner 1952: 140ff.) in which the luminosity of human faculties is referred to; it is found at the popular level in many Muslim societies, including those of South Asia (cf. Kurin 1984: 198ff.) It may not also be far-fetched to compare the Bakkarwal concept of *ōsh* to the Hindu notion of *tejas*, of "luminous power", of "triumphant glory", of "… the power … to do the good, (the power to uphold … [the] cosmomoral order". Though it is not clear whether ordinary mortals also possess *tejas*, or whether this is restricted to holy men and kings, Inden (1985: 147) notes: "To say that a person was endowed with (*tejas*) … was to say that he was commanded by a higher self. His intellect, the faculty of enlightened existence, directed his mind or will …." Remaining within the bounds of Islam, the concept of *ōsh* is also comparable to the Atjehnese notion of *akal*, which is "… similar to our concept of rationality.

Through the use of *akal*, man can know God's commands and control his instinctive nature, *hawa nafsu*" (Siegel 1969: 100). *Ōsh* lays the basis for knowledge, control, rationality and positive emotions. In Bakkarwal concepts, as I understand them, rationality and emotion are not opposites; positive and negative emotions are opposed, and while the former go hand in hand with reason, the latter are paired with unreasonableness. Someone who can feel for others, who has a big heart (*baṛo dil*), automatically also has enough *ōsh* to put him/herself in another's place. Positive emotions include empathy and sympathy and imply a broader perspective, and hence a better understanding (*samaj*) of situations. They are thus also the basis for reasoned opinion (*rāe*). Derived from the Arabic term *ra'y*, which covers both good and bad opinions (Shafiq 1984), *rāe* carries the positive connotation of opinion guided by moral judgement. Morality here, as apparently also among Hindus (cf. Miller 1994), is to be understood as that which is compatible with innate temper, which in turn is ultimately preordained by God. A person's moral actions lead to his/her well-being. Since persons are by definition social beings, well-being must be relational. As I shall show in Chapter 5, only those persons who are recognised as having enough well-being are entitled to impose their opinions on others and thereby resort to surrogate decision making. Through their well-being these persons have proved that they have enough *ōsh* to freely (*apṇi khushi nāḷ*) make the right choices for themselves, and can thus be entrusted with decision making for those who are less competent. On the other hand, those who do not possess enough *ōsh* – children as compared to adults, women as compared to men, shepherds as compared to their masters, in short those with less publicly demonstrated well-being – need help and supervision. Yet, we shall also see that there is an inconsistency built into this system in the form of various men, known as *khaṛpeñč*, who are considered rash and untrustworthy, but nevertheless wield much influence.

Well-being can, however, be diminished. This happens when a person *(bandā)* is affected either by external agents or by internal imbalances. An external agent, such as a *jin* or a *ban-buḍi*, can rob one of one's *ōsh* (i.e. make one *bē-ōsh*). Alternatively, internal imbalances of various kinds can affect one. Unlike among the Ilongot, where "deviance, illness, madness, and failure to perform are typically attributed to things outside the self' (Rosaldo 1986: 147), here the explanations are more varied and can equally be attributed to changes within the self caused by one's own mistakes. Most of these mistakes are traced to an excess of *nafas* over *ōsh*. Jima's brains (*magas*), for example, had progressively deteriorated the more his *nafas* grew and the prouder and more querulous he became. The fourteen-year-old headstrong Phullañ, whose *ōsh* had not quite stabilised and who was known to have a strong *nafas*, was prone both to attacks of giddiness with occasional nausea (*dil phirāñ*, lit. turning of the heart), when she nearly fainted, and to attacks of intense joy, when she laughed incessantly. It was the constantly changing balance between her *nafas* and her *ōsh*, between negative and positive emotions, which caused her head and her heart (both referred to in this context as *dil*) to turn. Some said that even Bahadura, whose brains had suddenly been so affected by a spell (*jādu*) cast on him by a jealous neighbour's wife that he made nonsensical statements and could no longer tell right from wrong, was partly to blame for his predicament; he should not have enticed away his neighbour's shepherd with the promise of better pay. Bakkarwal discourse also abounds in stories highlighting the well-being of neighbours and friends. Common to them all is the theme of *ōsh* pitted against and triumphant over so-and-so's selfish inclinations, which are all portrayed as directly connected to *nafas*. Agency – even when seen as primarily external – is thus inconceivable without the active participation of *nafas*, the control being mediated by *ōsh*.

Indeed, only in exceptional cases can humans attain wisdom without the collaboration of both *nafas* and *ōsh*. One such exception was the Bakkarwal Wali Jamal, who, so the story goes, became a *pīr* some "seven generations ago".

> He was grazing his animals in the forest when suddenly he saw flames on the mountains. Terrified, he ran away; the flames subsided and he returned to the spot, but again the flames sprang up. This happened seven times, and finally, Wali Jamal asked, "What are you?" The answer was, "I am *paighambar Khuda Khizr*. I bless you. Seven generations of yours will be *pīr* and *wali*, without even learning; after that also the generations will continue and have enough". [Legends about *Khuda Khizr* are popular in large parts of South Asia, and this figure is "… honoured as a god of rain in Sind and Panjab …". (Vaudeville 1993: 85, n.32; cf. also E.I.: *Kh^{w}adja Khidr*, *Al-Khadir*)]

Now, Wali Jamal had a great deal of *ōsh*, but not enough *nafas* to compel him to learn, but since he was an unusually good (*nēk*) man, God chose him out. The case of 'Ubaid Allah Bijrān, a well-known Bakkarwal *pīr* in the early years of this century was different; neither God nor his *ōsh* alone were responsible for his learning. His *nafas*, which created in him the intense desire to learn, also played a major part (Rao 1990). Now, it is a moot point whether God gives *ōsh* equally to all, but my interlocutors all agreed that the amount of *ōsh* a normal adult ends up with is interconnected with the amount of *nafas* he/she has. Too much *nafas* implies disharmony and lack of control – by *ōsh* and by society. As in most societies, so too among the Bakkarwal lack of control implies an unbounded state and signals danger. The ideal balance is attained when *ōsh* somewhat exceeds *nafas*. Here unlike, for example, in Islamic Sudan (Boddy 1988: 10), the legitimate amount of the latter is according to all informants greater for men than for women. Table 1.2 sets out the opinion of most Bakkarwal I spoke to concerning these ideals as compared to what they consider the reality.

Table 1.2. General opinion on gender-specific amounts of *nafas* and *ōsh*

Ideal		**Reality**	
Male	**Female**	**Male**	**Female**
Lots of *nafas*	Less *nafas*	Medium *nafas*	Lots of *nafas*
Lots of *ōsh*	Lots of *ōsh*	Medium *ōsh*	Little *ōsh*

When the balance between *ōsh* and *nafas* is upset and there is an excess of the latter there is usually trouble, insofar as the concerned woman/man does not fulfil the expectations of her/his fellows: she/he is not a good wife or brother, mother or son, shepherd or politician. In short, role expectations are not fulfilled, or as Leslie (1986: 45) has expressed it: "The problem occurs when one's nature somehow fails to coincide with one's function."

Hence in former times Bakkarwal political representatives (*mukaddam*) were chosen on the basis of the combined criteria of enough *nafas*, manifested through bodily strength, and *ōsh*, manifested through reflection and intelligence (cf. Ch. 5 for details). The legitimate boundaries of *nafas* are thus the limits to which a social role can be conceivably stretched. Every individual can and does, no doubt, incorporate several roles simultaneously; the more *ōsh* one has the better one is at playing these roles and the more numerous these can be. *Ōsh* and *nafas* are interdependent, for much the same reasons as "the notion of individual responsibility is essentially the problem of freedom of the will at one remove" (Hill 1993: 3). Only those with adequate *nafas* can receive enough *ōsh* to develop a sense of responsibility; those who can not control their *nafas* (and have it in excess) are unworthy of trust, and hence irresponsible. While it is *nafas* which enables a creature to take any action at all, it is *ōsh* which makes it aware of its actions, its rights and duties, its responsibilities: a man towards his father, a woman towards her husband, a horse towards its rider, a dog towards its master. *Ōsh* complements *nafas* and binds the potentially unbound and unbounded self into the comparatively bounded *bandā*, the social being – among humans the "public" person. This may remind us of Freud's concept of the ego controlling the id. In this non-Western model – if we use the terms "person" and "self" at all – it would be a mistake to try to use them as synonyms as Ingold (1991: 367) suggests in a rather sweeping attempt to generalise about "non-Western peoples" and "non-Western ideas". This native model also reverses Crawford et al.'s observation (1992: 117), that "... although reflection is an individual process, the capacity of human beings for reflection is premised on intersubjectivity". Here, the capacity for reflection is very much an individual capacity; it is the process of reflection which, being essentially social, is premised on intersubjectivity. Human reflection here is conceived of as a series of feedbacks between the various contextualised sets of what Goffman (1972: 80) considered a person's numerous selves, or more precisely between the different sequences of "I's" and "Me's" postulated by George Mead (1934).

A third property peculiar to humans only is that of *rū* (cf. Ar. *rūḥ*); a human baby enters the world with it (cf. Fig. 1.5). It manifests itself outwardly through great physical beauty and inwardly through religiosity. Although it is usually entirely subordinate to *nafas*, it is first through *nafas* and through *ōsh* that *rū*, which is basically dormant *(suto),* can be activated and awakened *(jāgeo).* It can be activated by *nafas* from early childhood onwards and then through *ōsh* usually around fifteen or sixteen years of age. In P's case cited above, her exceptional beauty in youth is explained by her *rū*, which was great. But her *nafas* subjugated *(dabāyo)* her *rū* completely, and this was inevitable, since her *nafas* even subjugated her *ōsh.* In most humans, however, *rū* is left more or less dormant throughout life. The notion of a dormant *rū*, activated only through religious fervour and/or possession, is attested in other Islamic societies as well; thus, for example, the Gnawa brotherhood speaks of normal humans – those never possessed – as the "living-dead" (Paques 1991: 138). At death, however, while both *nafas* and *ōsh* "dry up", what remains is *rū*. I shall return briefly to the fate of *rū* in the last chapter. It suffices for now to say that this concept includes what may be termed the capacity to be a complete individual, free of all bonds – except of that with God, one's ultimate Maker.

It should by now be fairly clear that to understand Bakkarwal concepts of human nature we must not look for contrasts in terms of nature versus culture, the biological versus the social. Durkheim's (1914) notion of *homo duplex*, presupposing conceptual differences not only of body and soul, but also of the pre-social and the social, the egoistic and the moral nature of humans, which has been so crucial in the development of so much of anthropology, does not lead us far with the Bakkarwal. Here human nature and human actions are conceived of as products of the combination of nature and nurture, of parentage and environment, of the innate and the learned.

Being Born

While in the womb, a child to be does not possess any of the above-mentioned properties fully. The blood in the womb *(pēṭ)* slowly grows in quantity from a drop (*bund*) to swell and become a baby: "Blood swells in the womb, like milk swells in a pot when you boil it. If you boil it down, it hardens through heat." Similarly the blood hardens day by day over nine full months.

There appears to be a very mild seasonality in Bakkarwal births (cf. Fig. 5.1), the peak period for 105 reported births lying between mid-June and mid-July (i.e. the month of *hāṛ*). The four births (*jaman*) observed by me did not vary much in detail. Three of the four babies born were girls, and no gender-specific distinction was made in the care of mother and child after the delivery. Bakkarwal camps in all seasons are small affairs, and at none of the four deliveries *(khalāsi)* I attended were more than five women present. Here there are no professional midwives as in certain other parts of South Asia, where women from specific low castes carry out this task (e.g. Fruzzetti 1981: 96; Gideon 1962). In each of the four deliveries the choice of the midwife was spontaneous and depended on the initiative taken by any given, elderly woman. Kin relationships were neither observed, nor reported to play any major part in the choice. One of the principal tasks of the midwife is to prevent the placenta, which is full of poison, rising up in deadly fashion to the mother's heart. Puerperal fever is imputed to the midwife having done a bad, or at least incomplete, job and having left "bits of the placenta" in the parturient's body (cf. Gideon 1962: 1225). The placenta is of a slightly ambiguous nature. On the one hand, as in other Islamic cultures (e.g. Nicolas 1972: 91–2), it is conceived of as the "companion" *(sāthi)* of a newborn baby, and in an easy delivery it is said that it comes out almost "with the infant". But when speaking of the mother the term used for the placenta is *jēr* (lit. poison, cf. Hd. *jāru* and Ur./Pers. *zahr*), which is said to be a tremendous source of danger to her. When the placenta does not "come out with the baby", it must to a certain extent be coaxed and threatened (*sharat*, lit. "wager") out of a woman's body, and this is the joint work of the woman and her midwife. Perhaps exorcist in nature, these acts consist of tapping the parturient on the head with a sickle, circling her head and then her abdomen with a lighted Kashmiri fire-pot *(kāñgṛi)* rarely used by the Bakkarwal otherwise, and banging on a metal pot with a metal spoon over her head. Before each act, the midwife pronounces the formula *Bismillā*, and in between adjures fairly loudly "In God's name!" *("Khudā ko nāñ", "Allāh ko nāñ")*. The afterbirth is buried together with some earth scraped up from the floor and the pine branches and needles or straw and leaves which serve as carpeting in summer and winter respectively. The burial spot does not appear to be of any importance.

Only after the placenta has been expelled is the newborn baby *(jātak)* attended to. To clear the cord of "blood seeds" *(rat ko bīj)*, which would be too "hot" for the baby, the midwife now takes the umbilical cord *(nāḷā)* in her right hand and smoothes it out with her left hand, in the direction of the placenta (cf. Misri 1991: 46, 57). She then uses any string at hand to tie three knots in the umbilical cord and, murmuring "*Bismillā*", she cuts it *(nāḷā kapāñ)* with a sharp knife *(čāku)* behind the last knot. In the meantime warm water is prepared for the infant to be bathed *(baḍēri)*. I was told that soap is used these days, but did not observe this. In all the deliveries I attended the infant was covered with a fair amount of *vernix caseosa*, a greasy whitish substance, which collects on fetal skin from the fifth month onwards. During the bath the infant is held by the midwife, while another woman ladles the water over it. With each ladleful, the formula "*Bismillā*" is pronounced. The infant's ears, head and nose are rubbed especially well by the midwife, who also holds it upside down for a moment, before throwing it up a tiny bit and catching it three times. The cleaning of the nose *(nak čakāñ)* is especially important, as only through this act of enlarging *(baṛo kario)* the nostrils will the baby be able to breathe freely and well. This is the first of a series of three compulsory ritual bathings every human must undergo – on birth, marriage and death (lit. three baths may not be postponed – that at the birth of a child, and that of the bridegroom and that at death: "*trē baḍēri ṭāl nai – yo jātak ki jaman ki baḍēri, te marāj ki baḍēri, te maran ki baḍēri – trē baḍēri durust e, ālā tālā kā ya manzūr e*"). It is through this first bath that, with God's acceptance, the newborn is prepared officially for its entry into the world of the living. The unwashed infant may be touched only by its midwife, and one who dies before this initial bath is considered "not to have lived", but to have "died at birth". In the phase between delivery and bathing, the newborn is of special danger to its own mother, and hence she should not even see it. It may well be that this first glance is avoided, as it is in many societies with high infant mortality, to prevent the mother from grieving excessively in case the child dies. But it could also be that since the mother is held to be in a special state of danger after delivery, she needs protection from this creature who is still marginal to human society (cf. Christinat 1989: 61). After it is bathed the infant is wrapped up and laid next to its mother, on either side. After burying the placenta and washing herself thoroughly, the midwife then utters a "*Bismillā*" and gathers up the infant in her arms. Holding its right earlobe with the fingers of her right hand, she holds the child out to its father or ideally to any man who knows the entire Qor'an by heart (an *āfij*), or parts of it (a *mullā*), or even someone who says his prayers regularly (a *marāb*), and tells him to "Read *(paṛ) bang*". *Bang* (cf. Pnj. *bang* = the muezzin's call) consists of whispering the *shahada*, the Islamic testament of faith, in the baby's ear. Once the baby has heard *(sunnā)* this, it becomes "one who has heard", i.e. a "*sunnī*", and thus a Muslim. The concept behind this folk etymology entitles the baby, should it now die, to a proper Muslim burial and to the reading of the *kalīma* at its grave. Only now, as a Muslim, may it be nursed by its mother, and hence the midwife now tells her to take it to her breast. The child is dressed in clothes only after it is at least five days old, and some mothers wait even forty days. The first clothes of a baby must be stitched by its own mother; there are no colour differences according to gender, but nowadays, more costly plain terrycloth is used for boys, whereas usually cheaper printed "*čhiñṭ*" is used for girls.

The Dangerous and the Endangered

Beyond the initial liminal phase, once humans and animals are acknowledged as belonging to their respective categories, they join their mothers in a common state of danger which may last for up to forty days. No longer do they constitute a threat to their mothers; on the contrary, together mother and child turn into the most vulnerable of all beings who simultaneously pose a threat to all others, especially all adult men. But in the transitional stage between the foetal and the newborn, just before and during birth, a baby, and especially its afterbirth, enjoys a certain restricted autonomy; although it does not possess any *ōsh*, it is said to have the capacity ("only Allah knows why", and hence "not explainable" to the author) to "choose" between poisoning and killing its mother or joining her in life. As certain acts at birth mentioned above show, everything depends on who wins the wager. Even if the afterbirth loses, to begin with both mother and child have a tenuous bond with life; it is this uncertainty, this indecisiveness between life and death, which makes them both endangered and dangerous. The term *lōs* circumscribes this very specific type of danger, which finds social expression in the mother and child's extreme pollution *(muč makru)*. During this period – also known as *lōs* – the mother sleeps alone and the only physical contact she has is with her infant. No food she may cook can be eaten by anyone else, and even the utensils she eats off are kept separate *(bāñḍā na rilāṛi)*. A woman in this phase is also known as *lōs*; she enters it *(lōs o gai)* when labour starts and ideally she leaves it *(lōs uṭhan lagi)* after forty days. Unlike Kashmiri Hindus (Misri 1991: 49–51) among whom mother and baby are affected by different periods of pollution, among the Bakkarwal ideally the period of pollution for both is forty days; as mentioned earlier, in practice it is often much shorter, but a minimum of five days is always observed.

As has been discussed above certain biological traits fix the basic pattern of each creature in a social matrix. This would suggest an extremely formalised social system with little room for flexibility and hence for autonomy. This is indeed also the image projected, especially when dealing with power structures from beyond the community. In practice, however, at every step decisions are taken and put into action which contravene all deterministic ideology. Thus, for example, various protective acts are undertaken to safeguard both the mother and her newborn from evil forces. These threats faced are partly external, but emanate partly from their own physical natures. Most important among the former are the *balā*, supernatural creatures who, following God's command, are especially active in the first five days following birth, but only between midnight and the morning's first *āzān*. They are of three kinds: adult males *(jin)*, adult females *(pari)* and children of both sexes *(pūtna)*. The last are particularly feared, as they are invisible to all except the specialised *pīr*. According to gender and age these three types of obnoxious beings fervently seek out a human – never, however, an animal – to satisfy their innermost urges. The *jin* are, vampire-like, drawn to parturients by "bad smells", and especially that of blood; hence every day for the first five to seven days, the somewhat soiled carpeting on which the woman lies is thrown out, and new bedding brought in, while she herself is washed every second day for forty days. The *pari*, who are invisible to humans though "one often hears their music", "live in the woods and mountains" and are desirous of "stealing away" babies to make them their own. The little *pūtna* claim the infants as playmates and are thus relatively harmless when compared to Pūtanā, the demoness of Hindu mythology, the nurse of the wicked King Kaṃsa who tried to poison the baby Krishna with the venom of her breasts; this demoness who also appeared as a vulture, a symbol of death, is widely held in India to be a great threat to children. To guard against the *pari* and the *pūtna*, the newly delivered Bakkarwal mother may not sleep on the first night after giving birth. To keep her awake she is fed a few pieces of *nukuḷ*, also known as *shirini kā phūl*. Before being administered to her this sugar-coated chick-pea is consecrated by blowing over it and repeating an incantation (a process known as *damnā*); it is also said to act as something of a painkiller. The only other protective measure observed against these creatures – as against all other potential sources of harm – is veiling *(parda)*. During the dangerous phase the face of neither mother nor child is visible; the headscarf is pulled low over the woman's face, and the baby is wrapped up and curtained off from the prying glances of all and sundry.

Whereas danger from supernatural creatures is dealt with in an apotropaic manner, potential danger from fellow humans, in the form of the evil eye, is warded off not by avoidance, as say in the Panjab (Gideon 1962: 1227–8), but by placating it *(nīt karnā)*. The term *nīt* probably derives from Hindi *nīti* (= good conduct, virtue) and in such contexts I often heard the sentence "*nīt kar li ki bal o jāī*", i.e. literally, "did something good so that (she) may get well". Placating consists of making a sacrifice *(banḍārā, or makhnā)*, while the term *bal* circumscribes the positive states of health, strength and happiness, which are some of the basic components of well-being. Indeed to thank God for the safe delivery, to protect both mother and child from further problems and to hasten the mother's recovery, the father is expected to sacrifice an animal immediately after the baby is first washed. Part of this meat is to be "thrown out so that the hungry may be satiated and God may be pleased". The rest "is to be cooked for guests", and distributed, along with cooked rice, to all the neighbours, who in their turn, are then expected to wish both mother and baby a long life. The sacrificial animal is led to the parturient and made to look at her (cf. Casimir and Rao forthcoming) before being taken out and sacrificed; if it is a chicken it is circled over her abdomen five times. In practice, however, after the first or second births, this protective act is often not resorted to in the stipulated manner. Unlike in the *kanḍūri* sacrifice mentioned below, mothers themselves play no role in the *banḍārā/makhnā* sacrifice, and hence women were often uncertain about whether or not their husbands had performed these rites for all their children. But they did say that the husbands of their neighbours or relatives had often omitted the act, and criticised them for this. Even in the four births I attended there was a certain variation in practice, as shown in Table 1.3.

Table 1.3 Animals sacrificed at or after the birth of four children

Case	**Birth Order and Gender**	**Gender of Siblings**		**Sacrifice**
		M	**F**	
1	4F	2	1	Chicken 1 day later
2	5F	3	1	Chicken 2 days later[1]
3	3M	1	1	Sheep after delivery[2]
4	3M	2	0	Sheep 1 day later[3]

Birth order and gender refer to the newborn baby.
[1]The husband said that he had "no time to do it that day".
[2]The meat was distributed as required by custom.
[3]People commented, however, that the animal sacrificed was anyway injured and had to be killed. In addition, the husband's younger brother tried to sell a portion of it on the sly; I never managed to find out whether the husband knew of this or not.

Both mother and baby are vulnerable in the postnatal period, especially in the first five days, to various illnesses imputed to internal deficiencies. The newborn infant can be affected either by having "too little blood" or by a wound on its umbilical stump. To prevent its forming, dried and powdered roots of *baṇvevo* (*Bergenia ciliata* or *B. stracheyi, Saxifragaceae*) are applied; if these do not help, and a wound forms or continues to bleed or fester, dandelion (*hand*) leaves are boiled in water and tied on to the stump. To prevent the infant from having "too little blood", it must be "kept hot" by not exposing it to draughts, not bathing it – after its initial bath – during the first five days, as well as by nourishing it with "hot" liquids. Unlike neighbouring Muslim Kashmiris among whom the very first milk of a woman is discarded, the Bakkarwal greatly value this milk (known as *krīṛ* and held to be very "hot") and give it to the baby. The first milk of a nanny goat (known as *bawḷi*) is also greatly valued and given partly to her kid and partly consumed as a delicacy by the herder's family and neighbours. Before an infant is nursed by its human mother, it must be given a few drops of goat's milk, or if this is not available, buffalo's milk. In addition to possessing certain medicinal properties, these drops of colostrum "bind" *(badāñ)* the baby to its future profession *(pēshā),* and teach it that the animal in milch *(liāri)* is like its mother, and that when older it "must take care of her". Sheep's milk would never be eligible for an infant, as it is "cold". The vast majority of Bakkarwal women I met had had little difficulty in breastfeeding their babies in the first few months after birth. The few who reported problems had started their babies on supplementary goat's milk a little earlier than usual. Although a woman does occasionally pacify a relative's baby by giving it her breast, I never came across a case in which an infant whose mother died at its birth or shortly after had been nursed by a foster mother; indeed I was told that "if in the first ten days (after delivery) a woman dies, usually the baby also dies soon after". If a woman's milk is insufficient, her baby is fed for the first five days with goat's milk, just as a puppy is. A cloth is dipped first in sugared water (cf. Gideon 1962: 1228; Lewis 1958: 48) and then in milk and given to the baby to suck. To increase her milk a mother may after the fourth day, for roughly one week, be daily administered a special porridge. This is prepared by lightly roasting and then boiling lentils (*masūr*, *Lens esculenta*) and foxtailed (Italian) millet (*kangṇi*, *Setaria italica*) in equal proportions, adding sugar and clarified butter and boiling the mixture in milk till it thickens.

For the infant, danger looms large even after the first five days; unlike Hindu babies whose fate is now largely secured through heavenly writing (e.g. by Bidhatapurush or by Bemata (cf. Goodwin Raheja 1988: 96)), for the Muslim Bakkarwal much is still open. Indeed it may happen that an infant does well for the first few days but then develops worrying symptoms. One such instance was that of Zaina's son.

> On 7 August 1981, twenty days after the child was born, Zaina took the rather unusual risk of leaving her camp to come and ask me for advice. I was at the time spending a few days in a Kashmiri village, some twelve kilometres away. "For the first five days he was o.k.", she said. "Then he started having problems passing stool. He has been crying a lot at night. Now look, his tummy is swollen and his liver *(kalīja)* has become hard *(tang*: lit. narrow)." Slightly warmed leaves of the mountain maple tree (*kanzil*, *Acer caesium* or *Acer acuminatum* – Sharma and Jamwal 1988: 151–2) placed on the lower abdomen had not helped, nor had the medicine bought by the baby's father without prescription at a chemist's shop in the nearest town.

Narrowness *(tangi)* is an important Bakkarwal concept and denotes lack of space (Rao 1992a: 97), constriction and hence a reduction of general well-being. As mentioned earlier, narrowness restricts the passage of body fluids; if these fluids are at a low level, as they are in an infant, such restrictions may ultimately lead to the "drying up" and hardening of internal organs, such as the liver. The causes for constriction may be mechanical, and thus curable by medicines; but they may also be supernatural, since certain *jin* are known to be especially fond of the blood flowing through the liver, which they try and squeeze out. Luckily Zaina's child ultimately responded to medicines, and there was no need to seek further help.

The day after the period of pollution officially ends the mother may begin to cook and participate in light housework. Whatever the real duration of her period of *lōs*, the fortieth day (the *čāḷi*) is the official day of release from pollution and from all varieties of danger, and is celebrated in the household. From today onwards neither mother nor child need be veiled when leaving their tent. As on the fifth day, so also on the fortieth the mother bathes and washes her hair and puts on new clothes which are given (or sent) to her by her parents. Her baby is also bathed and dressed in new clothes. Even in relatively poor families a good meal of rice and meat or chicken is cooked and neighbours and visitors fed.

The implications of feeding are of course not only social, but also religious, and carry connotations of sacrifice. In Bakkarwali there are three terms which can be translated as "sacrifice": *khayrāt*, *banḍārā/makhnā*, and *kanḍūri*; their context-specific use and meaning is set out below:

Type of Sacrifice

khayrāt	given to community to please and thank God
banḍārā/makhnā	given to nature and the hungry to please God; given to community members to gratify them
kanḍūri	given only by women to women (other mothers) to beseech Fatima

While the term *khayrāt* is widely known in the Muslim world (<Ar. *khayrat* = charities), *banḍārā* and *makhnā* probably derive from Hindi *bhanḍārā* (a feast given to mendicants) and *makh* (sacrifice) respectively. Among the Bakkarwal a *khayrāt* may be hosted only by men, and though it is a community affair, the primary invitees are also male; such sacrificial feasts are usually organised to celebrate and share with others and to thank God for His bountifulness. A *banḍārā* or *makhnā* can be organised not only after a birth, but (as it is in some Kashmiri Muslim villages too) in periods of incessant rain and storm to plead for better weather for men and herds; alternatively it can be organised after a series of accidents in which either animals or humans slipped on the high slopes, and were injured or died. In all these examples there were "natural" phenomena involved and some force had to be placated. Finally, the *kanḍūri* (<Pnj. *kaṇḍūrī*) is a small sacrificial feast hosted exclusively for women by women who have lost several babies either at birth, or shortly thereafter. It is attended primarily by neighbours, eventually also from other ethnic groups, and is given in honour of the Prophet's daughter, Fatima, whose *khirfa* (cf. Hd. *kripā* = mercy and Pers. *kerfe* = virtue/merit) is beseeched. The *kanḍūri* is thus one of the very few occasions for the public display – albeit only among women – of female

autonomy and agency. A brief comparison of the different contexts of sacrificial feasts and gender roles shows that whereas men can display agency in public both in contexts of community joy *(khayrāt)* and worry *(banḍārā/makhnā)*, for women such display is restricted to the framework of a very personal and specific social and biological role (that of mother) and that too only in the context of grief.

Chapter 2

Growing into Society

Becoming a Person

During fieldwork I grew interested in the demographic patterns and population dynamics of the Bakkarwal. Whenever I met a family for the first time, I tried to ask about household size. It was intriguing that very often the figures men came up with were lower than those women mentioned; the latter tallied in general with the numbers I myself counted when I got to know the family better. When I discussed this discrepancy with these men the response was always the same: "I thought you asked about the number of *bandā* (cf. Skt. and Pers. *bandā/bande* for slave, servant, bondsman, creature) in the household, but what you really want to know is the number of *shakas*." The women said they always automatically counted the number of human *shakas*, not just the *bandā*. Whereas the taxon *shakas* is neutral, unrelational and general, (cf. Ch. 1), *bandā* is specific, situational and social. Whereas *shakas* includes *bandā*, to go beyond the human category, the latter is restricted to humans, and indeed only to those identifiable with certain roles. A father, a shepherd, a Government veterinary doctor, a forest guard, a moneylender, a member of another ethnic group – each of these is a *bandā*. The ethnographer – also a *bandā* – can accompany another *bandā*, but not a *shakas*, to a wedding or to an office. *Bandā* indicates greater predictability of behaviour than *shakas* which always involves a certain ambiguity and uncertainty. Paraphrasing Fajan's (1985: 368) observation on New Britain's Baining culture, it is in the construction and action of a *bandā* that "… daily activities, relationships and symbols are integrated into a self-reproductive system". This boundedness and relationality are part of the definition of humanity as opposed to, say, animality, and Ohnuki-Tierney's (1991: 165) observations on Japanese society apply to the Bakkarwal too: "… humans are by definition *among* humans, an individual human can not be conceived of without reference to others …" And yet, in this culture as in large parts of India (cf. Östör et al. 1982 for several examples), not just humans are defined together with others of their generic kind; so too are animals, plants and fairies; unlike in Japan the self is conceived of here, I suggest, in the abstract – as the subject, an agent of action.

Within Bakkarwal society *bandā* include all those who are old enough to participate in household economy. However, a *bandā* is not necessarily a *kām karanāḷā* – an actual "worker" – since an aged parent too infirm to actually work is nevertheless a *bandā*, for *bandā*-hood ends only at death. *Bandā*, as different from *shakas*, is Radcliffe-Brown's (1977: 225) "… complex of social relationships" – and hence may be glossed by the term "person". The connotations of *bandā* seem to compare well to the philosopher-poet Iqbal's concept of the "efficient self" (cf. Ahmad 1986: 16–18); but the concept is also similar to Maurice Lienhardt's description of "the Person" in Melanesian society, a being "(qui) ne se connaît que par la relation qu'il entretient avec les autres. Il n'existe que dans la mesure où il exerce son rôle dans le jeu de ses relations. Il ne se situe que par rapport à celles-çi." (1947: 198)

Clearly, however, *bandā*-hood does not begin at birth; being born is not synonymous with becoming identifiable once and for all as a specific type of human. A newborn infant is not a *bandā*; it is simply a *jātak*, one who has been born. It has a gender, and it soon acquires a religion. It will have to wait a while before obtaining a name, and then some more years before it becomes a *bandā*, a human with social rights and duties. All this, of course, provided that it survives. Figure 2.1 illustrates the various steps in the social and biological transition of a *shakas* to a *bandā*, of a relatively unbound infant into one bound into human and ultimately adult

Figure 2.1 The components of social binding

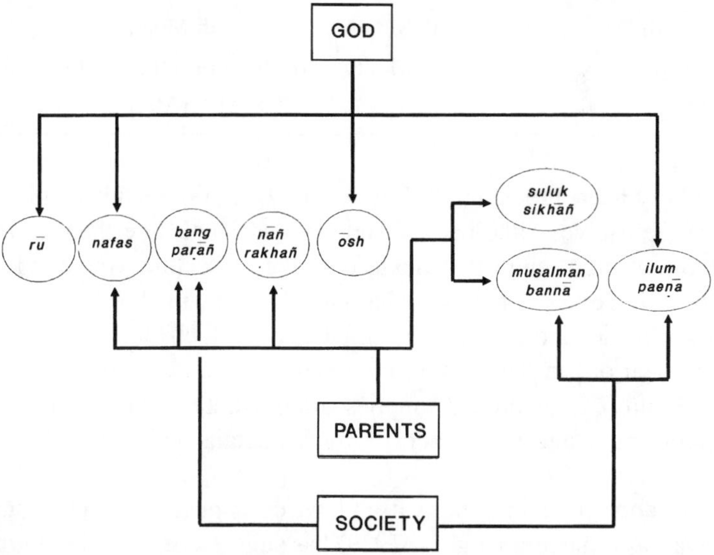

society; many of the roles played therein by society, by God and its own characteristics indicated here will be discussed in the course of this chapter.

In all societies a name is "… an important cultural device" (Fortes 1987: 251) in the process of becoming a person. Acquiring a name is at once an act of separation – as a specifically marked being – and an act of fusion – again as a new member of the specific group. Thus names and naming underline both individuality and collectivity. Samuel Beckett once commented that in Ireland an infant must survive four weeks before it is officially considered fit to live and hence to obtain a birth certificate. The concept of "fit to live" is of vital importance in a society with high infant mortality. The Bakkarwal mention three phases in the first year of life as being especially critical for a baby's survival – phases in which it is not clear whether or not the infant has enough *nafas*: birth to five days, then again to forty days and below six months. Babies who die within the first six months or so of birth often turn into spirits known as *but*. They are probably a specific form of spirits of the dead, who, for example, in Gujarat "assume the form of a child

Table 2.1 Breakdown of infant mortality in the first year of life

0–5 Days	12	3rd Month	6	6th Month	4
6–40 Days	16	4th Month	2	7th Month	1
41–61 Days	5	5th Month	4	8th–11th Month	0
				12th Month	5

and cry heart breakingly" (Enthoven 1914: 106). Bakkarwali *but* are themselves "like babies, and cry and laugh like them. They come at night and often tickle one; they also turn your food to water, but otherwise they are harmless". Following local concepts, it was decided to examine the infant deaths which took place in the first year of life. The results are given in Table 2.1, and illustrated in Figure 2.2; Figure 2.3 supplies and illustrates data on mortality according to age and gender (for further details on infant and child mortality cf. Ch. 4).

But does infant mortality itself have consequences for child survival, as Schapera-Hughes (1989) has suggested? In other words, do infant care and infant mortality among the Bakkarwal inform each other, and if so why and how? It has been hypothesised that intensive, time-consuming and non-conflictual child care in most preindustrial societies is a response to the twin phenomena of the desirability of numerous children and high child mortality. In a recent paper Hewlett (1991) explores this possibility as delineated by Robert LeVine, who

> … has hypothesized that such infant care practices are parental responses to the high infant mortality found in preindustrial populations and the desire of parents to have as many children as possible. When infant mortality rates are high, LeVine predicts that parents should have the physical survival and health of the infant as their overriding conscious concern and that infant care practices will reflect this. (Hewlett 1991: 16)

However, after reviewing the empirical data available, Hewlett comes to the conclusion (p. 17) that

> While it is reasonable to suggest that mortality rates influence infant care practices, the data … indicate that fertility rates or the number of children per parent may be just as important as mortality rates in

Figure 2.2 Infant deaths (in days or months) during the first year of life. For details see Table 2.1.

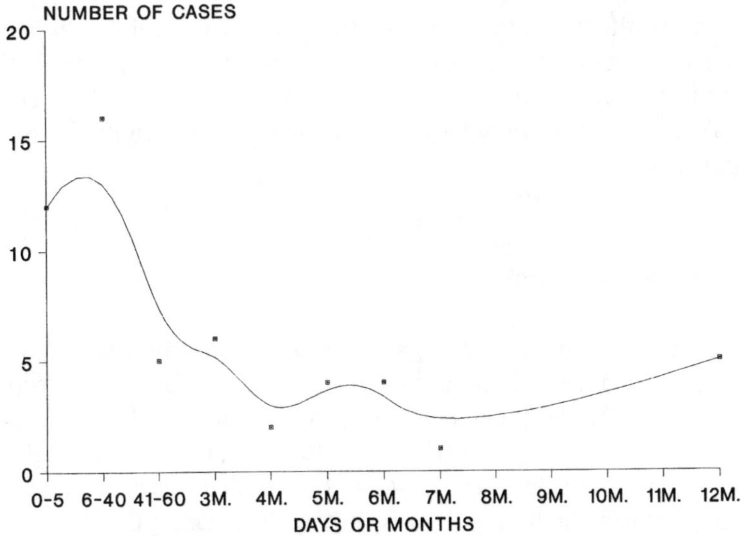

Figure 2.3 Mortality by gender expressed in percentage. For details see Ch. 4, Table 4.5.

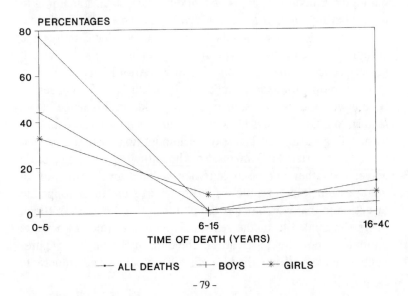

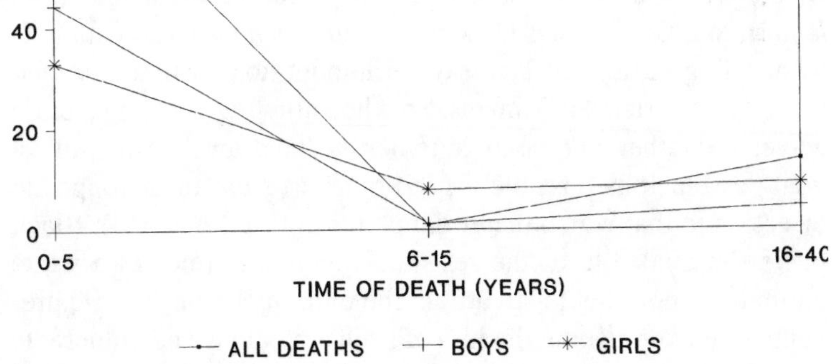

predicting patterns of "indulgent" infant care. Other factors, such as the mother's workload and ideology, in particular, can also be very influential forces that shape parental infant care.

Many of these factors have already been discussed by Whiting and Whiting (1975). I shall come to fertility rates in Chapter 4, but shall now briefly discuss certain strategies to which the Bakkarwal have recourse in order to protect their children from disease and death.

Acquiring a Label

On the Day of Reckoning, goes one *Hadith*, "you will be called by your own names and the names of your fathers. Therefore, keep good names". The daughter Zarina lost (see Ch. 4) had no name – she was known simply as *Niki*, "the little one"; her second daughter also was nameless. The daughter Bājā buried was called *Guḍi*, "doll"; this, I had been told, was "not really a name". Only *Shādi*, Zarina's five-year-old son, had "a real name" – Shahadat, shortened for convenience to *Shādi*. "Words", Francis Bacon wrote in his *Essays* (1597/1906), "are the tokens current and accepted for conceit as moneys are for values." It is the same with names. A name, the Bakkarwal say, is "a marker, a keepsake, something to remember by" (*nāñ nishani e, yādgiri e*). A name identifies, specifies and labels, and as such the "types of names that comprise the complete name set that is typical in any society suggest how that society conceptualizes personal identity" (Alford 1988: 78).

In keeping with widespread usage in South Asian languages, in Bakkarwali too, to call someone is to "take her/his name" (*nāñ lenāñ*); to give a name is to "keep it" (*nāñ rakhnāñ*), and with it its owner. To give the same name twice amounts to transmitting it, and this is not restricted to humans. So when after her wedding a bride leaves her father's home to go to her husband for the first time, a goat "as black as possible" is led out by its ear in the opposite direction to that which the bridal pair will take (cf. Ch. 3). Black plays the dual role of the resistant repellant; although a white animal is "more liable" to attract the evil, the herder's logic prevents him from risking the loss of such a precious and vulnerable animal. The black goat is repeatedly called out by the name of the bride, which has been transferred to it for the occasion, and left alone at some distance, to return on her own later. The evil powers that be may now affect the goat, but not the bride; thanks to the new label the goat is identifiable as the object of their evil intentions. To protect the goat ultimately, she is renamed after her return.

Identification has an element of certitude, and so therefore does naming. But to be sure too early is to be conceited. Labels attract and premature labeling attracts the destroyers of conceit. The destruction of conceit implies the destruction of certitude, the annihilation of the principle of identification – of the "marker" – and by extension of the identified. Premature naming thus involves the risk of premature death and is to be avoided. To stress their incertitude, their lack of conceit, their lack of autonomy versus the powers that be, Bakkarwal parents name their children only after they are reasonably certain that they will survive. Exceptions to this rule are made when a child is directly named by a *pīr*, since the powers of this holy man are held to be great enough to ward off threatening forces. Following the same principle, if a child is born following a vow made at a shrine, it is named at this shrine which the parents visit as soon as possible after the birth. The vow can be regarded as one side of a bargain hit between the parents and the Almighty or His representatives, and consists of the promise of offspring in return for the sacrifice of that very offspring. This ritual sacrifice, like all others, acts regeneratively.

Although I was once told that the Qor'an required a child to be named "before it is three days old", normally children are rarely named by their parents before they are about four, and even if they are, these names are used exclusively by their paternal male relatives. Indeed until they are about ten children are not called by these names either by their mothers and her relatives, or by their father's female relatives. A mother, a grandmother or an aunt will invariably use a pet name (also known as *nāñ*) till the child is about four, and often enough if this is the youngest child in the family, this name sticks, even after the child acquires a different, "real name" (again, *nāñ*, or more properly *asal nāñ*) later. Pet names are of two kinds – either openly fond and loving (e.g. *Pōtu/Bēṭki* (= sonny/little daughter), *Rāṇo/Rāṇi* (= prince/queen), *Guḍo/Guḍi* (=

doll), *Niko/Niki* (= little one)), or apparently derogatory (e.g. *Mandi Munji* (= inferior unhusked rice), *Kāḷi* (= the black one), *Kanḍo* (= thorn)). Whereas young mothers, who have not lost many babies tend to adopt the former type, grandmothers, or women who have lost many children, appear to prefer the latter, which are held to be apotropaic. *Niko* and *Niki* are terms which are also used by all and sundry to refer to any youngest child present. Even after a child has been officially named, it can be further called and referred to by its pet name, at times lifelong, provided it has no younger siblings. If it has younger siblings, it will be addressed and referred to by its mother and other close female relatives by a generic term of classification till it is about ten years old.

For the Bakkarwal a name *(nāñ)* is what is commonly called a personal name; examples for males are single names such as "Sarfaraz" or double names such as "Mohammad Ali", both types being common in other Islamic areas. In addressing or referring to Sarfaraz, however, one would never use the full name, but only a short form: *Phājā* or *Phājo* (the *f* being pronounced as *ph*). Similarly Ismael becomes *Melā*, *Melu* or *Shillā*; Mohammad Ali is contracted to form *Mā(w)ali*; and Ahad turns into *(H)ādeo*. In recent years, with increasing exposure to formal institutions in alien and public spheres beyond their own society, the Bakkarwal have, in keeping with the norms of this wider society, also adopted what they call "full names" (*pūro nāñ*). Thus one finds a Sarfaraz giving his "full name" as, say, Mohammad Sarfaraz. In intracommunity public contexts, however, someone may be referred to either as *Phājā* or as Sarfaraz. When it is not clear to the interlocutor precisely which of many eventual *Phājās* or Sarfarazes is being referred to, the name is often supplemented either with the name of the man's father, or with the name of the man's patrilineage *(zāt)* – for example, Bokuṇ or Kaḷo Khēl, or Bargaṭ – which functions in this case as a sort of family name. Although, as we shall see later, the patrilineage identifies, it is not generally considered part of a person's name, and most *zāt* names are not used as suffixes. Only those (e.g. Khaṭāṇā) with a clear connection to the Gujar, an ethnically and economically akin but numerically and politically more powerful community (Rao 1988b), are suffixed to the full name. The result of this is known either also as "full name" or more frequently as *isam*, a term which, though deriving from the Arabic (cf. also Pers./Ur.) *ism*, differs from it in construction (cf. Sublet 1991 for an excellent analysis of Arab names). An alternative suffix is Allaiwāḷ (or Ilaiāḷ), which denotes the region (Allai) of origin of a few numerically weak patrilineages with no Gujar connection. When I asked Shirā why he gave his name as Bashir Ahmad Allaiwāḷ, rather than as Bashir Ahmad Kāḷo Khēl (the name of his patrilineage), he answered: "You tell me which sounds better? Kāḷo Khēl sounds backward [*pičhṛa*: see below for a discussion of "backwardness"], doesn't it? Allaiwāḷ sounds good – one gets respect [*kadar*]." Three other possibilities are provided by the prefix Chaudhri and the suffixes Shah and Khan. All three are common in large parts of South Asia, the former as either prefix or suffix and the latter as suffixes; in Jammu and Kashmir whereas Shah can also be a Kashmiri suffix, it is very commonly associated with the so-called "hill people" (Pahāṛi) on either side of the Indo-Pakistan cease-fire line, and there is currently a movement to promote a unique hill-peoples' identity. The suffix Khan indicates a Pashtun ("Afghan") origin. The prefix Chaudhri, on the other hand, marks a clear distinction with the Kashmiri (as a suffix it is met with among Kashmiri speakers), while spanning a bridge to various traditionally land- and/or animal-holding communities in India and Pakistan. It is likely that with increased schooling and external contact in general these innovations in the traditional pattern of naming will accelerate, somewhat in the manner described by Zonabend (1980: 231) in her excellent paper on names in a French village:

> … daß sich durch den Vornamen ein Bruch zwischen der offiziellen Identität … und der – durch die Verwandten oder die Gemeinschaft – zugewiesenen Identität ergibt, und daß für den einzelnen im Lauf seines Lebens ständig die zugewiesene und die erlebte Identität auseinanderfallen.

Change is already evident in personal naming patterns, as shown by an analysis of the names of 560 women and girls and 1,186 men and boys drawn from two samples collected in the early 1980s. Since the two samples are from adjacent areas, they were pooled together for purposes of analysis. The first of these two samples was collected by me during fieldwork and the second was taken from unpublished documents of the 1981 Census of India.

Bisaria (1971: 99–101) also lists "common names" she found among men and women, but she does not identify those typical for the Bakkarwal, nor does she give an age-wise breakdown. From her list of "common male prefixes and suffixes" it is also not clear how extensive her sample was. Besides, she mixes prefixes ("Chowdhry") with the first part of compound names, such as "Noor"; thus Ahmad and Mohammad become prefixes or suffixes, rather than parts of names, as is usual throughout the Muslim world. For reasons of clarity, Bisaria's lists have thus not been included as an eventual third sample.

After pooling the names of 185 women and girls and 627 men and boys collected by me, and those of 375 females and 559 males figuring in the Census, all 560 female names and 1,186 male names were divided into three age categories as given in Table 2.2. While for reasons explained above, in the sample collected by me four years was the minimum age, the Census sample contains a few younger individuals, who have, however, also been considered for our purposes here as above four years. The oldest individuals noted in the unpublished Census sample are a women of eighty and a man of ninety; in my sample deceased parents and grandparents of informants were also taken into account.

Figure 2.4 Overlapping of names among women of different age-groups. The percentages indicate the overlapping (OVL) between age-groups. For further information see text.

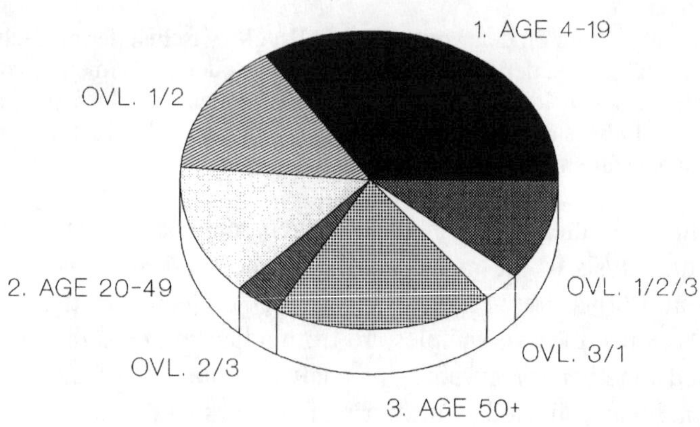

Table 2.2 Names of females and males recorded by me and in the Census (unpublished, 1981) and classified according to age

Age	4–19			20–49			50 +		
	Census	Own	N	Census	Own	N	Census	Own	N
Females	185	77	262	117	71	188	73	37	110
Males	269	160	429	184	269	453	106	189	304

It was found that between them the 560 women and girls had 181 names; of these 64 and 43 names were exclusively in my sample or the unpublished Census sample respectively, while 74 names were common to both samples. The commonest name in the female samples was Zaitun (14 and 7 times in the Census and my samples respectively). Similarly it was found that the 1,186 men and boys had 395 names. Of these 141 were exclusive to my sample (with 281 names in all) and 114 were exclusive to the Census sample (with a total of 254 names); 140 names were common to both male samples.

To ascertain variation in the choice of names the Bakkarwal give their daughters, the frequency of different female names in the different age categories was investigated. As a first step, the exclusivity, or alternatively the overlapping of names within and between each of the age categories, was considered. Figure 2.4 shows that for women while the maximum of exclusivity is among the youngest (34.2 per cent), there is a certain overlapping between all three age categories. However, significant overlapping is observed only between the middle and youngest female categories (14.3 per cent), and then again, between all three (11.0 per cent). The variation in the choice of names given to sons was also investigated by pooling together the male samples. This showed that unlike among other Muslim communities in India (Dua 1984: 245) here the names of the Prophet (Mohammad, Ahmad, etc.) are not the commonest, either singly or as prefixes or suffixes. The 11 following names (Table 2.3) appeared most frequently, all other names appearing less than twenty times. It was further found that, independent of age categories, these 11 names together make for 293 individuals, i.e. 24.7 per cent of all males and 2.7 per cent of the 395 names recorded. In other words, as few

Table 2.3 The eleven most frequent male names

Name	Variations and Vocatives	Frequency (N Individuals)
Ghulam	Gāmā, Gāmio, Gulama, Lima, Gula	43
Bashir	Shira, Shera, Sheru, Bashira	38
Rashid	Shida, Shido, Rashida	26
Abdullah	Dulla, Dullo,	25
Latif	Tifo, Tifa, Lito	25
Qasem	Sima, Kima, Simo	25
Mahbub	Būba, Būbo, Babu	24
Lal	Lālo, Lālā	22
Nazir	Jiro, Jira, Najira	22
Yusuf	Saiñf, Saiñfo, Sifo, Sufa, Sufi	22
Yaqub	Kuba, Kubo, Yuba, Yubo	21

as 11 male names (2.7 per cent of names) account for as many as 24.7 per cent of the individuals.

Alford's (1988: 73) computations indicate that in herding societies there is a fairly high reoccurrence of names, a phenomenon he interprets thus:

> Societies with high reoccurrence names … have no special need to submerge or restrict individuality … Individuality is de-emphasized merely by the use of high reoccurrence names … unique or near-unique names emphasize uniqueness and individuality … (Alford 1988: 74)

The sizes of the samples analysed here appear too small to warrant discussion of this matter.

In a second analytical step the Bakkarwal names in the two samples were classified into two broad categories: Islamic and non-Islamic. Each of these was further subdivided (I, II). Qor'anic names, or names considered befitting of a Muslim girl/boy (cf. Hathurani nd.) were classified under the sub-category Islamic I (e.g. Fatima, Khalida/Yaqub, Aslam). Names classified under Islamic II were such as are commonly found among Muslims in the surrounding regions, even though they may not be Qor'anic (e.g. Mahbuba, Zaitun/Mahbub, Mumtaz). Non-Islamic names were similarly subdivided into categories I and II, whereby I consisted of names common in a wide region (e.g. Hir, Rani/Jawahar, Sardar) and II contained names which were considered more exclusive to this community (e.g. Basnure, Jīmar, Makhṇi/Makhṇa, Miṭṭhā). The frequency of each name (i.e. the number of females/males bearing a given name) in each of these subcategories was then related to the three age-groups. Figures 2.5 and 2.6 illustrate the results of this analysis for women and men respectively. They show that while among women the frequency of Islamic names has risen steeply from 30.1 per cent through 55.2 per cent to 74.7 per cent, the frequency of non-Islamic names has correspondingly fallen from 67.1 per cent through 44.6 per cent to 24.1 per cent. The frequency of Qor'anic names has also risen steeply from 10.9 per cent among older women to 46.2 per cent among young girls, community-specific names having decreased from 31.8 per cent over 13.3 per cent down to 5.7 per cent. On the other hand, the two other categories (Islamic II and non-Islamic I) show less drastic changes across the generations. A closer look at the category Islamic I across all age-groups of females shows that of a total of

Figure 2.5 Diachronic change (expressed in percentage) in women's names

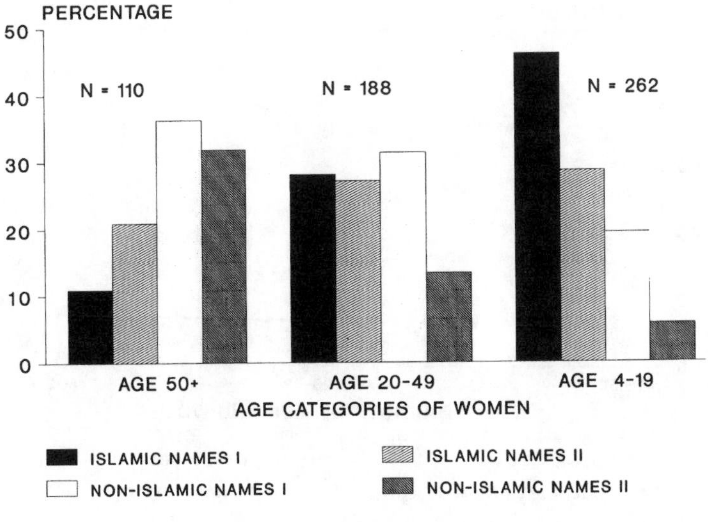

Figure 2.6 Diachronic change (expressed in percentage) in men's names

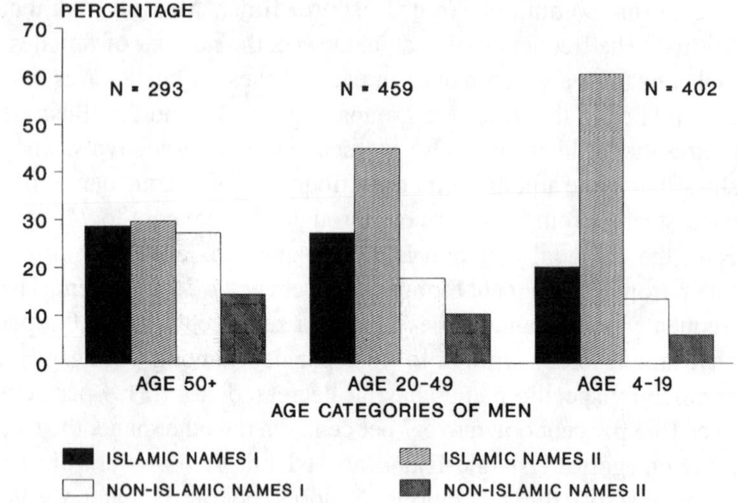

Figure 2.7 A comparison of gender-specific change (expressed in percentage) in naming patterns. M = men, W = women, ISL NAM = Islamic names, N-ISL NAM = non-Islamic names.

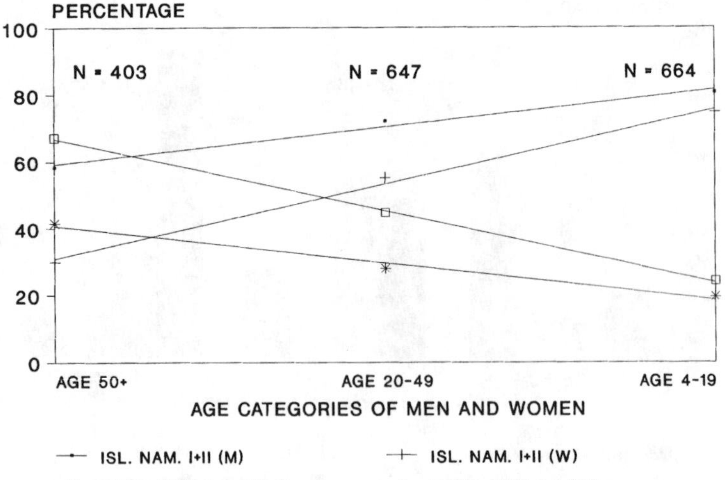

fifty-one (28.1 per cent of all) names, thirteen are basically male names modified with suffixes to form a female name. Thus Hassan becomes Hassan-*Bāno*; Hakim, Hakim-*Bibi*; Ershad, Ershad-*Begum*; alternatively, a final long vowel changes gender: Bashir*a*, Iqbal*a*, Suleiman*a*, etc. The frequency of such basically male names does not appear to have changed over the generations, however, with percentages of 25.0 per cent, 37.0 per cent and 33.3 per cent respectively from the oldest to the youngest age-groups.

Among men it was found that while Islamic and non-Islamic names held the balance (58.3 per cent and 41.6 per cent respectively) for the generation above fifty, among the youngest generation Islamic names represented 80.6 per cent of all names, only 19.4 per cent being non-Islamic; the generation in between had 72.1 per cent Islamic and 27.9 per cent non-Islamic names respectively. Unlike among women, however, no change was found in the frequency of Qor'anic names, which constituted from 28.7 per cent through 27.2 per cent to 20.1 per cent of all male names. Thus both male and female names showed a general trend towards Islamisation, but there were differences in detail between men and women. Figure 2.7 sets out the comparative data. While the use of all non-Islamic names decreased sharply over the generations, the fall in community-specific names (from 14.3 per cent through 10.2 per cent to 5.9 per cent) also marks an increase in the distinction the Bakkarwal formally make among men and animals; formerly there were more men called *Mehndi* ("henna") and horses called *Mehnda*, and both men and horses could be named *Čāndi* ("silver").

"Do names have meanings?" I once asked Makhṇi. "Some do", she said, "others are names according to the *sharā* [i.e. Islam], and still others are just names people give – nice names." The four categories used in the above analysis correspond roughly to the distinctions made by Makhṇi; Islamic II and non-Islamic I contain the names "people give – nice names", and Islamic I contains names attested to in Islamic tradition. Occasionally the first three categories do include names with a symbolic meaning for the Bakkarwal; "Nusrat Begum" and "Zulfiqar Ali", names given to children born in 1979, the year of Pakistani President Zulfiqar Ali Bhutto's execution, provide two such examples (for the practice of naming children after well-known people in another Islamic context cf. Littmann 1956: 93). But primarily it is the fourth category

Table 2.4 The most frequent women's names and their connotations

Positive Connotations		**Apotropaic**			
(Nature/Purity/Life)	**M/F**	**(Misleading)**	**M/F**	**(Negative)**	**M/F**
Bird/Sparrow	13/ 8	Secret	0/9	Thin	7/0
Henna	13/ 0	Another	0/7	Pain	2/3
Butter(y)	12/ 7	Yours	0/2	Thorn	0/1
Silver	8/ 0	Daughter-in-law	0/1	Crooked	1/0
Sweet Smell	1/ 5			Poor	1/0
Strawberry	0/ 8				
Doll	1/ 7				
Five Daughters	0/ 3				
Sweet	7/ 0				
White	0/11				
Happy	0/ 3				
Living	4/15				
Milky	5/ 0				

(non-Islamic II) which consists of such "meaningful" names, and this could perhaps also explain the overlapping between human and animal names. Among Bakkarwal women and men, sixty and forty-seven such names were found respectively, and these were divided into two broad types (for another typology of names in India cf. Ghosh 1975). Many names in the samples occur only once; those appearing most frequently are given in Table 2.4 in translation, and the frequencies are mentioned in brackets.

Many names among adults are not actually "real names", but pet names (e.g. *Guḍi*/*Guḍo* = doll) which have stuck on, so that the "real names" have been "forgotten". A few are also nicknames, acquired later in life, but early enough to supplant the names given by the parents (e.g. *Ḍōri* = deaf). Apart from the name "Five-Daughters" (*Pančdi*) which was always found to have been given to the fifth surviving daughter in a family, no correlation was found among either women or men between the name given and either sibling order or child mortality.

Unlike in many other societies, no ceremony marks the naming of a Bakkarwal child, except when it is named by a *pīr*. Perhaps in keeping with Alford's suggestion, but certainly conforming to notions about the evil eye, there is a general de-emphasising of the entire issue, and when the family has not lost many babies, there is an air of casualness about the choice of the name itself. The following brief narrative tells how the four-and-a-half-year old Nasir got his name:

> On 4 December 1982 Bakhti, the child's MBWZ, who was also his midwife, visits with her husband, on their way to their eldest daughter's camp. Also visiting is a Gujar from a nearby village. He fondles the infant and then asks its mother what name the baby is going to be given. She replies that they had not yet thought about it, but it is now time they did. Sipping tea, served by the baby's mother, its midwife suggests "Ghulam Nabi". "No", says the father (Ghulam Ahmad, known as *Gulla*). "That's the name of my elder FBS." The child's own ten-year-old eldest brother suggests "Ismael", but the fourteen-year-old eldest sister does not like this. Now the child's MBWZH suggests asking a *mulla*, but Gulla says, "We've no need for one". The visiting Gujar is asked repeatedly by the father to suggest a name, and ultimately he suggests "Nasir". "That's a really good name" is the overall consensus, and this is how the infant gets its name.

At home Nasir continued, however, to be called by his pet name, *Čāndi*, but gradually outsiders started referring to him as "*Sīra*" or "*Sīro*", derived from Nasir.

Age and Its Implications

All societies conceive of life as consisting of various stages, and Linton (1942: 593) suggested that although there is great variation in the number of such stages recognised by a culture, the minimum is four. Bakkarwali language does not distinguish between the terms "life cycle" and "life", both being known as *(jindagi)*. The human life (cycle) is divided into seven major phases (Table 2.5); it will be seen that terminological gender differentiation begins at about four years of age. A girl or boy in one of the first three phases can also be more generally termed a child (*bālak*), whereas from roughly the end of the juvenile period till one has a couple of children oneself, one is classified as *jawān*. After this, until one reaches old age there is to my knowledge no specific term of classification.

Stages of the life cycle are often subdivided, and unlike perhaps in Europe (cf. Ariès 1960) childhood has long been recognised in many societies as one such subdivision. Medieval Islamic texts

Table 2.5 Phases of the human life cycle. All figures indicate age in years. Gen = general term; Chd = child.

	BAKKARWALI			ENGLISH TERMS
AGE	Gen.	Male	Female	Male / Female
Birth - 4	BĀLAK	*jātak*	*jātak*	infant
4 - 6/7		*nikko*	*nikki*	child
6/7 - 10		*baḍēro*	*baḍērā*	child
10 - Puberty		*luṛā*	*bēṭki*	juvenile
Puberty - 1. Chd.	JAWĀN	*gadro*	*gadri*	adolescent
1 Child - Old Age	no term	no term	no term	adult
Old Age		*buḍo**	*buḍi***	adult

* or *bujurg* for males of well-being (cf. Ch. 6)
** for a woman this begins at menopause

reckon childhood as a stage beginning at birth and ending anywhere between the ages of seven and eighteen (Gil'adi 1992: 116); in the Hindu system of medicine childhood was subdivided into five such stages, starting with the foetal period and ending at the age of sixteen. Kashmiri Muslim farmers of high-altitude villages divide childhood into two subcategories, the *ku:r* (birth to about four years) and *bo:r* (about four to ten years), and the Bakkarwal distinguish four such subdivisions. The first four years of life are said to constitute roughly the first of these four phases. As we have seen, by the end of this phase the likelihood of the baby's survival increases, since its *nafas* now slowly stabilises. Several actions in this phase mark the first steps in the gradual transition of the human child from a *shakas* to a *bandā*. For about half of this entire period it is nursed (*čuči pīṇāñ*) regularly on demand and then only very occasionally during the day; at night, "to put it to sleep", however, it is given the breast as long as it does not have a younger sibling (babies up to about three years are put to sleep in the evenings, and not left around to fall asleep on their own).

There is no regular toilet training, but infants are often taken out of the tent and encouraged to urinate by saying "ps, ps, ps, ps". Among the Mandaṛ, a section of Bakkarwal probably of Pashtun origins, a baby is kept swaddled (*juṛan*) "for its comfort" till it begins to crawl (*goḍni karnāñ*). Too much kicking about (*kisiṭi marnāñ*) is not considered healthy for the little arms and legs. Infants are carried (*čaknāñ*) around, either piggyback in a sling – especially during migration – or in arms. A youngest child sleeps with its mother either till the birth of the next child, or till it is at least about seven years old. If a younger sibling is born, the older child sleeps, if male, with its father, if female, with an older sister or with its father's mother if she is a widow, or failing this, close to its own mother. As a baby grows, notwithstanding the presence of a younger sibling, the physical and verbal expressions of affection towards it by its mother continue and are supplemented by those of grandparents, father and yet older siblings. Thus with the transfer of care from mother to other household members there seems to be little loss of attention or affection.

In general the verbal expression of love and endearment of adults towards small children consists mainly of calling the latter by their pet names. Mothers – and adults generally – were not observed to converse with their young children, tell them stories, sing them songs, etc. Indeed the communication between different age-groups and especially between adults and children is, I suggest, largely expressed by and articulated through the body. Before I proceed to describe other aspects of childhood, I shall therefore briefly discuss certain salient features concerning the body and its relationship to manners and morals. I contend that these features also convey a great deal about Bakkarwal concepts of choice and the gender-specific capacity to take decisions at various stages in the life cycle.

Manners and Morals

Unlike Kashmiri Pandits who differentiate little between the genders in the early phase of socialisation (Madan 1992), the Bakkarwal start differentiating early, in little matters. Infant boys and girls are clad in long shirts reaching down to their ankles, but whereas from the age of about two years a girl must wear trousers *(suthuṇ)* to keep her private parts covered, little boys run around without trousers for much longer, sometimes till they are circumcised (see below). Over their trousers, girls wear a shirt *(ganḍai)* which stretches to a little below their knees. However cold it may be, girls wrap only a shawl around themselves, like their mothers and elder sisters, whereas men and little boys whose families can afford it keep themselves warm in woollen coats. The wool (for a small boy's coat, 11 *čhalli*, roughly 450 g) is carded and combed *(ōn tomnāñ)* at home by the women and given to a tailor.

It has been generally observed that in Islamic societies "clothes are an extension of the body" (Eickelmann 1984: 126). For the Bakkarwal being properly clad is part of being well mannered and well behaved – having *sulūk.* Since proper clothing is, however, also recognised as being related to purchasing power, really good *sulūk* is also attributed only to the wealthy, and there again especially to wealthy men.

> How can you expect someone like Alia, who's just a poor shepherd (*ājṛi*), to have good *sulūk* ? Think of who his mother and father are … To see really good *sulūk* you should go to Hajji's X's home; even his women have some *sulūk* …

My interlocutor was Alia's employer's wife's sister, and she was trying to explain to me why Alia had, the week before, been so unpleasant about helping her sister fetch food rations from the nearest town. The learning of basic *sulūk* begins in early childhood, first in passive fashion, and in a more active way when *ōsh* increases; it goes on till after puberty, although the principal elements should have long been mastered by then. These basic elements relate to dress and body postures, and are gender-specific in their details. Elements of *sulūk* beyond these basics depend on one's *ōsh*, and hence on a variety of other factors such as whom one mixes with socially. Perhaps the most important of the basic elements concerns the hair and head covering, and I shall now deal with this in some detail.

THE SYMBOLS OF THE HEAD As in many societies (for a recent discussion of Islamic contexts cf. Delaney 1994), for all Bakkarwal the head is a major focus of attention: long hair is a sign of female beauty and sexuality, and head coverings indicate honour, social power and levels of autonomy. At six months an infant receives its first haircut (*munnāñ*), an event celebrated by cooking a sweet dish *(alwā)* for the entire camp. At this stage, say the Bakkarwal, the head is pure (*sučo sir e*). Unlike other hair and nail pairings, which are thrown into running water, this hair, which is also pure, is hidden away from evil creatures in a hole (*khor māñ tariñ*). No gender differentiation is made at this stage, but after she is about two years old, a little girl's hair is never cut. Later, clarified butter will be regularly applied to her hair; it will be combed with short, double-edged wooden or plastic combs and plaited by her mother, elder sisters or aunts (see Ch. 3 for details on the sexual significance of oiling hair). Whereas girls grow their hair, boys and men are expected to shave their heads regularly.

Long before the first haircut, around one week after its birth, every infant gets a tiny cap *(ṭōpi)*. Made of ecru cloth, it has two earflaps known as *kanḍ* and is tapered (*kiāri*) at the back. It is embroidered with red, pink and blue or green silk (*resham*) thread, the generic term for the embroidered designs being "flower" (*phul*). In addition, coloured beads (*khōl*) are often sewn onto the top of the cap, and tassels (*maṇkā*) are attached to the fringes. A central tassel (*phumṛi*) is also sewn onto the top of the cap, while a fairly large black or white button (*birā*) is stitched on in such a manner that it is positioned just above the forehead; this button is partly decorative but partly meant to ward off the evil eye. Black thread is not used for a baby's cap, but, again as a protective measure, its eyes are ringed with collyrium and sometimes its cheeks are smudged with soot or collyrium. Above all, an infant is exposed as little as possible to the stares of strangers. A child retains this first type of cap till it is about four or five years old; only the size increases with the months. After this, however, a gender-based difference marks the caps of both boys and girls. Ideally, boys are shaved and given a flat, white, flapless – usually cotton – cap *(ṭōpi),* which resembles that of adult men and is embroidered like these in silk with white *sozani* (lit. needlework); on this a turban (*paṭko*) is tied. Usually, however, they wear either a cap or a turban, and sometimes neither. Contrary to men's caps, all those worn by females after infancy are made of black cotton cloth embroidered with coloured silk thread.

Caps among the Bakkarwal exemplify a number of meanings. The concept of keeping the head covered is of course an Islamic one and is otherwise also widespread in the entire region in varying ways. As Baso put it:

> This is our custom from Poonch and Gujrat and we'll never leave it. Some Khaṭāṇi (the name of a *zāt*) women have dropped it and have only their veils (*čādar*). But when they work these veils slip off, and it's a sin to be with uncovered heads. You know that – you have your head covered – but you're used to that; for us a cap (*lački*) is more comfortable." [I did indeed keep my head covered during fieldwork, usually with the common North Indian *čunni*, but sometimes also with a cap, which was a gift from Shida, a young Bakkarwal woman.]

And Hazrat Bibi, whom I never saw without her long-flapped *lački*, complained:

> Now there's no difference left between Hindus and Muslims. In my days it was all very different. I never allowed my boys and girls – however small – to run around without caps. Now look – no one bothers. They have caps, not that they don't! But they don't wear them; even when they're big they don't always wear them. And these newfangled caps (i.e. the small-flapped ones) – they don't cover the hair properly. *Toba, toba*!, Shame, shame!

But there are occasions when even women may go around without a cap and not be censured. Begāñ, for example, who lived next-tent to Hazrat Bibi and was closely related to her, one day simply took off her worn-out cap and put it away. Throughout the preceding winter she had nursed her little son, but he had died in early spring. After this she spent most of her time sitting around listlessly and often wept. "After Bubā ['s death] I just don't feel like it", she explained, when I asked her why she didn't make herself a new cap, or at least mend her old one. Other women could have made one for her, or lent her one of their older ones. But they didn't.

> "It might make her really sick to wear a cap now", Begāñ's cousin Jānā told me. "She's all hot with sorrow – others can be too cool with grief – you met Akma, she didn't cry much when she lost her son. She needs to be kept warm, otherwise she'll fall ill. But Begāñ is just the other way round – she needs cooling, otherwise her head may burst, and then she'll die."

Not only then do caps hide, they compress and prevent certain elements causing disease – in this case excess heat – from being expelled and curing the patient.

> This is also why five-year-old Nasima suddenly stopped wearing the beautiful cap her doting mother had made for her. Over the summer

months she had grown very weak, had lost appetite, and occasionally she had slight fever. As a contribution towards curing her, her cap was first removed; at a later stage her plaits were opened out at night. Finally her hair was let entirely loose and not combed at all.

Whereas bound hair is perhaps always a symbol of control by society (cf. Ch. 3), unbound hair may not always, I suggest, be symbolic of the contrary (cf. Ch. 3). In this case flowing and uncombed hair was not, as Hallpike suggests (1969) a symbol of being beyond society; on the contrary, at least Nasima's mother's cousin felt that her unruly hair could well divert the evil eye which had eventually fallen on the child.

Since head and hair symbolise such vital forces, it is not surprising that a Bakkarwal cap also symbolises honour, and to offer someone one's own cap is like offering one's honour, one's head, one's life. As discussed below and as indicated by Jana's concern for Begañ above, the head, the heart and life may well be considered semantic networks. Hence to offer one's cap is a sign of extreme humility, and thus of need; it is a gesture of supplication. In Bakkarwali – as in the Gujari spoken in the Kashmir Valley (Rao and Casimir 1985) – such a gesture is known as *swāḷu*, and the cap symbolises a very special request. Such a request can only be made from one much younger or inferior in status to one much older or superior. Such a request can never be denied, and Kāḷu had to present Jumma and his family with four kids and one nanny goat.

In March 1982 Jumma, the three-year-old son of Sona, presented his maternal grandfather with a beautifully embroidered child's cap. Sona and her husband had lost a great deal of his stock the previous spring, and were in dire straits. Ultimately Sona decided to ask her father for help. He knew about their hardship, but she found it rather awkward, as her father had often commented on her husband's carelessness as a herdsman. So before one of her visits to her parents in late winter she stitched and embroidered this cap. Jumma who had a nice cap himself, wore this one only on the trip to his grandfather. I was there the day Sona went back with her two children, seven-year-old Rajea and three-year-old Jumma, to her husband. Shortly before leaving she told Jumma to remove this cap and present it to her father, Kāḷu. The old man was now compelled to give the child a present – and the most obvious present was that of a few animals. Later Kāḷu commented, "What else could I do – after all the child came to me with such a request (*swāḷu āyo māro pās*) …".

THE BODY AND SOCIAL SPACE While the covering of the head is more explicitly associated with community traditions and Islamic prescriptions, body postures are associated with what I shall term secular social morals, summed up in the concept of *uṭhan beṭhan*. Literally translatable as "getting up and sitting down", this concept encompasses a complex range of norms and values impinging on social responsibility, sexual control, the domestic space and well-being. *Uṭhan beṭhan* is not conceived of in a vacuum, but within social space, which explicitly includes both non-Bakkarwal and non-Muslims. Space, as we have already seen, is an important element in Bakkarwal cognition, be it in terms of altitude or narrowness of bodily organs. Lack of space diminishes well-being, and hence those surrounding a sick person are told to "give him more space". As its converse, well-being can and is demonstrated through physical and social expanse. As mentioned earlier families who have demonstrated their well-being through wealth and good pastures spend the summers at higher altitudes where there is little crowding (Rao 1992a; Casimir and Rao). These families are considered better in every respect (Rao forthcoming) when compared to those at lower reaches. Crowding is associated with diminished well-being, with quarrelsomeness – and with women, the poor, the silly.

> Women, children and working hands like to sit huddled together", commented Hajji G., "they don't have enough *ōsh*, enough strength (*tākat*), enough heart (*dil*), enough *sulūk* to sit properly, quietly, apart from one another.

Hajji G. himself always sat at a certain distance from others, and this distance was automatically respected by all except infants. This was a pattern observed among all men of substance like Hajji G. When they entered a tent, people made way, they created space; they never did so for others. These men's wives were thought to be less desirous or needful of space – since as many women said, "they are women like we are" (cf. Ch. 4). Children are ignored even more than women and men of low status; they have no legitimate space of their own, and even the idea, when I broached it, appeared amusing. Space and its accompanying concepts and uses are always cultural constructions, and it has been suggested that everywhere a certain manipulation may take place to achieve a "selective control of access to the self" through "a process whereby people make their self-other boundaries permeable on some occasions and impermeable on other occasions" (Altman 1975 in Altman 1979: 97). In this nomad society, which is *per se* physically an open one, the quality and amount of space are hierarchisised, wealthy men having the most, poorer men less, women little, and children none.

As they grow older, however, gender differentiation expressed in body postures, in ways of getting up and sitting down, prepares boys and girls for their future social roles. For boys – especially for those from more wealthy families – the concept of *uṭhan beṭhan* encompasses social meanings, such as hospitality and control over one's large family. As we shall see in Chapter 5, the larger the number of descendants a man has, the larger his potential camp and the greater his prestige (cf. also Casimir and Rao 1995 for details). Physical control over humans (with their herds) coupled with social expansiveness, expressed in the generosity of a host and the kindness of an employer, are hallmarks of really good *uṭhan beṭhan* and the right *sulūk*. In other words, these concepts circumscribe the moral exercise of choice when shouldering responsibility for oneself and for others. For girls, on the contrary, immanent in these concepts are body postures which de-emphasise both physical space and social responsibility. Thus, for example, not only do women "crowd together", they should not laugh loudly or sit with outstretched legs in the presence of men. Women dropping in for a chat are not expected to be offered refreshments; men always are. For community feasts men are specially seated and served; women – even guests – sit wherever space is left. As we shall see in a later chapter, even social identity is verbally expressed by all women and less wealthy men in terms of attachment to a more well-known male individual. The practice and discourse of *uṭhan beṭhan* may indeed be said to underline the importance placed upon "… men's social graces… in constructing moral behavior" (Bauer 1985: 120), while de-emphasising women's capacity to develop these very graces. I can not say to what extent these concepts have been affected by external discourses regarding "backwardness", especially among those Bakkarwal increasingly entering into contact with various government representatives. But it is not unlikely that in the years to come such concepts will be strengthened through "modernisation". Even at the time of fieldwork, I was often told that learning *uṭhan beṭhan* depends on whom one mixes with. Not just notions of transactionalism, but also ideas about political and economic networks appeared to play a role here, and I shall return to these questions later in this chapter (cf. also Ch. 5).

The Autonomy of the Coddled

Various modern studies of child-rearing practices in India show that in the early years stress is laid on "… the avoidance of frustration … not encouragement of the child's individuation and autonomy" (Kakar 1979: 34). "*Lālayēt pančavarshāṇī*" goes the Sanskrit maxim, following which a child is to be treated with laxity in the first five years of its life. But is there an indispensable dialectic between indulgence and autonomy? "… [E]ven the newborn is considered partially autonomous – in the sense of having been born with a specific psychic constellation …" (Kakar 1979: 35). Every newborn Bakkarwal has the capacity to become more or less autonomous at a later stage in life. The degree of autonomy ultimately attained varies between children, depending on a variety of factors. Bakkarwal children are also brought up with great indulgence, which contrary to ancient Indian prescriptions does not end abruptly at any specific age. Simultaneously, from their earliest years children of both sexes are left to develop a certain physical autonomy. An unsteady toddler who stumbles is not picked up when it cries: "It must learn on its own", is the argument. Two crawling infants who shriek after a fight are not helped out: "In life the stronger wins", is the motto. If food is available, children – especially boys – of all ages eat without waiting for others: "Among us life is hard – one must learn to take in time, otherwise nothing will be left", is the explanation. On the other hand, when four-year-old Gāmā tries to snatch away a sweet given to his one-year-old cousin, their grandfather tells him, "Are you younger, or she? Come on, go off!" But I never noticed Gāmā or any other child ever being beaten or even severely scolded. Punishment would make no sense either, given that a child who is old enough to understand would most probably refrain from unreasonable acts anyway; if it does not refrain automatically, things have to be explained. If it nevertheless persists, the cause lies in its inherent nature and next to nothing can be done about that. But to expect reasoned behaviour from a child who is too young would in itself be unreasonable, and hence to punish it meaningless.

Lack of comprehension and reasoning is linked to the lack of awareness, but is not, I suggest, similar to the Western concept of childhood innocence. The notion of a child's innocence, neutrality and non-accountability was a controversial one in Islamic thought (Gil'adi 1992: 80ff.), and my field notes on this matter indicate that for the Bakkarwal it is the incomprehension and hence the inability of the child to undertake purposeful action which is of importance. A child below the age of seven or eight is too young to understand, because it does not yet possess enough *ōsh* to be aware of its actions. As in many Middle Eastern (e.g. Eickelman 1984: 190) and South Asian (cf. Hawley 1989: 30) societies here too increasing cultural competence is expected of a child from the age of about seven onwards. The juvenile period between about six or seven and ten years is in many ways critical. Though weaning is long over, chewing and hence digestion is a problem since some milk teeth (*duñd ke dandānā*), themselves largely composed of milk and almost as pure as a baby's first hair, are yet to be replaced by the second "stronger" set; in this liminal period both types of teeth "can be eaten away by worms" if, as with little Shidā and Bālā, enough care is not taken to stow away the milk teeth in a secret hole (among West Pashtuns too milk teeth are buried in mice holes, so that the teeth now cut may be as perfect as those of mice: Casimir, pers. comm.). Also critical in this period is the viscosity of body fluids, whose levels are slowly rising. Any constrictions within the body endanger the child's health. In the following case *tangi* had again taken place – no one quite knew how – but it was clear that it had to be got rid of.

> Phājā was six years old and had a small boil on his right shoulder; no one bothered much about it till some weeks later he developed a rash on his right cheek. Now his mother got upset and wondered what to do. Phājā had become quite cranky. Dulla, Phājā's uncle, then suggested that the best remedy for this kind of *tangi* would be "*kān saṛānā*", which consisted of branding (*saṛānā*) as follows: an iron rod with a wooden handle was held over the flames till red hot; it was then cooled for a few minutes and applied for a few seconds behind each of the ear lobes. Phājā's mother explained: "There is a vein joining the ear lobes to the cheeks and the shoulders, and in this *rag* somewhere

> there is *tangi*, so both the shoulder and the cheek have become ill. Now, both should be cured. Actually Sunday (*athār*) is the best day for this treatment ..."

Above all, however, it is at this stage that the basic amounts of *nafas* and *ōsh* should stabilise, and in keeping with this the child must increasingly be involved in the daily tasks of a herding household.

The Daily Routines of Play and Work

In the early stages of childhood here as in most other societies, work and play are intertwined. Toys are unknown, but when out herding children weave grasses, construct toy tents and play games individually and in twos rather than in groups. It must be remembered that throughout the year Bakkarwal camps are small and scattered and hence playgroups must be very limited in size. Children are also not allowed to wander off on their own, for example, to other camps. A child's world consists primarily of its own camp and this camp's members, and thus at this stage its access to social knowledge (*khabar*) is still very reduced.

In summer young children accompany their mothers who collect fuel wood and wild vegetables; in winter they go in groups of siblings and neighbours to fetch fodder and water, tend animals or wash clothes at the nearest stream. Whereas mixed groups of little boys and girls go gathering and collecting wood and fodder, fetching water is a purely female task, although a brother in arms may be taken along. Children start joining such work groups by the time they are about three years old, but are taken to steeper places only when they are about five. Till they are about eight, most tend to play more than they work; this is especially true of boys, who are anyway considered more immature than girls. But all children do in the process learn to recognise the right plants and trees, and practise how to handle the forests and negotiate the mountain slopes. Later in life, men forget much of this knowledge, especially that pertaining to medicinal plants. For example the dried roots of *Pinus wallichiana* (*čikṇi*) are used in every Bakkarwal household for a variety of ailments, and while all women, little girls and boys are familiar with it, adult men are extremely vague about it.

Milking and churning are arduous but essential tasks; while the latter is done only by the housewife, older children may milk if their mothers are sick, and younger children help their mothers by holding each animal being milked. Herding is basically a man's job, and only males go to the highest pastures (Rao 1992a). If there are no sons, shepherds are hired by the well-to-do; in less wealthy families little girls herd near home from the age of six or seven till about ten years; after this they may also go to graze during the day, but only if accompanied by their fathers or siblings. Boys start herding when they are a little older, since as children they are considered less responsible than their sisters. Particularly fathers tend to praise their little daughters and de-emphasise the importance of their young sons' labour in herding: "Our boys don't do anything – they play and quarrel and make mischief" is a commonly heard statement. Mothers, on the other hand, were often heard praising their sons and defending them, when their fathers accused them of laziness.

As they grow older the mixed work and play groups split according to gender, with girls increasingly helping their mothers with domestic tasks, and boys spending more time herding. Girls with younger siblings spend more time caring for them and practising their future role as mothers, for "just as puppies must be trained to catch hold of things, so also must girls learn how to mind younger (babies)".

The Acquisition of Knowledge and Information

Whereas the traditional practical knowledge acquired by a child is ascribed to its God-given *ōsh*, no specific term is used for this knowledge – it is a part of life, to be taken for granted, depending on the child's community, its place of residence and various other factors which all go to build its *mijāj*. This kind of knowledge is acquired at various ages, to various degrees by all normal persons. But there are other kinds of knowledge – specialised knowledge – which are acquired only by a few. That knowledge and access to it are graded is something I learned early in fieldwork, when I received differently worded, but stereotyped answers which could all be translated by "I don't know". When asked questions which I myself could not answer, I started off by mixing up these standard answers till, one day, old Ādeo decided he better clarify matters:

Ādeo: … Why do you say *"ke khabar"* when I myself saw you talking to that veterinary surgeon?

I: But he didn't tell me whether he had brought the medicine or not.

Ādeo: Then say, *"ke pato"* – you have his *khabar*, but he didn't tell you. O.K. And then why did you tell Farid [his grandson] that you didn't get *ilum* [*ilum paena*]?

I: Because I didn't learn the Qor'an like that …

Ādeo: O.K. you're not a *āfij* [*hāfiz*], but you told me you went to school for – how many years – fifteen, or even twenty? So your father saw to it that you got *ilum* …

Ilum is specialised knowledge to which high value is accorded, though it may be of little concrete use in day-to-day life. The term *ilum* was traditionally applied to knowledge of a religious nature, whose acquisition is in principle a strenuous and lengthy process. Access to it is not for all, nor is it meant for all. It is destined for the chosen few, whom God wanted to make *āfij* (<*hāfiz* = one who knows the Qor'an by heart) or *marāb* (one who prays regularly), or better still a *pīr*. These persons are seen as using their knowledge for the benefit of others, the common people without any knowledge. To acquire such *ilum* one must have certain special qualities which I have discussed elsewhere (Rao 1990). Unlike among many religious leaders in India for whom till very recently (cf. Salam 1996) the term *ilm* comprised religious knowledge alone, among the Bakkarwal *ilum* has for many years also applied to knowledge acquired through schooling. God has His hand in granting this new non-religious *ilum* too, but His ways here are less mysterious than they are in the former. As opposed to religious *ilum*, schooling, which for the Bakkarwal is primarily state-managed (but cf. Kohistani 1990: 257–8) is allegedly destined for all, and yet the acquisition of this "secular" *ilum* does not always appear to fit into recognisable cultural patterns. To begin with, it is not very clear what the benefits of this *ilum* are; many of its features appear to clash unreasonably with time-honoured usage, and finally, those dispensing it are viewed as humans who take rather than as those who give.

In the next paragraph I shall return briefly to schooling concepts and the new constraints imposed by these on autonomy and decision making. But before doing so I must refer to a third kind of knowledge – literally, information or news (*khabar*) – which one can acquire without either schooling or religious instruction. Like all other types of knowledge its acquisition depends on *ōsh* and *mijāj*, but takes place through mixing with the right persons, and hence it is linked to the practice of *uṭhan beṭhan*. This knowledge, which I shall refer to as social knowledge, is acquired, maintained and enhanced through what we would refer to as social networks. Obviously the larger a network, the greater the amount of knowledge available and the higher the likelihood of one's learning from the experiences of others within the network. Experience is linked not only to innate capacities and long life, but also to concrete instances of decision making through and concerning networks. Formerly, wisdom gained through experience was a proof of knowledge, and following the adage "he who is wise is powerful" (imputed to Firdowsi), those recognised as wise were also granted authority (Casimir and Rao 1995). However, neither in former times, nor nowadays does every Bakkarwal have access to large networks. As we have seen, mainly due to environmental constraints children have minimal networks; we shall see that women and men of low status also have small networks. Only those men whose well-being is also spatially wide enough, have really big networks (cf. Ch. 5 for more details).

THE INTERNALISATION OF "BACKWARDNESS"

An egg a day is more important than mother's love ...

— The Director of a Gujar-Bakkarwal Hostel, Srinagar, 1980

Backwardness *(pičhṛāpan)* is an important word in the political and educational discourse of most "developing nations", and so also of modern India. Through school textbooks children are told that "After [national] independence it was felt that the greatest obstacle for our citizens was represented by the backwardness of our rural citizens" (NCERT 1989: 13, translation mine). Illiteracy is linked to lack of knowledge, while not attending schools that are at least officially secular is projected as synonymous with being ignorant. Illiteracy and "ignorance" explain the "backwardness" of rural society (NCERT 1989: 14). This model applies particularly to women, who are "in a backward state" (NCERT 1989: 15). As for the Bakkarwal:

> They are backward ... and amongst the backward (in the State of Jammu and Kashmir) they are perhaps at the bottom of the ladder ...

> This backwardness is all-round, but it is particularly marked in scanty educational advancement, and unhealthy living conditions. Economically, some of them may be considered as fairly well off in comparison with other backward communities; at least this conclusion is reached by having a look at them in political, administration and urban hierarchy in the State, where some of them have good positions. (SOC. WELF. 1969: 1)

The other clear message is that the Government and its agencies attempt to "remove backwardness"; thus to improve the state of the Bakkarwal, the Government undertook measures "… for their settlement, educational advancement, economic uplift and improvement in the living and working conditions" (SOC.WELF. 1969: 2). Paraphrasing Nandy and Visvanathan (1990: 145) then, the removal of "backwardness" – or "development" as the process is usually termed – is a shorthand expression for attending to the overall needs of the poor, (still) nomadic, unhealthy and "scantily educated" Bakkarwal. The ideal agencies entrusted with this process are those of the Government and its urban or urbanised representatives. As early as 1916 the Government had given thought to the "problem" the nomadic population of Jammu and Kashmir presented in terms of schooling:

> Owing to their nomadic habits, it is difficult to arrange any educational institution for them. Even if moving schools could be arranged, the scattered nature of (their) … dwellings on the uplands would probably render any such arrangement inefficacious. The only plan which I can see is to encourage the children of such as spend the winter months in the lowlands of the State to come to the ordinary schools during that time. (Sharp 1916: 46)

This was still officially the colonial (and in Jammu and Kashmir the feudal) period; nomadism may have been a problem for the rationality of "law and order", but "backwardness" as such had not yet become a problem, perhaps because all the natives were considered backward. Today, however, schools in South Asia generally

> … act as agents of both cultural and ideological hegemony through the process of selective tradition…. The dominant culture in the school is passed off as the "tradition", or "the significant past" and thus legitimized as *the culture* that is common to all. The selection

process ensures that certain meanings and practices are chosen for emphasis while others are excluded. (Scrase 1990: 25)

This selection naturally tends to lead to the assertion of the values of the dominant sections of society. By accepting these values even superficially, one gains access to power networks of the dominant society, beyond one's community, thus enhancing one's status within it. Since in hierarchical societies this access is largely predetermined, schooling today often tends to reinforce old power structures, albeit in new forms – much as it did in the early colonial period (cf. Radhakrishnan 1990). Indeed, I suggest, that schooling could, at least to begin with, even decrease the autonomy of those who are lower in the community's hierarchy, because they are now doubly "proved" to be "backward" and "ignorant", and hence incapable of correct decision making. Bakkarwal children who had attended schools for longer periods certainly spoke with contempt about their community:

"You'll find out very soon that the Bakkarwal are a shameless people (*belehāz kaum*)", the eighteen-year-old Mohammad Yusuf told me when I first met him. He was studying in the 9th class and staying in a hostel specially meant for children of his community. On a visit to his parents with whom I was spending a few days, he insisted on his mother – who was "forward" enough to serve tea in cups rather than in tumblers or bowls – using saucers with these cups, and told her: "Otherwise sister [referring to me] will think you're as backward (*pasmanda*) as the other Bakkarwal women."

Ghulam Nabi had studied up to class 10 and informed me: "I'm not backward like the others here. I let my hair grow and don't wear a turban. I've told my mother so often not to let my sisters wear caps, to dress properly. But our women are all backward. Many of our rich men are not so backward. My late MB, Hajji I., was one of the richest Bakkarwal."

Fatima who had gone to school for six years also felt that the "Bakkarwal are a bad (*buri*) community". She was astonished that I had no problems eating Bakkarwal food, because she had problems ever since she went to school. "I can't eat at their homes, I get sick, they are so dirty… Everyday I have to take care how and what my mother cooks, to see that she does it the right way." Indeed Fatima's mother also had problems with her daughter: "She thinks she knows everything better simply because she can read and write! She has even stopped mixing with the other girls here", she told me.

Skinner's (1990) suggestion that through schooling children construct and create new ideologies and articulate their own emerging identities is, I feel, not applicable to all societies. These ideologies may differ from those of their families, and their identities may be in conflict with those of their parents, but this does not entail more cognitive autonomy, since these children like those in many other societies (cf. Bandura and Walters 1969) accept unquestioningly the cultural codes of the more powerful, dominant ideologies. Schooling involves mainly learning – *yād karnāñ*. To learn is to remember, to get by heart; the principle is not one of questioning and innovation, but of hearing, accepting and repeating till it is implanted in one's heart and head. When I asked their opinion on almost any matter, unschooled children I knew well and who were not otherwise shy with me were either silent, or answered "nothing", even when we were alone. Children who had been to school longer were no different, in that they had no opinions of their own; the difference lay, however, in their often answering by telling me what they had learned at school. By knowing these answers they demonstrated to the unschooled members of their camp that they participated in a superior culture.

From casual conversations it appeared that most Bakkarwal parents favour schooling. Of twenty-four men and women asked more pointedly, nineteen favoured schooling for sons and twelve for daughters (see Table 2.6 for details). When asked why they favoured schooling, fathers mostly replied in terms of the future economic well-being of their sons; mothers also mentioned future wealth and prestige, but most also linked this to their own old age security. Fathers who wanted to send their daughters to school cited a variety of reasons, all of which related to imbibing the culture of what they considered domesticity in the dominant culture; while they mentioned economic criteria only once, the mothers' arguments for schooling girls basically mirrored the fathers' economic arguments concerning their sons. The arguments forwarded by the eight parents not in favour of schooling their daughters tended to underline their fear of the child's learning evil ways. The two mothers who opposed their sons' schooling reasoned in terms of their health. Especially intelligent children (with lots of *ōsh*) are prone to attract the evil eye (*ak*). In 1984 Shafi died due to *ak*, "since he could write", his mother told me. Mothers feel that

Table 2.6 Responses of twelve mothers and fathers concerning the schooling of their children

	For Schooling		Against Schooling		No Opinion	
	Sons	Daughters	Sons	Daughters	Sons	Daughters
M	9	5	2	5	1	2
F	10	7	2	3	0	2

Note: M = mother, F = father

schooling also leads intelligent children to think too much, to reflect (*fikur*) and worry about things. Although it is good if a child understands and grasps (*samaj*) what he is told and taught, because he then considers (*fikur*) his actions, thinks about (*sōč*) them, and develops a sense of responsibility (lit. cares about someone, *is ko uskā fikur e*), too much pondering is bad, since it "cools" one down and can lead to sickness or early aging and a diminution in well-being – and ultimately perhaps even to death.

From various conversations and the very small sample of parents presented above it appears that schooling has a place in Bakkarwal ideology. To see to what extent this corresponds with practice, I considered a sample of 297 Bakkarwal men and boys and 231 women and girls between the ages of seven and forty-five years, obtained from the unpublished Census schedules of the official Census of 1981, and found that 57 (19.19 per cent) and 6 (2.59 per cent) respectively were classified as literate (which was implicitly defined at the time as someone above five years of age who was able to read and write: pers. comm. Census Office, Delhi). Table 2.7 sets out details concerning the males.

A comparison of these Census data with the opinions of parents discussed above points to a fairly great discrepancy between ideology and practice. Indeed, various intertwined factors are inimical to schooling. The shortage of mobile schools and of herding hands, the tendency of powerful families to monopolise such schools and exclude those not belonging to their power group, the shortage of teachers and their tendency to come from wealthy families, and finally the problem of the linguistic medium of instruction – all play a role in reducing the actual number of children going to school. I shall not enter into details here; suffice it to say

Table 2.7 Breakdown of 297 males according to age, and incidence and percentage of literacy as given in a sample population of the unpublished Government of India Census of 1981

	N	Literate	%
Age-Group 7–10 years	86	13	15.11
Age-Group 11–19 years	85	23	27.05
Age-Group 20+ years	126	21	16.66

that only those families who are really wealthy can afford to keep their sons in school for long, since they can afford to hire shepherds (Rao 1995). Additionally, these families are no longer entirely dependent on their flocks of small stock; most also have cattle and/or agricultural land, though the latter is rarely of high quality. A few of these families felt that sufficient diversification, i.e. a combination of land, cattle and small stock, or alternatively of land, cattle plus enough schooling, could lead a boy out of the constraints of a pastoral economy. Schooling, it is also felt, can lead to political influence, and this is borne out, it is said, by members of the Khaṭāṇā *zāt*, who have diversified the most – increasingly attending school and become increasingly wealthy and influential. It is still far too early to judge the impact of the Indian Government's current attempts to change this system by persuading the rich to open bank accounts and invest in private education rather than in cattle or land.

At the time of fieldwork one reason for labour shortage among the wealthy was the schooling of children, especially boys. Herding is basically a male job, though women and older girls help extensively in herd-related activities during the day. There is no prescribed lower age limit, and children start helping from the age of six or seven years, especially in the lambing and kidding periods. By the time he is about fifteen years old, a boy is expected to start taking on regular herding responsibilities under his father's or elder brother's supervision.

The End of Tending

In Bakkarwali usage both small children and animals are tended (*pāḷṇā*). Tending has many components, but one main goal –

survival. After all the necessary precautions have been taken a child is expected to survive. "Formerly those who fell sick died, but people were generally stronger", is the opinion of many. This attitude of the survival of the fittest applies all the more to orphans (*yatīm*), however young they may be. They have no parents – and following Muslim usage (O'Shaughnessy 1991: 35), especially no father – to tend them, but they are said to be provided for by God Himself. However, it is also said that they must have a strong *nafas* if they are not to lead a miserable existence. As mentioned earlier, the adoption of little children is not common among the Bakkarwal, and I encountered only one such case (for instances in which adults were adopted, see Ch. 6):

> Faruq, whose mother died at his birth, was adopted by his father's eldest brother, who had four daughters, but no sons. At the time of adoption, Zāro, the eldest daughter was sixteen, her younger sisters all above nine. In contrast, the oldest female in Faruq's household was his twelve-year-old sister, Shāzā, who, in addition to all the housework (and four younger brothers aged between about three and nine), simply could not manage to care for the newborn brother. (Later, Faruq's father remarried and had three more daughters by this wife.) Faruq had six elder brothers born of the same mother, and one elder brother, the son of his father's first wife, who too had died in childbirth. "For giving Faruq to my brother I got a promise of getting his two elder daughters (in marriage) for my first two sons", Faruq's father told me. The promise was kept.

But older children and even young men and women can sometimes be adopted by close relatives in times of need or labour shortage. This happens especially when a person has enough animals and pasture to survive, but no males to do the herding. In such circumstances, adoption, rather than the simple gifting of herds and pasture, is considered as something of a guarantee against ill-treatment.

A son, whether biological or adopted, is his parents' *wāris*, a status which signifies not only the right to economic inheritance but also the duty of moral responsibility, which is conceived of as individualised. To be a good *wāris* one must have enough *ōsh* to make the right choices at the economic and moral levels. A girl can also be a *wāris* though she has less *ōsh* and hence can not shoulder as much responsibility as a boy. A male *wāris* must represent *rag* in the genealogical sense of the patrilineage, and be able to compete with other similar sets of *rag*. A female *wāris* must bind these various, at times conflicting, strands together by asserting through her very being and her *batri* her female links and emotions of love. As mentioned earlier, it is around the age of ten that basic *ōsh* stabilises, and the foundation is laid for the capacity which develops variously in different persons to fend for oneself and be responsible. There is now no more need for elaborate care and tending. From around ten till they reach puberty a girl and a boy are termed *bēṭki* (lit. "little daughter") and *laṛā/luṛā* (cf. Hd. = *laṛkā* = boy) respectively, and this change of terminology marks the entrance into the next phase of the life cycle.

A PRELUDE TO PUBERTY Whereas a child below about ten is still considered fairly vulnerable (*nājuk*, <Ur. *nāzuk* = delicate, soft), a pubertal boy and girl are thought of as basically sturdy, strength being one of the elements circumscribed by the term *jawān* (<Ur. = young, youthful). Children in the phase in between are neither *bālak* nor *jawān*. A *bēṭki* and a *laṛā* have crossed one set of dangers which threatened mainly their physical life; they will face a second set when they are around sixteen or seventeen, and they must be prepared for this confrontation. These dangers are more social than physical, though they too stem from their own *nafas* and *ōsh*, which must at this stage be manipulated through socialisation. While this manipulation is required for both girls and boys, it is generally felt that "Girls are less of a problem on the whole than boys – if one is a little careful, they give less trouble. They also grow up much more quickly". This is partly because although by nature they end up with less *ōsh* than boys, in the early years they receive more of it than do boys of their own age, and partly because they are not as easily exposed to bad influences from outside the family.

Indeed mixing with the right persons is crucial at this stage, since it is explained that a good (*nēk*) person teaches others good things simply by his/her presence, and establishes harmony even in strained situations; by being with such a person even an enemy is turned into a friend (lit. "good person": *uske nāḷ dushman āto to sajjan banto*). Similarly, by keeping bad company one "goes bad" – a concept most Westerners should be familiar with. However, the essences transmitted among the Bakkarwal do not, I suggest, point to an ideology of dividuality, since what is really affected, even temporarily, is each person's unique level of *ōsh*. Akhtar's case is illustrative of such concepts.

> Akhtar disappeared suddenly six years ago, when he was twelve. He is remembered by relatives as being very bright and friendly, by his mother as being intelligent but mischievous, and by his father as disobedient and difficult. His FF felt that even before Akhtar's *ōsh* could reach its maximum (*pūro*), his parents had stopped controlling him, and had even sent him off on his own many a time to the village shop (near the winter area) where he had met "bad people" (*niphaṭ lōg*; lit. destructive persons); his FM was convinced that the man from this shop had used magic to "tie the boy's *ōsh*". Akhtar's father had informed the police, but to no avail. Then one day his mother told me "… a letter has come from someone who saw Akhtar in Bombay; Bombay's so far and so big and *pīr sāheb* says only prayers (*dua*) would help trace him out there. Akhtar's father says he'll go himself, but then he's so busy. If he's absent two days you see how many animals get lost. That's the trouble when there's only one man – that's why Akhtar used to be sent to the shop …"

Akhtar's was not the only case of boys aged between about eleven and fifteen disappearing, and the reasons given were all connected to *ōsh* having been diminished through contact with strangers. Perhaps that was also the reason why nothing much was undertaken by any relative to retrieve these boys.

It is important to bear in mind that Bakkarwal camps are always small, that children are usually not sent off on their own as Akhtar was, and indeed rarely get an opportunity to spend much time in the social world beyond the bounds of their camp. Hence the size of a child's social group is limited to its camp-mates, most of whom are siblings or other close relatives. Although camps split seasonally (Rao 1992a, Ch. 4), over the year camp-mates do not vary greatly. The children of a camp are, however, of various ages, so that genuine peer groups hardly exist. Even when they are out herding, boys are in charge of separate herd units, and have little opportunity to spend much time with those of their own age. Older girls spend most of their time in the camp, helping their mothers with all household chores; they leave it only to collect fuel, fodder and water, usually in the company of one or two adult women. Age difference between siblings is not manifested by an elaborate show of respect, nor marked by special terms of address. The authority older boys and girls exercise over younger siblings fades away by the time the latter reach puberty; decades later the younger may stand in a relationship of deference to the older provided that the latter do not occupy a patently lower socio-economic status than the former.

Gender differentiation in socialisation is publicly marked in this phase by male circumcision, there being no female counterpart to it. Circumcision (*soñt*, cf. Ur. *sunnat*), usually takes place – preferably on a Thursday (*vīrvār*) – when a boy is between the ages of six and twelve; it may not take place after this, but also not before the child is at least ten days old. This act finally confirms the boy as a Muslim (*musalmān bannāñ*), but it also affects him physiologically and prepares him gradually for puberty, when his seminal level will greatly rise. Were his prepuce not removed (lit. cut, *khatāñ*), it could some years later burst with the seminal pressure and the attending heat generated. This is why many families prefer to have their sons circumcised well before the levels of body fluids start rising rapidly. The circumciser is a local, professional Muslim barber (*nāi*), who comes in now and then to shave the heads of most men and older boys with his big scissors and blades, and is paid for his services in cash and in kind. He is now called into the boy's parents' home; no *mullā* attends, but the occasion is celebrated with a lot of food being cooked for the camp members. To prevent swelling and excessive bleeding the barber applies some medicinal plants on the operated area, and if this routine treatment does not help, the child's mother and other women take over to stop the bleeding, for with the blood goes the child's force, and if more than a certain amount of blood leaves the body "the seed will not be made".

The Rising of Fluids

"Certain things happen in the years [ages] between ten or eleven and sixteen or seventeen", said Janti, and these culminate in "a boy and a girl becoming *jawān*". It is established that universally between the ages of about eleven and seventeen certain biological changes take place among humans, and it is this period which is commonly termed "adolescence". These biological phenomena are usually subsumed under the term "puberty", which "… embraces a synchronised sequence of physical and psychosocial changes involving virtually every single tissue of the body over some three to four years" (Wu 1988: 89). There is further general agreement that in this

> ...period intervening between childhood and full adulthood, ... preparation for adult occupational, marital, and social class statuses and roles is initiated or intensified. (Schlegel and Barry III 1991: 3)

Ignoring ethnographic data on at least some non-Western societies (e.g. Baxter and Almagor 1978: 3–4), it has, however, often been suggested that "adolescence as a stage did not exist until extended schooling, which prolonged dependence upon parents, created it" (Schlegel and Barry III 1991: 2). Mamdani (1972: 131–2) corroborates this view for rural India.

> There is no adolescence in Manupur. There is only childhood and adulthood. The young in Manupur seldom display the carefree, spontaneous attitude that industrial society proverbially associates with youth. Children learn that if they are to be part of the family, they must contribute to it. Thus, children grow, not into youths, but into young adults.

Like most other South Asian children Bakkarwal girls and boys are "... profoundly enmeshed within the ... family hierarchical relationships ..." and "... adolescent issues of identity ... do not exist [here] as they do in ... Western societies" (Roland 1985: 100), partly because the options really available are so much more economically limited and socially circumscribed. But the fact that characteristics considered typical for a certain phase in Western societies are not displayed in others does not necessarily mean that the phase itself is locally held to be non-existent; other behaviour may be said to characterise this phase. In Bakkarwali there is no term specifically designating the period preceding sexual maturity or full adulthood. But it would, I suggest, be wrong to conclude that the Bakkarwal do not therefore distinguish this period from other phases of life; my data suggest that they do so both conceptually and in practice – for both humans and animals. Goats and sheep, for example, may be sold, sacrificed or eaten only after they are at least one year old, cows and buffaloes when they are two – in other words only after they can start mating and conceiving. To do so before would be a sin; even kids (*bakrōṭ*) and lambs (*lalūṭ*) may only be exchanged for food or grazing rights (Rao 1992a: 114), or gifted away after they are at least about six months old. This is how Shilla got the two-month-old pup, Arno, in return for a ten-month-old female kid, and many animals given as part of marriage transactions are not yet mature.

As always humans reach this preadult phase of life later than do animals. Girls and boys are now terminologically distinguished from those younger and older and are known respectively as *gadri* and *gadro* (cf. Gujari *gadria* and *gadroa* and Hd. *gadrānā* = developing youthful body). Physically much happens now, I was told: a boy's chest (*sīna*) expands and a girl's breasts (*čuči*) first develop, though they really grow only after marriage; wisps of hair appear on their bodies and on a boy's face. Both boys and girls grow in height and weight, since both increase in strength (*tākat*). But these changes are only the outward – one could say, physiological – manifestations of an internal, psychological – and as yet invisible – process. For it is now that the levels of blood in a girl and semen in a boy start to rise – slowly in some and faster in others, all depending on their *mijāj*, their innate temper or inherent disposition (cf. Fig. 1.1). They rise to reach a certain plateau, the level of which, again, varies individually. The attainment of this plateau manifests itself in the phenomenon of menarche and ejaculation, but is not synonymous with the maximum, for the levels of blood and semen do, and indeed should, spurt at regular intervals all through the adult phase. When these spurts take place regularly one is considered a young adult. I was often told of cases in which menarche had taken place much earlier, but had not been followed by regular menstruation. These girls were not yet considered fully *jawān*, and hence even if married they were not yet considered ready for sexual intercourse (cf. Ch. 3).

The term *jawān* and its derivatives constitute something of a semantic network which stretches between positive connotations such as strength, bravery and sexual maturity through ambivalent ones such as romanticism to negative ones such as rashness, heedlessness and irresponsibility. To help his "strength ripen" a boy must now start accompanying the family's animals to the high pastures. In these expanses (*wasi*, cf. Ar./Ur. *waḥshi* = wild, uncultivated) with few constrictions (*tangi*) of any kind, he can test his mettle and experience the beauty and hardship of a herder's life. Many of the life histories collected reflect this romantic and idealised phase of life to which older men – but never women – hark back. And yet this phase is in many ways ambivalent, above all, perhaps, because it is now that the social binding of a person is to be successfully completed. Errors at this last stage may have devastating effects on all. This ambivalence is built into the term *jawāni* which is associated – as far as I could gather, exclusively in men – with what may be described as a carefree disposition. Romance and adventure are part of it, but so too are thoughtlessness and the lack of a sense of proportion. *Jawāni* in a person who is physically just about *jawān* is accepted as perfectly normal, but it is not considered befitting those who are well into this phase. The term sums up Bakkarwal disapproval of a phenomenon which is probably universally frowned upon: "Although we sometimes idealize childhood, we have little tolerance for life's permanent children, the 'childish' adult…" (Burgoyne 1987: 40). Up to a point *jawāni* can be excused and at times appreciated even in a young adult, just as boyishness is in English society. As opposed to childishness, which implies the lack of reasoning, boyishness evokes reason tempered by spontaneity and youthful dynamism. *Jawāni* expresses precisely this ambivalence, and if its negative aspects are not curbed in time they *may* lead to a man becoming *shoñki* later in life (cf. Ch. 5). A man who is *shoñki* has little *ōsh* and excessive *nafas*, and this is what makes him excessively "hot".

Heat must always be regulated, since it has negative as well as positive effects. In the phase in which they gradually become *jawān* every boy and girl tends to be humorally hotter than ever before, and to avoid problems in later life their intake of heat must be carefully tuned to their gender-specific requirements. The level of heat socially accepted in boys and men is considerably higher than that in girls and women, who are, however, supposed to be "hotter by nature". It is this natural female heat which attracts the snowman (*baraf ko ādmi*) to young girls and impels him to try to abduct them away from their summer pastures into his abode in the highest mountains. Thus also while girls should avoid "hot" foods such as raw onions, eggs, too much salt or fat, there are no similar restrictions for boys. As mentioned in the previous chapter, excessive salt can dehydrate a girl and render her sterile. Hot foodstuffs and especially fat, on the other hand, symbolise wealth (large herds, much milk, and hence much butter oil), and a good life – and the richer the food, the more enjoyable it is supposed to be. All this conjures up luxury, which, however, connotes self-indulgence and passion on the one hand and impotence on the other, and the consequences of excessive rich food as of salt are compared to those of an excess of fertiliser. Hence to abstain (*parēj rakhāñ*) from hot foods is a metaphor for self-control. In keeping with this logic the annual fast (*roza*) enjoined by Islam to be first observed in this phase of life (girls at menarche, boys at around fifteen) is also said to help "cool them down". Several mothers, however, also felt that the reason why a boy was now allowed to break off an engagement if he really wanted to was that he was apparently "not yet hot enough".

The general increase in heat in boys and girls in this phase of life leads to a rise in the levels of body fluids, and this in turn to the physical strength achieved in the years to follow. But this rise is also associated with the development of certain undesirable wishes in them, and hence special care must be taken to achieve and maintain a highly sensitive equilibrium between "hot" and "cold". Excessive heat could make a girl sexually too demanding, and this in turn could make her ill and even barren (*ōtar*); alternatively she could later in life become so egocentric as to become a witch (*ḍākini*), turning others ill and barren. A boy with excessive heat is likely to become too power-loving and hence cruel (*ḍaḍḍā*). It is in this phase that *ōsh* stabilises, what we call character forms and beauty really develops. Here again, if a girl's parents are not careful enough, a pretty girl could grow so hot as to become too aware of her own beauty, and a sturdy boy overly conscious of his own strength. As mentioned in Chapter 1, beauty is also an outward expression of *rū*, which is basically a non-material component, and can from now on be influenced and "awakened". Somewhat like the Sufi concept of *latifa* (Hermansen 1988: 1–2), the awakening of the spiritual element in *rū* may lead to the good of one and all when by dint of his strong *nafas* a boy goes through arduous spiritual practices to ultimately attain the powers of a saint (*pīr* or *ajrat*). However, this concept does not conform to the mystical theories propounded by most Sufis, whereby a saint has to annihilate his *nafs* in order to enable his *rūh* to communicate with God (cf. Gaborieau 1989: 218). Also diverging from Islam, the awakening of *rū* may equally lead a girl to develop evil powers and grow into a witch (*ḍākini*). Once awakened, a *rū* is hard to put to sleep, and both saints and witches remain active even beyond death. But most persons do not activate their dormant *rū* even in their lifetime; to do so is to exercise one's will (*marji*), though ultimately, of course, the capacity to do so depends as we by now know on a variety of factors – and ultimately on God's will (cf. Hussain 1990 for a recent discussion of the concept of human capacity, free will and predestination in Islamic theology).

THE SPOILING OF CLOTHES With the onset of menarche, known variously as *čiṛa kharāb ōṇa* (clothes being spoiled), *rat čalnāñ* (blood flowing) or simply *kapṛā* (cloth, cf. Hd. *kapṛoñ se hōnā*), a girl attains a new social status and participates in new productive activities. Most girls and women asked said they remembered their first menses because they also kept the first ritual fast (*roza*) following this. Recollection data gathered among seventy-four girls and women gave an average age of 14.3 ±2.9 years. Phāta, who became a great-grandmother in 1983 observed:

> Formerly it was different. The first time a girl's clothes were soiled she was much older – it all happened later than it does now. Since the new salt came in, things have changed. Normally a girl was sent to her husband only after her blood has been flowing regularly – these days also it's like that, but some people are now thinking that if a girl's breasts are developed she's mature (*jawān*) and can sleep with her husband. And now many girls have too much blood and still have small breasts. It's all upside down these days.

From the day when a girl's clothes are soiled for the first time she is classified in the category of those who should possess modesty and the sense of shame (*lāj*). If necessary, she may now milk and churn, except during her monthly period, but till she herself marries and becomes a mother she may no longer go to the highest pastures, nor may she be present at the birth of a baby, since she herself is no longer pure. A girl who has reached menarche may no longer be careless about wearing her cap, and indeed her mother now makes a new cap (*lački*) for her. From now on it would be a real shame (*sharam*) to be seen with bare head (*sir nango*) – it would indicate that she does not have the emotion of *lāj*. A young girl now openly acquires the label of *aibdār*, imperfect, since her innate imperfection is now obvious to all, and yet she is simultaneously considered weak (*nājuk*) and vulnerable. Each month when the moon wanes (*čan katāwar āveñ*, lit. "moon gets frightened") she feels a hot wind rising up in her (*phūk čaṛho*); she feels dizzy and giddy (*dil phiro*), overcome by *asāyā* (cf. Hd. *asahāy* = helpless), when the *jin* take hold of her, pollute her and render her polluting (*makru*) for the rest of society. Till the next waxing of the moon (*čan čaṛhtāwar āveñ*) she may touch no cooking pot, no milking pail, no horse or goat.

Menarche, and with it menstruation, acts perhaps as the most ambivalent of diacriticals in a young girl's, and later a woman's, life. No longer a child, she is not yet a married woman, but a being in between, as indeed she will be in various ways for the rest of her life – between two families, eventually two *zāt*, etc. Menarche underlines on the one hand her imperfect female nature and calls for modesty on her part, but it also signals her fecundity (cf. Leslie 1986: 32 for similar observations on Hindu society). Fecundity and fertility – and thus menstruation – is associated with physical strength, which is an expression of a strong *nafas*; this in turn is associated with sexual desire. The more blood a woman loses at menstruation, the more excess blood she is supposed to have, and hence the stronger she is considered; the greater her strength the more her *nafas* and her sexual appetite and the larger the number of children she can bear. To say that a woman has "a lot of blood" thus amounts to making an ambivalent remark about her, and often older women are teased about "still having so much blood", in other words still being sexually active (cf. Ch. 6 for details). Excessive sexual desire is disapproved of among both women and men, and as in a variety of geographically distant cultures here too "… losing as much menstrual blood as possible" (Skultans 1970: 643) is considered a female body's way of keeping itself in natural balance by ridding itself of excessive heat, although menses which last many days are also considered debilitating. To preserve humoral balance and prevent menstrual pain a woman should not consume chillies which are too "hot" or buttermilk which is too "sour"; only sweet foods like milk and salty items like bread and salted tea should be imbibed. The roots of *Pinus roxburghii* (*čīr*) are drunk, boiled in a little milk, while the roots of *kāzabān*

(*Arnebia benthamii, Boraginaceae*) are ground, boiled in a little water and drunk. It would seem that menstrual blood is a category apart, considered basically different from blood exuding from any other part of the body. It is definitely considered "bad blood", as is also evident from the expression *čiṛa kharāb ōṇa*. This is why, though many women complain of the pain and inconveniences of excessive menstrual bleeding, they seem to accept it as something positive. What they fear is excessive clotting since this indicates constriction (*tangi*) and the accumulation of bad blood which could turn into poison (*jēr*) within the body.

A girl must be engaged before she reaches menarche and becomes nubile (cf. Ch. 3, Fig. 3.4). In principle the earlier the better, for her and for all others, since the chances of her becoming sexually dangerous to herself and to others must be minimised. Both ideally, and as far as I could gather in reality, a girl is a virgin (*kuāri*) till her first marriage. Sexual intercourse with a girl who may "look *jawān*", but is not yet regularly menstruating is considered sinful and to insinuate this is to insult a man and his entire family, including its female members. So when Pālki told me that her husband had slept with her before she had her periods regularly, although she was already thirteen years old, her daughter-in-law, Māto, who was present, took strong exception. Māto, who was also Pālki's husband's elder brother's son's daughter, accused her of lying and insulting her and her family, and finally cursed Pālki's male ancestors (*thāroñ bujurgoñ kā dāṛi no mār!*, lit. may the "beards" of your male elders be hit!). Once periods are fairly regular there is in principle no hindrance to intercourse, and transient adolescent infertility is sometimes used as an excuse to delay sending the young bride to the groom's home.

In Bakkarwal society although there is anxiety among young girls and their parents over future marriage, and especially about their having to leave the natal home, this anxiety appears to stem not only as it does in other South Asian societies from the role changes that accompany the transition from unmarried daughter to married wife, but also often from the great physical distance between natal and marital homes. Bakkarwal children and youth are brought up in relative seclusion. Throughout the year their settlements (*ḍērā*) and local exploitation groups are small. In summer and winter, settlement sizes vary from one to nine tents ($N = 42$; $\bar{x} = 3.4 \pm 2.3$) and one to seven dwellings (N = 23; $\bar{x} = 3.5 \pm 1.6$) respectively. An investigation of forty-six settlements (twenty-three each in summer and winter) revealed that none consisted of more than three generations. It is only during migration that young girls get a chance to meet persons from beyond their nuclear or immediate extended family. They are hence not necessarily familiar with even close relatives, such as first cousins. Leaving the natal home thus entails entering a whole new world and eventually meeting one's parents and younger unmarried siblings only during migration.

Chapter 3

PRODUCING NORMS

All normative systems constitute a link between cultural concepts and social action. The social action embodied in many of the rites which mark the process of binding the individual *shakas* into the communal *bandā* have already been discussed. The final and perhaps most crucial, being the most comprehensive, of all these acts of binding is that of marriage. Here, as in most societies, marriage binds not only two individuals, but also two families – sometimes two factions, two sets of people, each possessing a whole bunch of varied interests. Through marriage not only is a new husband-wife relationship established, but old relationships between families are reaffirmed and new ones formed. Formerly perhaps strangers, friends or even relatives, these two sets of families now enter into a (new) bond, that of *kuṛum* (cf. Hd. *kuṭumb* = kith and kin). This communal aspect of group reproduction reflects the general South Asian concern with establishing appropriate alliances through marriage, and is explicitly recognised by the Bakkarwal when they say that the respective patrilineages, the units of social and genealogical identity *(zāt* or *khēl*) are of utmost importance in the choice of bride and groom. Or when a man says that "before deciding on a groom for my daughter I must ask the *birādari*" [lit. "ascertain the will – *marji* – of the *birādari*"]. The basic principle underlying this role of the community is that of narrowing down the degrees of choice, so as to make other, future decisions less risky. When choosing a spouse for one's child, abstract rules matter little; what is aimed at is the concrete likelihood of husband and wife matching each other optimally and hence of minimising unpredictability for all those closely associated with them. The less the spouses (or their families) know of each other, the greater the unpredictability, and the higher the risk involved. The risks of bringing in a stranger can be both immediate and long-term, affecting both present and future generations socially, morally and economically. Marriage among the Bakkarwal is the prerequisite for sexual relations, premarital sex being as far as I am aware largely restricted to the few young men who may go off to urban areas singly in the winter to run errands for their parents. Obtaining access to reproductive resources is thus also linked to access to productive resources, in terms of produce, capital goods and, indirectly, power, and thus ultimately to decision making. Although this pertains more generally to men, it is also applicable to women who may alienate productive resources from both their natal and marital households in the form of dowry and dower.

One way of assessing autonomy can be to ascertain whether a person can dispose of him/herself in matters of sexuality, whether eventual individual emotions and desires in this sphere are publicly sanctioned. Ideally, I was told, such individual interests are taken into account when arranging a marriage; additionally most informants simultaneously projected these as usually concording with the interests of the larger group. All opined also that paternal authority was absolute, and the father's decision in the matter final. The reality is more complex and more individuated. I came across three instances in which young men and women who felt attracted to each other managed to convey their feelings – without ever mentioning them explicitly though – to their respective mothers. In two of these cases the mothers got these matches arranged, the public expression of these arrangements being constructed via the respective fathers; in the third case the mother was overruled by her husband. Equally, however, I encountered cases, discussed in some detail later in this chapter, in which the wishes of young women and men were explicitly ignored and subsumed under the interests of older, more powerful individuals. Running counter to the dominant ideology of paternal decision making were cases I also came across in which mothers were accused of having used charms and magic (*phūñk*) to entice a future son-in-law. While one such accused I once asked contemptuously dismissed such talk as envious gossip, most women I spoke to explained that by blowing on persons weaker than themselves persons with very strong *nafas* can bring about changes in the former, and even get them to carry out the blower's intense wishes. Blowing as a means of transmission has been observed in other Islamic societies, in contexts of healing and blessing as well (e.g. Donaldson 1938: 181–2, Sharif 1975).

Units of Identity

Whoever the actual decision makers may be, as already mentioned *zāt* and *khēl* identity is crucial in the choice of a spouse. These taxons are semantic keys to the historical identity of the entire Bakkarwal community. "*Zāt*" probably derives from the same Indo-Iranian root as the "*jāti*" (Ansari 1960; Ali 1978: 24; Steingass 1973: 605) of the Hindu *varna-jati* system. "*Khēl*" denotes various units of social organisation (e.g. Barth 1959: 24; Glatzer 1977: 119; Anderson 1982: 7; Rao 1982: 119; Orywal 1986) in areas of Pashtun influence, and is transcribed in neighbouring contexts as *k͟hel* (or *xel*). Although taxonomically different, *zāt* and *khēl* among the Bakkarwal are today organically and functionally indifferentiable; but they indicate different origins. The community today is composed of thirty-seven *zāt* and two *khēl*. Thirty-six of the former form one subdivision, that of the *Kunhāri* (or *Kunāri*); the remaining *zāt* and the two *khēl* form a second subdivision, that of the *Allaiwāḷ* (also pronounced *Alaiāḷ, Ilaiāḷ* or *Ilahiwāḷ*). Whereas the taxon *khēl* is used exclusively to denote *Allaiwāḷ* subsections, the taxon *zāt* is used by members of both subdivisions to denote subsections of *Kunhāri* and *Allaiwāḷ*.

Bakkarwal *zāt/khēl* are unequal in size, and most Bakkarwal have some idea of the relative size of every such unit. Appendix A lists twenty-nine *zāt/khēl* whose relative sizes were estimated spontaneously on different occasions by forty-four Bakkarwal women and seventy-nine Bakkarwal men of various *zāt/khēl*. The estimates showed great consistency. The names of these twenty-nine *zāt/khēl*

Table 3.1 The spontaneous naming and ranking of *zāt/khēl* undertaken by fourteen Bakkarwal, examined further according to their own estimates of relative size of these units

Estimate of Informants' *zāt/khēl*	Total *zāt/khēl* Named	Estimated As Large	Medium	Small
Large (4)	20	4	10	6
Medium (4)	20	9	7	4
Small (6)	30	10	10	10
Total		**23**	**27**	**20**

were chosen by me out of the total of thirty-nine *zāt/khēl*. The remaining ten *zāt/khēl* can be classified as extremely small according to self-perception estimates done independently by between five and nine members of each of these ten *zāt/khēl*. It was also found that except for a handful of politically influential and ambitious men, no Bakkarwal, when asked to rattle off the names of all the *zāt/khēl* that came to mind, could think of more than a few. As an indication, a very small sample of fourteen men and women named an average of 6.3 (± 2.2) *zāt/khēl* (5.8 per cent of all 39 units). Each of these ten men and four women who themselves belonged to six "small", four "medium" and four "large" sized units, named their own unit first. This is hardly surprising; of interest, however, is the question, which other *zāt/khēl* did they name, and furthermore, was there any ranking involved in terms of perceived *zāt/khēl* size or typological frequency? In other words, were the more abundant "small" *zāt/khēl* named more and before, say, the numerically stronger but less abundant "large" or "medium" *zāt/khēl*? To answer these questions it was decided to examine which first five units each of the fourteen respondants named after having mentioned his/her own unit. It was found that irrespective of the *zāt/khēl* size of the respondant, the first five units named were those perceived of as either "large" (in twenty-three cases) or medium (twenty-seven); in twenty cases the so-called "small" *zāt/khēl* were named (see Table 3.1). Had these listings been at random, i.e. according to typological frequency, one could reasonably expect all informants to name more "small" *zāt/khēl*. That this was not so can be explained in terms of geographical distribution, but above all, I believe, in terms of relative influence and power of patronage, both in the past and now (cf. Ch. 5).

A Bakkarwal *zāt/khēl* is generally classified as either *Kunhāri* or *Allaiwāḷ*, following the principle that its ancestors (Rao 1988a) originally came into Kashmir from the valleys of either Kunhar or Allai (cf. Fig. I.1) in present-day Pakistan. Khatana (1976a: 87) suggests that these subdivisions do "not have any direct functional relevance today". This is true insofar as Bakkarwali language has no taxon for them; they are, nevertheless, considered distinct units of neighbours *(amsāyā)* with important and well-recognised differences. Dress and vocabulary are said to be some of the outward expressions of these differences, and *Allaiwāḷ* men are supposed to sport fuller beards and pay bridewealth for wives rather than dowry to their daughters (Rao 1997). Even today each of these subdivisions is preferentially endogamous (cf. Table 3.2).

Originally possessing only geographical implications, the two terms *Kunhāri* and *Allaiwāḷ* took on historical ones for the Bakkarwal, and in the early phase of the formation of this community in Jammu and Kashmir (Rao 1988 a, b) still more connotations got added. While the *Kunhāri* are considered akin to the Gujar of the Kashmir Valley (Rao and Casimir 1990), the *Allaiwāḷ* are said to contain more Pashtun elements. The pasture areas of the two subdivisions are largely distinct and until about 1989 there was also the connotation of two sets of affiliations with regional and political parties, leading to what could almost be considered two factions. These more recent aspects have resulted partly from the political nature of the Bakkarwal institution of *birādari*, a kind of corporate group, to which I shall return shortly.

The ancestors of the Bakkarwal immigrated in small groups, each of which was composed of one or more *zāt* or *khēl*, probably one dominant and a few other numerically weaker ones. These *zāt/khēl* are comparable to clans, insofar as each of them constitutes a "compromise kin group" (Murdock 1949: 66–8), consisting of a group of men and women who claim common ancestry but are not able to trace it. A solitary exception reported – but not met with personally – was that of the *Bōṭa-Bokṛā*, who I was told had formed as a separate *zāt* through the segmentation of the *Bokṛā* (or *Bokun*) *zāt*. Their ancestor, Bōṭa, had "so many descendants that they separated from the rest"; in other words social and biological networks provided them with a base to publicly demonstrate autonomy by splitting from the larger group and establishing a separate identity. New *zāt*, I was told, can come up even today, depending on "whom one marries, where one lives and how many descendants one has". Some *zāt* names – such as *Āwāṇ* or *Gakkaṛ* – are names of ethnic groups in present-day Pakistan, while the name *Bokṛā* is traced to *boka* (pail) and to the blessings of the Biblical Joseph (Yusuf):

> Between Misar (Egypt) and Kinhan, the Prophet *Hazrat* Yusuf *Paighambar* (son of Ibrahim al Islam Alai Salām – may peace be on him!) had eleven brothers, and they threw him into a well (*khu*). *Hazrat* Yusuf and the youngest, *Hazrat* Biniamin, were of one mother; the other ten were of another mother. *Hazrat* Yusuf went hunting with his ten brothers, while Biniamin stayed home. There *Hazrat* Yusuf was beaten up by his brothers and thrown into the well – but he did not die. A caravan of traders was passing by and decided to encamp there. Their cook (*babarči*) had to fetch water and went to this well with his pail (*boka*). When he threw his pail in, *Hazrat* Yusuf came up with the water. The cook reported to his masters that a prince (*shāzādā*) had come up with the water. Since then the name *Boka* stuck, and *Hazrat* Yusuf blessed the cook, saying, "He who saved me, his descendants should always be blessed".

But the majority of Bakkarwal *zāt* names are also caste names among several Hindu and Muslim communities of the subcontinent, and hence it is pertinent to ask whether Bakkarwal *zāt* can be considered as castes. A historical link between Bakkarwal *zāt* and caste units can not be dismissed entirely, but can not be discussed here. As for the contemporary situation, however, the answer must be unequivocally in the negative: Bakkarwal *zāt/khēl* are not hierarchically ordered, though some are patently bigger and on the whole even richer than others. Members of all *zāt/khēl* share the same occupation, there being no further specialisation within the community. Finally, no ideological restrictions inhibit daily social intercourse among members of the various *zāt/khēl*. Yet there are certain inhibitions imposed by the ideology of purity on those embarking on long-term social (and physical) intercourse; hence a marriage partner should be chosen preferentially from within one's own *zāt* (or *khēl*). As Wikeley (1991: 69) wrote of the Gujar, who share many *zāt* names with the Bakkarwal: "No one of [their] clans can claim any definite superiority over the rest, but some are more exclusive than others as to whom they give their daughters in marriage." However, as Honigman (1960) has pointed out for Sind, Wakil (1972) for the western Panjab and Ahmad (1976: 50–1) for Swat, even a higher rate of *zāt* endogamy would not necessarily point to *zāt* being a caste-like element among the Bakkarwal.

Although a *zāt/khēl* is generally classified as being either *Kunhāri* or *Allaiwāḷ*, there are instances in which it can be classified as both *Kunhāri* and *Allaiwāḷ*. This is where one grasps the pertinence of the *Kunhāri* and *Allaiwāḷ* divisions and reaches the nexus between the concepts of *zāt* and *birādari* (Rao 1988a). Derived from Persian *berādar* (brother), the term *birādari* is used extensively in northern India and Pakistan to denote, strictly speaking, the patrilineage. By extension, however, it is frequently used to refer to a kind of sodality, to various formal and informal associations, even those beyond kin connections, all of which nevertheless have in common the concept of "belonging together", of mutual cooperation to various degrees and in various spheres. The Bakkarwal speak of "doing *birādari*" (*birādari karāñ*) when a matter is to be solved amicably, in cases where mutual trust between the partners involved is of crucial importance. Not to help fellow *birādari* members amounts to being impious, irreligious and faithless – *bedīnī*. Help can come in many forms; one of the commonest is that of lending money.

> "One of the good things about a *birādari*", commented Qasim, "is that within it one can borrow money without interest for up to one year. On government loans – or with outsiders – one has to pay interest even for a few days, and if one can't pay back one's animals are seized and one is ruined." However, even here there can be nuances, as Shilla observed: "It's true that within the *birādari* no one can take interest, but then two men are always different: take J and N. J takes no interest but lends only to the rich; N also takes no interest, but out of the goodness of his heart he lends to the very poor (*lāčār*)."

Indeed, were lending money within the *birādari* always so simple and automatic, no Bakkarwal would need to borrow money from shopkeepers and other non-Bakkarwal as they so often do, nor would hired shepherds run up the debts they do (Rao 1995).

When the ancestors of the Bakkarwal first came to Jammu and Kashmir they were few in number, and "*nātedāri* created the *birādari*". In other words, they intermarried (cf. Pnj. *nattā* = a relationship created by giving a female kin in marriage), and with these first steps towards creating a kinship network in their new land, they created the various *birādari* with their elementary genealogical connotations. At this level of usage the term *birādari* denotes a patrilineage to which one belongs by birth; hence, whatever one's crime, one can never be expelled from one's *birādari*. Furthermore, since the alliances the ancestors entered into were limited in number, "there are no new *birādari*, although there are now many more Bakkarwal". In the early years of immigration most male members of a *birādari* also belonged to one *zāt/khēl*, although dependant members of other *zāt/khēl*, who had migrated along with them, were also considered fellow-*birādari* members. Soon, however, daughters and sisters were given in marriage in limited numbers to men of other *zāt/khēl*, who then came to be considered as fellow-*birādari* members. Gradually one could "change" one's *birādari* and be recruited into one. The original and single patrilineage connotation of the term *birādari* was thus affected and additional connotations now emerged (cf. Ch. 5). One of these concerned marriage and alliance. Today, both *zāt/khēl* and *birādari* operate at the level of biological reproduction, and hence the terms are often used synonymously to denote a patrilineage. A *birādari* is actively involved in regulating the autonomy of its members, for example, in the choice of marriage partners and in marriage negotiations; it also participates in solving marriage problems and on rare occasions may even instigate separation and divorce.

The Accountability of Endogamy

A daughter-in-law of one's own zāt is one's own;
a daughter-in-law of another zāt is from outside.
— a Bakkarwal

For the Bakkarwal the taxon *zāt* subsumes a number of connotations, some of which act as nearly absolute constraints on one's degrees of freedom. These are the connotations of race and breed, applicable to humans and animals alike, and explicit, for example, in the statement: "Just as we have different *zāt*, so do our goats, our horses, our dogs – they too have different *zāt*, different *nasal* (literally, pedigree, genealogy)." Implicit in this statement is a qualitative difference, which is however not globally ranked for either goats, horses, dogs or humans. But ranking may be situational. Thus, as Shafi explained,

> There are three kinds of horses, *Zānskāri*, in Ladakh, *Kāshir*, locally, and among us and the Gujar, *Paryum*. The *Paryum* are bigger and taller than the *Kāshir*, and their legs are also thicker, so if you want heavy loads carried as we do, it is better to have a *Paryum*. But then, they are also more expensive than the *Kāshir*. Also, if you want to ride fast, a *Paryum* is not so good.

Similarly, remarked Dulla, there are two types of dogs – *Kāshir* and *Bakarāḷi*: "The *Kāshir* eat a lot and bear a large litter, the *Bakarāḷi* only bear one or two puppies at a time but they eat less and are very good as watchdogs."

> "You see", said Daud, "the *Kāshir* litter is so large that the mother's brains get distributed among all her children, and each gets only very little (cf. Ch. 4). Since the other litter is so small, each puppy gets a lot of brains. When someone plans a theft a *Bakarāḷi* dog even far away gets to know about what's going on in the thief's head, whereas a lone *Kāshir* dog has problems catching the thief, even after he's there. But a *Kāshir* dog is also much cheaper, so either you can have two or three or four *Kāshir* dogs or one *Bakarāḷi* dog to do the same job. Also you can make money selling the extra *Kāshir* puppies you don't need."

Then again, as Kalea commented,

> There are certain types of goats who give a lot of milk, others who give a lot of hair, and still others who breed well. Similarly, there are big *zāt* and small *zāt*; different *zāt* have different traditions and customs (*rawāj*).

It is generally agreed that in terms of numbers as well as in terms of generational depth (*bujurgi ke isāb se* – traditionally counted as "seven generations"), the *Khaṭāṇā* are the most important among the *Kunhāri* Bakkarwal *zāt/khēl*. Among the *Allaiwāḷ*, the *Bijāṛ* are ranked first numerically, with *Kāḷo Khēl* and *Mandaṛ* following. But once again, everything is relative: the *Khaṭāṇā* may be the most numerous, wealthy and nowadays even the least "backward", but they are also universally held to be greedy, oppressive and cruel (*zālim*); the *Wānā*, on the other hand, are known as very poor, dirty and gentle, while the *Čēči* are said by many to "have both poor and rich" among them, to be ill-behaved, and "artificial (*nakli*), not genuine (*asli*)" and hence untrustworthy, though good-looking. For many *Bijāṛ*, the *Bargaṭ* are "a useless (*bekār*) lot – like the *Dihāṛ* among the Hindus. You'll find them everywhere in small numbers". And as Alia, also a *Bijāṛ*, concluded, "They were bad from the very beginning. They're not given to [in marriage] by any, nor taken". The basic unit at stake is that of biological, and hence also social, reproduction. The term *nasal*, which the Bakkarwal confine to animal usage, is indeed met with among other subcontinental Muslims in human contexts as well, and Roy (1984: 391, 395, 396) notes that among the Asna Ashariya of Uttar Pradesh "… the concept of *nasab* or *nasal* … emphasises … the purity of blood and its retention by close inbred marriages".

Precisely because of this idealised coherence between biological and social units of reproduction, *zāt* for the Bakkarwal, very much as for other communities in Kashmir, helps identify the "essence or inherent nature" (Madan 1972: 109; cf. also Madan 1994: 171ff.) of an entire group, and hence of every one of its members. This innate temper is, as we know, intergenerationally transmittable, primarily through body fluids. "Giving and taking in marriage" is the ideal framework for the transmission of inherent nature and its accompanying qualities, as well as for the specific traditions which are the typical expressions of the latter. As good Muslims, rejecting all notions of absolute hierarchy, the Bakkarwal nevertheless recognise differences in "traditions and customs" (*rawāj*), and reserve the right to prefer some, tolerate others and reject still others outright. Since traditions are transmitted primarily by blood, and since one may not want to obtain (or transmit) certain traditions, one must be careful about whom one mixes one's blood with. A child is as we know the product of the mixing of blood and semen; it is expected to be also the defender and transmitter of the right traditions.

At the level of bride and groom, marriage involves the transfer of semen in exchange for the gift of a hopefully worthy inheritor (*wāris*). At the level of the families involved in the immediate marital transaction, the exchange of bride and groom involves opening one's home to newcomers, obtaining inheritors and forging or cementing alliances. At both levels there is a certain risk involved; the risk of the unknown, the risk of taking the wrong decision, of making the wrong choice (Rao forthcoming). Security and dependability are at stake here and only one's own *zāt/khēl* can ensure these as far as possible, as far as God's will allows. A pure (*čhaṛā*) thing is always good, be it grain, medicine, water – or blood. Mixtures are no doubt sometimes necessary, and many can even be beneficial, but one must be wary of them. Excessive mixture (*ṭhis mis*; cf. Pnj. *miss tiss* = "mixed grain", Maya Singh 1972: 754) is, however, always bad as it implies chaos and impurity; in the case of blood this is especially so – it leads to ruin. "We know what we get" expresses the emotional and moral security provided by the familiarity of one's own *zāt/khēl*, which represents one's own blood. Minimal mixture of blood also increases the chances of legitimate autonomy, since the general risk factor is reduced. Purity of blood connotes purity of character, and this is of utmost importance as far as a woman – and a future mother – is concerned. Character, in its turn, is said to show in the face, and thus "a person's *zāt* is always recognisable". An investigation carried out using twenty coloured photographs of fourteen adult Bakkarwal men and six women belonging to ten *zāt/khēl* showed, however, that such "recognition" consists largely of guessing. The photographs, taken by me or my husband at different places between July 1980 and March 1983, were partly portraits and partly full-size. On different occasions between July 1983 and July 1985 these pictures were shown individually to eight men and seven women of twelve different *zāt/khēl* who we thought were unlikely to know the persons photographed. They were asked to identify the *zāt/khēl* of the person and if possible explain their choice. Of the three hundred replies obtained (fifteen answers for each of the twenty pictures), only twenty-eight (9.33 per cent) were found to be correct. The failure to recognise was imputed by the respondants to the quality of some of the photos, to the observers' incompetence coupled with their relative youth and lack of experience. "Our old people could do this much better", said Jima, and Pari, who had three answers correct, concluded: "*Zāt* does tell you everything you can want to know – if you know the *zāt*, you know all, for good or for bad."

It is this allegedly predictable nature of *zāt*, the accountability of one's fellow *zāt/khēl* members and the corresponding reliability achieved through endogamy that Bibo was trying to explain when she said, "it's safer to give and get within the same *rang*". "Of course even [within] the same *rang*", said Gama, "we must consult the elders"; he was talking about the offers which had come in for the marriage of his eldest daughter. "All these offers [were] from a different *rang*", and so Gama "hadn't even bothered to talk [i.e. consider them]". He was waiting for offers from his own *rang*. *Rang* literally means "colour", but Bibo had pointed to the veins (*rag*) in her arm. In the context of identity *rang* signifies the "blood flowing through the veins", and in Chapter 1 it was seen that blood is conceptually bilateral, and connected to both *batri* (the female link) and *rag* (the male link). Types of blood indicate types of identity. As Khana put it,

> There are various types (of *rang*). The Gujar are of one type, the Kashmiri of another, the Sayyed of still another, and the Bakkarwal again of yet another – we're of the *Kasāṇā* (*zāt*), others are *Bokṛā* (*zāt*), still others are *Allaiwāḷ* … (lit. *kisam kisam kā ōta e. O Gujur bi aur rangā e, kishmiri aur rangā, Sayad aur rangā, Bakrāḷ bi – am Kasāṇā e, koe Bokuṛ e, koe Ilaiāḷ e …*).

Zāt (or *khēl*) endogamy thus ensures a maximum of security through purity of blood – through non-mixture, the opposite of *ṭhis mis*. This semi-mystical nature of the ties of blood has been described by Kurin (1990: 107) for the Nunari of western Panjab:

> The conversion (to Islam) entails a transformation wherein Rajput blood, as the basis for identity, is superseded by *nur* or light. The light is understood as both a metaphor and a metonym of *ruh* or the spirit of Allah which is present in all human beings. What was hidden before conversion was made apparent through it and became the basis for group identity. In a basic way, the Nunari were defined as a spiritual community, and each person a spiritual brother.

The concept of the purity of blood plays an essential role in the practice of alliance among Muslims and Hindus in large parts of South Asia (e.g. Ahmad 1978: 5; Donnan 1988: 127, 130; Parry 1979: 85–6). The idea that this purity is best represented by one's own social or religious group is also attested over a wide area (e.g. Goodfriend 1983: 121 for Delhi Muslims; Canfield 1973: 69; and Casimir pers. comm. 1979 for Central and West Afghanistan respectively).

Table 3.2 Extent of *Kunhāri-Allaiwāḷ* intermarriage

Kun – Kun		**Kun – All**		**All – Kun**		**All – All**	
N	%	N	%	N	%	N	%
80	96.4	2	1.1*	8	4.3**	82	87.2

Note: N marriages analysed = 172. Percentages are calculated on all marriages analysed and the division of the male partner is indicated first.
Kun = *Kunhāri;* All = *Allaiwāḷ.*
*2.2 per cent of all *Kunhāri* marriages
**8.7 per cent of all *Allaiwāḷ* marriages

Levels of Marrying "One's Own"

The principle of endogamy is enjoined within every unit of Bakkarwal social organisation beyond the nuclear family, Islamic rules governing the categories of permitted (*jāez*) and prohibited (*nājāez*) sexual partners. Table 3.2 sets out data on degrees of endogamy at the subdivisional level of *Kunhāri vs. Allaiwāḷ*. These have not changed substantially over the last roughly seventy years, and ranged for the seven age groups (-20 to 70+) between 90.9 per cent and 100.0 per cent and 60.0 per cent and 100 per cent for the *Kunhāri* and *Allaiwāḷ* respectively. Endogamy at this level was least for women now aged thirty-one to forty years, i.e. for those who married between 1957 and 1973 (period of marriage calculated from Tab. 3.10), a phase in which two wars between India and Pakistan also affected Jammu and Kashmir. The situation of the group as a whole and the social relations among the various families during the Indo-Pakistan war of 1965 were also described by several Bakkarwal as mixed-up (*ṭhis mis*), chaotic and confused.

Marriage (*nātedāri*) between *Kunhāri* and *Allaiwāḷ* can lead to a change in subdivision; this was said to happen especially when a man without stable pasture rights marries a woman who has access to pasture, but no brothers to manage it. The groom then comes and lives with or near his wife's parents and is henceforth considered a member of their subdivision.

An analysis of another sample of 187 first marriages contracted by women belonging to 29 different *zāt*/*khēl* showed that the question of

Table 3.3 Frequency of first-ever marriages contracted by a woman within her paternal *zāt/khēl*

Zāt	Marriages	*Zāt* Endogamous		*Zāt* Exogamous	
N	N	N	%	N	%
29	187	101	54.0	86	46.0

Note: The term *zāt* is used to cover both units.

Table 3.4 Frequency of first-ever marriages contracted by a woman within her maternal *zāt/khēl*

Zāt	Marriages	*Zāt* Endogamous		*Zāt* Exogamous	
N	N	N	%	N	%
16	31	17	54.8	14	45.1

Note: The term *zāt* is used to cover both units.

Table 3.5 Frequency of 180 first-ever marriages contracted within their paternal *zāt/khēl* by women over a period of seven generations

Zāt/Khēl	Ages of Women	Marriages	*Zāt/Khēl* Endogamy		Marriage Period (ca.)
N	N	N	N	%	
14	–20	27	17	62.9	1983–1985
16	21–30	45	25	55.5	1967–1983
13	31–40	17	9	52.9	1957–1973
13	41–50	19	10	52.6	1947–1963
14	51–60	18	8	44.4	1937–1953
0	61–70	0	0	0	1927–1943
17	70 +*	54	28	51.8	before 1927

Note: The cut-off point here was taken as 1985. The term *zāt* is used to cover both units.
*This category includes deceased women whose daughters reported.

the extent of marriage within a *zāt* or *khēl* is more complicated than that of subdivisional endogamy. Of the 187 women, 101 (54.0 per cent) married men of the same *zāt/khēl*, while 86 (46.0 per cent) married men from other *zāt/khēl* (Table 3.3). This indicates a high preference for *zāt/khēl* endogamy, i.e. for marrying a man whose *zāt* or *khēl* is the same as one's father's. Had these marriages been randomly distributed within these 29 *zāt/khēl*, there would have been only 6.4 marriages (3.4 per cent) in each of these 29 *zāt/khēl* provided that these units were all relatively equal in size. Similarly, their random distribution among all Bakkarwal *zāt/khēl* would have yielded a frequency of 4.8 (2.5 per cent) marriages per *zāt/khēl*. As discussed earlier, however, these units vary in size, and it will be shown below that the larger such a unit is, the greater the degree of endogamy practised.

A closer look at the 86 marriages in which a woman did not marry a man of her fathers' *zāt/khēl* shows that in 55 cases (63.9 per cent) her parents had been endogamous, while in 31 (36.0 per cent) instances the parents of these women had been *zāt* or *khēl* exogamous, i.e. their maternal and paternal *zāt/khēl* were different. In the 55 cases a woman and her husband's mother shared a *zāt/khēl*; i.e. while the wife's parents were endogamous, those of the husband had been exogamous, and the woman married into her FZH's family. The 31 women whose parents were exogamous belonged to a subsample of 16 *zāt/khēl*. Once again, assuming that the social units were equal in size, had these marriages been normally distributed, one would have encountered 1.9 (6.1 per cent) marriages per each of the 16 *zāt/khēl*. But it was further found that of these 31 women, 17 (54.8 per cent) had married men belonging to their mothers' *zāt/khēl*, and 14 had married into a third *zāt/khēl* (Table 3.4). Again of these 14, in four cases the *zāt/khēl* of the mothers of the spouses was identical, and only in ten cases was an immediate *zāt/khēl* link between the spouses entirely absent. Figure 3.1 illustrates the detailed breakdown of the marriages analysed, and shows that, not surprisingly perhaps, parental endogamy favours children's endogamy.

The above data show a clear preference for a woman being married within her paternal *zāt/khēl*, and failing this within her maternal *zāt/khēl*. As shown in a subsample spanning about seventy years (Table 3.5), these trends (Fig. 3.2) appear to have changed somewhat

Figure 3.1 Detailed breakdown of 187 marriages according to *zāt* endogamy and exogamy over two generations

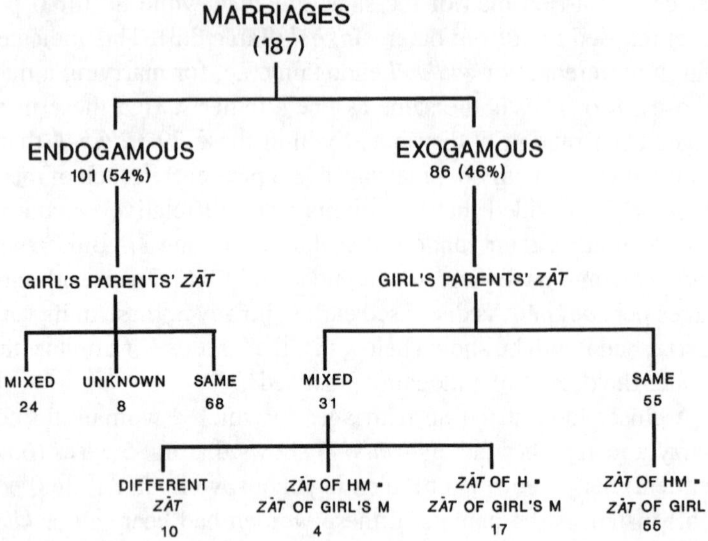

Figure 3.2 Percentage change and related regression in extent of endogamy in 180 marriages contracted over a period stretching from before 1927 to 1985, in relation to change in overall population over the same period

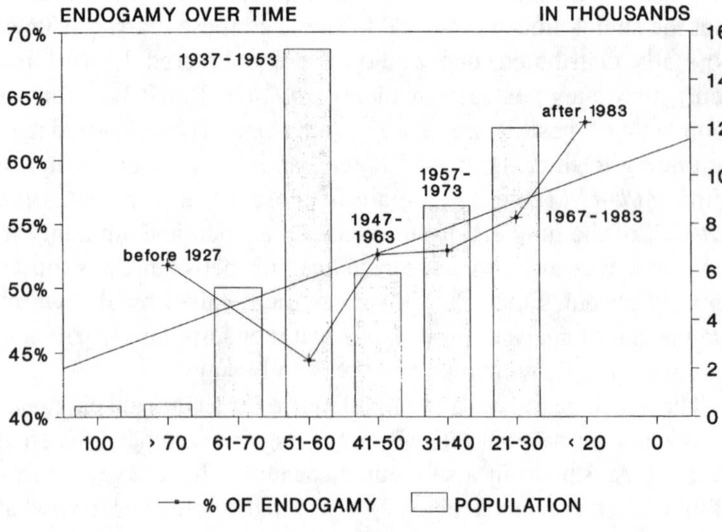

over the last few generations. The sample is perhaps too small to allow firm conclusions to be drawn, but the limited data appear to contradict the oft-heard lament: "Formerly there were more marriages within the *zāt/khēl*; now people go in more for wealth and other things." Especially since 1947 endogamy seems to have steadily increased as it also has, for example, among the Muslims of Delhi where consanguineous unions rose sharply from 15.98 per cent (between about 1869 and 1947) to 37.85 per cent in the period 1947 to 1969 (Basu and Roy 1972). Figure 3.2 also shows that women now aged fifty-one to sixty years were the least *zāt* endogamous, although from data presented earlier it appears that most of them married within their respective subdivisions. These women married between 1937 and 1953 (calculated from data in Table 3.10), a phase which began with a somewhat inexplicable spurt in the overall Bakkarwal population (Census of India 1941). I can offer no explanation for this all-time low of 44.4 per cent *zāt* endogamy, but suggest that it may be partly related to the 1947 partition of the Indian subcontinent which caused considerable population dislocation in Jammu and Kashmir (cf. Zutshi 1974), and is also remembered by the Bakkarwal as a period of extreme confusion.

A further examination of a subsample of 118 first marriages revealed that 61 (51.6 per cent) of these had taken place between persons who formed an "effective kinship circle" (Marx 1967: 162–9) and thought of themselves as related in some manner even before marriage, while 57 (48.3 per cent) were between those who considered themselves unrelated. Examining the latter more closely I found that a relationship could be traced, but when I pointed this out to the relevant persons, they invariably felt that it was too "far" (*dūr*) a link to be considered (cf. Tapper 1991: 50ff. for a discussion of relative distance among Durrani nomads). Disregarding the degree of perceived proximity, if all marriages between kin are considered it appears that endogamy rose sharply from 46 per cent in 1971–80 to 87.5 per cent in 1981–85. Since *zāt/khēl* endogamy is preferred, only those who can not resort to it, say the Bakkarwal, are constrained to marry out. The bigger a man's *zāt/khēl*, the less he "needs to look outside" for a spouse for his child. The problem is recognised as being one of numbers, and this is borne out by data presented in Table 3.6 and illustrated in Figure 3.3.

Figure 3.3 Percentage of endogamy and exogamy according to *zāt* size

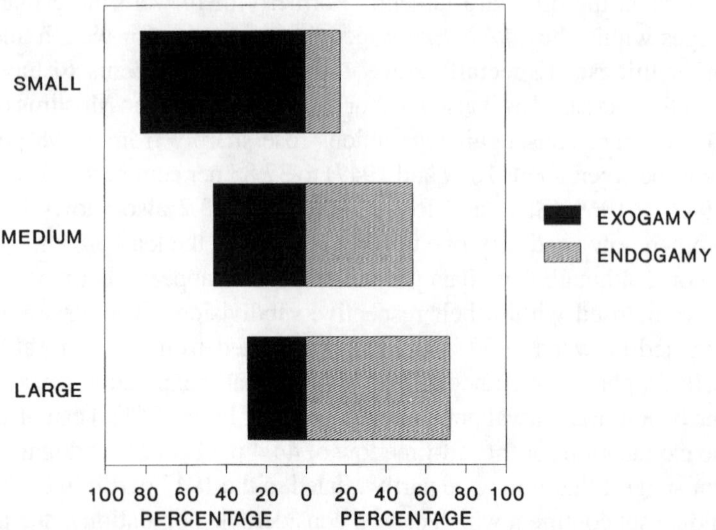

These data were calculated according to the spontaneous scaling mentioned earlier of 29 *zāt/khēl* by 123 men and women according to size (for details see Appendix A). It can be seen that for the "large" *zāt/khēl*, endogamy is as high as 70.6 per cent. Had the endogamous marriages been equally common in all three *zāt/khēl* size classes, about 54 per cent (101 out of 187) of all marriages in each size class should have been endogamous. But this is not the case; significantly fewer marriages are endogamous in the small-size class, and significantly more are so for the large-size class. One such "large" *zāt* is that of the *Khaṭāṇā*, and here one is confronted not only with the demographic, but with a political aspect of *zāt*. In the early years of this century Wikeley (1991: 69) referred to the *Khaṭāṇā* – a *zāt* name which is not confined to the Bakkarwal community – as either exogamously hypergamous or endogamously isogamous. Among the Bakkarwal the *Khaṭāṇā* are widely known to be "big in numbers and in influence". We shall see in Chapter 5 how these factors coincide (also see Casimir and Rao 1992; 1995); for now it suffices to quote an informant who expressed this interdependence in the following manner:

> They're the most powerful and the most numerous ... the grandfather and father [of a well known *Khaṭāṇā*] had two or three wives each and many many children. To get so many wives you need power. With so many wives and children you get more power.

Large in numbers, thus, is a pointer to high status; as a corollary, small in numbers must indicate low status.

Unlike in many other Islamic contexts (e.g. Ballard 1990: 231; Das 1973: 17; Holy 1989), here a girl's father's siblings do not enjoy the *right to expect* that she will be the bride of one of their sons. They consequently also do not have the *duty* to offer her parents their sons. Although for many generations now a girl is apparently preferentially married to her patrilateral parallel or cross-cousin (19.6 per cent and 9.8 per cent respectively of 118 first marriages), many feel that such marriages are of an ambiguous nature. Many Bakkarwal women were of the opinion that the most harmonious mother-in-law/daughter-in-law relationship is the one where the latter is her own brother's or sister's daughter. Although preferable to a "complete outsider", the daughter of her husband's brother, and especially sister, is comparatively disfavoured by future mothers-in-law. This is perhaps partly because, as Sant Cassia (1986: 41) observes of southern Tunisia, the husband's sister's daughter could threaten a woman's position in her son's household. A Bakkarwal mother is thus especially watchful about the future wife of her youngest son; it is on her that she will most probably have to depend entirely in old age. Formerly, it appears, marriage prestations were lower in cousin marriages. But many men and women are not clear

Table 3.6 Frequency of endogamous and exogamous first marriages resorted to by 187 women in relation to estimated size of their paternal *zāt/khēl*

***Zāt* Size**	**N *Zāt***	**N Marriages**	**Endogamous**		**Exogamous**	
			N	**%**	**N**	**%**
Small	13	34	6	17.6	28	82.3
Medium	11	78	42	53.8	36	46.1
Large	5	75	53	70.6	22	29.3
	29	**187**	**101**		**86**	

as to whether marriages between the children of two brothers really tantamount to incest or not, whether they are *jāez* or *nājāez*. Following Qor'anic injunctions, children nursed by the same woman are considered siblings, and milk-kinship (*rida'a*) is a barrier to marriage. Among the Bakkarwal a women does now and then briefly nurse her own child and the whining infant of her husband's brother, when the baby's mother is absent for a few hours fetching water or fuel. Whether this concern for a rare milk-kinship is genuine or is used in the Middle East on specific occasions as "… an ingenious device to preclude customarily preferred marriage arrangements", as Altorki (1980: 243) suggests, remains an open question. The best marriages, I was often told, are between those who are "neither too far, nor too near", and these are marriages between *tēr-patēr*. Perhaps deriving from the Kashmiri *tēr* ("degree of collaterality in cousinship", Madan 1989a: 304), the term *tēr-patēr* designates the relationship between a woman and her FFBSS (or FFBSD) or alternatively between a man and his FFBSD (or FFBSS). This indicates that among the Bakkarwal the preference for real and classificatory cousin marriage is "… a particular expression of a notion of higher generality – that of preference for marriages between close kin …" (Holy 1989: 34). Of 118 first marriages, 19.6 per cent and 13.1 per cent were found to be between patrilateral classificatory parallel and cross-cousins respectively.

Whereas most young girls and women questioned said they would like to marry (or were happy to have married) men related to them prior to marriage, most men said the opposite, and it would seem that many perceived their autonomy as shackled by kin relations. Shafi, who had managed to get out of an engagement with a cousin told me: "A man prefers not to marry a very near relative – especially a cousin – because we can't control or scold the wife so much." "If you marry your father's brother's daughter or your mother's brother's daughter you can never do what you like for the rest of your life", said Būba, and nearly echoing the saying Centlivres-Demont (1981: 121) noted in northern Afghanistan, Ali Jan commented: "It isn't much fun to marry a girl you've known all your life"; (cf. Rosaldo 1989: 204 for similar sentiments among the Ilongot, and cf. Ch. 5 for data on the relation between polygyny and marriage between close kin). Although small camp sizes do not really make for intimacy among prospective marriage partners, most members of a *birādari* are related to one another in more than one way, and as in most Muslim societies, whether in faraway Oman (Eickelman 1984: 94) or in across-the-border Mirpur, so also here, "rarely does a bride join a household of strangers ..." (Ballard 1990: 231). On the other hand, as mentioned in Chapter 2, the familiarity with all but very close relatives can never be as intense among these nomads, as it is among many sedentary communities of the area.

Choosing a Spouse

Ideally a girl's father, the latter's father and brothers, the girl's elder brother and her mother's brother have the right to bestow her hand on whomsoever they consider most suitable. At least officially, the agency of the future bride and groom is entirely denied, and most fathers spoken to gave the impression that "... marriage partners are commodities to be manipulated for the greater good of the family" (Joseph 1974: 398). The criteria of social identity represented by *zāt/khēl* and of kinship in the choice of prospective brides and grooms have been discussed above. Partly from these follow two additional criteria, namely the reputation of the respective mothers in terms of character, and the economic status of the two families. The two mothers, it is said, must not be mean (*kamīn*); this is especially important as far as the bride's mother is concerned. In other words, women are considered as criteria in decision making, even if they are not acknowledged as decision makers. The criterion of financial assets and economic power will be discussed in some detail below. Other criteria of choice of bride and groom vary according to the gender of the offspring (see Table 3.7) to be married, and also on whether one is *Kunhāri* or *Allaiwāḷ*.

The burden of marriage prestations in initial marriages falls entirely on the parents of the prospective partners, and no extended family or communal contributions come in. For subsequent marriages the prospective groom alone is responsible for the payment of bridewealth. In marriages in which siblings, cousins or other relatives are exchanged, ideally bridewealth is lower. In conversations it appeared that such marriages are favoured by prospective fathers-in-law more than by prospective mothers-in-law. The former are

Table 3.7 Gender-specific criteria in the choice of a marriage partner for son/daughter

Properties of Future Son-in-Law	**m/f**	**Properties of Future Daughter-in-Law**	**m/f**
Proper social unit (*zāt/khēl*)	m+f	Proper social unit	m+f
Proper age	m(+f)	Proper age	m+f
Should not live "too far away"	m(+f)		
Good-natured and honourable (*sharif*)	m+f	Good-natured	m+f
Good-natured mother	m(+f)	Good-natured mother	m+f
Handsome	m	Pretty	m
Hard-working	m+f	Healthy, strong and hard-working	m+f
Sound financial status (should be able to provide wife with "enough food and clothes")	m+f	Good financial status	m+f

Notes: *m* and *f* indicate respectively the interests of the mother and father of the son/ daughter to be married. N informants of various *zāt/khēl* = 48 women between the ages of about thirty and sixty, and 21 men between the ages of about forty and fifty-five.

keen on saving, the latter perhaps more concerned with the stability of a marriage (cf. Centlivres-Demont 1981: 122 for a similar ambiguity in northern Afghanistan). "If one part of such a marriage goes bad, the other is bound to follow", said Aji. Women whose daughters are unhappy in such a marriage are in an embarrassing situation; as Baso put it, "if my daughter is ill-treated, I shall have to ill-treat my daughter-in-law, even if she is good and gives no cause". One could expect both women entering into such an exchange marriage to be treated well, as a guarantee for the other, so to say. But Lāli disagreed: "The mothers-in-law may treat them well, but not so the husbands. What does a man care for his sister's marriage? He cares only for his own happiness." Ultimately, however, all Bakkarwal conclude that the criteria of choice are subservient to Providence, for who after all can change one's preordained fate (*takdīr ko kōṇ badul sakto*; cf. Pugh 1983 for a brief discussion of concepts of fate among North Indian Muslims).

In most societies, a marriage alliance also entails specific economic transactions between the families involved in the alliance. The Bakkarwal have two terms to designate marriage prestations: *samā* and *duniya* (Rao 1997). The former represents the daughter's share in the paternal property and consists today of cash, jewellery, and when the parents can afford it, herd animals and eventually also pack animals. This share is promised to the daughter at the time of the wedding, but (except among indigent families with nearly nothing to give) handed to her over a period of time, depending on the economic situation of the family. Only after the entire dowry has been given may the girl's parents, brothers, and other kinsmen and women "eat at her home". But even giving this "dowry" entirely does not end the parents' debts towards their daughters. Gift giving goes on, theoretically, as long as they live; practically in most families it is carried on for the first "five to eight years" after the daughter has moved to her conjugal home. The gifts given vary greatly and depend entirely on the economic status of her parents. While not all Bakkarwal parents give *samā*, all – or nearly all – give *duniya*, which may be glossed as bridewealth. Most informants felt that the amount demanded as *duniya* had increased drastically over the last few years (Rao 1997). "Formerly", said many, "so much *duniya* was never paid, poverty mattered little." Even now, not every family demands "excessive" amounts, and some families are known as especially fraudulent and deceitful *(ghadar)*. Reshma told me that when her brother "got married to our *māmā*'s daughter [MBZ] – he was five years old then [i.e. *ca.* 1930] and our *māmā* had died – and his wife demanded three hundred *rupees* it became a scandal." For, as Longu explained, "formerly a *duniya* was at the most a question of one hundred *rupees*, and even among the Gujar, at the most one took a cow [in return] for one's daughter – now they demand ten thousand".

In the 1980s Bakkarwal bridewealth ranged between Rs. 500/- and Rs. 350,000/- in cash and kind. As old Fakira put it,"since [his] father's time" even the *Kunhāri*, who till then reportedly gave only dowries (Rao 1997) began "selling their daughters for a living (*laṛkiāñ na bēč khāṇ lag giyo*)". Apart from bridewealth, heavy expenses are often incurred unofficially by both *Allaiwāḷ* and *Kunhāri* grooms during marriage negotiations. Often, influential men who can make or mar a marriage settlement have to be bribed, with the highest bidder usually getting the bride. Either cash, animals or even another woman can be given as bribes; as the Bakkarwal say, "the *kharpẽñč* (for details cf. Ch. 4) take both money and women". Not a week passed, I believe, when some story involving such men was not recounted to me, either by gossip-happy neighbours, or by people who had been left high and dry, caught between the receiving and giving ends of such incidents. Trying to trace such stories to the end was not always possible, nor did one usually get more than a mass of confused and contradictory versions; but Saiñfo's reasonably straightforward story will serve as an illustration of this practice. All the persons involved in this case were *Kunhāri*.

> My father died in 1947 when I was one year old, and my mother married again. She became the second wife of my father's brother ... Some twelve years ago I wanted to get married. For this I sold 22 animals to pay *Hāji* A Rs. 1500/- as bribe *(baddi)* for getting my wife. The girl's father wanted to give her to some *Khaṭāṇā*, who, however, was prepared to give *Hāji* A only Rs. 1000/-. The girl's father was too poor to give her animals as dowry, so the *Khaṭāṇā* was not interested in paying that much; he's L's real WFeB, and one of L's sisters is married to one of my father's brothers. So L, and both my father's brothers spoke to *Hāji* A ...

Another possibility is that the girl's father takes money surreptitiously from the prospective groom, and plays up one possible match against the other. This was what had happened in a case which was discussed on 14 January 1983, at the "*kameṭi*" meeting of the *B birādari*, which met at *Haji* J's place; again all the persons involved were *Kunhāri*.

> Potu *B* had married his daughter to a *Paswāḷ*, who had only one arm. She was unhappy and kept running back to her parents, and she had the full support of her mother, who told me that the husband was in addition impotent. In any case the couple remained childless, and many apparently felt that the marriage had been a mistake. So after six years of married life, Saida *B* approached her father, Potu *B*, and told him that he would like to take the girl as a bride for his own son. He gave Potu Rs. 1000/- to be paid as *khulli* to the husband, so that he may grant his wife a divorce and free her from their marriage. The girl now returned to her parents and when after about one year, Saida's preparations for his son's marriage were ready, he heard that Potu had in the meantime married his daughter off to another man of the *B zāt*.

The rumour was that the father had again taken money (Rs. 1500/- this time) allegedly for paying the *khulli*; but since this had already been paid, Potu simply pocketed the sum. There were now two men claiming the girl as wife, and her father was trying to bargain with each of them.

Such cases can be encountered in interethnic contexts as well. The following incident, which took place towards the end of my field work, is a case in point, and also involved other mobile pastoral groups such as the Gujar and Pathan.

There was a young girl of about sixteen in a Pathan hamlet in the western Liddar Valley. In 1981 she had been engaged to a Gujar youth, some four years older than herself. This boy had been "asked for and brought" (*mangta lāyā*) into the Pathan household as a grazier. As a live-in future son-in-law he had a low status and even five years later, in 1986, it was not clear when he and his family would have put by enough money for the wedding to take place. In the summer of 1986 this boy had gone to live with his own parents not very far away, and I was told by his aunt that a *Kunhāri* had come through one day in spring 1986 and enticed the Pathan girl away. He had then taken her to the nearest town and married her officially. She became his second wife. On 5 August 1986 the Gujar youth's father called in the police and lodged a complaint of abduction against the Bakkarwal. On 16 August this Gujar's brother died, and the Pathan girl's father appeared at the funeral as a gesture of goodwill. He came again a week later to pay condolences, but above all to try and settle the case out of court and without the police. It now came out that he had taken Rs. 1800/- from the Bakkarwal a year earlier for paying the Gujar the compensation money (*khulli*), and then again Rs. 4200/- in spring 1986 for the actual marriage agreement. Instead of paying the compensation, he had pocketed the entire amount, and was of the opinion that he owed the boy nothing, since he had fed him for so many years.

That not just fathers, but brothers – and allegedly even husbands – "sell" their daughters, sisters and wives to the highest bidder is a common theme in Bakkarwal conversation. In all these cases influential Bakkarwal men use their autonomy to make and break matches. It is common knowledge that when these men are not allowed to play their highly profitable roles, they do not hesitate to take revenge (*badlā*). This is just what happened in Nazira's case in 1984.

Nazira's husband had died six years earlier, leaving her with a son and a daughter aged five and two respectively. Theirs had been an intra-*zāt*

> marriage and after her husband's death she had stayed on at her parents-in-laws' camp. But with two small children, no extra hand and about sixty herd animals, she simply could not make both ends meet. So she decided to remarry. There was apparently no eligible man in her deceased husband's family, or at least no offers came. But her brother fixed a match with a man of another *zāt*. Her husband's family protested, but as she expressed it, "I had no way out. They didn't help feed my children, nor did they lend a hand with the animals." Her fiancé borrowed money from the head of his migration unit, and paid Nazira's brother and her father-in-law Rs. 5000/- each and ultimately it was all settled. However, a week before the wedding, to which I also had been invited, the head of her own *zāt* intervened; he got his men to beat up the fiancé so badly that he had to be hospitalized. The reason was that he had not got his share, either from Nazira's brother, or from her father-in-law, or again from her fiancé. Since the two former men were from his own *zāt*, he had apparently picked on the weakest of them all, "the outsider", as Nazira's sister put it. Finally, the police intervened; but as I heard later, they took seven hundred *rupees* from Nazira for not filing a charge of trespassing and theft against her fiancé!

In all the above-mentioned cases the "loser" continued to be so in all aspects of life, for, as among the Durrani nomads, here too a family "... which demonstrates weakness, by failing to control ... their independence in the arrangement and completion of a marriage loses honor and credibility and find themselves ... extremely vulnerable" (Tapper 1981: 393).

A woman is asked for and given, the Bakkarwal feel; for a man to be asked for – as in the Pathan-Gujar case narrated above – is considered a source of shame. Although most women criticised the "buying and selling" of female kin by the menfolk, they did not condemn it outright. This way or that "a woman has to be given and taken", and the "prettier" or "better" she is, "the more men there are to take her", and obviously, "to take one must pay". Thus, although "a woman may feel sad" at being given to a man who is ugly but rich, she "should also feel happy" that he "wanted to spend so much for her". In other words it is a woman's very beauty, which is a manifestation of a non-material ingredient, *rū*, that makes her an object of material transactions among her current and future male guardians. A woman is expected to fufil the physical (sexual, nutritive) and psychological (caring) needs of her husband as long as he fulfils her physical (material, sexual) needs. The question of an adult woman's freedom to decide whether she wants to have sex with her husband or not is considered irrelevant. Rape within marriage is an alien concept, for rape is perceived of in this society, I suggest, not in terms of the humiliating loss of a woman's personal autonomy or a brutal imposition on her wishes, but only as the illegitimate alienation of sexual resources. The humiliation and shame inevitably associated with rape stem from this illegitimacy and from her helplessness to prevent the alienation; these can, of course, never happen within a legally recognised marriage where the husband is considered the legitimate "owner" of these resources.

Echoing the misogyny of Hindu canons of law, both Bakkarwal women and men say that "women always want to marry rich men" and that no woman wants to have a poor man as a husband. "To be given to a poor man is shameful (*sharam*)." These feelings of shame are exploited in taunts, especially among sisters and sisters-in-law. According to certain women relatives these feelings can even lead to sexual problems between the spouses and symptoms of illness and disease for the wife. But even here there are exceptions, such as that of pretty Sonio, who was in love with poor Bashir, her brother's hired shepherd (*ājṛi*). But she was not allowed to marry him, and was married off instead to a rich man much older than herself as his second wife in a polygynous marriage. This man paid her brother a handsome bridewealth and bribed various community elders into pressurising and threatening Sonio and Bashir into giving up.

When I began fieldwork I had heard about these *ājṛi* from various non-Bakkarwal; they were known as extremely poor and utterly exploited. "The (*ājṛi*) as a son-in-law is not as common as you think", Phullāñ told me when I started on the topic once again; "this is because a girl doesn't like to be given to a poor man." She conceded, however, that "from the girl's father's point of view it's good if the son-in-law is a good shepherd and stays at least for a while". Most informants agreed that well-to-do *Kunhāri* and *Allaiwāḷ* fathers were not averse to having a prospective son-in-law work for them temporarily or even permanently. This kind of bride service is reported to have been especially frequent between 1947/48 and the early 1970s, since "those days there were many more young men whose parents were too poor to pay either the bridewealth or to give their married son a decent portion of animals as inheritance". On condition that they work as shepherds and live with their employers, these men often manage to get a wife. Although they are happy to get work and a wife, these men are in an ambivalent situation. On the one hand they are praised as selfless men, but they are also pitied and even despised since their capacity for self-assertion and autonomy *vis-à-vis* their wives' parents, and even their own wives, is now considered minimal. On the whole, the families of both the shepherd and the employer stand to gain by such alliances, albeit in very different ways: the employer gets an extra hand to work and simultaneously retains the girl's presence and labour, and obtains those of her eventual children. In return for his labour the shepherd receives food and a wife; after marriage he may continue to be fed and sometimes even obtain a few animals and/or access to pasture. Investing in such a shepherd is also tantamount to investing in his family and thus maintaining, or obtaining and expanding, the network of clientele. The young shepherd's parents get him married without paying bridewealth, and through him they generally obtain access to persons of influence. This kind of reciprocity tends to suppress undue discontent within the community. When both employer and shepherd are from the same descent group solidarity is further stressed, especially since rich families tend to marry within their descent groups, and those employing shepherds are invariably rich. Hence it is important for a shepherd's parents also to be a party to such marriage negotiations. Like all other freshly married Bakkarwal men, a shepherd also has a right to his share (*mā*) of his father's meagre flocks and/or grazing lands. Unlike other men, who may directly "take their share and go", or "decide to stay" on with their father, a shepherd has no choice: he must go to his father-in-law. But if he goes without his own father's permission, he is entitled to nothing. Baja's marriage in 1970 exemplifies this last point.

> One day Jijo, Barhim's eldest son, came and persuaded my elder brother, Bājā, to go with him. He said, "We need an *ājṛi* and we'll give you a wife." So Bājā went – without our father's consent.... My other brother Saiñ had died working for Barhim's elder brother – these people get all the work done and don't give you a thing. *So our father didn't want Bājā to go ... But he went*, and he got a wife – and what a wife! She's deaf and dumb! Anyway of what use is he now to us, *since our father didn't speak to them before and decide to give him*

there [in marriage].... He's of no use to us – *so our father decided not to give him his share of animals*. [emphasis added]

The Time to Go Asking

An important criterion the respective guardians keep in mind while negotiating a marriage is the age difference between the prospective partners. Since premarital sexual relations are as good as non-existent, age at first marriage acts, albeit not consciously, in determining population growth. The Bakkarwal are in their overwhelming majority what is known as a "natural fertility population", i.e. a population in which reproductive behaviour is not deliberately curbed in order to limit reproductive output. (The post-partum taboo imposed by Islamic norms is not *aimed* at limiting family size.) Hence of prime importance for fertility rates is the age at first pregnancy, which is influenced by the age at menarche and the average age at first cohabitation. For the Bakkarwal, the commonly debated question of whether "... age at first conception may have more to do with age at marriage than age at menarche" (Spielmann 1989: 329) must thus be reformulated: both factors are of importance here.

But to marry one must first be engaged, and engagement (*mangṇai*) in this society is closely related to menarche. The onset of menarche marks a girl's first participation in the ritual fasting (*rōza*) enjoined by Islam. This in turn acts as a diacritical in recollecting all major subsequent events. When asked about their engagement, for example, women tried to remember whether it had taken place before or after their first *rōza*, i.e. prior to or following their first menses? If it took place after the menses, how many times had one fasted before one was engaged? The fasts are recollected in the further context of migration patterns, i.e. in the summer or winter camps. An analysis of the first-ever engagement of fifty-five women now aged between fourteen and seventy-five years showed that while in sixteen cases the ceremony of *mangṇai* took place in the same year as did the onset of menarche (and the keeping of the first fast), in thirty-eight cases there was a difference in timing (Table 3.8). Of these thirty-eight again, twelve (21.8 per cent) women were engaged after their first period had taken

Table 3.8 Relation between age at menarche (M) and age at first engagement (E)

Years	E After M (Cases)	E Before M (Cases)
1	8	6
2	2	9
3	0	2
4	0	1
5	0	2
6	0	1
7	0	2
8	0	0
9	0	0
10	0	0
11	0	2
12	1	0
13	1	1
Total	12	26
Percentage	21.8	47.2

Note: Years = difference in years.

Figure 3.4 Difference in years calculated for thirty-eight women between her engagement ceremony and the time she reached menarche

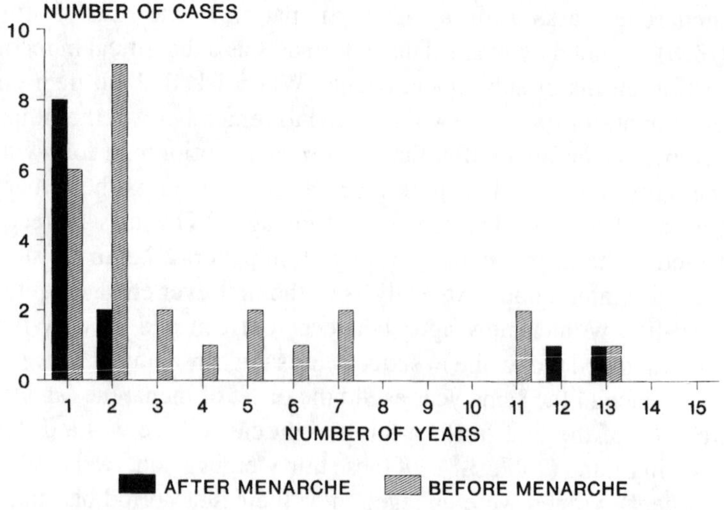

place and after they had fasted at least once, while for twenty-six (47.2 per cent) the engagement ceremony had taken place before they reached menarche, in other words before they had ever fasted. Figure 3.4 illustrates these findings.

Most Bakkarwal women are thus engaged before their first menses, and for an overwhelming majority the formal engagement ceremony also takes place either before this or in the same year. This ceremony seals an agreement which may have been reached either shortly before or several years earlier between the respective (male) guardians of the girl and the boy. In the sample of fifty-five women, one woman reported having been engaged at as early as one year, and the oldest at twenty-nine years. Similarly, out of a sample of forty-eight men (spouses of the fifty-five women above) the earliest age at first engagement a man could recollect was five years, and the latest thirty-nine. Table 3.9 sets out the number of cases per gender and age (for details of the ages recollected by each individual see Appendix B). The average age at engagement for girls and boys is 13.2 (± 4.09) and 19.0 (± 5.9) years respectively (see Figs. 3.5a, 3.5b and 3.6), and this appears to be in keeping with the trend reported for other Islamic communities in northern India (cf. Aggarwal 1976; Roy 1979: 150, 153, 191, 192). Ideally, a girl should be four to five years younger than her husband, and data show that at the time of their engagement ceremony, girls are on an average 5.7 (± 4.2) years younger than their fiancés (Fig. 3.6); the only case in which the girl was older than the boy was not taken into account in this calculation.

Theoretically, engagements can take place even at birth: suckling babies can be engaged and even married (*nakā khwāṇi)*; and till divorce is declared, these unions are valid. Invalidation can take many forms and have several reasons, but in general, as a child "a man can marry only once", and he can repudiate his wife only after "he is about fifteen, or sixteen, or twenty years old", in other words when he has reached or completed the pubertal phase. In such early engagements the bridewealth is very low (as it is also for a widow, or in a levirate marriage). But early engagements are today neither frequent, nor recommended; I was repeatedly told that "so many things can happen by the time the two have grown up. Such engagements and even such marriages break up (*ṭuṭ jāyo*) very often". One of the partners may die, as happened in the case

Figure 3.5a Age (in years) at engagement of fifty-five women

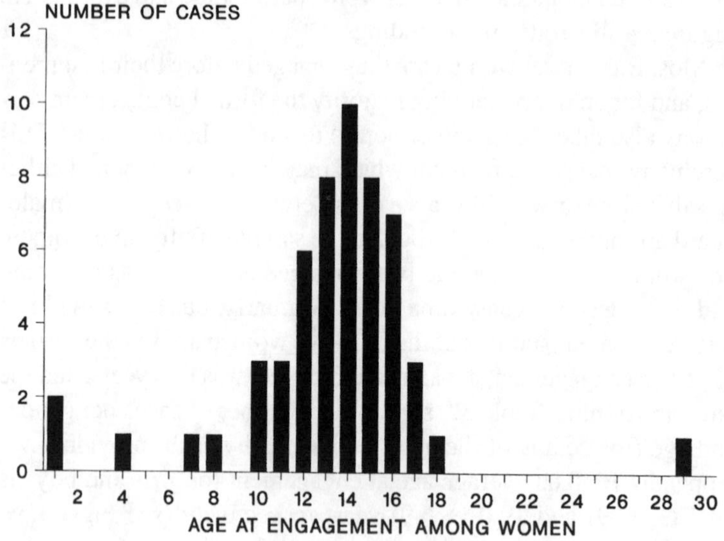

Figure 3.5b Age (in years) at engagement of forty-eight men

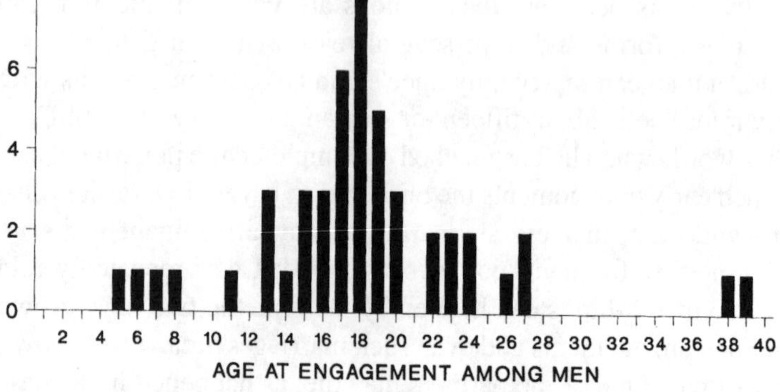

Table 3.9 Recollected age at engagement according to gender and frequency

Age at Engagement	Women	Men
1	2	0
2	0	0
3	0	0
4	1	0
5	0	1
6	0	1
7	1	1
8	1	1
9	0	0
10	3	0
11	3	1
12	6	0
13	8	3
14	10	1
15	8	3
16	7	3
17	3	6
18	1	10
19	0	5
20	0	3
21	0	0
22	0	2
23	0	2
24	0	2
25	0	0
26	0	1
27	0	2
28	0	0
29	1	0
30–37	1	0
38	0	1
39	0	1

of Ajrat Bibi, who was married when she was eight years old. "I was sent off straightaway", she said, to her conjugal home. "There I spent only one month, then my husband died. So I returned to my mother for four years. In the fifth year, my present marriage took place and I was again sent." Her second husband was her first husband's younger brother. Another case is that of Zulfāñ.

She was married and sent to live in her conjugal home when she was eight years old. So she was "like a daughter" to her husband's mother (who also happened to be her father's sister), and who brought her up. Her husband was six years older. When he grew up (and became twenty-one) he married a second wife (in exchange marriage for his younger sister). He had two children by this wife; then, in 1981 she died of tuberculosis. In 1982 Zulfāñ, then sixteen years old, got her first child. In late 1982 her husband again married; this wife was his deceased wife's younger sister. At this, Zulfāñ left and went back to her own parents. In the meantime Zulfāñ's younger brother had been engaged to her husband's eldest daughter (by his second wife) and was living with them as a hired shepherd.

My data indicate that the age at which an engagement or a wedding takes place also appears to be related to a question raised by numerous authors (e.g. Das 1973: 37; Joseph 1974; Altorki 1977; Leamann 1978) concerning the extent to which in South Asia and the Middle East the formal paternal authority to bestow a child in marriage coincides with the father's actual decision-making power. For the Bakkarwal this coincidence is absolute at the level of the dominant discourse, and as discussed above material transactions

Figure 3.6 A comparison of the age (in years) at engagement of fifty-five women and forty-eight men

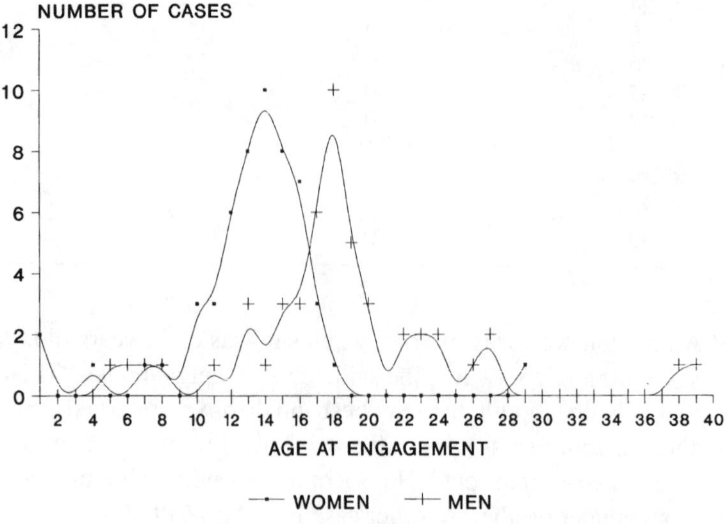

are manipulated by several males. It is acknowledged that mothers can and do express their opinions regarding future spouses for their children, but the final decisions are said to be entirely paternal affairs. Even widowed mothers have no authority to decide, and in the absence of all male paternal kin this authority is abjudicated to male maternal kin. This is perhaps not so surprising when we consider the degree of endogamy among the Bakkarwal and hence the extent to which the distinction between patri and matri kin must be a formal one. Case histories suggest that it is extremely difficult to generalise about who actually takes the decisions in this sphere. I did indeed encounter instances in which mothers had no say; however, in others, which I could follow from start to finish, it was the mother who took the actual decision over and above the heads of the girl's father and other paternal male kin – and yet neither these women nor others acknowledged these decisions as anything other than those taken by the respective fathers. Even when an engagement takes place against her wishes, a girl's mother can use the famous "weapons of the weak" (Scott 1990) to delay the wedding and eventually even subvert it by pronouncing that her daughter is physically far from mature enough to "be sent" to her husband. For a variety of reasons – to keep them company, to help them in their chores and to spare them the eventual problems of the conjugal home – mothers like to keep their grown-up daughters with them as long as possible. When I discussed this with Makhṇi, she suggested that mothers "say less" in marriage negotiations when the daughter to be married is very young, and more in the case of an older daughter. This is not corroborated by data on fifty-three marriages (cf. Appendix C), but it may underline the more general hypothesis that young children do not enjoy the same emotional status older children do, that in practice they are perceived of less as individuals. The gender-specific mother-daughter bonding perhaps also increases with the daughter's age and is reinforced by constant interaction throughout the day. Once the daughter has left her mother's home, this intimate daily interaction must take place between mother-in-law and daughter-in-law:

> "I haven't yet found a suitable girl for Dulla", said his mother. "I want a girl who's clean and well mannered, and a girl whose mother doesn't

always interfere … I know such girls, my brother has two such daughters, but then they'd never give them to us … I know others who'd gladly give a girl, and Dulla's father wouldn't mind taking them. But I don't want them; after all I've to be with the girl all day."

Not surprisingly, then, are women in particular wary of whom they "bring in", and of when they part with their older daughters.

The Rituals of Asking and Receiving

Proposals are always sent by the boy's family; it is for the girl's family to accept or reject. It is said that "it's the boy's side which goes asking", but it is also said that "a man takes a woman, and not the other way around". Asking and receiving do not in the final account necessarily amount to taking, for a boy has the individual right to dissolve an engagement; a girl or her family do not. If they want to annul an engagement agreement, it has to be "a *birādari* decision", and even this is "not good for the girl". Also, whether *Kunhāri* or *Allaiwāḷ*, her father then has to pay the boy's family "whatever they ask for". The social and communal importance of engagement is symbolised for a girl by her outward appearance; for a boy there are no such symbolic status markers. An affianced girl applies collyrium (*surma*) to her eyes and henna (*basma* or *methi*) to her hair. The combination of red (henna), black (collyrium) and white (considered to be the girl's own ideal skin colour) serve an apotropaic purpose, but are also *par excellence* the colours of matrimony. All this does not, however, mean that an engagement agreement is always adhered to by a girl's family. Depending on how influential one is, or how one goes about it, there are ways and means of getting around such a promise. The case mentioned below is illustrative of such tactics not seldom resorted to by women, but publicly represented as male decisions.

Basso and Nawab had two daughters and three sons. The elder daughter was married to Basso's ZS and lived near Basso's F, who was an influential man. The eldest son was engaged to Nawab's BD. The second daughter, Rina was fifteen years old and had been engaged two years earlier to Phājā, Nawab's MBSWBS, who also happened to be Basso's BWZS. Now Basso apparently never liked her brother's wife much, and claimed to have met the latter's sister only after the engagement had taken place. "Why did you agree to the engagement?" I asked her. "Well, I only wanted the child's happiness, and so when

> Rina's father told me of the decision, I said 'yes'", was the reply. Rina's eZ remembered, however, that at the time Nawab and Basso were badly in need of pasture for their growing herds. Phājā's family had some excess pasture, and had let it out to Nawab for a pittance, probably to pave a smooth way for the engagement. Rina eZ also remembered her mother saying at the time, "when the time [for the wedding] comes, we'll see about it". "About one year after the engagement", Basso felt "more and more that Rina wouldn't be happy with those people"; but she kept quiet. This year, at *Id*, when Phājā's mother sent Rima a set of clothes, Basso returned them with the excuse that they "didn't fit", since "these people are so stingy even now, they don't buy enough cloth – what will they do later!". In fact, Rima didn't even try them on at the time. Three months later, before the engagement was officially broken, Phājā's mother insisted on Rima's wearing the clothes "to prove that Basso had been lying". By then they really had become too tight …

Custom requires that after the engagement ceremony and till the wedding twice every year – at the New Year and at *'Id-e Qorban* – the fiancé's family present the fiancée either with a set of clothes or with its equivalent in cash. To return these items implies automatically that the bride's family has decided to break the engagement.

For a first proposal to be made, a male relative or friend of the boy or his father is sent to the girl's father. Ideally this is his mother's brother, and can never be an agnatic relative of the boy; but even a friend can act as go-between, as was the case for example when Mahwali married Fatima; the other go-between here was Bashir, Mahwali's FZS. "For two years, Mahwali and his father used to visit me twice or thrice every month in summer, and try and persuade me to persuade [Fatima's] father, who's a friend of mine", this friend, a Kashmiri villager told me. In these highly ritualised negotiations it is for the girl's family to react after they receive the first proposal: "Now the girl's side must talk", it is said. To talk is to show interest, and this can be done in many ways and to various degrees: a visit paid by a uterine kinsman of the girl a few days later shows really great interest; a similar visit by an unrelated friend of her father indicates less interest. Later visits are evidence of still less interest and signify that even if further negotiations do take place, the going will not be easy for the boy's family. If the first visit takes place within a season there are more visits from the boy's side, and if the girl's people have really shown interest, the boy's father's sister or other female relative may even accompany a male on one of the future visits, and get talking about this, that and the other to the girl's family. If both sides are really keen, negotiations now begin in earnest and centre around the financial transactions. The bride's family now officially raises the question of the dower (*mār* <Ur. *mahr*), which consists of animals (*māḷ*) and jewellery (*bast*) to be handed over to the girl in case of divorce. If the girl dies leaving her husband a widower, he is expected to spend a sum amounting to roughly what he promised her as dower for the ritual feast (*khayrāt*) in her memory. Unlike among many urbanised Muslim families in India (Rao 1992b), here the amount of dower promised depends on the actual economic status of both the families; in 1986 it ranged from Rs. 11500/- to be paid in cash among the rich, through some twenty herd animals and jewellery worth Rs. 2000/- among the less wealthy to about five animals and Rs. 500/- among the poor.

This is also the time to raise the question of the bridewealth and eventual payoffs. Among "good families" this should be done unobtrusively; common friends or relatives are sent to casually intimate that the honour of both families requires a certain amount to be paid. This unofficial bargaining can go on for months, but before the agreement is finally reached the amounts must be fixed; they must be paid – either in instalments or at one go – for the wedding to take place. Bargaining on other issues can also take place in this phase, and thus a boy or a girl may at this stage lose out to a preferred sibling. Normally, older siblings are married first, irrespective of gender, but there are cases in which a younger one is favoured by visiting friends or relatives of bride or groom. This was the case with Zāro, whose parents decided, midway in the negotiations to marry her to Baādura rather than to his elder brother Kima, for whom the proposal had originally been made. Zāro's mother told me how and why this reversal took place.

> They had come to ask for Zāro for Kima, their elder son. Zāro's father was agreeable, but he hadn't yet told them so. Then, once my sister's husband and his brother and his wife visited them – from our side. This brother-in-law's wife is also a distant cousin of mine. And she came and told me that on her visit she'd seen Kima, and he seemed very slow and stupid. But his younger brother looked just the opposite. And he's not too young for Zāro – he's two years older than her. So I told Zāro's

father, and my sister's husband also told him and we all agreed that it'd be better to give her to Baādura. So when they next asked, we said "No" to Kima, but then we also sent my brother's wife's brother to say that we'd have no objection to the second son. So that's how it happened.

If after several months of negotiations both sides finally come to an agreement, a promise (*lafaz*) of engagement leading to marriage is made and everyone comes to know informally. Now no other boy's family should approach and ask for this girl's hand. This agreement or pledge is, however, to be distinguished from the *akad*, which is the agreement to actually marry, i.e. for the wedding to take place. The engagement pledge is sealed by the girl receiving sweetmeats and one set of new clothes in any bright colour from the boy's family. As mentioned above, this gift giving will continue annually till the wedding. At the making of pledges, as also later at the engagement and wedding ceremonies, the girl is represented by a man, older than herself, known as her *vakīl* or *dīni pāi*, and who is either her mother's brother or another maternal relative or the husband of one of her elder sisters. Unlike among certain other neighbouring Muslims, such as the Ghorbat of Afghanistan (Rao 1982: 191), here an agnatic relative can never be her witness on these occasions, because "for her [paternal] family her being given is a question of shame – *is māñ sharam oe*". After the wedding the *dīni pāi*'s duties and obligations towards the bride are over, and he has no claims on her offspring. The connotations of the terms *taram* and *dīn* should perhaps be mentioned here. Once when I asked whether the term *dīni pāi* could in analogy to the *taram pēṇ* (see below) also be called *taram pāi*, I was told that the two were entirely different: "*taram* is tradition – *dīn* represents Allah's commandments" (*taram rawāj e – dīn Allāh tālā ko ukum e*). On another occasion I was told that *dīn* refers only to the Holy Prophet (*Rasūl Allāh*), whereas *taram* "is our Bakkarwali thing" (*amāri Bakarāḷi čij e*). The opposition between these two terms could perhaps be considered thus:

dīn	***taram***
ideology	practice
universal	local/specific
learned	imbibed
male	female

There are no restrictions as to the month or season in which an engagement can take place, but the days considered "best" are Friday, Thursday and Sunday. No engagements may take place on Tuesdays and Wednesdays, for on these days "all – including animals – are mad *(sodo* cf. Ur. *saudā*)". The symbolic significance of Wednesdays could perhaps be explained as a reversal of that attested among Pashtuns, among whom "Shoro (Wednesday) is so called as God is said to have begun working on the world on this day" (Ahmed 1984: 316). It was, say the Bakkarwal, on a Tuesday and a Wednesday that "the she buffalo became so itchy [*khurkuṇ*], that she dug her horns into the earth – so our Holy Prophet does not allow us to do any [important] work on these days [*mhēsṇi ne singni ḍuboyo jamīn māñ, te mārā sarkār pighambar ne kuṇ ne diti koe kam*]". An engagement pledged on these days is thus bound to go wrong.

The engagement ceremony takes place at the girl's home, and is attended by five elderly male relatives of the boy (his father, his elder brother, his father's and mother's brothers); as far as possible the boy's paternal and maternal relations must be represented. Only if no males are available, may the boy's mother go with elderly female relatives. On the girl's side no females should be present in the immediate vicinity, although they can be nearby cooking, etc. Her paternal kin can be present, but only in the background, and they may not participate in the ceremony. There must also be at least three male witnesses present, who are related to neither the girl nor the boy. The fiancés themselves may not be present at the ceremony, but on return home after the ceremony the elders should tell the boy: *"t(h)ārā bad āyo*" – your turn has come. Although the engagement ceremony takes place at the girl's home, it is not a subject of conversation with her. I never happened to attend such a ceremony, but was told by all I asked that the proposal of marriage is now once again formally made, the ritualised sentences running as follows:

Boy's father:
"Ye meri čoḷi e. Khudā ki to khudā ki rasūl ki.
Ūṇ nāto mango pūt vāste. Ye gadri miṇe čak de."
This is my lap. God's and God's Prophet's [witness] now I ask for an alliance for [my] son.
Lift/carry this girl and give her to me.

The eldest male who represents the boy's side then asks:
"Tu dyā?" Will you give?

Answer (usually girl's MB and two other men – never her father or any other paternal kin, who are totally in the background):
"Am de čhuṛeo, am de čhuṛeo, am de čhuṛeo – pāñḍa saṭh čhuṛeo."
We have given, we have given, we have given – We have joined the pledges.

The repetition of the last sentence (*am de čhuṛeo*) thrice symbolises the "promise of giving the girl" (*gadri ko zabān karāñ*), and must take place in the presence of the unrelated male witnesses. The boy's side now presents sweets (*shirīni*) and cash (Rs. 200/- to 1000/-), which symbolise the *pāñḍā*, the pledge for the joining (*saṭhāñ*) of fortunes. This cash should ideally be spent by the girl's father on buying her clothes, etc., but "many eat it up themselves". The girl's side also offers sweet tea and sweets to the guests. As so often, once again satiating sugar represents the mutual satisfaction of the families and the harmonious relations between them. Salt would no doubt bind (cf. Ch. 1) the families together, but it would also have an undesirable heating effect and act as an appetiser, both financially and sexually. Indeed, from now on till the wedding the fiancés may not see each other, and the fiancée in particular must be kept in a balanced humoral state. This balance is represented outwardly on the one hand by two cosmetics used by her: collyrium, which is classified as "hot" (*tattā*), around her eyes and henna, which is "cold" (*sarad*), in her hair. As a further binding step she may no longer wear her hair loose or unkempt, but always properly combed into neat braids.

The wedding (*byā*) can take place at the earliest eight days after the engagement. Wedding dates are fixed according to the lunar calendar and may not take place on the seventh, thirteenth or eighteenth days of any month; nor were Tuesdays or Wednesdays permitted by the Prophet, for the same reason that he forbade engagements on these days. The best day is Thursday, so that the bride may go to the groom's home on the Friday following. As among most other Muslims, it may not take place in the *doashure*, the period "between *Shab-e Kadar* and *Korbāni kā Id*", or as some put it "between the two *Id*". Many Bakkarwal felt that most weddings take place "around November to December (*mangar*) or February to March (*phagaṇ*)", while others mentioned March to

April (*čait*). Those I could personally observe did take place in early winter, after the families had settled back into winter quarters. By now excess herd animals had been sold and the annual debts paid off; the farmers had also brought in their maize harvest, so that the Bakkarwal had by now bought this primary staple (Casimir 1991) for the winter months and had also rented their winter grazing lands (Rao 1992a). The peak kidding and lambing period was yet to begin, so there was enough leisure time and, hopefully, also enough money in hand. Shopping for the wedding is also generally easier and cheaper in winter, with urban areas less distant than they are in summer. Women can more easily go and choose cloth to their taste and bargain with both clothsellers and tailors. Jewellery is the only item which appeared to be bought during migration from specific jewellers in the summer area. Friends and relatives to be invited also live "more together", that is, somewhat less scattered in winter than they do in summer, and communication is easier. However, although attending the wedding of a near relative is important, the matter often appeared to be dealt with relatively informally. At a fairly early stage of fieldwork when Zābo got married I found, for example, that her father's sister's family had sent only one representative, her FZSS; the two families were, I found later, on very good terms, but "someone had to look after the herd and home". Similarly, at Pipi's wedding her father's brother and his wife came, but their children did not, although the groom was their maternal uncle.

The Marital Process

Let those who find not the wherewithal for marriage,
keep themselves chaste, until God gives them means
out of His grace ...

_ Qor'an (XXIV/33)

For the wedding to take place the only formal condition to be fulfilled is that bridewealth has been fully paid. The last installment of payment marks the *akad* (cf. Ar. '*aqd*), the agreement for the wedding. Marriage among the Bakkarwal, as in neighbouring societies (e.g. Centlivres-Dumont 1981) is a long, drawn-out process. This processual nature is indeed even legally recognised by some states. Thus in Pakistani law "'marriage' includes betrothal, *nikah* and *rukhsati*" (Pak DBGR 1982). All these elements are present in the Bakkarwal process of marriage as well, which is clearly punctuated by the eight following ritual acts:

- *lafaz* (the promise of an engagement)
- *mangṇo/mangṇai* (the engagement)
- *akad* (the promise to wed when all the dues have been paid)
- *byā* (the wedding at which the marriage contract – *nikā* – is sealed)
- *ruksati* (the first departure of the bride for her husband's home for one week)
- *sātmoñ* (the bride's return as a virgin to her parents)
- *duphēra* (the bride's final return to the groom)
- *sagaṇ* (ceremony culminating in the consummation of the marriage and marking the bride's freedom to visit her natal home in the future)

In the previous pages I have already discussed the first three steps; to some extent these three form a cognitive unit, since of a girl in all these three phases it is said that "she's a given-away-one" (*de čhuṛiya*). Similarly of a girl in any of the last four phases it is said that "she's a sent-off-one" (*bhēj čhuṛiya*). The wedding – the fourth ritual – is thus the point of transition, the liminal act: it turns one who has been given away into one who will be sent off. One may never speak in the active tense of a virgin who has gone: the passive tense marks her decency and virginity which for women in general, and young women in particular, is symbolised by their extreme lack of autonomy. In the following, the term wedding will indicate the actual ceremony of marriage.

Both first and subsequent marriages and weddings of men and women are known as *byā* (cf. Hd. *vivāh*). An analysis of the marriages which had remained monogamous shows that the mean age at (first) marriage (wedding) among men and women is 21.30 (± 6.09) and 16.23 (± 3.49) years respectively (Table 3.10), the minimum and maximum being three and thirty years and twelve and thirty-four years for women and men respectively. Data obtained on the recollected age at marriage of each partner in a subsample of forty-eight couples is illustrated in a scatter diagram (Fig. 3.7a).

Table 3.10 Mean age at first marriage of Bakkarwal compared to that in Jammu and Kashmir in general

Bakkarwal			**Year**	**Jammu & Kashmir**
Women (N = 126)	Men_1 (N = 97)	Men (N = 106)		
			1961	16.1
			1971	17.8
16.23±3.49	21.30±6.09	22.47±7.65	19??–1983	

Notes: The data for Jammu and Kashmir in general are given in Zachariah and Patel (1984, Table 5). While all the Bakkarwal men in this sample had remained monogamous, Men_1 indicates their age at first marriage, while Men (N = 106) includes data on subsequent marriages by divorcees or widowers.

Table 3.11 Comparison of two sets of data (own and unpublished Census of 1981) on the age at marriage of Bakkarwal men whose spouses were marrying for the first time

Age (Years)	**My Data (N = 106)**	**%**	**Census (1981) Data (N = 109)**	**%**
–20	44	41.5	30	27.5
21–30	47	44.3	69	63.3
31–40	8	7.5	8	7.3
41–50	3	2.8	2	1.8
51–60	4	3.7	0	0

These data may be compared with those obtained on sixty-seven marriages from the unpublished Census records of 1981 and presented in a second diagram (Fig. 3.7b). The two sets of data concur in showing that men between twelve and thirty-six years of age tend to marry women between about twelve and twenty-five years old. The age of most Bakkarwal women at first marriage is slightly higher than that reported among rural Muslim communities in India (Aggarwal 1976), and compares favourably with that reported for urban Muslims (Roy 1979). If, however, one considers the ages of all the men who – irrespective of whether they were

Figure 3.7a A comparison of the age (in years) at marriage of forty-eight women and men illustrated by a scatter diagram in which each symbol represents one or more couples. These data were collected by myself.

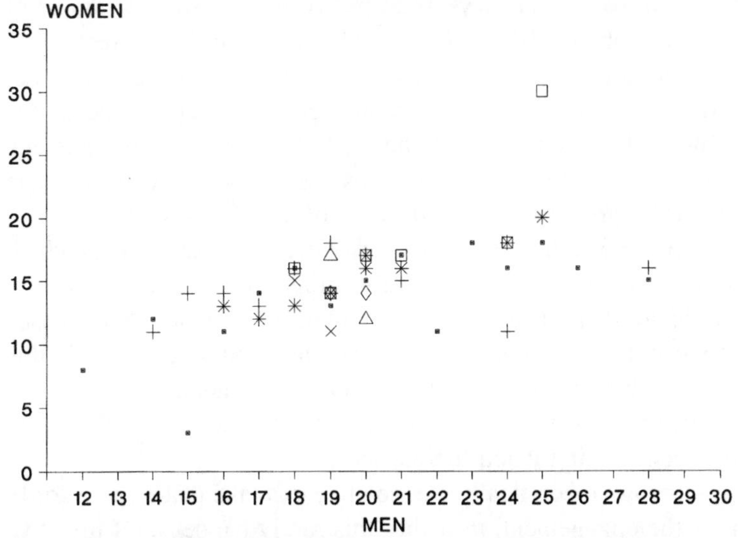

Figure 3.7b A comparison of the age (in years) at marriage of sixty-seven women and men illustrated by a scatter diagram in which each symbol represents one or more couples. These unpublished data were collected by the official Census of the Government of India in 1981.

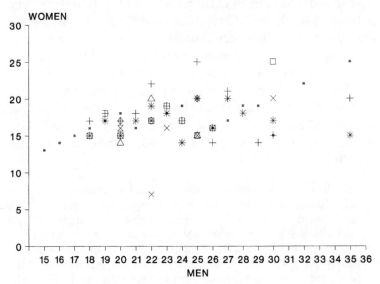

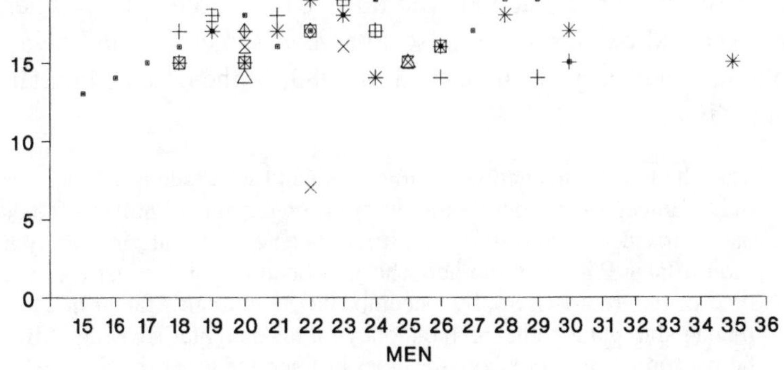

ever married or not – became first husbands, one obtains a slightly different average; the average age at which 106 husbands wedded a virgin was 22.47 ± 7.65 years, the minimum and maximum here being twelve and sixty years respectively. In a similar sample of 109 men obtained from Census (1981, unpublished) records, a median value of twenty-three years is recorded, with minimum and maximum values at fifteen and forty-nine years respectively. Table 3.11 sets out my data and the Census data according to age groups, while Figure 3.9 compares the two sets of data. The age categories are those followed by the official Census.

Figure 3.8 indicates a discrepancy in the two sets of data which is difficult to explain conclusively at this stage. It may result from the distinction made in my sample but not in that of the Census between the ages at engagement, wedding and sending off; in this case the discrepancy probably reflects the advantages of an ethnographic microstudy over a formal government survey, especially in overwhelmingly non-literate societies.

Although theoretically the wedding can take place very shortly after the engagement, in reality this rarely happens. Of fifty-five women I asked, fifty-one (92.7 per cent) recollected that there had been a gap of one to twelve years between their engagement and marriage. Here too the period of waiting is reckoned by both women and men in terms of the number of ritual fasts (*rōza*) kept in between (cf. Table 3.12 for details and Fig. 3.9 for the graphic illustration of the difference in timing). The delay in the full payment of prestations is the major cause of this gap, but there can be other reasons too, all of which are basically financial.

After paying the prestations the boy's family must have enough money left for the actual wedding costs (Table 3.13). Other unexpected expenses may also intervene sometimes and delay planned weddings, as happened in 1983, in the case of Phullāñ and Zima.

> They had been engaged in autumn 1980 and were due to be married in December 1983. Four months after the engagement Phullāñ's father had married a second wife, and it had been a costly affair. Hardly a month later Phullāñ's mother who had been ailing for many years, died of tuberculosis. So, by December 1983 Phullāñ's father had not managed to put together all the money for his daughter's wedding. But he was under pressure from his elder brother and other relatives, who

Figure 3.8 A comparison of my own and Census data (1981, unpublished) on the age at marriage of men of different age groups. For details see Table 3.11.

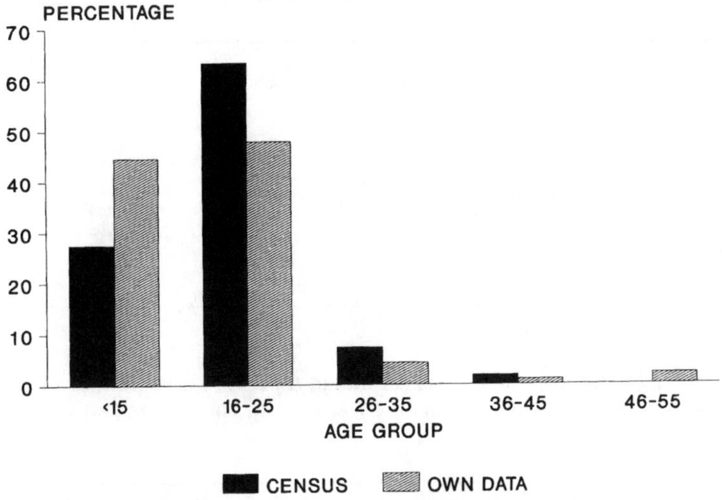

Figure 3.9 The difference in number of years between the time of engagement and marriage of fifty-one women. For details see Table 3.12.

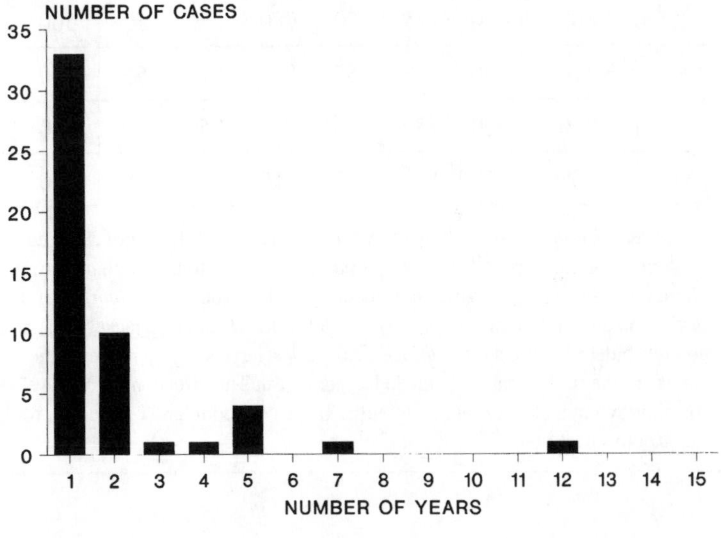

Table 3.12 The period (expressed in years) a fiancée recollected having waited before her wedding

No. of Years	No. of Women
1	33
2	10
3	1
4	1
5	4
6	0
7	1
8–11	0
12	1

Table 3.13 Approximate costs (in Indian *rupees*) – apart from bride-wealth and jewellery – run up by six grooms in 1983, 1984 and 1986

Case	**Wedding**	**Bridal Apparel**			**Groom's Apparel**			**Gifts**
K/Al	Feast	Suits	Ch	Shoes	Suits	Turban	Shoes	
Al	4,000	500	180	55	750	200	55	750
K	2,000	400	120	52	700	170	55	550
K	2,800	400	175	50	780	230	50	560
K	3,500	600	175	55	950	210	55	700
K	3,200	500	150	50	900	250	50	470
Al	4,000	420	150	55	850	220	55	450

Notes: K = *Kunhāri*, Al = *Allaiwāḷ*. Although the colours have not changed, the texture of cloth has – from rough cotton to terry cotton. Wedding garments are: a long shirt (*ganḍai/kurti*) and matching baggy trousers (*suthuṇ*) with a bridal cap and veil, a turban (*paṭko/pag*), a waistcoat (*angi*), a jacket (*kōṭ*) and an embroidered white shawl (*tolia*). Ch= *čhipṛi* (large shawl with veil); the shoes are the traditional, handmade leather *čhitar.* The gifts consist of shawls for older women closely related to either bride or groom, and of a turban for the groom's best man.

anyway disapproved of his second wife, to get the wedding through by December 1984.

A wedding may also be deferred occasionally since "after marriage the boy may want to separate, and we couldn't afford this. We couldn't afford to lose him as a working hand (*bandā*)".

THE WEDDING The wedding ceremony lasts two to four days, depending on the economic status of the families – "the poor do it in two days, the rich in four, and most in three". Although all the days are covered by the term *byā*, this term applies more specifically to the day on which the marriage agreement is sealed by the "reading" of the marriage contract (*nikā badāñ*). The essential ceremony lasts two days, any extra days being for feasting and merriment. I shall now describe the two principal days, which must be consecutive, and in both of which the bride plays an entirely passive role.

The first of these two days is more properly speaking called *māigora* or *mendirat* – after the name of the ceremony which takes place on this day at both the bride's (*bōṭi*) and the groom's (*marāj*) homes. This ceremony is basically a preparatory one and symbolises the transition from the prewedded to the wedded phase. The highlight of this transition is a bath which the bride will be given in the presence of unmarried and married women of her peer group; her last bath was immediately after her last menses. To stress the importance of this ritual bath and its role as a preparatory act, the bride may not wash or comb her hair in the preceding weeks; as a result she may take part in neither household nor pastoral activities. As Janti explained, "she's so sad in these weeks, she doesn't wash or comb and behave like before"; here as elsewhere in southern and southwestern Asia a bride must manifest her sorrow at leaving the natal home. Like a mourner she too is one who is breaking bonds. This bath is the second ritual bath (*baḍēri*) in the triadic series which every human being must take; the first was at birth and the last will be at death (cf. Ch. 1). On the morning of the *māigora*, or on the previous evening, the groom's family sends a covered basket to the bride's mother. This basket contains henna, clarified butter (*ki*) or mustard oil (*tel*), a cake of soap, collyrium, two suits of clothes of *čhiñṭ* a new cap and a golden nose stud (*long*); a ring (*čhāp*) or a pair of earrings may also be included. All these items are to be used by the bride at the *māigora*, and the first – and preferably only – person who is allowed to see them before they are actually used is the bride's mother. In the afternoon the plaits of the bride are opened out and she is undressed. Although young friends and relatives help in the entire process, known as *sir kholāñ* (lit. "opening out the head"), two women in particular do most of the work. These are the two women whom the bride chooses to be two "sisters in faith" – *taram pēṇ/bēṇ*, or *tarbēṇ/tarpēṇ* – to both her and her future husband throughout their wedded life. The couple's children will address them as "maternal aunt" or "paternal aunt". These two women are usually unmarried, though this is not compulsory; they may not, however, be either close agnatic or affinal relatives of either bride or groom. They can be uterine relatives, and this ritual strengthens the existing bonds of kinship. Both women have to be compensated with gifts (*tār*) of a set of clothes (*līr*) and money (about Rs. 100/- in 1984) by the bride's and groom's fathers. Further research is required to establish the similarities and differences between the Bakkarwal concept of siblings "in faith" and, for example, concepts of "bond" siblings (*dharam behen/dharam bhāi*, Bhasin 1988: 132ff., 259) among the Gaddi, Hindu pastoralists of neighbouring regions.

No substantially older women are present at the Bakkarwal bathing ceremony, since "to be naked before elders is a matter of shame". The bride is rubbed from top to toe with a mixture of the henna and fat sent by the groom's family, then soaped and bathed in warm water. Apart from the cleansing effects of the bath, the henna paste represents a balance between hot (the fat) and cold (the henna). The body of the bride is thus rendered "neither too hot, nor too cold". Too much heat would be inadvisable, since as we shall soon see, the bride will have to wait some time before she can consummate her marriage. Too much cold could, on the other hand render her disinclined to cohabitation, and even infertile. The warming is preparatory for sexuality, the cooling for the period of waiting. Once again the symbolic combination of the colours red (henna), white (fat) and black (the "dirty" girl) appears. As Werbner (1986: 237ff.) has argued for other South Asian Muslims, here too henna is a transforming agent, but the transitional states at play are different and less antithetical. After her purifying bath, the bride is dressed by her friends in the new clothes sent by the groom's family. It is the bride's future mother-in-law (*sasu*) who chooses the colour, which nowadays is not specified except that it must be dark. Apparently these clothes were formerly black; I observed printed dark green, blue, red and orange as being common. Two suits are worn, one on top of the other, the darker one of the two being next to the skin. Nowadays pure cotton cloth is also despised, and even the poorest families get a tailor in the nearest bazaar to stitch the "*ṭerikāṭ*" wedding clothes of both bride and groom. While the bride is being bathed and dressed women guests keep coming; they sit and chat and drink tea, and many older women do not even take much notice of the bride.

During this period, a basically similar, though apparently much less elaborate, ceremony of bathing and dressing (*pallā lagānāñ*) takes place at the groom's home. Like the bride the groom is also rubbed with henna and fat before his bath. He is then shaved by a professional non-Bakkarwal barber (*nāi*) who receives a new suit of clothes and cash worth Rs. 100–300 in return for his services. While many Bakkarwal regularly keep their heads shaved or at least very closely cropped, the ritual shaving at the wedding is of special importance, since "the Prophet enjoined it" explicitly. During the ceremonies, many young men arrive as guests, and the groom chooses one friend as his *dosat* – his special friend. This man, who can be a parallel or cross-cousin, will help him dress and will tie his wedding turban (*pag/paṭko*) for him; he will also accompany him throughout the wedding ceremony. In return for his services at the wedding he must receive a white turban (*čiṭṭā paṭko,* or *dastār*) from the groom. His duties and rights end with the wedding. No colours are specified for the groom's suit, but white may not be worn; generally these clothes are also of a dark shade (blue, grey or brown) and his waistcoat (*angi*) is often dark grey or black. Only the turban must be pure white. On it the *dosat* places the *sēro*, a kind of gold-tinselled crown whose red, white and golden fringes and tassels hang down low over the groom's forehead (cf. Ur./Hd.: *sehrā*, a kind of chaplet fastened on the groom's head in large parts of South Asia). His eyes are now lined with collyrium and his fingers or hands decorated with henna by the woman he has chosen as his *tarpēṇ*; she can be his own sister, his brother's wife or a niece. While the groom is being dressed a large round metal tray (*thāl*) is kept in front of him; on this a scarf (*guluband*) and sweets are placed. This is a signal for the ritual of *n(y)eñdro čakāñ*, and each man present now places some cash in this tray. Each amount and the name of the donor is loudly announced by one of the groom's relatives, and eventually another man writes them down. This is because of the "business of give and take" (*neñdro leñdro ko sawāḷ*); at every wedding each male guest has to pay and the quasi potlatch principle is that "what I or my people have paid at your wedding or those of your people, you and your people have to pay at our weddings". The term *n(y)eñdro* is probably akin to the Panjabi *neundra* (Maya Singh 1972: 812), and the custom, which originally may have been designed to help the groom's family pay the bridewealth, is known elsewhere in South Asia (Vetscher 1973: 396; Good 1991: 100). Traditionally, among the Bakkarwal the amounts given and received are not high, and this too appears to be in keeping with regional custom, for while Pakistani law, for example, officially recognises it, it does not consider it to be a "present" (Pak DBGR 1982). The principle underlying this custom is, however, known well beyond South Asia, and among the Ghagar of Egypt, Hanna (1982: 65) notes:

> *Nokoot* is like a loan payment which the Ghagar are obliged to pay on certain occasions and which must be repaid on a similar occasion.... [At weddings] ... it is called a *sineia* (tray) because the money is collected on a tray by one of the groom's kinsmen. He delivers the money to the groom. Someone is selected to write the name of each contributor and the amount which they have paid. Generally the payer writes it too which guarantees the amount will be repaid.

It is afternoon by the time the groom is ready and all the money has been counted. Now lunch is served to all present – except the groom.

In the afternoon at the bride's home the preparations continue, and usually the assembled women sing (*bait paṛāñ*) traditional wedding songs. These songs are, however, no longer sung among a few families who prize themselves on being "really good Muslims", and one bride's mother even told me that her husband "would be made to divorce" her, were she to allow songs at her daughter's wedding. Henna is applied to the bride's hands and feet by one of her *tarpēṇ*, while the other *tarpēṇ* oils and combs (*kangi pherāñ*) her hair and then plaits (*miñḍiāñ guññāñ*; cf. Pnj. *mendhiāñ* = braids) them in the fashion typical for a married woman. Among certain "modern" Bakkarwal women these traditional plaits are no longer made, and the hair is done up in one central plait only. For the traditional hairstyle, first a central parting (*ṭanḍi*) is made and then a second central parting (*paṭh*) is drawn at right angles to the first. Numerous lateral plaits (*miñḍiāñ*) are now made with the hair which has been combed to the sides of the head. To keep these plaits from getting dislocated, the first and last lateral plaits are braided together on each side. Then, a central plait is formed with the longest hair combed back; below this thick plait several other smaller plaits are braided with the remaining hair at the back. The number of the plaits depends on the amount of hair a girl has. Finally the ends of all the plaits are braided together with traditional tasselled (*proñḍi*) coloured thread decorated with coloured beads. These beads, known as *aḍḍi*, were formerly of bones, but are now of plastic. While the bride is being prepared, little girls and young women all around her also apply henna to their own or each other's hands and feet; small boys who are present also get this treat. Little girls sometimes also manage to pester their elder sisters or cousins into doing up their hair like the bride's and flaunt their braids to playmates for weeks on end after the wedding.

Finally, the bridal cap (*lački*) sent by the groom's family is placed on the bride's head. The cut of the cap depends on whether she is *Kunhāri* or *Allaiwāḷ*. Again no special colours seem to be prescribed, and we have the usual red and golden embroidery against a black background; in addition, however, little coins (ideally gold and silver, but in reality copper or even tin) are sewn on to it. Collyrium is now applied to her eyes. Then either her mother or her elder sister decks her out in all the jewellery she may have received from the groom's family. Only once did I see a – very modern – Bakkarwal woman wearing a wrist watch; these are held to be male prerogatives, and irrelevant for women. Two shawls (*čhipṛi*) are now thrown round her shoulders: the first is red (*ratti*) and covering this a second golden (*jarīn*) one. While both shawls are important, the golden one is of mystical significance: it symbolises the young, especially virginal, bride as the material and earthly manifestation of *Nūr Allāh* – God's own light, pure Light, that unsoiled by the heat of sexual passion. This manifestation empowers her with potential fertility, but simultaneously constrains her in all activities, for it underlines her extremely vulnerable status. Vulnerability is a sign of low predictability which, especially in the midst of omnipresent danger, must lead to a suspension of action – and hence to lowered autonomy. Thus, once the bride has been clothed she may not leave the tent or hut, for the dangers (*khatar*) of the evil eye and other malevolent forces loom large. Most important among the latter is light (Casimir and Rao forthcoming b), whose most potent symbols are said to be the sun and fire. Young brides are often referred to as "*nikki lō̃*", literally "small light", or dawn, the time just before the sun rises and ideally the first milking of the day takes place. Neither this "little light" nor by extension her golden shawl should be dazzled by exposure to any other powerful source of stronger light; hence no fire may be lit near her and even photography using a flashlight is frowned upon. It is interesting to note a somewhat similar, though much more elaborate act of sequestration practised by the Newar of Nepal during female pubertal rituals:

> A girl is at that time sequestered for 12 days in a dark room; during that time it is forbidden to her to see the light of the sun, Surya, who is of course a male god, as well as the men of her household. The latter are protected by the … ritual from the dangers of the girl's menstrual blood. (Vergati 1982: 280)

Among the Newar the sun is said to become the husband of the girl on the twelfth day; like all males, he too should be protected from the female forces of procreation manifested through menstruation. In Chapter 1 we have seen that in keeping with ancient concepts spread over a wide region (cf. Gnoli 1966/67) the sun's rays are compared by the Bakkarwal to semen, and both can be dangerous to just these female procreative forces. It could then be suggested that the sequestration of the bride represents a reversal of more widespread regional notions concerning the female power of procreation. Here the bride and her virginity are vulnerable, and require protection from the sun, who could impregnate her and rob her of her virginity (cf. Tod 1983: I/191).

Partly, I was told, to avoid the bride's "having to go out" and getting exposed to various dangers, but also as part of the general scheme of humoral balance and of maintenance of purity, neither she nor her groom may eat, drink or sleep till the following day. Eating and drinking can not only disturb the sensitive humoral balance so essential at this liminal stage, but can also lead to the discharge of bodily substances, such as urine (*pipi*), which not only defile (*mandas ōṇā*) the carefully cleansed bodies, but through their impurity also attract undesirable creatures such as the *jin*, who act as further pollutants. The purified bodies of bride and groom, just like that of a bathed and prepared corpse, are especially attractive for the *jin*, and on both occasions great care must be taken to keep these at bay. It is again as part of the protective measures against the *jin* that the bride and groom are also not allowed to sleep on this night. The reasons are again similar: *pollutis nocturnae* or other unconscious soiling attract the *jin*, and in sleep one is hardly aware of the visitation. Both bride and groom are thus kept awake by their respective friends and young relatives, by singing songs, chatting and telling jokes.

Early on the following morning there is hectic activity at the bride's home. In well-to-do homes especially, while the bride was being prepared the day before, her father and brothers had been busy procuring large quantities of meat, vegetables and fuel wood for today's midday feast, known as *langar ko ṭukṛo*. The term *langar* normally designates the kitchen of a holy place, such as a mosque or a shrine, and the food cooked therein and distributed to the gathering. Its use on this occasion perhaps emphasizes both the communal as well as the non-profane nature of the wedding feast. Days, if not weeks earlier, the bride's family had bought enough rice, flour, tea, sugar, salt and sometimes pulses. A couple of days earlier the bride's father had gone round neighbouring camps and requested the families to "keep milk ready" (*duñd/tutio jamā rakhyo*) for today; the groom's father had done the same in his neighbourhood, for large quantities of milk will be needed today. Very wealthy families even arrange for professional male cooks from local sedentary communities to come with their utensils and prepare the meal; poorer families have to obtain extra pots and pans, large enough to cook such a big meal. All these expenses are borne by the bride's family. Formerly, I was told, "every guest brought an animal along as a gift, but now they only eat at [the bride's] father's home".

Today the guests start coming from around ten o'clock; most of them are of course Bakkarwal, but neighbouring farmers and the local veterinary surgeon and his assistants are also invited. Few, however, really expect the last to participate in the meal; caste and/or class barriers are generally too great to permit commensality. The women guests all go straight to the completely darkened tent in which the bride is sitting veiled and huddled up in one corner, more or less in tears. Nobody seems to bother much with her. Beside her on a large green cloth the clothes, jewellery and household goods she has received as dowry and trousseau from her parents are spread out; covering them all are bits of red cloth, or one large red sheet. Also displayed are presents – invariably embroidered textiles for personal or household use – which the bride may have received from close female friends or relatives. Indeed this is the only occasion when women work together to openly express solidarity. Every woman guest who enters takes a look first at the bride and then at these objects; uttering *"Bismillā"*, she then places a little cash either on the red sheet, or in a box kept there for the purpose. Closely related men also enter the tent now and then, even the veterinary surgeon comes in for a few minutes, but none of the men get even a glimpse of the bride. The other women present here are busy; at the far end of the tent on a very low fire, rice pudding is being cooked and served to the children. The entire atmosphere is extremely noisy, the noise being punctuated now and then by women singing wedding songs. Formerly, I was told, there was more singing at all weddings, but as mentioned earlier, in recent years, in response to what some consider increasing "knowledge of Islam", certain influential Bakkarwal men "have forbidden" these songs and threatened those women of their circle of influence who persevere with divorce proceedings.

Shortly before noon the coming of the groom and his party of about ten men is heralded by crackers or gunshots. This little group is known as *janj*. In response, the bride's male relatives, including little boys, also fire crackers or shoot in the air. At least the groom, if not his company, comes on horseback; among them are the groom's *dosat*, as also the man who is addressed as *"Mullā"* and who will "read" the *nikā*. By the time the groom reaches the bride's camp, most of the women and children have rushed out to see him; only the bride remains in her tent. Before the groom dismounts, he must be welcomed by the bride's mother, who must wave before him an earthen pot containing the glowing seeds of *arbambal*, the wild rue *(Peganum harmala*); this is designed to protect him against the evil eye and the *jin*, "just as wild rue and camphor protect the dead" (cf. Ch. 6). Once the groom has descended, he is challenged by the bride's younger brother, or another younger male relative, to lift a heavy stone, known as *buḍkur* (cf. Hd. *baṭkhara* = weight), placed there beforehand for this purpose. This contest, the Bakkarwal say, was decreed by the Holy Prophet Mohammad himself, "in order to test and prove one's strength". The groom's honour (*ghairat*) is now at stake, and theoretically he can not get the bride unless he, or one of his men, manages to lift the stone. Not only is the groom expected to feel shy (*sharminda*) and behave bashfully *(mu jari karāñ)*, he is also pelted with water and mud (*kučur*). But he has a way out even if he and his men fail to lift the stone: he must put a coin in the hands of each of the women present. The motif of the "difficult task as prerequisite to the bridal bed" has, as Campbell put it (1949: 344) "spun the hero-deeds of all time and all the world". The stone-lifting theme in particular has something of an "Indo-Germanic" flavour, but one is also reminded of the concept of the *Kshetrapāl*, the local overlord-cum-hero turned presiding deity, who is symbolised by a stone (Enthoven 1914: 138) and must be pacified if he is not to carry the bride away himself. Yet another aspect of this mock challenge is that of marriage by capture, met with symbolically in many parts of northern India and encountered in subsequent stages of the Bakkarwal wedding ceremony (cf. infra).

However he may have solved the problem of weight-lifting, the groom is now led to the tent reserved for male guests and seated right at the back, in the darkest portion of the tent. His *dosat* sits on his right. The women return to the bride's tent, for except at the groom's arrival and departure, the gender-specific spatial arrangements allow no mixing. Now as part of the *nikā*, the *mullā* sends two men, known as *agwā* (cf. Hd. *aguvā* = a matchmaker), who have accompanied the groom to obtain the bride's acquiescence (*jāb kabul karāñ*, lit. "obtain answer"). The semiritualised formula runs as follows:

> The son (*pūt*) of X has come to ask for Y's daughter (*gadri*). May she present (*baksheo*) the boy with her domicile (*nawās*)

> in return for the dower (*mār*). Are her parents pleased to agree? (*Isne apṇe nawās is gadro nāḷ, badlā mār ko. Iskā mā bāp kā khushi e ke ṇe?*).

These two men approach the bride's representative, her *vakīl* or *dīni pāi*, who, as mentioned earlier, can never be an agnate, and is often the bride's sister's husband (*benoi*) or maternal uncle (*māmā*). He asks the two emissaries how much the dower (*mār*) will be; all three men then return to the *mullā* and the latter orders the groom to specify the amount. Now it is for the groom's father to place the cash component of the dower on a metal tray and display it to the assembly. The rest of the dower – consisting of animals – must also be specified now, but will be shown later by the groom to the bride, when she reaches his home later that evening. The bride's representative then formally gives his consent to the marriage on her behalf. The contract is sealed by the groom's young friends throwing crackers or firing in the air once again.

In case the bride and her future mother-in-law share the same name, the former must officially be given a new name by her representative, at the latest when he is approached by the two *agwā*. If this is not done, "it would be disrespectful" towards the future mother-in-law. The same applies to the groom, in case he shares a name with his future father-in-law or the latter's elder brother. Henceforth this new name is ideally used by all. This is, however, of little practical consequence. In her natal home the bride's former name continues to be used; in her conjugal home she is addressed and referred to by the appropriate kinship term, except by her husband's seniors – all of whom except her HeBWs may use either of her names. Her HF may indeed tend to use her former name, since at this stage in the cycles of life and household he does not usually address or refer to his wife by her name. While both men and women may refer to their parents by their names, the concept of *sulūk* discussed in the previous chapter enjoins on a woman to refrain from pronouncing the names of her husband's parents. A bride's change of name publicly stresses just these aspects of submissiveness and obedience expected of a well-brought-up young woman.

Once the solemn ceremony is over, it is time to feast. Lunch is served separately to the assembled men and women by the bride's

Figure 3.10 Sequence of events in the final stages of the marital process. For further information see text.

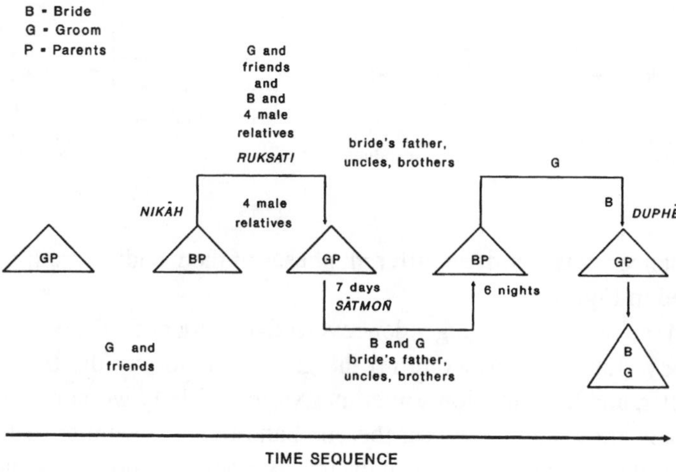

young relatives. After the meal, salted tea is served to the guests; finally each is given a cup of sweet tea. As mentioned earlier, neither bride nor groom may partake of this feast, which marks the end of the *byā*. The last four acts of the marital process may now begin. Figure 3.10 illustrates the sequential relationship between the *byā* and the ritual acts of *ruksati*, *sātmoñ* and *duphēra*.

TAKING LEAVE The bride must now take leave (*ruksati*) of her natal family and home. If it is her first marriage and she is a virgin, she will leave amidst drumbeating and even music (played for the rich by *mirāsi*, hired professional musicians); if not, she is likely to leave in silence. If her destination (*pinḍo*) is far and she has a long way to go, she will leave before sunrise, if not she will leave just before darkness (*aingat*) sets in, since excessive exposure to sunlight is detrimental for her. The difference between the send-off of a virgin and a non-virgin was explained by most as the greater pride of "taking a virgin home". Before the bride leaves the tent she is wrapped in a *khēs* (cf. Pnj. *khēs* = plaid shawl; Ar. *khes* = black goat's hair shawl), a large white shawl with a red border; neither her clothes, nor her cap should now be visible. The colour

Figure 3.11 The colour sequence for the bride in different phases of the wedding

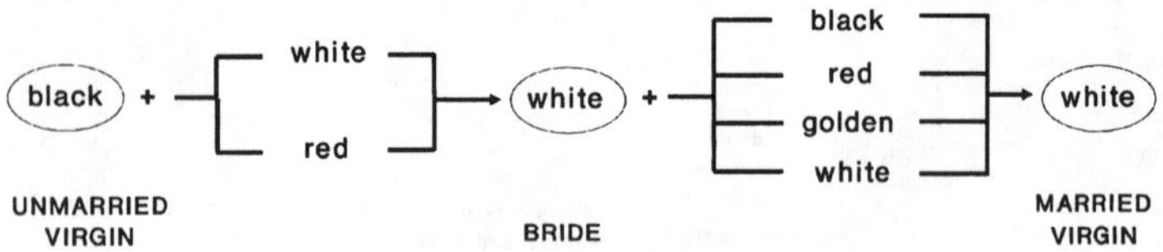

sequence for the bride in different phases of the wedding are illustrated in Figure 3.11.

In the meantime, in a gender-reversed reminder of a Rajput ceremony (Lambert forthcoming) the groom has to pay the bride's mother, and by extension sometimes various elderly women some money, known as *leñdr*. On the one hand this is a symbol of his gratitude for her having brought up his bride and nourished her with her milk (cf. Ch. 1); on the other hand it is a sort of compensation for taking away her daughter. As the bridal couple prepares to leave, the women now start singing the refrain: *jin o giyo, lō lio* ("he's snatched away the light and gone"); once again the light referred to here is the bride, radiant with fertility and the purity of God's light. The bride is now helped to mount the horse – or enter the *ḍoli*, a wooden box used specifically at weddings in large parts of northern India – by the groom and her mother's brother, some other maternal relative or her elder sister's husband. If a *ḍoli* is used, four men must carry it (*janā čār čake*). Her agnates always remain entirely in the background, and in fact one of her younger brothers or agnatic male cousins leads a black goat in the opposite direction to the one the bride will shortly take. Holding her by the ear, and calling her by the bride's name he says, "the little one's asking for a buyer" (*niki kharidār mānge*). The goat is left at a certain distance to return home later on her own; she is then given a new name. This essentially apotropaic act has already been mentioned in Chapter 2, but I suggest that this rite also stresses the apparent uninvolvement of the bride's agnates in the bride's transfer from the paternal to the conjugal home. The suppression of agnatic activity and the correspondingly intense participation in the betrothal and wedding ceremonies of affinal kin could point to ideological remnants of marriage by capture. This thought is reinforced by certain songs sung by women of the groom's family in which he is praised for vanquishing the girl's family and stealing her away. One such song runs as follows:

Marāj lāl o jui āgeo/ Look, the dear groom has come
Sātmoñ mārak** diye marāj lāl na/* With the seventh battle, the dear groom
*Bōṭi jin ke āgeo/*Has snatched the bride and come

* Lit. the seventh, this term also designates the seventh day after the wedding on which the bride's agnates and non-agnates go to her conjugal home to fetch her back as a virgin.
**cf. Hd. *marak* = battle, destroyer; Pashto *maraka* = delegation of marriage proposal (Tapper 1991: 168).

The bridal pair is accompanied by four adult male affinal relatives of the bride. Depending on the distance between the two camps and a variety of personal factors, these men stay at the groom's camp for one or two nights, returning home at the latest on the third day. On their return home, each is gifted a turban by the bride's father. Formerly, I was told, very young brides were also accompanied by a much older woman; referred to as her foster mother (*duñd māñ*), she could either be an affine, such as her mother's sister, or an agnate such as an older married sister; for an unmarried agnate to accompany the bride would be "shameful". This woman would stay with her at the groom's place for seven days and then accompany her back to her parents. The bride's vulnerability as well as her low level of autonomy are stressed by the presence of all who accompany her back and forth, as guarantors of her safety and well-being.

Among Kashmiri Pandits a woman's social bonds with her natal household are snapped "... literally in the span of a few hours ..." (Madan 1975: 221) following her wedding. Among the Bakkarwal a woman remains socially part and parcel of her natal family – and yet with this first journey to her conjugal home the bride is turned into a traveller (*musāphir*) for her agnates. This ambivalent allegiance of hers condemns her to remain a foreigner (*pardesiñ*) to her husband's family. Some women felt that this status was of relevance only in contexts of conflict with the husband's mother, or between the bride's father and her husband's family. Here too *zāt* endogamy helps diminish this foreignness. I did not, however, get the impression that the verbally affirmed status of an eternal traveller affects Bakkarwal women negatively. This may well be because of the general context of migration and nomadism which affects the entire society. Indeed, somewhat like the annual *rōza* fasts, this coming and going helps in later years to remember certain vital events, such as pregnancy; they act as units of measuring time specific to women.

As the bridal pair approaches the groom's camp, the women there welcome them, beating tambourines (*goḷa*) and singing. These songs also stress the joy of victory, and reminded me of Kolenda's (1984: 106) remark on North Indian Rajput (Hindu) brides going "… as hostage to another fortress …". One of the songs I often heard on these occasions was:

Kuluf da kunji kariye mānge avāle/Placing the key in the lock … ask to be entrusted
Paradesiñ[1] *diyāñ da ke dāwā*/Having given the foreigner the promise, challenge
Tu ki ke dāwā min paradesiñ ta bāwā[2]/You who challenged promised my/to me foreigner's father
Mērā jogiwālā[3] *phēra paradesiñ čal gayi*/My bridegroom returns, the foreigner has left
Diyāñ musāphir[1] *bābul*[2] *mērā asi ke dāwā*/The traveller gave my father this challenge
Učaṛi[4] *meñ khaliyāñ*[5] *mērā*/In ruin is my granary
Bābul mērā najar i na āyo/My father is not even in sight
Učaṛi meñ khaliyāñ mērā/In ruin is my granary
Māmā mērā najar i na āyo/My maternal uncle is not even in sight
Bēn mērā paradesiñyā/My sister is in a foreign land
Bīr[6] *mērā najar i na āyo*/My brother is nowhere in sight
Mērā rain[7] *rain ḍērā* /My home/house has been mortgaged away
Mērā jogiwālā phēra/My bridegroom returns

[1]*paradesiñ/musāphir* = lit. foreigner/traveller, here: bride; [2]*bābul/bāwā* = father; [3]refers to the bridegroom as "he who was abroad"; in large parts of Hindu India the term *jogi* refers to the God Shiva, who is also often ritually depicted as a bridegroom (e.g. Fuller 1984: 8) – the term *jugi* also designates the bridegroom in East Pashtun marriage songs (Ferdinand 1978: 131); [4]*učaṛi* = ruin; [5]*khaliyāñ* = granary – probably a reference to an agropastoralist, or agricultural past; [6]*bīr* = brother; [7]*rain* = in ruin/mortgaged.

Before the bride dismounts, her four attendant relatives shout out *(pīt mār čhuṛi)* to demand that she be given a gift *(isna de tar)*. Her mother(s)-in-law and elder sisters-in-law now draw back her veil a little and kiss her on the forehead; all the older women assembled follow suit. Each woman also gives her a coin; the coin is kissed by the donor, held up to the bride's forehead and then, saying "*Bismillā*", put into a basket held out for the purpose by one of the men accompanying her. This money, also known as *n(y)eñdro*, belongs entirely to the bride. If and when the bride is accompanied by her so-called foster-mother, she too will have to be paid very handsomely (cf. Ch. 1). The bride now dismounts and together with her attendants is led by the groom to his herd. A similar custom obtains among the Gujar of the Kashmir Valley; before crossing the threshold of her new home one of her attendants demands a female kid or a calf as part of the dower and says, "I'm holding the doorway, give a calf" (*buo pagṛāni, kaṭṭi de*). The bride then holds the ear of the animal and calls her attendants as witness; this animal and her offspring will belong to the bride alone. The Bakkarwal groom now points out (*dasalāñ*) the animals which he has promised her as part of the dower. The demanding tone of the bride and her people are just the reverse of what Madan (1975: 233–4) notes of Kashmiri Pandit weddings, where it is the groom's relatives, and especially his sister who refuses to let the bride in till she gets a gift.

In the meantime, the goods brought by the bride are unpacked and closely scrutinised and commented on by the women present. Sweetmeats brought by the bride are also distributed. Traditionally these consisted of an *alwa* of semolina, set with bits of coconut, but today they also include a bagful of toffees. The more and the prettier the objects the bride has brought, the more she is loudly praised and the greater her prestige. She is now brought into the women's tent and seated comfortably in the middle, surrounded by young girls and little children, all vying with one another for a glimpse of her face, which is still heavily veiled. She is served with sweetmeats (*miṭai*) and sweetened milk. Shortly after, food is served amidst much singing and merriment, and at last both bride and groom may also eat. There is still no commensality between men and women, and the bride at least is not expected to eat much. Many of the guests spend the night at the groom's camp. The women guests sleep in the same tent as the bride and the other women of the camp, while the men share a tent with the groom and other men. These guests will participate in a meal to be served around midday the following day, which must include bread and either butter or buttermilk and is of great symbolic importance, since the bread and the milk products have been – at least ideally – baked and churned by the bride. It is thus the first meal to be cooked by her in her husband's home. In practice the bride only touches the pots and pans containing the food. To partake of this meal is to testify to the fact that the bride is *suči* (cf. Pers. *suč* = pure, and Skt. *shuči* = pure, light, radiant, white – Mawet 1980: 286), in other words that she is unsoiled and auspicious. Similar rites observed in Kabul (Janata 1962/63: 70) and among certain Hindus in India stand as a testimony to the fact that she has been accepted in her new status as a member of her husband's family.

THE RETURN OF THE VIRGIN The bride's purity also symbolises her potential fertility, and the transformation from virgin to mother must carefully be watched over. She stays at her husband's home for six full days and nights, but during this period no sexual intercourse may take place. The honour of the groom and his family is at stake here, for were intercourse to take place the marriage could be annulled by the bride's family, or payment of heavy compensation could be demanded. The person held responsible for guarding over the bride's virginity is her mother-in-law, or if the latter is not alive her husband's nearest female agnatic or affinal relative. This is indeed one of the few occasions when female responsibility is publicly acknowledged. Bisaria (1971: 82) mentions a ritual in which the bride's brother hands over white wool to her mother-in-law, asking her "… to send his sister back to him after seven days, as white as the wool." This custom was not observed by me, nor was it familiar to my informants, but unlike in, say, neighbouring Kumaon (Sax 1991: 124), here as among the Rajputs Kolenda (1984: 100) wrote about a marriage may be consummated only on the second visit (*dūji ṭūri*) of the bride to her conjugal home – for the Bakkarwal an average of 1.46 years (± 2.02, N = 50; cf. Appendix C) after the wedding, for the Rajputs some two years later. Formerly in the Panjab, it was also customary for "… several years to separate the [wedding] from the change of residence." (Hershman

1981: 169). Among the Bakkarwal the sequence is not limited to wedding and consummation, but to wedding, coresidence – i.e. when the bride is finally sent (*rawānā karāñ* or *duphēra*) from her natal home to set up permanent residence in her conjugal home – and consummation (*muklānā*). I shall deal with these in some detail in the next section. As for why a bride must wait so long for the consummation, and why her virginity in this period is of such great importance, Rima commented laughingly: "You don't churn a pot with only a day's milk, do you?" Basso explained: "The longer you keep the milk, the more quickly comes the butter." A young girl is, as we already know, often compared to milk, and Makhṇi is a common name. The extraction of butter from milk by churning, a process the Bakkarwal explicitly compare to sexual intercourse, is perhaps in keeping with wider regional concepts understood in Marriott's (1976: 110) words as

> … subtler substance-codes … emerging through processes of maturation … subtler essences may … be ripened, extracted, or distilled out of grosser ones (as … butter from milk); and grosser substance-codes may be generated … out of subtler ones….

This may well apply to the generation of life in general; the longer the milk is kept, the greater the pleasure in churning and the more the butter you get.

On the morning of the seventh day (*sātmoñ*; cf. Hd. *sātvāñ*) the bride's father, accompanied by two or three non-agnatic male kin of the bride, comes to fetch her and the groom, as they also do among East Afghan Pashtuns (Ferdinand 1978: 133). While she now returns to her parents for a minimum of six nights, the groom stays with the bride's family for exactly this period. The period of the bride's stay at her natal home depends on several factors, which will be discussed below at some length; the shorter her stay is planned, the more she is made much of by her parents and siblings. Since she retains her affiliations to and identity with her patrilineage now, as on all subsequent visits to her parents, she is treated as a full member of her natal household and takes part in all household activities, including cooking.

THE FINAL SEND-OFF Although after the *ruksati*, the bride is referred to as a "sent-off one", in reality she will become one only with the *duphēra* (lit. second round, second return), or the *dūji ṭūri*, the second going, the first *phēra* being reckoned as the wedding immediately after which the groom brought his bride home. Till the birth of her first child, each return of a woman from her natal to her conjugal home is referred to as a *phēra*, each trip to her natal home in this period being called *bārā*. At every *phēra* among both *Kunhāri* and *Allaiwāḷ* she brings back presents (shawls and other clothes, bread, butter oil, and perhaps even an animal as part of her dowry) for herself and her husband.

The question of the length of the bride's first stay at her natal home after her wedding, or alternatively the gap between the time of wedding and the time of coresidence has been raised above. Recollection data (Appendix C) reported by fifty-three Bakkarwal women showed an average difference of 0.94 years (± 1.54) between the time of the wedding ceremony and the bride's change of residence, the maximum being seven years. These women themselves said that usually a bride is "finally sent to her husband" (*rawān karāñ*) within one migrating season, i.e. one year, but "if she is very young, she may be sent after several years". This seems to be borne out by the small sample given in Appendix C. Officially it is the groom and his parents who decide when the *duphēra* will take place – "according to the wishes of her master" (*usko mālik ko marji nāḷ*) Zuleika would be sent, said her father. But Zuleika and her husband, Gāmā, lived with her parents for almost three years after their wedding, because, as she herself explained: "I'm the only grown-up woman to help my mother." In reality several factors – such as household labour availability, the girl's health, her attachment to her mother, the latter's relations with the bride's mother-in-law, etc. – determine a bride's period of stay at her natal home following her wedding.

The best days for the send off are Fridays, Thursdays and Sundays, Wednesdays once again being forbidden. It is also forbidden to send the girl during her menses, during *rōza* and in the time of *doāshure*. At her *duphēra* a woman may for the first time publicly exercise her freedom of choice in taking or leaving behind some or part of her dowry. She is now also given several pieces of wheat flour flatbread, molasses and butter oil as presents. She is fetched by the groom and the couple return to the latter's residence, where the *sagaṇ* (cf. Pnj. *sagan*) ceremony takes place. After this ceremony, which marks the public recognition of coresidence, the bride can – at least theoretically – return any time to her parents' place and stay there for a while if she chooses to. The ceremony consists basically of presenting the couple with small gifts in cash or kind. This is followed by lunch. The guests are mostly men, only close women relatives being obliged to attend. Although male attendance at this ceremony is important, many men delegate others to go; thus at Alia's daughter's *sagaṇ*, Mirio (his WB) gave Jumma a kid, and asked him to present it. Jumma's son was married to another one of Alia's daughters, and as a *kuṭum* of Alia he had to attend the *sagaṇ* personally.

The *duphēra* marks the bride's change of residence, but not necessarily her change in status as a virgin. The *sulūk* of the groom's family demands that his sexual impulses be controlled, and that the girl get mentally adapted to the new surroundings before being physically exposed to her new position. In most cases when it is felt that the couple is ready to cohabit, they are given a separate tent for the first few nights. If the bride is still considered very young, she will be led there by the groom's mother. In a subsample of fifty-one women the difference between the time of first coresidence and cohabitation was found to be on average 0.27 years (± 1.31), the maximum here being nine years. In an earlier section it had been mentioned that in a sample of fifty-five women twenty-six had been engaged before menarche. Data in Appendix C show that many weddings also take place before a girl has her first period, and this I was told is one major reason for the marriage not being consummated immediately upon coresidence. The average gap between cohabitation and menarche is 1.46 years (± 1.58, N = 50), but two cases were reported in which consummation took place prior to menarche. In both cases the brides were considered "to look grown-up enough", and yet since they were not yet "really mature", their parents had brought them back after a few months. One of these marriages ended in a divorce.

That this phase between coresidence and cohabitation can be problematic and potentially conflictual is illustrated by the following case, recorded in 1983, but not included in Appendix C.

> Emina is fourteen years old, very pretty and outgoing. She had her first period two years ago. Since then she has had them off and on, and

> she complains a lot about the pain she has each time. Neither she nor her mother considers her properly *jawān* as yet. When she was eleven, she had been engaged to a man in his twenties, and last year I had attended her wedding which took place when she was thirteen. After the usual wedding ceremonies and a short stay at her husband's home, she had returned to her parents. A few months ago her husband's father (his mother had died) requested her parents that Emina be sent back to them; her parents agreed on condition that, since she was still not quite ready for intercourse, she "be treated by her husband like a sister". She was sent to her husband's home, and the first week everything went well. Then, one night, her husband tried to approach her and there was a scene. A couple of nights later he tried again. This time Emina fled to her father-in-law and asked for help. But the old man led her back to his son, and Emina's mother told me that Emina was then raped by her husband and became very ill. On the fourteenth day Emina was brought back to her parents. While her father told me that she would be "sent back when she's older – now her mother says she's too young", her mother has resolved to get the marriage dissolved and "find her a more suitable husband when she's old enough". Emina herself feels she "will be old enough in five or six years".

This case also illustrates a point referred to earlier, i.e. that within the framework of marriage rape is tolerated – the legitimacy granted to intercourse is linked here to both partners being considered physically adult enough.

Chapter 4

PERPETUATING LIFE AND PRODUCING VALUES

Unlike in some societies (Chodorow 1974), both women and men among the Bakkarwal tend to perceive themselves in the early years of marriage as fairly intimately connected to and even defined in various degrees through others. As the years pass, and the new bonds grow old, these others come to be part of oneself and one's own identity – as Makhṇi said, the "distinctions between oneself (*apaṇ*) and others (*pare*) get wiped out (*miṭia*)". In the early stages of her wedded life in her conjugal home, a girl tends to think of herself in terms of her natal family. She generally visits her parents each year – often after the autumn migration, or at other slack periods of the pastoral work cycle. Each time she brings back presents; these may be clothes, some cash worth between Rs. 10/- and Rs. 100/-, sweetmeats, a shawl, an embroidered shabrack or saddlecloth. On the very first visit her parents may, if they can afford it, even present their daughter with a herd animal. This is how Zarina got her three sheep: the first at her first visit to her parents, the second at her first pregnancy visit, and the third at the visit after the birth of her first baby. She hopes she will get a fourth one when her next child is born. Here, as in certain other South Asian societies a married woman is entitled to visit her parents and stay with them without being accompanied by her husband. Her absence from her husband is not construed, as it is often enough in Western societies, as a sign and a source of marital discord. But unlike among, for instance, the Tamang (Fricke et al. 1993), it is problematic to relate the degree of a Bakkarwal woman's autonomy with the frequency or intensity of contact with natal kin. This is partly because, given the context of intense endogamy, it is so hard to effectively distinguish between natal and marital kin, but also because this contact is intimately connected to pastoral timetables in both the natal and conjugal homes. The young woman already has a stake in the herds of her conjugal family and most probably still has one in those of her parents.

Until he sets up his own "household", a married man is socially defined exclusively through his father, and even after this he will be contextualised through his agnates. (The use of the term household is not unproblematic, since its meaning changes in different phases of the life cycle.) Within his natal family he is now additionally perceived of together with his wife, with whom he is expected to spend as much of his leisure time as possible. Indeed, if he does not do so, she can complain of being neglected and the young husband's elders tend to concur and consider that "he's going bad". This is why Jima decided to sell off his son Shila's truck; "he goes off with it at any time and is away for hours on end, and is never at home with his young wife", he explained. A young husband's lack of interest in his newly wedded wife is interpreted by women either as a sign of his general sexual inadequacy – imputed to his weakened *nafas* – or his lack of interest in this particular woman. The former – if ascertained through the indirect questioning of his wife by slightly older sisters, sisters-in-law and cousins (cf. Das 1976: 6) – is imputed to the malevolent influence of extraneous evil forces, such as *jin* who may be jealous of the new relationship; the latter is viewed variously depending on the individual case. In the former case various remedies are sought, to begin with by the women at home, and failing a cure, by the boy's father at specific shrines. Only if the wife is considered outstandingly ugly does one sympathise with the husband, but whatever the reasons for indifference, the neglect is a serious matter of concern to both families. Although most forms of public demonstration of affection between husband and wife are frowned upon, such affection is very obvious in many cases and there are several subtle expressions of it, which are approved of. Gama usually helped his wife wash her beautiful, long hair, and the neighbours praised him for it. Dulla's neighbours thought well of him because, even three years after his young wife's death, he was so miserable at losing her.

A husband – variously referred to with a tekonym, as *khā(w)ind*, *kārāḷo* or *buḍo* according to age and status – is, however, never defined through his wife (*ṭabri* or *buḍi* according to age); he is also not defined through his affines, unless he is a live-in son-in-law, in which case his father-in-law acts as the defining element. A married woman, on the other hand, is explicitly defined not only through her natal family, but also through her husband and his family. The husband is officially said to be his wife's master (*mālik*), just as a man is of his herds, an employer of shepherds, and God of all that exists. It is a woman's duty to look after her husband and her "household" – which may well include his parents and other relatives – in every manner. If for whatever reason a woman fails to comply, her husband may even take another wife, and while this may not always be considered the right thing to do, it is nevertheless thought of as "in a way natural for a man in this case". "The sign of a good (*nēk*) woman", said Zaro, "is how she cares for her husband." And Jimdi felt that Yasin's mother was "a really good woman because she looks after her old man so well, even when he's ill". Symbols of these additional criteria of definition a woman has are pieces of jewellery and hairstyles. Thus a married woman, however poor, must wear a pair of either *marīda* or *kaṛā* bracelets, and nowadays a number of plastic (formerly silver) ones. Most married women are also expected to apply collyrium to their eyes and dye strands of their plaited hair with henna.

Another important expression of a woman's relationality is the fact that she "… is never left alone (*ekelā*)". To be alone in Western societies can be a sign of autonomy, of being on one's own, of being independent, but it can equally signify helplessness, especially in old age. How is "being alone" denoted, and what are its connotations in this society? Bakkarwal camps are never crowded, and it is not rare to find sites with just one or two nuclear families. And yet these families are not considered as being alone. On the other hand, adult women who had to be hospitalised for a while were thought to be alone. To "be alone" then is, I suggest, a question of being with people other than those of one's family or close community. All Bakkarwal I met were struck by the fact that over long periods of time I used to be "alone", i.e. without my own agnates or affines. My husband used to come and stay for several weeks at a time, and once my mother also visited me, but I was on the whole perceived of as "being alone". The fact that I was with these women and their families apparently did not count in this context. In a previous chapter it has been shown that keeping physical distance is an important aspect of testifying to being well mannered, to having learnt *sulūk*, to show respect. Lack of space and crowding are signs of poverty just as much as of a lack of good breeding, and both tend to diminish well-being. Being apart can thus signify strength, reasoning, good manners, high status, manliness, and hence also plenty of capacity for decision making. But being apart is not the same as being alone, and as Salzman (1992: 40) comments on a neighbouring pastoral society: "To be Baluch, and to be human, is to wish to be with people; to be alone is an unnatural state, and to wish to be alone is an unhealthy state, or worse." To be Bakkarwal is to wish to be with certain people – depending on one's gender, age and economic status. "Who will listen to one who is alone?" goes one saying, which means, "a man with few or no agnates can never hope to have a say" (cf. Ch. 5). Not being alone can thus signify strength. To simply be together is also an expression of mutual care and especially feminine emotions. To leave a woman alone is not to care for her. Not "being alone" is for the Bakkarwal perhaps a much watered down form of what Delaney (1991: 38–42) describes for Turkey as "being covered":

> … women must be "covered"; a woman must always be under the mantle of a man (whether father, husband, brother, or son) … Women without cover … indicate that they are without protection …

In the early stages of fieldwork, most men and even some women breathed a sigh of relief every time my husband reappeared; as Alia once put it, they now felt "less responsible" for me. When my "being alone" became part of the routine, interpretation not being the monopoly of the anthropologist, these women also interpreted my situation in their own way. "Your husband's a real man", Jano commented one day. "Our men don't ever allow us to go far alone." Begāñ echoed similar sentiments, when she said: "We can never spend a night alone. Even in the day we're usually with others. But sister, my brother [referring to my husband] lets you spend days and nights alone. That's a real man." But what is a "real man", a *saččo mard*, and would Begāñ and Jāno and all the others really like to "be alone", I asked. "A real man", so I was told on many occasions by various women, was a man who had things under his control (*bas māñ*). But not every man who has things under control was a "real man"; physical strength (*jismāni tākat*) and bravery (*baāduri*) were no doubt necessary requisites, but so were intelligence (*čālāki*), the capacity to sympathise and empathise (to feel *amdardi*), generosity (lit. to have a big heart, *baṛo dil*) and soft-heartedness (*dil ōṇa*). Without these four characteristics, one could perhaps be a *khaṛpēñč* (cf. Ch. 5) and hence a man of influence, but not a "real man". In other words, a good measure of *ōsh* was essential to being a "real man". Sometimes young men also were present at these conversations – younger brothers or cousins, sons or nephews. While they generally agreed with the views expressed, they also felt that even a "real man" would not let any and every woman "be alone". "If our women were alone they'd go bad (*kharāb*); now where can they learn bad things like smoking or joking loudly – they hardly go anywhere. To go somewhere, to be alone you first have to have *sulūk* …", explained Shafi.

To be able to "be alone", a woman must thus have certain qualities; if she does not, "it would mean ruin (*tabā*) for all". Most women agreed and indeed thought that since they lacked these qualities, they would be afraid to "be alone". And as for women who "ruined one and all", there was the contemporary case of Bibo, whose story was repeated to me over and over again, by men and women, in as many versions (cf. Ch. 5). The basic story was one of a woman who separated from her husband in winter 1982, after several years of marriage and shortly before the wedding of their own daughter. In summer 1983 she demanded her legal right to maintenance. Bibo was condemned by one and all as a "bad woman". The qualities that Bibo lacked – but which were explicitly ascribed to me, as they also are to "… strong women among the Durrani …", Pashtun pastoralists of northern Afghanistan (Tapper 1980: 74) – were those which made of a normal woman, a manly (*mardānā*) woman. A comparison of this concept with that mentioned by Mines and Gourishankar (1990: 762) for "leading women" in South India may be interesting. These qualities are primarily those of reflection, reason and comprehension, subsumed under the term *dyānat* and linked to the capacity to discriminate, to choose between right and wrong, and to exercise discretion.

As mentioned in Chapter 1, all these qualities depend on the amount one has of *nafas* and *ōsh*, those properties discussed in earlier chapters. Most women, the Bakkarwal feel, have little or no power of discretion, and in this too they echo Delaney's informants (1991: 41). As mentioned earlier, women are generally held to have less *ōsh* than men, and hence only if a woman is credited with as much *ōsh* as a man of fair well-being, may this manly woman also be credited with the capacity to take decisions which are publicly recognised as such. As discussed earlier, most phenomena recognised as decisions take place in public space. It is this de-emphasising of decision making in the private sphere which precludes the construction of women's autonomy, either singly or as a category, and is the primary cause of their lack of authority in the wider polity. Only a manly woman can thus be granted more autonomy in public space – and is perceived of as having more of it also in the private sphere – than an ordinary woman. But unlike among the neighbouring Hindu Gaddi, among whom sexual identity rather than gender identity stands in the way of expressing personal choice (Phillimore 1991: 335), here a manly woman is considered physically fully as belonging to the female gender and the female sex. I was often told by both men and women that, when compared to me physically, Bakkarwal women are "like men" since they can carry infinitely heavier loads of water and wood, and walk much longer distances without fatigue. Manliness in the context of the manly woman is thus a metaphor for certain ascribed qualities marking neither physical nor social identity. This is also borne out by the hierarchy of manliness in which any man of sound mind is allowed more autonomy than a manly woman: he can theoretically always be on his own and is recognised as taking certain decisions. He may not, however, indulge in surrogate decision making beyond his own nuclear family – only some men can do that, as we shall see in the next chapter. Whereas publicly acknowledged decision making remains extremely limited for women even in adulthood, a man may, once he is successfully established in life, slowly assert his "ego boundaries"

(Chodorow 1974: 57). The greater his perceived well-being the stronger this legitimate assertion, and the less permeable the boundaries from without. Explained in Bakkarwal terms, the extent of well-being is, of course, bound up with the question of the legitimate amounts of *nafas* and *ōsh*. In practice, it depends on factors such as a man's socio-economic status, which again is related to, for example, the number of children he has and the size of his flocks – in other words on the degree of well-being he can attest to (Casimir and Rao 1995) publicly. I shall return to these points in the following chapters.

Being a pastoral people, the Bakkarwal criteria of male definition and relationality include, reasonably enough, not only other people, but also herd animals. Economically and socially the young husband is defined more than ever before in terms of the well-being of his flocks, or rather his father's flocks, part of which he will inherit one day. A woman is also entitled to a share of her parental flocks, and following Islamic norms this is half that of a son's. Though not all women get their shares, those who do receive them as part of their dowry (*samā*). This share is intergenerationally transmittable and ideally a woman leaves 40 per cent of her animals to her sons and 60 per cent to her daughters; but if she dies without heirs, they become the property of her husband or his heirs. In case of a divorce initiated by the husband, the property remains hers, and she is also entitled to dower (*mār*) from her husband. As mentioned in Chapter 3, even when she receives animals as dowry she does not take them with her at once, but transfers them gradually from her natal to her conjugal home, and this can take many years. These animals form the core of a married woman's theoretical herd and together with their eventual offspring are legally considered her exclusive property. But, "since most families have everything together" – in other words, since there is no de facto separation between a man's and his wife's property, this exclusivity is only theoretical. However, when animals obtained in dowry or their offspring are sold, the money obtained is considered the woman's, and in the early years of marriage she has to be given the amount. Were this not done, she would have a legitimate grievance and could complain. This money is usually put aside by the young wife to be taken along if and when she and her husband separate from her parents-in-law. She is also free to gift these animals – as also those she may receive as dower – to anyone in her own or her husband's kin-group.

In the previous chapter reference was made to certain ritual aspects of social relations among the Bakkarwal. In this chapter other aspects of the relations between persons will be discussed. These aspects affect the reproduction of Bakkarwal society in all its facets, including those of autonomy of each of its members, and its eventual articulation by them.

The Desire to Beget

Baggo and Shafi had only one daughter, even though they had been married a long time. They had been very unhappy about this for many years, Baggo said, but had apparently reconciled themselves to their fate. "At least our fate has been better than that of Shilla and Janti", she added. Shilla, Baggo's brother, and his wife never had any children. He was many years Baggo's junior, but looked very much older, I felt. Shafi agreed and explained,

> People who have no children often grow old through sorrow (*duk*). Those who have children have many cares and worries, but they're not alone – the children always help. Those without children get no help … It's difficult, especially nowadays, to live without children."

To have children is a basic necessity; it is also a deep-rooted wish, a *manshā*. A woman who does not conceive could well be barren (*ōtar*), for here as in most other South Asian societies infertility is considered commoner in women than in men. It is a source of sorrow and worry, for though it does not lead to repudiation or divorce, it may lead a man to take a second wife (cf. Ch. 5). A woman may be barren because of her own temperament (*mijāj*), which "is too cold"; alternatively it may be created in her by extraneous, obnoxious forces which "make her too cold". Either way, here as elsewhere in South Asia "… a barren woman is (too) 'cold'" (Mani 1981: 195), and in certain contexts extraneous forces can, at least temporarily, alter inherent nature. "What can she do, poor woman, if her *mijāj* is that way" – in other words the woman can not be held responsible for her innate disposition. Yet measures are taken to modify such a temper and warm the woman enough to enable her to conceive. If it is felt that she is inherently cold, she may be cured through traditional medication, or failing this through modern medical methods, including occasionally surgery. Three standard traditional pharmacopoeia are the roots of the willow (*bōṛ*) tree, those of a kind of sorrel *(khaṭri: Rumex nepalensis*, considered hot), and those of the wild rhubarb (*pombačāri*: *Rheum spec.*). All these are dried in the shade – this is important, for the effect of the sun would make them "too hot" – and then powdered. The willow root powder is mixed with brown sugar and a little *ghi*, dissolved in cool milk and drunk. The roots of *khaṭri* and *pombačāri* are eaten mixed with whole meal wheat flour, *ghi* and sugar. When sterility is traced to a supernatural but unidentifiable evil force, the latter's negative influence is often sought to be overcome by certain locally mainstream religious practices. For example, to counter the evil eye (*ak*), usually cast by a female witch (*ḍākini*, cf. Chs. 2, 6), an amulet (*tawīj*) may be tied with a special string (*goḷeo*) round the waist or upper arm; both the string and the amulet should be specially made for the supplicant by a man well versed in the Qor'an. If this has no positive effect, or if it is felt that not just the evil eye but some other supernatural force is at work, the disappointed couple may go and seek the blessings of one or more holy men (*pīr* or *bāji*), who promise to pray for them and intercede on their behalf. Here the woman receives another kind of amulet (also known as *tawīj*) containing specific curative powers in the form of a spell (*mantar*, cf. *mantra*) to wear around her neck. If this too does not work the couple usually takes a vow at one or more shrines, symbolising their innermost wish to receive from God a child whom they will hold in trust on His behalf. This pledge known as *manti* or *mannat* (cf. Ur./Pers. *amānat* = deposit, custody, trust, faith) also involves their promising to show their gratitude by giving gifts known as *khayrāt* or *shirinī*, which usually consist of some cash plus a goat or a sheep; in acute cases, the hair of the desired child is also pledged.

A *mannat*, which can also be made if a couple has lost many young children, is valid as a response only to certain kinds of *manshā*, not simply any desire or wish. In this it differs from the use of the term *manat* (vow) as observed among Hindus, for example, at the temple of Bakreshwar to which men and women go in the hope of a number of things such as recovery from illness, obtaining offspring and safeguarding "household welfare", but also in the hope of solving family disputes, passing examinations and getting jobs (Chaudhuri 1981: 57–8). A Bakkarwal *mannat* can not be made for settling disputes or obtaining grazing land or livestock; it can, however, be made for the protection and recovery of livestock extensively and repeatedly subject to loss. This in turn is because one can not have a *manshā* for more money, more livestock or nice clothes; a *manshā* for the Bakkarwal is an intense and deep-seated desire for non-material things. With it one leaves the domain of the profane to enter that of the sacred, which in all societies informs life-giving and life-preserving acts. Eight women and five men whom I asked for examples of a *manshā* all mentioned the desire for offspring; six of the women and four of the men mentioned recovery from serious illness, four women and three men mentioned the well-being of their children and their flocks respectively, and one woman mentioned the happy marriage of her only child. A *manshā* thus seems to imply the desire for generation, preservation and continuation of life (birth, recovery, sexuality) – and the concomitant release from the dangerous, hung state of pseudo-liminality which expectancy and waiting, and thence indecision, amount to.

Although sterility is feared, women who are considered too fertile are partly laughed at and partly censured; the former because "she's like an animal" and the latter because "she doesn't control her heat". Both animality and heat are expressions of excessive sexuality. This ambiguity is reflected also by Vieille in his paper on Iran (1967: 120), where "… a woman who has many children is censured, but helped very little; her too great fertility has become a fault". Bakkarwal women talking of a youngish woman with many children, blame her for being unthinking and irresponsible, for having too much *nafas* and too little *ōsh*. But they pity her too for having to do so much work and bear so many children. For several reasons single births are also preferred by all, frequent twins (*dukuṛ*) and multiple births – in 1984 a Kashmiri woman some Bakkarwal had heard of had "even three at a time!" – being ascribed to the impending end of Time (*ākhirzamānā*). Most Bakkarwal said that roughly 20 per cent of their goats (among sheep it is rarer) gave birth to twins (*jotrā*), but did not view this entirely positively: "Whether it's a goat or a woman, twins are always less intelligent than others. The mother's brains (*magaz*) get distributed and each gets only half." The mother's strength gets divided up similarly, with the result that each of the twins is weaker than a single baby would be; opinion diverged on whether such siblings were equally weak. With multiple births, the part each receives of the mother's brains and strength is even less, and yet nothing can be done to prevent such births.

Bringing children into the world is thus recognised culturally as partly being an act of human decision, in which women and men can, and at times should, exercise discrimination and choice. This exercise of choice was also imputed to me, and my being childless was interpreted by most women as the temporary result of a perfectly logical decision taken by someone who "had to be away from home for so long on work". In the course of numerous conversations I had in 1983 with sixty-four married women, between the ages of sixteen and fifty, I happened to ask them whether they wanted more children; all had been pregnant at least once, and many had lost children. We also spoke about the number and gender of the desired children. Figure 4.1 illustrates the answers to the basic question "would do you like to have more children?" in relation to the number of living children per woman (N = 58). Not taken into consideration here are six women who were undecided; these women had three or more children living. The figure shows that in this small sample, not surprisingly perhaps, the more children a woman had, the less her desire for further offspring.

In most parts of South Asia there is a strong preference for male offspring, and what Levine (1987: 287) writes of Tibetan communities in northwestern Nepal is fairly representative of the entire area:

> This ... general preference for male children ... [is] articulated in terms of four characteristic rationales, all future-oriented. The first is that sons will contribute to their parents and natal household, whereas daughters will benefit their husbands and husbands' households. The second is that sons can provide diversified economic contributions ... Third, sons can be expected to support their parents politically; and fourth they perpetuate their father's clan.

It is hence all the more interesting that conversations with the twenty-one Bakkarwal women who wanted more children revealed no essential gender preferences; they tended to want children of the

Figure 4.1 The relation between the number of surviving children and the desire for more among fifty-eight women

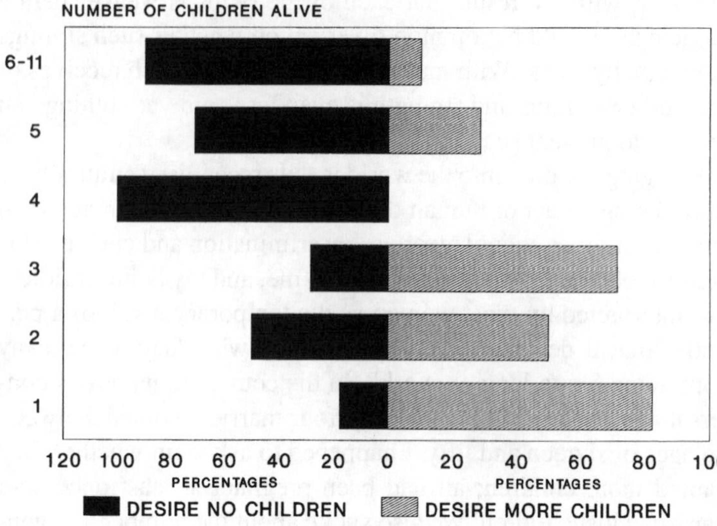

opposite gender to those they already had. Their statements are supported by the fact that, unlike Kashmiri Hindus (Madan 1965: 76–77) or Muslims, for example, in Iran (Massé 1938: 10–11), no interest is evinced in the sex of the foetus, and no methods used to prophesy it. But this apparent absence of gender preference does not concord with their overall sex ratio (cf. Casimir and Rao 1995 for a brief discussion), nor with other demographic data collected. It is suggested that, at present, religious ideology acts as a barrier to conscious gender preferences and sex discrimination (but cf. Khan 1979: 105ff. for different observations among urban Indian Muslims). Even this may, however, change in years to come with increased schooling of Bakkarwal girls (cf. Das Gupta 1987: 95). Paradoxical as this may sound, the process of what I have termed "debackwardisation" (cf. Ch. 2) is, somewhat like Sanskritisation and Islamisation in other parts of India, already contributing to negative changes in the status of women and the value of girls. Fatima is a case in point. She was one of the very few Bakkarwal women to have attended primary school; as a result she considered herself less "backward" (*pasmandā*) than most of her relatives and neighbours. One day she told me:

> I didn't want any daughters – these days a girl is a burden – what shall one do with them? Even to marry them off you need money these days. I'm not that backward; when I marry my daughter I shall have to give her a dowry. If I've two daughters I have to get two dowries. And then only backward women work, so of what use is a girl?

Now to return to the twenty-one women who wanted more children, the reasons they gave were of four kinds: either, and this was the case with those desiring sons, they mentioned economic requirements (six cases), and more specifically herding labour; or, when they wanted daughters, they said they wanted someone to take care of them, to talk to them, to keep them company (four cases); ten women simply wanted more children, because they "liked children"; and finally one young woman said she wanted children as this was part of having sex, which she greatly enjoyed. The thirty-seven women who definitely did not want any more children also gave their reasons; here their own health considerations (weakness, menstrual problems, body pains) predominated (twenty cases), with general workload (nine) and poverty (eight) following. Incidentally, one unmarried girl who was present during one of these conversations volunteered the answer that she did not want any children at all, because she had seen the physical suffering of others during pregnancy and labour. One older woman told her that then her future husband would drive her out, while another advised her to "have one or two, but no more". While running parallel to the intense belief held by all that ultimately God grants children and takes care of them and the entire family, it appears that concepts of *mijāj, nafas* and *ōsh* discussed in earlier chapters, as well as perceived economic necessities and demographic constraints interact intimately to create contexts in which decisions regarding family and domestic affairs are embedded. Some aspects of these necessities and constraints which inform daily or seasonal discourse will be discussed in this chapter.

Regulating Reproduction

Sexual practice is a topic on which it is relatively hard to obtain more than anecdotal ethnographic information. It is standard knowledge that intercourse is allowed and resorted to anytime except during a woman's menses and at a late stage of pregnancy;

to have sex while menstruating is a sin not only for the woman but also for the man, and religious precepts (*yo sharo e, ādis e*) enjoin upon a woman to refuse her husband on these grounds. She sins if she does not, and if he nevertheless insists, he becomes the sinner. Either way the proverbial "seven generations [of theirs] will burn in hell" (*sat pīri saṛiygi, mardi[h]i jānum māñ*); in other words, these heinous sins of the parents are visited upon their offspring, who may be born blind or otherwise disabled and deformed.

Bakkarwal women (and possibly also men with whom I as a woman could never broach the topic) believe that sexual intercourse leads to pregnancy, the only normal exception being a nursing mother. The capacity for breast milk is first generated when a woman first conceives; it remains constant till she reaches menopause (cf. Ch. 6), when it starts to diminish, to cease completely at death. Occasionally old women well past their menopause were observed giving their breast to a whining grandchild, and although only a few drops seemed to flow, it was enough to pacify the child in its mother's absence (cf. Krengel 1989: 42 for a similar observation in the Kumaon Himalayas). This is especially resorted to with recently weaned children, whose mothers are again pregnant. Breast milk itself is regenerated through the basic capacity each time a baby is born. The connection between and interconvertibility of milk and blood discussed in Chapter 1 (cf. Rao forthcoming) also explains why a woman can not become pregnant as long as she nurses her child regularly. This contraceptive effect of suckling, widely known in northern India, is explained here by the principle that a woman's "blood does not come as long as she is giving her breast"; in other words, she does not menstruate regularly as long as she is breast-feeding (*čuča deṇāñ*). This is because her strength (*tākat*), normally manifested through menstrual blood, goes into the milk (*duñd māñ jāwe*), and "what is then left for the blood (*te ōr ke bače rat vāste*)?" This concept is in keeping with traditional Islamic medical views wherein "... breast milk [is] formed from the menstrual blood which was not shed during pregnancy" (Gil'adi 1992: 25). Thus I was often told that a woman who is three to four months pregnant should no longer breast-feed her previous baby; the milk thus saved will turn into blood (*rat baṇ jāe*). If she does not abstain from nursing, she will not have enough "good blood", and the placenta (*jēṛ*), whose function it is in both humans and animals to "absorb the bad blood" – i.e. the poison in the blood – will have no recourse but to release this "bad blood" into the womb and kill the child.

Indeed in societies where breast-feeding is on free demand – and this is the case among the Bakkarwal – the frequent stimulation of the mother's nipple has been observed to delay the onset of renewed menstruation (Spielmann 1989: 329). Data gathered among forty-one Bakkarwal women, with a total of eighty-four births indicate, however, that for reasons I can not yet explain regular breast-feeding did not, in most cases, lead to prolonged post-partum amenorrhoea (see Fig. 4.2). Most of these women nursed their babies for between eighteen and thirty-two months; for the majority the renewed onset of menses followed in the first fifteen months after delivery. Further, as shown in Figure 4.3, forty-three out of sixty (71.6 per cent) women conceived once again while nursing their last child, and continued breast feeding for a maximum of five months after renewed conception. Seventeen women (28.3 per cent) had already stopped nursing (minimum one month earlier, maximum twenty-one months earlier) before becoming pregnant once again. All these data were obtained by asking women to recollect how long they had nursed, when after delivery they had "again started bleeding", and whether they were still nursing when they conceived again. Most data relate to the last two or three children of a woman, or alternatively, with an older woman, to her first two or three, as most women did not remember such details about the children born or conceived in between. The themes about which these data were collected systematically are those that preoccupy Bakkarwal women and recur in their own conversation. The discrepancy between the principle – projected as a reality into the idealised past – and the reality today is of concern to many.

Pregnancy, menstruation or the absence of it, as well as nursing and weaning are, not surprisingly, subjects which preoccupy Bakkarwal women a great deal. Young mothers are often asked by others whether they are "already bleeding again" and advice is often given on how to prolong eventual amenorrhoea, as this will then delay the next pregnancy. Older women often narrate that whereas formerly one did not usually become pregnant as long as one was nursing a child, nowadays things are different. "Nowadays", grumbled old Bakhti, young women have "one child at the breast and

Figure 4.2 The nursing span and the onset of the next menses among forty-one women with a total of eighty-four births

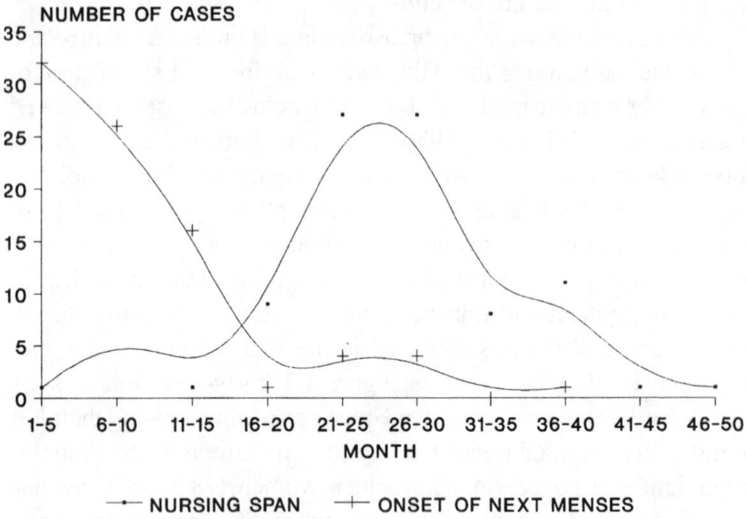

Figure 4.3 The relation between the end of nursing and the start of the next pregnancy among sixty women

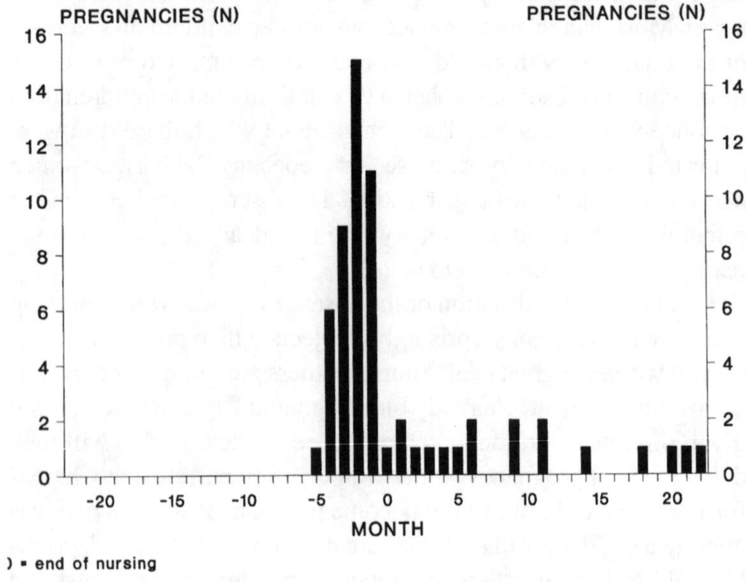

Figure 4.4 Interval (in months) between consecutive births in sixty-four cases

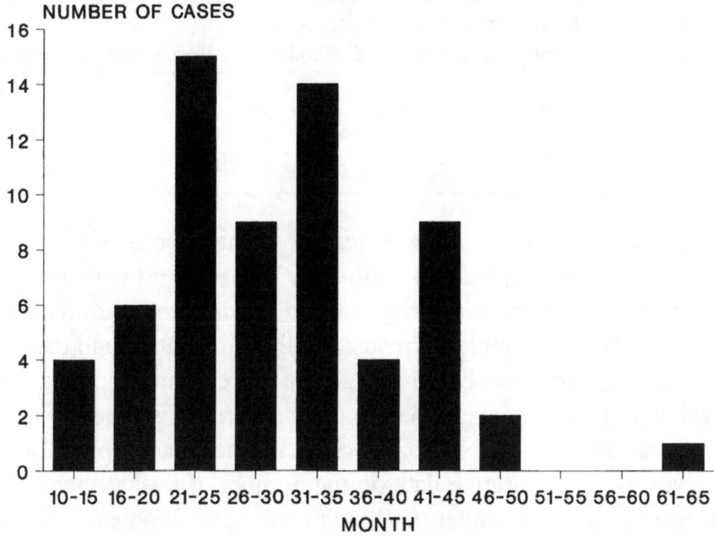

the other in the tummy". The reasons for this are numerous and rather diffuse; but they can all be linked to the increase in "heat" in everything, which in its turn is related to the increasing wickedness of the world. The general increase in heat has led to an increase in the frequency of pregnancies (cf. Ch. 1), and also to an increase in miscarriages. Data gathered on birth intervals are illustrated in Figure 4.4, which shows that while siblings can be separated by a gap of only ten to fifteen months, most (59.37 per cent – thirty-eight of sixty-four cases) have a gap of twenty-one to thirty-five months between them.

One result of frequent and hence excessive pregnancies is said to be that miscarriages (*kaččā baččā*, lit. "raw child") and stillbirths (*pičhāñvāñ*) are much more frequent today than they used to be. The quantitative recollection data gathered from 152 women are, however, at variance with this view. In this sample there are thirty-four women of various ages who had completed the fecund spans of their lives, the rest, between fifteen and forty-nine years, still being fecund. The thirty-four women aged ≥50 years had had a total of 288 conceptions, the rest having between them 405 conceptions. Contrary perhaps to all demographic logic, it was considered

Table 4.1 Comparison of the variation in perinatal mortality between women ≤49 and ≥50, with a total of 693 conceptions

Age Category	No. of Women	No. of Conceptions	Miscarriages & Stillbirths	Miscarriages	Stillbirths
≤49	118	405	37	25	12
≥50	34	288	41	28	13

meaningful to take the younger, fecund women into account while reviewing miscarriages and stillbirths. When an old woman says "now there are more miscarriages, or stillbirths", she is thinking of her neighbours, relatives, friends and their daughters and daughters-in-law, irrespective of their ages; in this cognitive context it is irrelevant to the speaker whether the woman she is thinking of is nineteen or fifty-nine. Not so, of course for the demographer. Table 4.1 sets out comparative data on the number of miscarriages and stillbirths among younger (≤49) and older (≥50) women. Since in Bakkarwali a terminological distinction is made between miscarriages and stillbirths, information on these two phenomena is set forth separately. Bakkarwal women are probably as little aware of very early miscarriages (up to about three months) as are women in other societies, and thus eventual miscarriages in this stage could not be taken into account. Indeed, I was told that one can be really sure of being pregnant only when one has missed two consecutive monthly periods. Table 4.1 indicates that the number of miscarriages has not increased among younger women, and perinatal mortality has indeed even decreased over the years, but no conclusive results can be presented.

Miscarriages may, however, be induced. Basically, Islam forbids abortions, but exceptions may be made up to a period of three months. Bakkarwal women abort very rarely, and when they do so it is interpreted as bringing on menstruation, and hence not considered sinful. Since a woman is considered pregnant only after she has missed two consecutive periods, any measures taken after missing only one menstrual cycle are not considered abortive. This two-month period is also the time in which the liquid element, *nafas*, first begins to "flow into the child", and it is only at the end of this phase that a child's existence in the womb is recognised.

This is in keeping both with Aristotelian tradition, where the spirit is said to enter the foetus between forty and ninety days (for males and females respectively) after conception, as well as with contemporary notions in parts of western Asia (e.g. Nicolas 1972: 47 for Bergama, where abortions are permitted within fifty days). To induce a woman to bleed and hence abort, hot sugared milk (in which the tiny seeds of *āḷu* (cf. Pnj. *hālõñ*) a kind of cress (*Cardamine macrophylla*) are boiled) is administered to her. This "makes her hot", engenders "excess blood" and brings on menstruation. Each time a woman is to be "made hot", i.e. should bleed, or is in labour, this cress is used in the entire region, not only by the Bakkarwal but also by rural Kashmiri sedentists who cultivate it in small amounts in the upper valleys.

One reason for the decline in perinatal mortality discussed earlier could be the increased access to medical facilities, at least at certain times of the year. This access in turn also appears to have contributed to the development of the idea of eventually regulating the number and spacing of children by means unknown earlier. Most Bakkarwal women I met were aware that they could be sterilised (*āpreshan*) if they so desired. But they were understandably frightened of such an operation; many knew of other women who had undergone sterilisation, and the general view seemed to be, "it suits some, but not others – it's a question of temperament (*mijāj*)". Some of the younger women were also aware of other methods of family planning available, but this knowledge could not always be translated into meaningful action, since acknowledged decision making even at this level could be in the hands of others. Nazira's is a case in point:

> Nazira has already had five children, of whom one died. One day she starts on the topic of family planning, in the presence of her husband and his mother. They all agree that the couple – they are both literate – does not want any more children. Both women are afraid of an operation, although Nazira's husband has told them that "it's only a small thing". Nazira's HyBW Shida has one baby and has started on the contraceptive pill with her husband's consent. Shida's father is literate, and her husband has frequent contact with urban folk, and yet she undergoes no regular medical check-ups. Nazira says that once she "tried Shida's pills", and now wants me to bring her some more from the town: "But don't give them to *Hājī*", she says, referring to her father-in-law; "he doesn't know about either Shida or me, and will be

very angry." Later she tells me that I should not give them either to her mother-in-law or to her brother-in-law, since she would feel "shy to take them from them"; I could, however, give them to her own husband. This case testifies to a young woman trying to take decisions and even implement them by a combination of secrecy *vis-à-vis* those in real authority (her father-in-law) and attempts to take into confidence others of only slightly less subaltern status than herself (her husband and mother-in-law). Although I appreciated Nazira's attempts at asserting her freedom, I felt I could not take the responsibility of getting her contraceptive pills (which are available without prescription) without her being examined by a gynaecologist. Since I could not convince her of this, I got her no pills.

"Having Another in One"

Pregnancy is in a way a state of ill health. Generally known as *bimāri* (sickness), but more specifically, as "in [a state of] someone with another in her" (*aur nāḷ māñ*, cf. Ur. *dujān*, lit. "two lives/bodies"), the idea of illness is implicit, and most women complain of giddiness (*čakkar*), nausea (*kē āṇā*), extreme backache (*lak māñ darad*) and general weakness (*kamjori*, cf. also Casimir 1991: 211). But it is not considered proper for a poor and in addition nomad (*khānābadosh*) woman to complain; it is both shameful and pointless, since "it's all part of a woman's life".

Most women are eighteen years old (± 3.2, N = 96) when they first conceive. In the early stages a woman speaks openly about her pregnancy only to her mother and elder sisters, or, if she lives with them, to her husband's brothers' wives, and to his mother or married sisters if she has a warm relationship with them. She does not mention it to her husband, especially not if they are a recently married couple. He learns about it either explicitly from his elder sister-in-law or mother or elder sister, or implicitly since his wife no longer observes her monthly menstrual taboos relating to domestic chores and cohabitation. Sometime during the third or fourth month of pregnancy, she pays a formal visit to her parents and stays there for anywhere between one week and one month. The length of her stay depends on various things, such as the distance between the parental and marital homes, the frequency and duration of her previous visits, the degree to which her labour in the marital home is indispensable, her relations with her husband and mother-in-law, etc. Generally, however, at her first pregnancy she stays a full month, the length of her stay decreasing with every subsequent pregnancy. However long her stay may have been, on her return to her marital home, her parents give her several presents to take back. Among well-to-do families these can include a lamb or kid, among others, clothes and money for herself. No other ceremonies mark a pregnancy, but all pregnant women, and especially younger ones, observe numerous precautions to protect the foetus (lit. "child in the tummy", *pēṭ māñ baččā*) and themselves from various evil influences.

As mentioned earlier, a woman three or four months pregnant weans the child she has been nursing; this is done at one go and the child is now given goat's milk with some molasses (*guṛ*) dissolved in it. To prevent pain, bleeding and an eventual miscarriage, dried dandelion leaves (*and*, *Taraxacum spec.*) are boiled and eaten at least once every month. Certain dietary restrictions are also maintained quite strictly, following the basic regional principle that specific disproportions in the consumption of "hot" or "cold", "sour" or "sweet" foods will lead to imbalances and hence illness. Chillies (*mirči*) and buttermilk (*lassi*) are avoided as being respectively too hot and sour; the former would create too much heat within her, the latter too much cold. Excessive heat could lead to an excess of blood in her body and hence to bleeding; it would also arouse in her passion, making sexual abstention difficult for her. Excessive cold, on the other hand, would lead to debility. Sweet substances are good for her, for they satiate; salt is less benign, for it creates thirst, cravings and heat, which in turn can lead to swellings in various parts of the body. Sweet substances always fill and fulfil, and hence sweet tea, rather than the more commonly imbibed salt tea (Casimir 1991: 205), is drunk during migration. The theme of sweet versus savoury recurs often as a symbol of saturation versus craving (cf. Ch. 3). At this point in life any disproportion in the qualities of foodstuffs should if at all tend towards sweetness, all other qualities being kept at a minimum. An ideal food for the pregnant woman, and one administered to her at least twice a month, is made of flour (*āṭo*), turned in clarified butter with sugar (*khanḍ*) and cinnamon (*dalčini*). The sugar satiates, the fat "strengthens", the flour "nourishes", and the cinnamon "protects, pleases and heals" her.

The carelessness of a pregnant woman can have grave consequences for her baby. This is specially so during eclipses, which are periods of general danger. In the first-ever eclipse *Garo* (cf. *graha* below), who shares a father with the two real brothers *Čan* (moon) and *Din* (sun), gobbled up (*nawaḷ lio*) the latter, and the sky (*āsmān*) grew red (*ratto*) with their blood. With every new eclipse, this fratricide is re-enacted. This story is probably one of many versions of the Hindu myth of the planet (Skt. *graha*) *Rāhu*, the colour red perhaps signifying a warning of an impending bloody battle (Gurumurthy 1981: 349). Hindus in India neither cook nor eat during an eclipse; the Bakkarwal light no fire at this time (*gaṛi*). If a pregnant woman ignores these prohibitions and puts bread to bake on the usual iron griddle pan (*trokhṛa*), her child will be born with the red stamp of *Garo*'s five fingers (*hath*) on its chest, "for *Garo* would want to make it his own inheritor (*wāris*)". This birthmark (*čangarlē* – lit. "seized by the moon", cf. Hd. *čandragrahaṇ* and Kashmiri *grōn*) results from the violation of a principle noted in a wide region, and Massé (1938: 843) reports of Iran that "if a pregnant woman touches herself during an eclipse of the sun or the moon, the corresponding spot on the body of her child will have a dark spot". Another widespread concept also shared by the Bakkarwal is that during an eclipse a pregnant woman should touch no metal object. If she uses a knife to cut a radish the child will be born with only one nostril; were she to cut a potato the baby would have a cleft chin. Among Kashmiri Hindus cutting a potato in this period would make the baby harelipped; indeed, "… a pregnant woman should not see an eclipse nor do any work during its duration, or else her child may be born malformed" (Madan 1989a: 65–6). This fits in with the general concept noted by Crooke (1896: I, 22; cf. also Lapoint 1981: 337) in his compendium on South Asian folklore:

> A pregnant woman will do no work during an eclipse, as otherwise she believes that her child would be deformed, and the deformity is supposed to bear some relation to the work which is being done by her at the time. Thus, if she were to sew anything, the baby would have a hole in its flesh, generally near the ear; if she cut anything, the child would have a harelip.

BRINGING INTO THE WORLD Unlike in many South Asian societies, where especially young women usually give birth in their parents' homes (Jeffery et al. 1985: 19), first births among the Bakkarwal

Figure 4.5 Percentage of births in 105 cases according to place of delivery

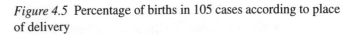

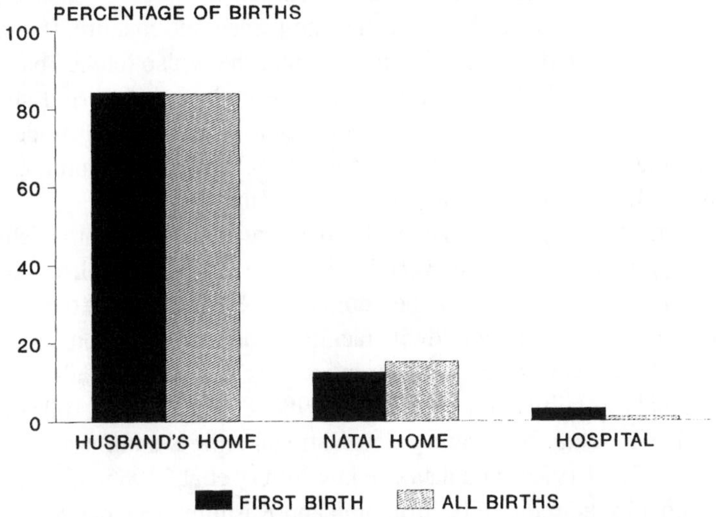

ideally take place in the husband's home. Of thirty-two reported first births 80 per cent were found to have taken place in the conjugal home, and again 80 per cent of 105 births (N = 34 women) also took place in the conjugal home, irrespective of the order of birth (see Fig. 4.5). Later births can, reportedly, take place even during migration or in other circumstances where little midwife help is available, for "an older woman delivers (*lōs ōe*) where she is". Strictly speaking, all the married women present at a woman's wedding have both the obligation and the right to help her deliver, but in reality very few women are present. Sometimes, especially for a first delivery, the woman's mother comes and spends a few days with her.

After at least forty days the couple and their child – or mother and child – visit her parents; the duration of her stay with them depends on the season, on the distance between the two home, etc. She and her infant now receive gifts from her parents, as she had when she visited them during her pregnancy. If the birth takes place in the woman's natal home, her mother now also performs a ceremony to offer thanks to God for His bountifulness and to pray for the couple's continued fecundity. I never witnessed the ceremony but was told that a he-goat or a ram is made to urinate in a pot which is buried in the earth. The idea of male urine as a fertilising agent is also met with in northern Pakistan and Nuristan (Snoy 1962: 160–1), and once again one encounters the analogy between the womb and the earth, between urine-semen and manure. If and when a woman delivers in her natal home, she is also fetched back by her husband after forty days. At the end of this period she becomes *ari* (cf. Hd./Pnj. *āhāri*, "the eater"), since she has undergone the rituals which make her clean (*pāk*) and enable commensality. She can now also start on a normal diet.

Parturition in general is considered a very real and potential danger to a woman's life, for very little can be done if complications arise. Most women feel that their nomadic lifestyle stands in the way of their obtaining better midwife facilities, and would welcome easy access to doctors in case of complications. The official all-India maternal mortality rate for the period 1980–87 was 340 per 100,000 live births (data from various international reports summarised in Ahooja-Patel 1993), and data cited by Jeffery et al. (1985: 15) indicate that in the mid-1970s in Jammu and Kashmir, 83.9 per cent of all births were attended to by "untrained personnel". By far the overwhelming majority of Bakkarwal deliveries are "natural ones", and only occasionally do women give birth in hospitals. One such case was that of Kāḷi, who died during my fieldwork in November 1984.

> In February 1983 Kāḷi had given birth to two girls by Caesarean section, but both died after one day. In November 1984 she was due to deliver again, and although the doctor had warned her that she would once again have to have a Caesarean, she "couldn't be taken to hospital, because there were other things to be attended to", as her grieving mother-in-law explained. She died in childbirth and the infant, again a daughter, died twenty days later.

This brings us back not only to the question of degrees of choice in terms of access to medical care, but also to that of the priorities which define such choice. The demands imposed by herding schedules constitute the temporal framework for daily and seasonal routines of work and leisure. Hence they are also crucial for what Hendricks and Peters (1986: 665) described as "… the individual consciousness … in the manufacture of time". Adult men are the manufacturers of time for all contexts beyond those of the domestic sphere, and thus eventual access to medical care operates almost exclusively via one's father, husband or older son. The importance of herding schedules struck me rather dramatically when I first met Bibo and Makhṇi on 18 April in the gynaecological ward of a Jammu hospital.

> Both had given birth a few days earlier – Bibo to her fourth child on 14 April, Makhṇi to her second son on 16 April. While Makhṇi's family was preparing to migrate to summer pastures (they left on the 20th), Bibo's had left on the 16th. The doctor in charge of the ward told me in a very matter-of-fact manner that both women "had gone mad temporarily", and would be kept in hospital for some more time. On my daily visits till the 25th, neither of them spoke a word; while Bibo simply stared into space, Makhṇi wept bitterly, but silently. I learnt from the nurses on duty that both women had been sterilised without having been explicitly asked. When they regained consciousness they were simply informed that they would not be able to conceive again. Bibo had been brought to hospital by her husband, but he had never again visited her; Makhṇi too had been admitted by her husband, and her mother-in-law and elder sister had come to see her a day after she had delivered. Since then no friend, no family member came – till sometime in June Makhṇi's husband's elder brother happened to come to Jammu and take her back with him to the high pastures. I met her again a few weeks later at her mother's camp; she had apparently told her family about my visits in the hospital, and her mother wept and praised me for my "kindness", but added "we *Bakarāḷ* can not afford to be so soft-hearted – for us first come our animals and then our children". Bibo was left in the hospital without any contact till the family returned to winter quarters in late October. When I met her in December she said: "You city people are soft-limbed and soft-hearted; we live in the wilderness and are tough in body, but also hard-hearted. There is no one harder than a *Bakarāḷ* – for good and for bad."

The most critical period for both mother and baby are the first five days after delivery. This applies to animals just as much as to humans. On many an occasion did I observe migration units split, with the healthy animals going off, and a part of the family staying behind for up to five days for a newly foaled mare and its young to recover. Newly delivered women may sometimes be seen riding rather than walking. But not every woman is taken care of for five days after each of her deliveries (cf. Jeffery et al. 1989: 164). If she is on migration, she may rest only for a day or two and then set off again. Twice I saw young women who had delivered three days and eight days earlier respectively walking slowly at the tail of their

Figure 4.6 The frequency of births according to month in 105 cases. See Appendix D for the names of the months.

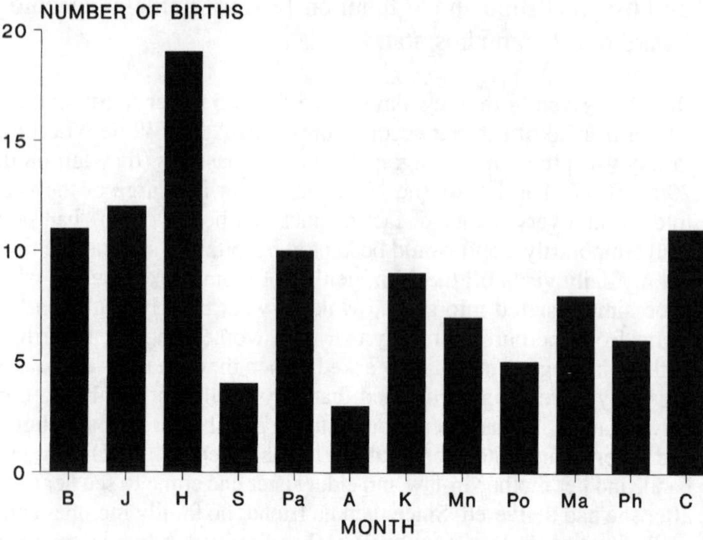

migrating group, their newborn infants fast asleep in a cloth sling on their sides. I was told that when a woman gives birth at critical moments during the spring or autumn migrations – for example, when fodder is in short supply, or weather is bad and the herd is in danger of depletion – "she must be left alone to fend for herself". I never saw or heard of any concrete case, and this reported violation of the more general norm that women are not be left alone can only be explained by the temporal imperatives of the pastoral economy, which in turn informs most decision making. Figure 4.6 shows that there is a very mild seasonality in human births, the peak period lying between mid-June and mid-July (the month of *hāṛ*).

The Bakkarwal share the concept widespread among South and West Asians that the mother's well-being is reasonably assured only after the sixth day following parturition, (e.g. Goodwin Raheja 1988: 96 for Hindus in India; Rao 1982: 203 for Afghanistan). The end of the first most dangerous five days is ideally marked by a small feast at which, after bathing and washing her hair for the first time, the mother joins her relatives and guests at a common meal of rice and meat. By now it is clear that the placenta (*jēṛ*) has been entirely expelled and the credit for this goes to the midwife.

Accordingly, on the preceding day she is sent a gift (*bakshish*) of new clothes (*līr*) and money, and is invited to the meal. If she lives too far away, these are given to her later. The cash paid varies between Rs. 25/- and Rs. 100/-, but does not depend on the infant's gender, as it does, for example, among Hindu Jats (Lewis 1958: 48).

Becoming a Parent

Socially for a man the birth of his first child signifies less than it does for a woman, and fatherhood is socially marked only through the increasing use of a tekonym. Indeed, it could be suggested that the specific father-child relationship is publicly perceived in a uniquely biological manner, the social and legal aspects of this relationship being transferred to the patriline. This uniqueness is symbolised in language. Whereas the reference terms for "mother", for maternal and paternal kin, for siblings and for children are applied to show respect and/or affection even beyond the pale of kinswomen and men, the terms of both reference (*peu, bāp*, *wālid*) and address (*abbā*) for "father" are reserved for the genitor. Motherhood, on the other hand, is marked socially much more explicitly. With the birth of her first child, the ritual cycle of a woman's wedding – symbolised by each of her visits (*bārā*) to her parents' home and her subsequent returns (*phēra*) to her husband – comes to an end. But at her first pregnancy and after each of her first few deliveries she visits her parents and receives gifts. When she has children, they too are given extra presents of clothing.

What is it like to be a Bakkarwal parent? The answers can naturally be of many kinds. I shall restrict myself here to the relationship between demographic constraints and certain parental emotions. Expected death, and high child mortality in particular, can, I suggest, seriously affect the perceived uniqueness of persons. Additionally, the latter certainly stands in the way of a parent's choosing between conceivable alternatives for his/her child.

Counting (on) Children

There is considerable controversy as to whether women in non-literate societies recall the number of children they have borne.

Older studies postulate that such data, were they available, would be unreliable. More recent studies suggest otherwise. Data from St. Barthélémy in the French West Indies (Brittain 1991) indicate clearly, for example, that here women are well able to remember the number of children they had borne, and Eickelman (1984: 22–23, 183) writes that in Oman:

> I … also discovered that when I asked women the number of children they had, they usually included their dead children…. To my question, "How many children do you have?" women of Hamra answered by telling me the number of times they gave birth to a live child, regardless of whether the child was still alive or not.

I was luckier still, since the Bakkarwal women I asked mentioned all their conceptions, including even the miscarriages they had had at a later stage in pregnancy. Whereas women could narrate a good deal about the infants of their brothers and sisters and husbands' brothers and sisters, with men I usually drew a blank on this topic. Below a certain age, I felt, children literally do not count for the menfolk. Most men did not even know how many little children their own brothers, living next-tents, had; their wives and sisters knew, regardless of whether they lived together with these families or not. Even the grief evinced by a father at the death of a small child of either gender is different from that when an older child dies.

> On 12 August 1984 Guḍi died. She was not quite three years old and had been suffering from a "bad cough and fever". The death took place early in the morning. The body was bathed and shrouded by her bitterly weeping mother, her fifteen-year-old elder sister and another woman relative and neighbour. The burial took place around 10 a.m. that day. All the men got together and took turns at digging the little grave. Guḍi's father, Bājā, sat silently nearby, looking on. After the burial, the others went home, but he stayed back and we started chatting. "God gave and God has taken away", he said, asking me if I had a match to light his cigarette. "So what's the use in one's pondering about it (*fikur karāñ*)? If one ponders too much one gets sick, and anyway, she was just a *jātak*. With an older child it's different, isn't it?"

It would be pointless to speculate on what Bājā and others like him really feel when one of their infants die. It could be that since men spend relatively little time with their infants, the attachment is less strong than it is to older children; this has been attested to in other societies (Gil'adi 1992: 91). But it is equally possible that in a society where high infant mortality is very much a reality, studied cautiousness is the better part of paternal love and hope. As Rajwali observed, when I asked him what he wanted his son to be when he grew up (cf. Awasty 1982: 62–63 for comparable data among sedentary herders and others in a winter area of the Bakkarwal):

> When a *Bakarāḷ* child is born, its parents' only wish is that it should survive and grow up and live on by whatever means. It's not as with other parents who say: "My son will be a *tehsīldār* [officer in charge of a *tehsīl*, an administrative unit], or this or that."

Although the problem of child mortality is certainly not as acute here (cf. Ch. 2 and below) as it is in many other societies, some of its effects are perhaps similar to what Scheper-Hughes (1989: 12) describes for the shantytowns of Brazil:

> Part of learning how to mother … is learning when to let go of a child who shows that it … has no "knack"… for life. Another part is learning when it is safe to let oneself love a child. Frequent child death remains a powerful shaper of maternal thinking and practice. In the absence of firm expectation that a child will survive, mother love … is attenuated and delayed with consequences for child survival.

The following bits of conversation with Zarina, a woman in her mid-thirties, convey some of the conflict that goes on in the minds of Bakkarwal mothers who have lost young children:

> "She's a black one (*kāḷi*)",* she said, referring to her only daughter, born two years earlier, during the spring migration of 1981. This daughter was known simply as Beṭki – "daughter" – and was the youngest of Zarina's seven surviving children. Beṭki had already survived much longer than her elder sister and Zarina's only other daughter, who had died "exactly fourteen months before Beṭki's birth". She had been "nearly three months old" and had died of "pneumonia". "It was a very cold winter; she died and so did many of our flocks", said Zarina simply. Did she sometimes think of her dead child, I asked. "Yes, sometimes I see her in my dreams, and then when I give my breast to Beṭki at night to put her to sleep, I think of the little one (*niki*). She used to cry a lot, but now God has taken her and she's quiet and happy, because she was innocent (*beguṇā*, lit. without sin)." Did Zarina worry about losing Beṭki or any of her other children? "May God have pity (*raam*)!" she replied, hugging

Beṭki close. "What's the use of worrying? It would be a sin (*guṇā*) to worry – it's all in God's hands."

* The use of the term black is often of apotropaic value.

Six months after this conversation Zarina lost another child – the five-year-old Shādi, her youngest son. He fell from the string bed they used to sun themselves on in the winter camp. Medical facilities were not close at hand, and besides it was right in the middle of the peak lambing period, so "one did not have time to take Shādi to the Doctor", his father explained when I met him again the following winter. Again subsistence priorities outweighed all others; publicly set by Shādi's father, they appeared to be entirely accepted by his mother as well. Zarina's tears flowed as she brought home to me the crucial connection between availability of labour and decision making in every sphere of pastoral life:

> ... there was no one who could have taken him to the doctor – his father was with the nanny goats, Jia (Shādi's FyB) was with the ewes, I myself had to look after the lambs and kids – there was no one I could have sent to call someone. If I had gone myself, the jackal could have eaten them all up ...

Though lower than the all-India figure of 98 per 1,000 live births in 1988 (Ahooja-Patel 1993), child mortality in Jammu and Kashmir is quite high, and varied between 71, 69 and 70 respectively for the years 1988, 1989 and 1990 (provisional figures, Sample Registration System 1990). In the rural areas of the region neonatal mortality rose from 37.0 in 1970–72 to 44.9 in 1976–78, and accounted for 45.1 per cent and 60.7 per cent respectively of all infant mortality rates here in this period (Visaria 1988: 98–99). Intrauterine and perinatal mortality among the Bakkarwal, i.e. foetal deaths in the first couple of months of pregnancy or shortly before or at delivery were discussed in Chapter 2. Table 4.2 sets out two separate sets of data on mortality in the early years of childhood.

The first sample was recorded by me during fieldwork; the second was taken from the official but unpublished Government of India Census schedules of 1981. Whereas in the first sample the age at death was recorded, this is not so for the second sample; thus the two data sets are only partially comparable. In my sample 40 out of 115 mothers (34.78 per cent) had lost at least one child

Table 4.2 Comparison of two sets of data on mortality

	Mothers			Bereaved Mothers		
	N	44≥	≤45	N	44≥	≤45
Sample 1	. 115	93	22	40	18	22
Sample 2	36	24	12	17	8	9

at some point of time after birth; 22 (55.0 per cent) of these bereaved mothers – and 61.11 per cent of all the women in the sample – had attained menopause. In the unpublished Government Census sample 47.22 per cent (17 of 36) mothers reported loss of offspring. These 36 women had between them borne 177 live children, which gives an average of 4.92 (± 2.64) children per woman. There is, however, an as yet inexplicable male bias in the number of children born alive: 105 boys (59.32 per cent or an average of 2.92 ± 1.79) and 72 girls (40.70 per cent or an average of 2.00 ± 1.37). Of all the children born, 35 (19.77 per cent) died, i.e. an average of 0.97 ± 1.38. Here the gender proportion is not unusual: 18 males (51.43 per cent) with on average 0.50 (± 0.77) and 17 females (48.57 per cent), i.e. on average 0.47 (± 0.81). Twelve (33.33 per cent) women in this Government Census sample were forty-five years or above, and could thus be expected to have reached the end of the fertile period of their lives. Between them they had 83 live births, of which 20 (24.10 per cent) died subsequently. This gives an average live birth of 6.92 (± 2.50) and an average child loss of 1.66 (± 1.72) per woman. Tables 4.3a and 4.3b set out some details of the official Census sample. Table 4.3a deals with the entire sample of 36 women, whereas Table 4.3b is limited to subsample data on women of forty-five years and above. Gender-specific mortality in both cases is reasonably similar; for the entire sample average male deaths were 0.50 (± 0.77) and female deaths were 0.47 (± 0.81), whereas in the subsample averages were 0.92 (± 0.79) and 0.75 (± 1.21) respectively.

In my own sample the forty women had among them borne 277 live children (153 sons and 124 daughters), i.e. an average of 6.97 children per woman (± 2.64). Of these 277 children born, 88 (31.8 per cent) had died during the lifetime of their respective mothers;

Table 4.3a Mortality of offspring reported by thirty-six women of various ages in a sample of the un-published Government of India Census, 1981

Children Born Alive			**Males Born Alive**			**Females Born Alive**			**Children Died**				
N	$\bar{X}$	SD	N	$\bar{X}$	SD	N	$\bar{X}$	SD	N	$\bar{X}$	SD	M	F
177	4.92	2.64	105	2.92	1.79	72	2.00	1.37	35	0.97	1.38	18	17

Table 4.3b Mortality of offspring reported by twelve women aged forty-five and above in a sample of the unpublished Government of India Census, 1981

Children Born Alive			**Males Born Alive**			**Females Born Alive**			**Children Died**				
N	$\bar{X}$	SD	N	$\bar{X}$	SD	N	$\bar{X}$	SD	N	$\bar{X}$	SD	M	F
83	6.92	2.50	52	4.33	1.30	31	2.58	1.68	20	1.66	1.72	11	9

Table 4.4 Percentage completeness of registration of infant deaths

Age Group	**Rural** **Males**	**Rural** **Females**	**Urban** **Males**	**Urban** **Females**
Less than 1 week	18	17	40	39
1 week to 1 month	24	20	36	31
1 month to 6 months	30	26	50	45
6 months and over	46	36	59	47
Under 1 year	27	24	45	41

Note: From Registrar General, India, Sample Registration System, 1980.

half of these (44) were sons. Table 4.5 gives the breakdown of these deaths according to age and gender. It shows that for both sons and daughters by far the largest number of deaths (68) took place in the age group birth (O years) to roughly five years. In this age group there was little gender-specific difference, the slightly higher value for boys (39) being corroborative of the universal tendency, also noted in India. The following table (Table 4.4) is cited in Desai and Krishnaraj (1987: 225) and has been interpreted by them as representing not only the reported data, but also actual mortality patterns.

Table 4.5 Age and gender-wise breakdown of mortality

Age Category	Deaths N=m+f	% of All b/d	Deaths N (m)	% of All b/d	Deaths N (f)	% of All b/d
0–5*	68	24.5/77.2	39	14.0/44.3	29	10.5/32.9
0–1**	54	12.2/61.4	29	10.5/32.9	25	9.0/28.4
2–5	14	12.2/15.9	10	3.6/11.3	4	1.4/ 4.5
6–15	8	2.9/ 9.0	1	0.3/ 1.1	7	2.5/ 7.9
16–40	12	4.3/13.6	4	1.4/ 4.5	8	2.9/ 9.0

Note: b = births; d = deaths. See Figure 2.3.
*Each of 22 women lost sons or daughters up to age five years.
**Up to age one year, 17 women lost sons and 18 women lost daughters.

Since the maximum number of deaths among the Bakkarwal took place in this first category it has been further broken down into two subcategories (0–1 and 2–5 years). It is in the next age category (6–15 years) that gender-specific differences, based on cultural manipulation, are evident. These data corroborate the general Indian trend whereby for females the "sex ratio becomes increasingly adverse with rise in age" (Desai and Krishnaraj 1987: 225). For the last category, the sample is too small to speculate on the eventual effects of childbearing on the values for women's mortality.

In an interesting article on age and gender preferences among Iranian parents, Vieille (1967: 121) observed that only theoretically, in keeping with Islamic injunctions, is

> … the idea of choice … strongly rejected. The concept of equality of beings, and especially equality in death, the concept of equality in grief provoked by the death of children of whatever age, is strictly opposed to such an admission…. But this is only a question of a ritual assertion, in a very stereotyped form …

Though Muslims, the Bakkarwal openly have preferences. I believe Kima echoed the sentiments of most fathers when he said: "Formerly the child who looked after the animals best was his parents' favourite. Now also it is the same among most. But among some it is the child who studies." Gender preferences are rarely if ever openly expressed, but data on child mortality as well as those on various age groups illustrated in Figure 6.1 seem to point to the neglect of daughters (Casimir and Rao 1992: 282–3). The perhaps subconscious choice involved in the neglect is rationalised, and Janti's explanation of why she could not give her breast to Rafie, the twin sister of Yusuf, sounded logical enough: "I could not give my breast to both, so I gave [it] to Yusuf. Rafie got goat's milk and those days *Hāji*'s mother (her husband's aged mother) was still alive so she also gave Rafie her breast." Rafie is lucky to have survived as well as Yusuf has. Incidentally, Janti had earlier borne two male twins, and remembered having given her breast to only one of them. Both sons survived, and both are long-married men; the one she gave her breast to still lives with her, whereas the other one has formed his "separate household". The former is known as a bully, the latter as kind and thoughtful, and neighbours impute the differences in character between the two brothers largely to the "different milk they drank".

In Bakkarwal society the framework for all relations – and thus for relative autonomy between groups and individuals – is provided primarily by the domestic group, or "household". A Bakkarwal household's very right to exist – as well as its need to do so – is based on two components: children and herd animals. While discussing the structure and organisation of the domestic group, I shall thus also briefly touch upon certain aspects of herding.

The Incipient Herder-Householder

Mobile pastoralism requires great flexibility. It entails a great deal of on-the-spot decision making by each husbander, but it also requires intense cooperation between herd owners. As Goldschmidt (1979: 20) expressed it, mobile pastoralism represents "… a flexible social order capable of providing mutual protection while preserving individual autonomy". In other words, nomadic pastoral life is a continuous oscillation between relative isolation – especially marked in the summer terrain of the Bakkarwal, which enforces and sustains greater autonomy – and cooperation and collective activity, particularly visible during the biannual migrations of spring (*bāñdh*) and autumn (*shard*) – which is essential as a buffer against the great risks every herder is exposed to. At the long-term social level risk may be minimised through the right marriage alliances (cf. Chapter 3). At the economic and political levels risk is negotiated through the right networks and the right clientele (cf. Ch. 5). At the daily level risk is managed through domestic and herding labour. Moral responsibility and trust represent the two essential components of practice at all these long-term and immediate levels. On the ideological plane independence and cooperation emanate equally from one's innate nature, and the ideal striven towards should be a balance between the two. This balance, an expression of one's well-being, is hard to achieve – once again those credited with well-being are also said to have struck this balance.

At least since the first decades of this century Bakkarwal economy has been market orientated. The mainstay has been the sale or exchange of animals on the hoof, goat hair (*jaṭ*) and to some extent sheep's wool. As among all pastoral populations (e.g. Glatzer and Casimir 1983; Beck and Klute 1991) here too herd size and hence well-being are intimately connected to labour availability and input: "The more hands (*bandā*) a man has to look after his herds the richer he is." The richer he is, the greater his political influence both within the community and beyond (cf. Ch. 5). Such a man also has better, or at least more frequent, access to State veterinary services than does a poorer, less important herder (Rao 1992a: 106). As Gama observed:

> Those who have enough labour to go and report illness get the medicines; those who have few working hands can not go and so get nothing. In the office they know the rich; they know they can not afford to ignore their request for medicine.

A rich man is thus likely to remain so even in the face of epidemics, hailstorms or other pastoral crises.

Access to all principal resources is acquired, managed and lost by individual domestic groups. As a rule herds are owned by *kaṇṇi ḍērā* – which for lack of a more precise term I shall have to gloss as "independent households" – and each such household obtains and processes milk separately. Ideally a man may not sell his wife's animals or their progeny without her permission. But

> if a marriage is good and not very new, a husband basically does what he likes with his wife's animals [and] unlike the peasant (*zamindār*) women in [the] winter [area] who graze theirs separately, among us a husband grazes his wife's animals for her.

Beyond a two-generational extended family there are usually neither common grazing areas nor joint herding units, but occasionally more distantly related families may, in summer, build a common herd (*ghalā karāñ*; cf. Pnj. *ghala mala* = counsel for helping one another, Maya Singh 1972: 378), provided that each of them has less than about seventy animals, and the relationship between them all is very warm. Herd animals are obtained through

- male inheritance (anticipatory or otherwise) and among the wealthy female dowry;
- at weddings as part of bridewealth or as gifts brought by guests to the young couple;
- as dower to a divorcée;
- as part of the salary of a hired shepherd.

While access to water is generally unrestricted in the summer area with its ubiquitous streams, in winter water rights with their surrounding salt-lick areas are mainly leased from the State or from peasants. Access to pasture obtains through inheritance, marriage, employment, exchange, borrowing, purchase, lease or usurpation (Rao 1992a). Though the lease and sale of pasture is not officially recognised by the State, it is de facto tolerated. Two broad categories of pasture space are distinguished within the community, and elsewhere (Rao 1992a) I have referred to these as "directly productive" and "indirectly productive" spaces. Both sets are situated in what is broadly termed *jangal* (lit. "forest", but in keeping with wider South Asian tradition, the "wilderness" or any area which does not include fixed and permanent settlements of villages or towns). The overall term denoting both types of space is *jā* or *jū* (lit. "place"), but when referring more specifically to the former, the terms *čhēṛ* (cf. Pnj. *čhera* = a herdsman, Maya Singh 1972: 222) and *pathrā* are used in summer and winter respectively. Directly productive space consists of grazing and browsing areas, sources of water and salt-lick areas, while indirectly productive space includes camp-sites for families, resting sites at night, locations yielding fuel and eventually wild plant foods or any materials such as wood, reeds, etc., required for the construction of temporary dwellings or household equipment. Known as *kāṛ*, this is where mostly milch animals "sit and sleep" rather than graze or browse; it is also here that the family camps. While long-term rights of appropriation are recognised for the directly productive spaces, or parts thereof, they are not for the indirectly productive ones, unless permanent dwellings have been constructed in it. Every herd owner has a right to at least one productive space (*čhēṛ/pathrā*) of his own in summer, and this right is transmitted intergenerationally along the male line.

Since daughters usually shift residence at marriage, and since "they can't take a *čhēṛ* with them", women do not have pasture rights. A daughter's son or an only daughter's husband can, however, obtain pasture rights if he is adopted as heir (*wāris*). Normally, when the paternal herd is divided, so also are the *čhēṛ/pathrā*, both these divisions being termed *mā* (cf. Skt. *mā* = "to measure, mark off"), with the proportion of pasture depending on the number of animals the father has at the time. In principle, all sons should inherit an equal share of the paternal herd. In reality, if the sons are unequal in strength and influence, as they often are, influential men of the community intervene and settle the matter in such a manner that the strongest son gets the largest share, and they themselves get their cuts. The Bakkarwal comment on this practice by using the commonly heard North Indian proverb "he who has the stick (also) has the buffalo" (*jis ki lāṭhi us ki bhaiñs*). If, however, the sons are on good terms, they may keep their herds together and use parts of a common pasture; although no territorial markings (*nishāṇā*) are then used, each is well aware of his own territory. Rights to pasture include not only complete and exclusive rights of access, but also a set of well-defined rights of obtaining, maintaining and losing access. One maintains a *čhēṛ/pathrā* by having a large enough herd, enough male labour and the concomitant of these, namely enough political clout within the community. Access is lost principally through conflict with more powerful competitors, State intervention and the loss of too many animals resulting in short-term or long-term abandonment or sale.

The ḍērā

Generally, a newly married Bakkarwal couple lives with the husband's father and his nuclear family, provided the latter is alive and has enough animals and pasture. Living together may not always involve sharing the same tent, although if the dwelling is a hut it is shared for at least part of the year, or alternatively for at least part of the day. But living together does mean cooking together over the same fire for at least part of the year and budgeting together in all respects throughout the year. One speaks in such instances of the father's *ḍērā* – not the son's – whereby the *ḍērā* is viewed by all as a single unit in all socio-economic transactions with non-members. The factor of commensality is also crucial in the definition used by the Government Census of the term "household", namely the unit of persons who regularly ate together in the period of counting, i.e. in the winter months. In the early span of his married life a young man when referring specifically to his wife, their children and their personal clothes, bedding and utensils will use the term *ṭabbar* (Rao 1988a: 212–4). As opposed to the use of the term in Kangra (Parry 1979: 157) or Panjab (among Jat villagers, Kessinger 1979: 43–44), here the term *ṭabbar* can be glossed as an almost always incomplete nuclear family (cf. Eglar 1960: 75; Jettmar 1961: 84). Through eventually polygynous marriages, as well as through the marriages of the offspring of the *ṭabbar*-head, a *ṭabbar* can and usually is transformed into a *ḍērā*. Figure 4.7 illustrates the different types of domestic units eventually formed in different phases of a person's life span.

These domestic units, and indeed the very concept of "living together", are imbued with a certain inconstancy, which is the outcome of seasonal migration and of sets of summer pastures and winter grazing areas often being non-contiguously distributed over a large area (Casimir and Rao 1985; Rao 1992a). The greater a family's well-being, the more this flux, since the more numerous its herds and the larger the number of grazing or browsing areas it requires. When members of one *ḍērā* simultaneously use two or more pastures in summer or grazing areas in winter, they are parted temporarily; while the milch animals remain with most of the family in the lower summer pasture, the dry animals are taken by some of the younger men to graze at higher altitudes, sometimes almost

Figure 4.7 The sequential development of domestic groups according to gender and age. ME = menarche, MA = first marriage, P = first pregnancy, MP = menopause. The hatching indicates the time span between the earliest and the latest occurrences. The terms *ṭabbar*, *ḍērā* and *kumbā* are explained in the text.

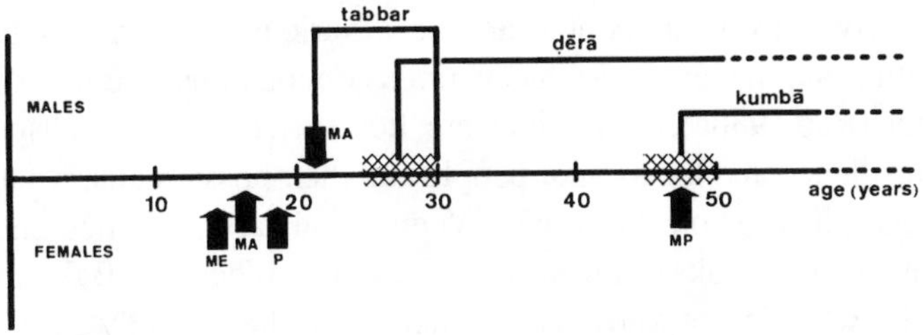

a week's journey away. Similarly in winter, the various herd and pack animals can be grazed in different forest "compartments" spread over a wide area, and different *ḍērā* members in charge of each of these units can be separated by a day's walk. Splits also occur during migration, when during the day only the men and animals of several *ḍērā* join together, separating from their respective families to follow time-honoured routes (*rāsto*) of travel. At night, however, each family gets together and camps on its own, close to other similar families. At different times of the year a *ḍērā* can therefore split into cooking, eating, sleeping and walking units, and is thus comparable to one aspect of the term "domestic group" as used by Ingold (1986: 176):

> In all human societies for the majority of individuals during most of their lives, habitations are not just places at which they stop to cook, eat and sleep. They do, nearly always, in the company of others, who together compose a micro-community that we call the domestic group.... When we plot the space-time trajectories of these persons, we find that they form a bundle whose various strands may tend to separate during periods of motion, but which converge, over and over again, during periods of rest.

But *ḍērā* also denotes nuclear and extended family or kin-group and may, at times, even extend to cover all material belongings, including herd animals, and especially milch animals. It is this aspect of *ḍērā* that is taken into account when, for example, government food ration cards are applied for *ḍērā*-wise, with the eldest male member of the *ḍērā* entered as "head of the family".

Then there is the aspect of *ḍērā* expressed in a sentence such as, "there are three *ḍērā* in this hut", i.e. there are three units of individuals who cook and eat separately, though they are usually closely related and may even constitute one loose unit for production purposes.

Derived from the Arabic and used variously in large parts of South Asia, the term *ḍērā* has various connotations in Bakkarwali usage (Rao 1988a), all of which are, however, connected to aspects of residence and location of people and their possessions, whether in one place or on the move. When a Bakkarwal invites one to visit, he/she speaks of the *ḍērā* – of "home". When two Bakkarwal adults who do not know each other meet, they usually ask each other one of two questions: "Where is your *ḍērā*" (*ḍēro kit jāy e*)? or, alternatively, "With whom is your *ḍērā*" (*ḍēro kisko nāḷ e*)? Each of these two questions is meant as an introduction (*shanākhat denāñ*), and implies a specific manner of perceiving the other's identity in terms of economy, kin-group or both. The first question implies that the respondent has an independent unit of his own; the second question implies that the respondent's identity – and thus perhaps even his physical habitat – is linked to someone else's. In both cases the person (*bandā*) is very much bound up; but while in the first he is embedded in the wider environment – and thus related to his parentage and group – in the second he is primarily subservient to one specific person. The answer to the first question is straightforward: a camping area is named and with it, generally, both the *zāt* and the *birādari* at various levels of connotation (Rao 1988a) become fairly clear to the enquirer. The answer to the second question depends partly on the respondent's gender, but predominantly on his/her economic status and social position within the kin-group. If in answer to this question a man replies, "With A.", he means either that he is part of A.'s migrating unit at some point of time, or that he camps with A. In either case A. is a point of reference. He is considered by the respondent to be a widely recognised important man, with an independent identity, under whose umbrella and through whom other less important men obtain a dependent identity. If A. is not recognised as such by the enquirer, further details may be asked for – such as "which A.?" (*kēṛo* A.) – in which case the respondent names another man higher in the umbrella-hierarchy. This relational connotation of the term *ḍērā* is perhaps comparable to the use of the same term among Kashmiri Hindus, who use it foremost in the context of rural-urban migration to denote a temporary/fixed abode away from home and under the tutelage of some important person or a broker who helps find employment (Madan: pers. comm.).

The Use of Time

Both domestic and herding activities are organised according to season and type of space, and in fact it is often hard to draw a rigid line between them. They must not only be coordinated in terms of mutual cooperation at the level of the household and beyond, they must also be linked to the biological schedules of the herd animals. The pastoral economy requires a woman not only to do the domestic chores commonly associated with women in southern Asia, such as cooking and baking – "the lighter a woman can bake bread, the better" – cleaning, washing, fetching water and firewood, sewing, spinning, child care, etc., but it also enjoins upon the housewife to milk her family's animals twice a day in summer, to prepare milk products (butter, butter oil, whey/buttermilk and cheeses), gather wild vegetables and dry these for winter (Casimir 1991), feed the dogs, mind the horses and participate generally in animal care. She also sets up and dismantles the family tent and does the packing for migration. She is assisted in much of her work by her children, especially her daughters, and most men also participate in at least some domestic work. The older men butcher occasionally injured animals and cut up meat, while the young ones often help collect and slice vegetables. When there are women available, no man cooks, but occasionally they help in tidying up the tent. Socio-economic rank rather than simply gender determines the chores a man does, and while better placed men rarely fetch fuel wood and never fetch water, hired shepherds often do both. If there is a great quantity of milk, sons and husbands may also help in milking. But it is always good if "the same hands always milk the same animals". Men may not churn, only a "pure" or "clean" woman may, and the cleaner she is the greater the yield of butter; if she has "a good hand" the goat butter oil, which is always warm, can be "really hot and good". All women also comb, spin and dye wool. Sheep are shorn thrice each year – just before the spring migration, in mid-August and in mid- or late November. Shearing (*katri*) is a male task, and when a family has many sheep to be shorn, friends and neighbours are requested to help; in return they are fed and given a small portion of the wool. Prior to about 1947 wool was rarely sold, nowadays only the shawls and the men's jackets are made of wool. Goat hair (*jaṭ*), which is clipped once every spring or summer, is sold primarily to carpet manufacturers in the Kashmir Valley, but also woven by women into ropes, pack lashings, lengths of webbing and other equipment for tying luggage. They also convert goat/sheep hides (*khāḷ*) into storage bags (*kharḍi*). Both men and women concur that "in winter there's more work than in summer". This is partly because winter is the peak lambing and kidding season. But generally, as Bibo said: "In summer we women have more free time than in winter." Makhṇi who came from a poorer family with few animals to milk, felt that "the main job in summer is fetching wood and water, we don't have to mind the horses or weave or care for sick lambs ...". When I asked Baggo, who was in her forties, whether she had more time "for herself" in summer or in winter, she first said that she didn't quite understand what I meant; but then she added:

> I have more time in summer to sit and watch the water flow by, and the tall trees. I have more time to walk up the slope and look far out at the mountain peaks. Down there [in the winter area] I have no time; there's always so much to be done. Here, if you don't do something now you can do it tomorrow; there it's different. Here I feel free (*ājād*).

Women's work is, however, rarely recognised as being such by the men, and as Mioñ lamented, "another of our problems is that our women do not work". Mahwali was more precise when he informed me that "we men don't do the small work (*nikko kām*) – child care, cooking, washing, bringing fodder for horses, milking goats, making *kī*, fetching water and fuel – stuff like that". Only sixteen-year-old Sadiq, who had been to school and was still unmarried, felt that "our women work in the house[hold] and even in herding much more than our men do". That the women themselves think they work very hard was amply illustrated in their conversations, and as I have shown elsewhere (Rao 1988a: 215–7), joint domestic units split mainly when one or more of their women perceive their workload as being excessive. The partition is principally triggered by the ratio between the number of persons to be cared for – the so-called "eaters" (*khāṇāḷā*: children below about twelve years, the aged and the infirm) – and the number of women and older girls who regularly participate in the daily productive activities and hence consider themselves as "workers" (*kām karanāḷā*). When the workload of each adult woman in a household rises above a certain level, tension increases to such an extent that the decision to split is taken. In an extended household, Aji explained, "it's true that all tasks are shared – but this does not mean that each woman has less work to do". The bulk of the cooking, for example, is usually done by the eldest son's wife, irrespective of the number of mouths to be fed. Most women felt that in a nuclear domestic unit a woman has more work to do if she has no children old enough to help. This was the case with Phullāñ, who had four small children and who had moved out of the extended family because her sisters-in-law had found the workload excessive; she remained on excellent terms with them and waxed nostalgic over the days when "formerly, one of us fetched wood, another water, yet another did most of the cooking, and so it went. Now I must do all this myself". But even this might be preferable to looking after other people's numerous children "who eat, are noisy, crawl all over the place and dirty everything" – somewhat like the worm-like children among the Ilongot (Rosaldo 1986: 194). As with the Ilongot, here too the number of children is a major factor in the splitting of a joint household. As Janti, who had three small children, said:

> Till six months ago we lived with my husband's parents – my father's brother – near here. There were five children – our three and my husband's eldest brother Bashir's two. Then, when Bashir's third child was born it became too much work for me, and I told my husband it would be better if we separated (*kaṇṇi ōṇāñ*). It was just too much work – I was the only grown-up woman to help my mother-in-law; Bashir's wife died in *asu*. Now we must find another wife. My poor mother-in-law looks after all those people, but we are still near one another both in summer and in winter, and I often go over to help her.

A man usually breaks away from his father's extended household when he and his wife have children and at least one of his younger brothers is married and also has children. Well-being in terms of both human and animal fertility are thus the basis for such a split. At the end, one is generally left with a male ultimogenitural form of residence. A sample of twenty nuclear families in which the parents were between about thirty and forty years of age shows that for an average of 2.4 workers there are 4.3 persons to be cared for. In such a family the workload of the woman is very high, but then the possibility of splitting is also nil, since the "eaters" are too young to split. As shown in Figure 4.8 such a nuclear family starts off on its own with on average 2.0 adults and 1.8 children (N = 20) or 2.1 adults and 1.1 children (N = 12). Data on ten extended families just before a married son left to form his own domestic unit show that here the proportion of working adults to non-working adults and children is on average 5.7/7.5; the parents in these households were aged between forty-one and fifty-four. Table 4.6 compares two sets of "eater"/"worker" ratios. One set of results may be described as the outcome of the analytical approach, wherein the workers are also assumed to eat; the other set represents the attitude of Bakkarwal women, for whom the categories of "eater" and "worker" are mutually exclusive. It will be seen that in the analytical count the "eater"/"worker" effectives vary minimally throughout the development cycle; but from the local perspective the ratio of 1.3 in an extended family capable of splitting may be considered an approximate threshold value. The ratio of 0.5 found in a sample of 14 other extended families which could have split, but chose not to, appears to strengthen this suggestion. The ratio of 1.2 for families with parents above fifty-five years is as high as for those who split, but here again there is no member who could leave to form an "independent" unit.

A Question of Achievement

On separation a son receives his entire share of animals as anticipatory inheritance, but to begin with he generally leaves them in his father's herd. Only he and his *ṭabbar* move out to form a separate (*kaṇṇi*) cooking and new sleeping unit, a *ḍērā*. When in the second phase of asserting his identity as an autonomous animal husbander, he draws his animals out of the common herd to become

Figure 4.8 The development cycle of domestic groups. Each ellipse represents a phase in this cycle, and within each are given clockwise from the upper left section the age-group, the sample size, the number of "eaters" and the number of "workers" – *a* and *a'* are both starting points for a young household, whereas *b* and *b'* indicate mature households.

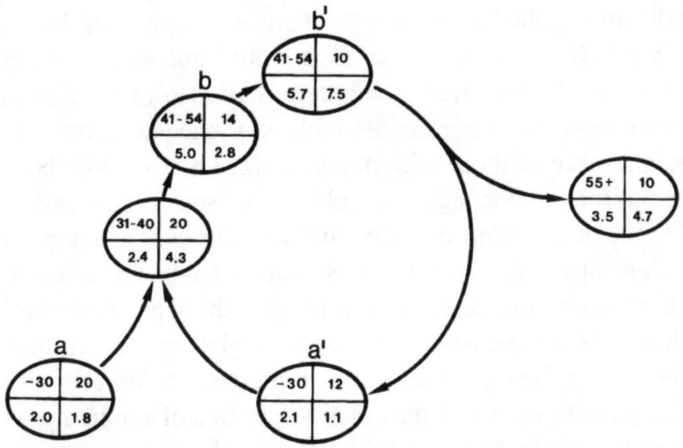

Table 4.6 "Eater" to "worker" ratios among eighty-six households in different phases of the development cycle

	Average				Ratio	
Parents' Age Group	HH	E	W	E+W	E/E+W*	E/E+W**
≤30(a)	20	1.8	2.0	3.8	0.4	0.9
≤30(a')	12	1.1	2.1	3.2	0.3	0.5
31–40	20	4.3	2.4	6.7	0.6	1.7
41–54(b)	14	2.8	5.0	7.8	0.3	0.5
41–54(b')	10	7.5	5.7	13.2	0.5	1.3
55+	10	4.7	3.5	8.2	0.5	1.2

Note: HH = households; E = "eater"; W = "worker".
* Represents the "analytical" approach
** Represents the approach of women members of households

economically independent as well, he usually takes his share all at once, not bit by bit as a daughter does. Since ideally a herd is always "divided equally among all sons", each son's share depends on the size of the father's herd and the number of male siblings at the time of separation: "If a man has say, one hundred animals and five sons, he keeps thirty and distributes seventy equally among the five. If later this number increases or decreases, it's fate." Since, however, all five would not want to separate simultaneously, and since daughters may also receive animals, often enough brothers start off with very unequal herds. This is especially true of those with medium-sized herds, while both the poor and the rich manage to roughly equalise among themselves.

The open assertion of individual identity begins when a man starts establishing his own "household" (*ḍērā*). Since too much work (with children and animals) triggers the separation, it is also the first public expression of prosperity and hence of well-being at the level of both human and animal reproduction. We are now also squarely confronted with the practice question of autonomy, which is almost entirely denied till this stage at the normative level. In Chapters 1 and 2 we have seen that irrespective of age, gender and status the assertion of identity in the social context as a specific though composite *bandā*, as opposed to other basically similar but different *bandā*, is achieved through the force of one's *nafas*. Thus a battle of *nafas*(es) is a prerequisite for such an assertion. This battle is formally recognised when a son first indicates that he wants to separate from his father. With this separation the son will now become a *kārāḷo*, i.e. a man who not only works, but gets work done – a man who chooses and decides for himself and at least partly also for others. Separation thus leads to acknowledged agency, for *kārāḷo* (deriving from the Sankrit root *kṛ*) and like the term *kartā* means "he who independently performs … actions for his house … and his bodily dependents" (Inden and Nicholas 1977: 7). The very fact that he is able to separate and form his own economically viable unit is a sign of his and his father's well-being; on the other hand, the separation could entail the risk of a decrease of this well-being for all involved. The ambiguity of this process of separation and filial assertion is reflected in sentences such as "a good son remains with his father throughout life", but also, "after marriage a son always separates – be it after ten days or ten years – he eats separately and the herd divides" or again, "if we brothers remain apart we get on better; if we're together we'll quarrel". Jima thought he found a way out in the idealised past to solve the problem of the primary struggle between the *nafas* of fathers and sons on the one hand and of brothers on the other: "In the old days among us there was no question of herd-splitting or pasture-division. As soon as a son was born the father died, so there was only one male child in every generation...." While a son's basic desire to break away from his father is recognised by all and criticised by none, an extended bi- or multigenerational household is often projected as an ideal. The fact that in reality such households generally create more problems than they solve is partly imputed to women. They, it is claimed by men and women, are instrumental in putting into effect the son's desire to assert himself *vis-à-vis* his father, and the timing of the separation is said to be governed by the relations between mother-in-law and daughter-in-law.

In a nuclear household, apart from the question of the workload discussed above, a woman has undoubtedly more autonomy than she does in a joint one; it also enables her to retain contact more easily with her natal family. Her parents may visit her and stay for a few days, something they could rarely do were she living in a joint unit. Even in joint households, however, the unmarried kin of a daughter-in-law may come and spend some days with her. This is how eleven-year-old Čiṛi and I went to visit her elder married sister Bedāñ and stayed with her and her parents-in-law for almost one week. Whereas gifts must always be given on such visits to an extended family, there is no such compulsion when a woman lives in a nuclear household, and these visits are "simply occasions for rejoicing". This greater female autonomy is however not seen as authorising individual interests which would counter those of the household as a whole, since the well-being of the individual is normatively held to be inseparable from that of the household. To take a decision that runs counter to the well-being of one's household is considered foolhardy if not outright abnormal and even immoral. Those men who have publicly proved a virtual coincidence of their individual and household interests by exhibiting a high degree of well-being – measured in age, wealth and demographic and political status – are indeed credited with knowing not only what is in the interest of their own households, but also in that of several related households. Somewhat as in the case of the Durrani (Tapper 1991: 213):

> The idioms of responsibility and honour and shame constitute a male-dominated discourse and afford men many opportunities to expound a point of view in which they define themselves as responsible and their personal interests as honourable and in accord with those of the wider community.

Only here one can not generalise for all men, for not all men have the right balance of *ōsh* and *nafas* to be accepted and acknowledged as responsible and honourable.

Acknowledging Bondage

Separating to form an economically viable, independent household is undoubtedly a sign of paternal, and hence also filial well-being. But a son's separation from his father either before or after marriage does not always carry such positive connotations. A very poor man must always separate from his father's household and join another domestic unit as a hired shepherd/goatherd. This bondage of a son to a household other than that of his father is the public acknowledgement of a drastic lack of well-being, of the father's economic and social impotence. The very existence of dependent men is largely the outcome of their innate temper (*mijāj*), whose hallmark is an insufficient amount of *nafas* (selfhood) and *ōsh* (personhood). It is *ōsh* given by God but related to parentage which enables a man to tend his flocks well, day and night, to be intelligent and brave enough to overcome his laziness, his desire for self-gratification and his fear of the dark and of wild animals. Lack of *ōsh* leads to laziness, cowardice and the incapacity to do the right things at the right time (cf. Ch. 5). This incapacity precludes the possibility of such a man's autonomy, and he has no choice but to become – and in all probability remain – a hired goatherd/shepherd (*ājṛi*), dependent on those who have considerably more well-being and are hence capable of being more responsible.

Undoubtedly, since herd sizes fluctuate, a man whose grandfather was wealthy could himself become impoverished, and two (N = 57) such men were found to have been reduced to working as

Figure 4.9 The intergenerational transmission of the status of shepherd and dependant. The figures express the percentage of cases in which a man who is presently a shepherd (EGO) also had a relative (father, father's father, mother's father) who also had this status.

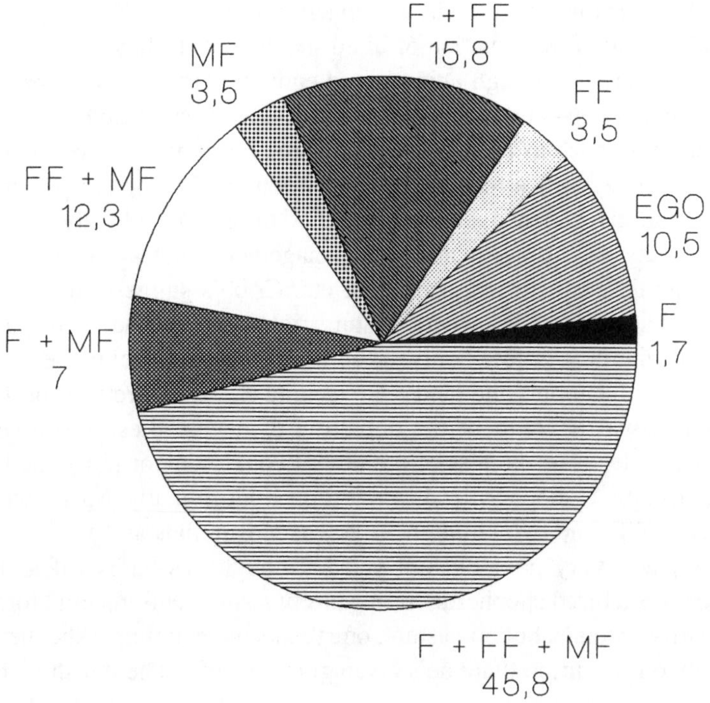

hired shepherds. In spite of such fluctuations, however, economic status does not change very rapidly over the generations. By and large the children of the wealthy tend to remain wealthy and those of the poor rarely manage to become rich (cf. Black-Michaud 1986: 114 for similar observations on the Iranian Lurs). Figure 4.9 sets out data on fifty-seven men who were hired shepherds at some point of time in their lives. While nineteen had ceased to work as shepherds at the time of fieldwork, thirty-eight were still doing so. All fifty-seven men could well recollect the status of their fathers and grandfathers, but they could not do so with any certainty for still earlier generations. It is clear from the figure that in a vast majority of cases (45.8 per cent) the fathers, the FF and the MF of these men also had been shepherds, live-in sons-in-law or other dependants. Only six (10.5 per cent) were first-generation shepherds; of these four young men had quarrelled with their fathers (two because of *mésalliances*), and two had suddenly lost most animals.

From about the mid-1970s onwards only a man who had no way out (*čārā*) took on a job as a shepherd (cf. Rao 1995 for a historical review of the situation of hired shepherds). To have a way out means having enough animals and enough pasture (also *čārā*) in normal years – and at least access to enough cash in times of sudden need, such as marriages or sickness. Elsewhere I have shown (Rao 1992) how a man can lose his traditional claims to pasture; animals can be lost over a longer period of time or suddenly, due to a variety of reasons such as mismanagement, shortage of fodder, epidemics, hailstorms, accidents, etc. Cribb's suggestion (1991: 39) that in societies where pasture rights are individuated, pastoral viability is lost "only when all three major components – herds, kin support and land – are lacking ..." is theoretical for the Bakkarwal, since here the depletion of one of these resources quickly leads to the loss of the other two. How poor must one be to become a shepherd, was a question I put to many. Mirio, who had a wife and two children, eighty-seven animals and some pasture, was very poor but not yet, he thought, as badly off as to become a hired shepherd: "If one has two small children and forty to fifty animals, but no pasture, one thinks of becoming a shepherd only on condition that one's given grazing area." The threshold of others can be lower, and Ghafur opined that "today with a herd below 150 for a family of five, labour of some kind is a must – otherwise one just doesn't have enough to eat". Many who do not want to engage themselves as shepherds try to borrow money to tide them over, but usually this only makes matters worse. One such case was that of Daud.

> I met him first in July 1984 when he came down to Sekwas to beg and eat at the homes of the Gujar (mobile buffalo breeders) and Pohol (professional Kashmiri shepherds). At one Pohol's he was given a proper lunch, but when he then begged for some salt for his animals, the housewife got angry and threw him out. Daud said he worked for his MeBS, Kima, but was not really his shepherd. His sons helped tend Kima's animals and his daughter helped fetch firewood. He possessed three goats, four sheep and one horse, but no pasture land.

> Kima had given him "a cheap loan [Rs. 1200/-] since last March … I'll probably have to give him the horse and maybe one goat in return", he said. Later he explained that if he went as a shepherd (*ājṛi*) elsewhere, he'd get "Rs. 400–600 for six months and food and one set of clothes – that's what Kima gives each of his three shepherds – but then I'd not be independent (*ājād*) anymore – perhaps never again".

The concept of a herder's independence or autonomy is thus not confined to subsistence; even a man who is patently not subsistent and goes begging considers himself independent as long he is not officially recognised as someone else's bondsman (*bandā*). Sirajo's case was perhaps more complex, but less hopeless.

> Sirajo's status *vis-à-vis* Shilla was something of a combination between an unofficial shepherd, a neighbour and a friend. Usually Sirajo ate at Shilla's home, though his own family also lived there and he had his independent flocks. Shilla's wife also managed Sirajo's horses along with her own, while Sirajo helped herd Shilla's animals. Though neither of these two families came up with any explanations, Sirajo's cousin told me much later that Shilla did not possess traditional grazing rights in that area, which was indeed a *Bokṛā* (name of a *zāt*) area; Sirajo was a *Bokṛā*, and was thus entitled to live there, but he was not very well off and had borrowed money from Shilla (who was from the *Teruā zāt*). So the two men had struck a deal, whereby "each helped the other".

Another similarly ambiguous case was that of Jalil.

> He worked for Mahwali and their respective flocks were together. Mahwali had lent him money and in return Jalil had to herd, cut fodder, fetch Government food rations, etc. He was not (yet) considered Mahwali's shepherd, "but if we get poorer", said his wife, "he'll have to try and become" that.

Finally, here is an extract from the life history of Jumma, as he narrated it to me.

> "Formerly I worked as an *ājṛi* for Maulvi M. I worked for him for six years. Then I was young, but now I'm too old for that. Every year I got one bad goat and Rs. 300. When I was a child, my father used to go to Dras till [1947/48] the border that side got closed. We had some two hundred animals of our own – that was a lot those days. But we lost these slowly … and so I had to become a servant (*naukar*). Now I have only ten animals – I got them all as payment as a shepherd (*ājṛi*). Only three of these give milk right now, since the grass is so very bad."

A hired shepherd is a bound man, economically and socially, and is perceived of – by himself and others – as a man who has little freedom of choice, little liberty to take decisions concerning even his own life. But a man who is able to set up his own "independent household" is also not an entirely autonomous, "indivisible, bounded unit" Marriott (1976: 111); he remains bound (*bandā*) by wider economic constraints and social norms and above all to God. And yet this bound state is unlike that suggested by Marriott for Indian society as a whole – the degrees of boundedness to all but God can vary with time; and if and when a man is in a position, in terms of age and wealth, he asserts himself by demolishing certain boundaries and erecting new ones, for himself and others. The very capacity to assert himself successfully in this manner is the ultimate sign of his well-being. If he fails to do so he runs the risk that others more capable than himself may permeate his boundaries and take away his pastures, his wife and even his freedom. The boundaries of a man of great well-being are permeable only from within: he can expand them to include others. Those of a man with little well-being are permeable from without: his space can shrink till he becomes a bondsman. In the following chapter I shall discuss the transition from the first possible open assertion and social recognition of autonomy as a herdholder and a householder through the phase in which a man may receive or wrench power to finally express authority.

Chapter 5

Reproducing Values

... the common good differeth not from the private;
and, being by nature inclined to their private,
they procure thereby the common benefit.
— Thomas Hobbes (Leviathan, XVII: 111)

In the previous chapter I mentioned that in practice every household strives towards a balance between independence and cooperation, the nature and degree of which vary according to context. This is fairly typical for pastoral societies, and what Spencer (1984: 63–64) writes of East Africa is also applicable here:

> A basic dilemma with which … pastoralists have to contend is the need to reconcile their immediate interests with those of the longer term. Pastoralism enforces a considerable degree of dispersal.… the more [a herd owner] isolates himself from others the greater his freedom of choice. However he cannot survive alone … the resolution [of this contradiction] lies in the context ….

"Choice" is exercised through decision making in different "contexts", at different levels of social organisation; those of the *ḍēṛā*, the *birādari*, the *kumbā* and the *ṭōlā* (see below for details). Thus, for example, within each *ḍēṛā* the adult women decide whether they have enough excess butter oil to sell; the sale itself is usually negotiated by the men, and the price is ultimately decided by the buyer, depending on local market rates. Similarly, every herd and *ḍēṛā*-owner decides within his *ḍēṛā* when and which animals to sell; to which butcher and where he sells them depends more on his *birādari* networks, and eventually on his *kumbā* leader. The migration halts depend on the heads of the *ṭōlā*, and hence it is they who also negotiate the fallow fields used en route as pasture. The more successfully a person manages to choose (*čunāñ*) and decide (*phesla karāñ*) within and between these various contexts, the greater his well-being. Indeed, as mentioned in the last chapter, the very capacity to testify in this manner to his agency is a sign of his well-being. The greater one's agency, the greater one's well-being. To paraphrase Sen (1990: 43, a "… person's success as an agent [can not] be independent, or completely separable from, his success in terms of well-being". Bakkarwal ideology and practice go further: the extent of a person's success as an agent and the extent of his well-being are mutually dependent; for agency to be conceded one must be recognised as having well-being, and to attain well-being one's agency must be acknowledged.

Measures of Well-being

The concept of *bal ōṇā* – which I have glossed as well-being – indicates nearly ideal amounts of *ōsh* and *nafas*, expressed in a whole gamut of positive states, such as physical power, economic and demographic prosperity, and mental happiness. Related to innate temper, the degree of well-being and hence also of autonomy are expressed in Bakkarwali through certain terms listed and explained in Table 5.1. This indicates that while herd animals form the basis of economic well-being, increasingly agricultural land is also important and in many cases is encouraging sedentarisation (cf. Khatana 1993 for data on Bakkarwal and allied communities). The staple of Bakkarwal diet is maize bread (Casimir 1991: 113–210), which is generally bought directly from non-Bakkarwal producers. However, men of the last two categories mentioned above meet a part of their families' annual requirements in maize and sometimes also in wheat from their own lands. Depending on the amount of land held, the area and the rainfall – it is almost always unirrigated land – the crops mostly suffice for consumption in either summer or winter, but rarely in all seasons.

Table 5.1 Factors and expressions of well-being

Term	Herds/ Flocks	Level of Subsistence	Brothers No.	Brothers Status	Sons No.
miskīn	few	poor	irrel.	poor	irrel.
khāto-pīto	medium	fair	medium	irrel.	irrel.
gujārāḷo	fairly large	good	medium	irrel.	fairly large
māldār	large	surplus	medium	irrel.	fairly large
baṛo ādmi	very large	large surplus, increasingly land	large	rich	large
safedpōshi	very large	very large surplus, land	large	wealthy	large

Note: irrel. = irrelevant

Whereas the first two meagre degrees of well-being expressed by the terms *miskīn* and *khāto-pīto* also connote an extremely limited degree of agency, the last three degrees imply a great measure of decision making power and autonomy, with the *gujārāḷo* taking up a position in between. Men classified as *baṛo ādmi* or *safedpōshi* may be further classified as men of influence. Of the last three categories it is also expected that they are generous hosts, so that "although they no doubt have many animals, they also have a lot of expenses". This explicit social aspect, as well as the data on brothers and sons, underlines the fact that well-being is relational; complete autonomy is impossible since the agent is a *bandā*, tied above all to God, but in varying contexts and to varying degrees also to fellow beings.

Well-being and Agency

As discussed in earlier chapters, the ability to take the right decisions is the outcome of the right amounts of *nafas* and *ōsh*. Since a person imputed with much well-being is also credited with a large measure of *ōsh*, he is logically authorised to openly express opinion and exercise choice not only for himself, but through and for others. It is *mijāj* which both enables and constrains well-being and autonomy. Consequently, those with greater well-being have not only the right but also the duty to care (and decide) for those who are less *bal*. Logically, the former must know better than the latter what is right and good, since they have for a variety of reasons managed to attain and maintain the state of *bal ōṇā*. Concepts of transactionalism thus legitimise the practice of domination. A man's (for women are intrinsically incapable of shouldering much responsibility) acknowledged right to surrogate decision making flows from the recognition of his enhanced well-being, which in turn is related to his innate temper. Of such a man it is said that his goals are compatible with those of persons for whom he decides. As among Durrani pastoralists, here too such men are entitled to "… define … their personal interests as … [being] in accord with those of the wider community" (Tapper 1991: 213). In this vicious circle of power the legitimising idiom is that of *sulūk*, discussed in earlier chapters. In keeping with this logic even the Government (which is taken to be synonymous with the party in power) is conceived of as an ideal person, with an abundance of *ōsh*, which should lead it to display unbounded generosity, bravery, loyalty to its followers, etc.; if it fails to comply with expectations it should be condemned, just as a Bakkarwal man with well-being must, if and when he contravenes the norms of *sulūk*. In other words, the greater one's well-being the greater should be one's accountability.

Decision making *per se* denotes some degree of agency and autonomy, and hence the "… ability to form goals, commitments, values, etc., …" (Sen 1990: 41). But to judge a person's success as an agent one must know what decisions she/he may, does or must take, and for whom and to what extent these decisions can then be implemented, and by whom. Decisions which women and men must and can take in other cultural contexts, such as "what do I cook today", or "when do we want to have our next child", are not decisions for most members of this society, since the options implicit in such decisions either do not exist, or are not perceived to do so. To quote Sen once again (1985: 201) the "capability set", i.e. "the set of functioning vectors within [a woman or man's] reach" is extremely limited. This limitation is set not only by the

Table 5.2 Decisions and decision makers as observed by me and perceived by thirteen Bakkarwal women and men

Decision Taken	Deciding Agent: My Observations	Women's Views	Men's Views
Where to camp (exact location)	W	not a decision	not a decision
Whether to sell butter oil	W	not a decision	not a decision
When to send one's married daughter to her husband's home	W (girl's mother)	W (girl's mother + evtl. her HM)	not a decision
When a married woman visits her parents	W (+M) (the woman + evtl. her HM and her H)	not a decision	not a decision
Whether to sell wool	W (+M)	(W) + M	M
When to split a household	W + M	(W) + M	(W) + M
Whether and how much dowry to give	W + M	(W) + M	(W) + M
When to start migration (time of day)	W + M (+ *kumbā/ṭōlā* leaders)	M + *kumbā/ṭōlā* leaders	M + *kumbā/ṭōlā* leaders
Whether to divorce	(W) + M (+ men of influence)	M + (men of influence)	M + (men of influence)
Whom to marry one's child to	(W) + M (+ men of *birādari*)	(W) + M (+ men of *birādari*)	M + (+ men of *birādari*)
Which animal to sell	(W) + M	(W) + M	(W) + M
Whether to hire a shepherd	(W) + M	M	M
Whether to diversify (invest in land/houses)	M (+ close agnates)	M	M
Whether to accept new sheep breeds	M (+ men of influence)	M	M
Whom to vote for	(M)/men of influence	(M)/men of influence	(M)/men of influence
Whether to slaughter an animal	M (depends on availability of injured animal)	M	M

Note: W/M = women/men; H = husband; HM = husband's mother; the brackets indicate reduced participation.

economy, but also by a mixture of political and economic structures and the ideologies that sustain these. Table 5.2 sets out sixteen topics of decision making observed by me and/or referred to by eight women and five men informants and classified according to the decision-making agent(s) I observed or they mentioned spontaneously. These data exhibit a certain discrepancy between local views and my views; specially striking is the fact that decisions I classified as having been taken exclusively by women are not considered by Bakkarwal men to be decisions at all. Not only then, are "… definitions of … autonomy … culture-specific" (Basu 1996: 53), but concepts of choice and decision making are also cultural constructions; so we must first as: "Who considers what a decision?"

In Chapters 1 and 2 we saw that an adequate amount of *ōsh* lays the basis for intelligence, competence and the shouldering of responsibility. We also saw that inherent nature – which is gender-, age- and to a certain extent family-specific – regulates *ōsh*, and hence also the capacity to choose and take the right decisions (*sai phesla*). A person deemed incapable thus hardly gets the opportunity to take decisions beyond a certain level. While as an empirical observer I may think that the choices these persons make are also decisions, culturally they are not considered so; these choices are not recognised as such, and the importance of these actions is deemphasised. For a decision – at whichever level of social organisation it may be taken, and to whatever domain it may pertain – is *per se* considered something important. For the psychologist or medical practitioner the very notion of "competence" may be "decision-relative", rather than "global" (Buchanan and Brock 1989: 18); here the notion is gender-specific, partly age-specific and generally status-specific. Something done by a person who is not considered competent enough to take a decision can not be of any importance, and hence can not be a decision (*phesla*). In this vicious circle only "choices" made by those who are important are granted the status of a "decision", and by dint of making choices recognised as decisions, these persons retain and eventually enhance their power and authority. All other choices are no choices, but simply work (*kām*), custom (*rawāj*), profession (*pēshā*); for echoing John Stuart Mill (1927: 72: "He who does anything because it is the custom, makes no choice." Day-to-day decisions taken by children, women and low-status men are relegated to the domain of habit and tradition, and not elevated to the status of *phesla*. It is not the object of decision making, nor the sphere it pertains to that matters, but rather the subject – whose agency is simply denied. This denial is almost universal, with only a handful of hired shepherds and even fewer women even vaguely entertaining "subaltern" ideas. Thus, for example, although a hired shepherd must often enough take quick decisions to save his employer's flocks, rarely are these decisions publicly acknowledged as such. In practice, however, they are valued, since employers do distinguish between good and bad shepherds, between intelligent and hard-working ones and dull and lazy ones. In practice – though this idea is neither acknowledged nor encouraged – hired shepherds must take short-term surrogate decisions about their employers' herds, and hence about the latter's economic well-being. This potential power, denied over the years and perceived apparently by none, surfaced after my main fieldwork was over against the background of the repression, turmoil and violence in Kashmir (Rao 1996) and has been discussed elsewhere (Rao 1995).

A second incoherent feature in this ideology of agency and well-being is embodied by the various *kharpēñč*, men of influence who are disapproved of as fanciful (*shoñki*) for many of their ways, and yet feared, admired and followed (see below for details). These are the men who indirectly usher in change, though as Poirier (1992: 771) concludes for a very different society, here too according to ideology innovation is the prerogative of "… the elders, those who … have reached an understanding … of the balance between two basic values of their society, namely autonomy and relatedness …". Innovation does not have to be at the level of the entire community; change can be introduced at a purely personal level. As we know, personal aesthetic criteria come into play when a woman makes herself a cap. But here too there are constraints in shapes, sizes and colours, and purely personal choice is circumscribed by overarching cultural norms and technical possibilities. When Zarina asked me to bring her some thread "of a different colour than the usual ones", what she was trying to do was experiment, eventually innovate and thus assert her individual identity. At more complex levels however, a *bandā* is so intricately bound that there is little she/he can do that does not affect at least her/his immediate family and *ḍēṛā*. Nazira, who asked my help in obtaining contraceptive pills (cf. Ch. 4), is a case in point. The *ḍēṛā* forms the basis for the creation, attainment, maintenance and eventual increase in well-being. Not that everyone within the family fold attains a high measure of well-being, but to be beyond it is in a way inconceivable. When I persisted with presenting hypothetical situations in which a man or a woman would be without his/her family, I was often told that "the household, the profession and the community are the same" (*ḍēṛā te pēshā te kaum ek e*), or again I was asked what I thought one could possibly do without a family (*ḍēṛā na oe te am kit jāe*). The centrality of the family demands that it becomes a unit of reference in all processes of decision making, whereby the degree of reference as well as the definition of the unit vary contextually.

Daring Change

Yet there are occasions on which the family is not taken into account or contravened even when the decisions taken deeply affect the daily life of most of its members.

> Tifo, the son of a man of influence, and himself something of a *kharpēñč*, hit upon the idea of hiring a truck to transport his family's enormous herds part of the way. Tifo's elder agnates disapproved of the idea as being too costly. But Tifo went ahead anyway, paid from his pocket, then split his herds from his father's stock. He made friends with the truck owner, invested some money in his business and ended up with a profitable share in the transport undertaking.

The most obvious example of such contravention is, however, provided by a man who decides to take a new wife; he does so notwithstanding the objections of his existing wife, his older children, her parents and often enough his own parents. A second marriage is for most men the second public demonstration of well-being (the first being the formation of an independent household), and polygyny and its premises are considered by both women and men as rather vehement assertions of a Bakkarwal man's autonomy. These men are now old enough to act independently of their fathers and have large enough herds to express their own wishes in and through these second marriages. Of 274 existing marriages analysed, twenty-eight were found to be polygynous (of these nineteen still existed intact, while in nine cases one or more of the partners had died). While collecting genealogies or life histories, I came across another eleven cases of polygynous marriages which had existed prior to the time of fieldwork. By pooling together these data we get a total of 285 marriages of which thirty-nine (13.68 per cent) were or had been polygynous. Polygyny can thus be considered fairly frequent among both *Kunhāri* (twenty cases) and *Allaiwāḷ* (nineteen) men.

The Bakkarwal usually speak of polygyny and divorce in the same breath; indeed it is surprising how frequently women and men speak about divorce and convey the impression that it is commoner than it is – just 1 per cent of 277 existing marriages. A person's first marriage is invariably arranged by her/his parents, and generally one has little say in the choice of one's first spouse. The divorce rate apparently does not reflect unhappiness with this low level of autonomy; could it be that polygyny does? In a society where both divorce and polygyny are allowed, why is it that the assertion of autonomy is directly linked only to polygyny; or could it be that there is a link between polygyny and divorce? An examination of eighteen divorces shows that in all of them the divorcée remarried and entered into a polygynous union; in another unpublished official Census sample of eight divorcées, again six wedded married men. Since the remarriage of a divorced woman apparently carries no stigma, the high percentage to which these divorcées become second or even third wives probably points to the subtle relation the Bakkarwal make between divorce and polygyny. Divorces, like marriage negotiations, are often contextualised in terms of the corruption of specific men of influence within the community. As Kalea explained: "If a man takes a young married girl as wife the *birādari* persuades the girl's father to get her home. For this most of the big men [in the *birādari*], especially Alia, Saiñ, Būba, and the others … take money … from this man." And according to Gam: "Whenever there's a marriage discussion Nura forces the boy's side to give him Rs. 500–1000, and he never allows the girl's father to agree unless he gets a share. He also induces divorce and makes money by reselling the poor girl."

Nura, Alia, Saiñ, Būba and many others who were mentioned in other conversations were all either known as *khaṛpēñč*, or as aspiring to become so. They were rich and polygynous, with large herds and considerable muscle power. They expressed their autonomy by manipulating others and counted as followers other, similar men who dared the risk of upsetting family members by setting their eyes on pretty women, getting them divorced if they were married, and then making them their second, third, or even fourth wives. Interestingly, in all thirty-nine cases recorded by me the first marriages these polygynous men entered into were contracted with women they considered as related. A breakdown of these first marriages shows that in twenty-two cases (56.4 per cent) a man married either a patrilateral (parallel (eleven cases), cross (five cases)) or a matrilateral (parallel (one case), cross (five cases)) cousin. All patrilateral (*patēr*) marriages pooled together form the overwhelming majority (thirty-one = 79.48 per cent), with matrilateral (*matēr*) marriages following (six = 15.3 per cent), the remaining two being exchange marriages; this is also the basic pattern found in the monogamous marriages. A further examination of the marriage sequence shows that while the second marriages took place nearly equally between relatives (twenty-one, of whom *patēr*: three and *matēr*: eight) and non-relatives (eighteen), in the third and fourth marriages the partners were predominantly non-relatives (16:4 and 5:0 respectively). Figure 5.1 illustrates these data and compares them with corresponding data on monogamous marriages. These data also concur with unpublished official Census data in which in all twenty-four polygynous marriages investigated the partners in the first marriage of a polygynous sequence were either paternal (FBD fifteen cases) or maternal (MBD nine cases) cousins. The Census data further indicate that a woman entered into a polygynous marriage mainly (sixteen cases) between the ages of fifteen and seventeen, while in four cases each she was either below fifteen or between nineteen and thirty years old. My data on thirty-three women (fourteen *Allaiwāḷ*, nineteen *Kunhāri*) who were married more than once show that at the time of their second marriage eighteen of them were divorcées and all of these entered polygynous unions. While in five cases their first husbands had not been related to them, in twelve cases they now married non-relatives. On an average these women (N = 13) were 21.8 (± 2.8) years old at the time of their second marriage, and the age difference (N = 15) between them and their new husbands was 22.5 (± 9.1) years. While their former husbands (N = 4) were on average 24.2 (± 6.1) years old at the time of divorce, their new husbands (N = 13) were on average 44.1 (± 8.3) years old.

"Divorce", said Čhattāñ, "often takes place with an old man because the young wife doesn't wash his clothes, obey or massage (*dabānāñ*) him enough.... Among us a man can't be without a wife. So the *birādari* approves him, if in anger he divorces such a wife." But Čhattāñ was wrong in generalising; men divorce their wives by and large when they are fairly young, and because they

Figure 5.1 Relatedness of spouses prior to marriage in thirty-nine polygynous and 103 monogamous marriages

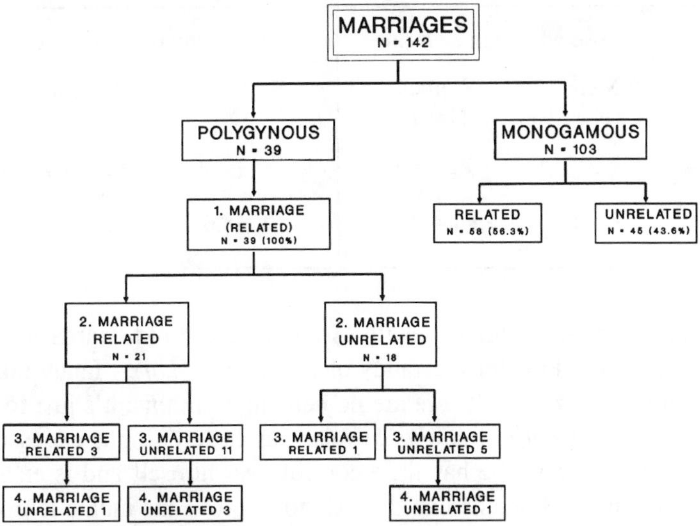

are forced to by more powerful men. The latter either marry these divorced wives or get them married elsewhere and take their monetary shares in the transactions. Men marrying divorcées are not very young; the above sample gave an average of 44.1 (±8.3) years, and from the independent sample of thirty-nine polygynous men mentioned earlier it was found that the fourteen men marrying divorcées as second wives were on average 44.9 (±8.6) years old. These women were on average 19.9 years old (±1.7, N = 11). But not all men marrying a second time are this old; nineteen men in the sample who took unmarried girls as their second wives were found to be on average 27.1 (±7.0) years old, their brides (N = 16) being on average 15.1 (±1.4) years. It appears then that a man who can demonstrate his well-being by asserting his autonomy between the ages of about twenty and thirty-five years is also likely to get a virgin as second wife, whereas a man who must wait till he is between about thirty-six and fifty-two years is more likely to try to use his power to get a woman divorced in order to marry her. Table 5.3 sets out these different data.

Whereas polygyny was always spoken of negatively, men resorting to it when older were more severely criticised than younger

Table 5.3 The two types of men who marry polygynously

Age at Marriage			
Those who marry virgins		Those who marry divorcées	
Men (N = 19)	Women (N = 16)	Men (N = 14)	Women (N = 11)
x̄ = 27.1	x̄ = 15.1	x̄ = 44.9	x̄ = 19.9
±7.0	±1.4	±8.6	±1.7

men were. As Phullāñ put it: "Some of these old beards marry often. They do it for the fancy of it (*shoñk ke nāḷ*) – fancy takes over (*shoñk ā jāto*). There are no benefits from this; it's just foolhardiness (*bekufi*)." A *shoñki* man has little *ōsh* but excessive *nafas*; as a result he has little control over himself and is excessively "hot". Since he can do little to improve his innate temper, and since he is wealthy and powerful, he may be criticised, but this does not prevent parents from giving him a daughter in marriage. There are many such *shoñki* men; of those I came to know well I would like to mention Yatmir and Būba.

> Yatmir's first wife was also his father's younger brother's daughter. The couple had no children, and at least when I met her Makhṇi, his by then fifty-year-old first wife felt it was his fault. "How could I become pregnant", she said, "He rarely slept with me – he simply didn't like me, he wouldn't come near me." Yatmir's second wife died in childbirth, leaving Makhṇi eight stepsons and one stepdaughter to raise. About a year after she died Yatmir married Zāro as his third wife; she gave birth to three daughters. Rumours were that Yatmir now fancied Ājra, the wife of his brother Kima's hired shepherd.
>
> In 1986 Būba who was in his late forties married his third wife; she was about twenty and had been engaged to his son for the last three years. In this period Būba found his son a new fiancée, but could not proceed with the wedding since he had spent most of his money on his own bridewealth and wedding. Būba's other two wives by whom he had four sons and six daughters, his mother and even his old father highly disapproved of his decision, but apparently there was nothing they could do.

Both Yatmir and Būba are wealthy and reasonably influential; not so their earlier wives. Thus, although they were criticised, their

Figure 5.2 Kinship relations in a case of divorce and remarriage. For details see text.

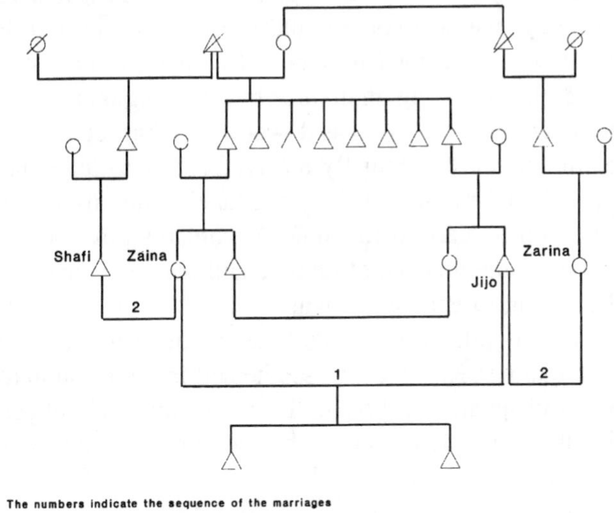

Note: The numbers indicate the sequences of the marriages.

decisions were accepted. *Shoñki* men with wives from families as rich and influential as their own can have greater problems, as the following case shows (cf. Fig. 5.2 for the kinship relations).

> In 1979 Jijo, who was roughly thirty, had been married for about fifteen years to Zaina, his father's elder brother's daughter, who was in her mid-twenties. The fathers of Jijo and Zaina were two of eight wealthy brothers. Theirs had been an exchange marriage, and they had two sons, aged ten and eight years. At a wedding in winter 1979– 80, Jijo saw Zarina, also a relative, and fell in love with her. Zarina was only sixteen, but looked grown-up. In the summer of 1980 Jijo often visited Zarina's father, whose camp was not very far away from his. Jijo was much wealthier than Zarina's father, and the latter apparently felt quite flattered. In winter 1980–81, Jijo decided to marry Zarina as his second wife. When his father and uncles got to know about this, they strongly objected; so did Zaina's father. Ultimately, in winter 1981–82, Jijo divorced Zaina, and sent her back to her father while he kept their sons with him. This drew the fury of his entire family. A few weeks later he got engaged to Zarina. To teach Jijo a lesson, his family now helped marry his ex-wife Zaina to Shafi, who was much more influential than Jijo. Pretending not to bother about all the rumpus, Jijo married Zarina in summer 1982.

The level of autonomy enjoyed by a man in a second marriage certainly does not hold for a woman, whose publicly acknowledged agency is all the way through almost nil: she *is* married, she *is* sent away, she *is* divorced, and she *is* remarried. Following Islamic precepts, women may not of course divorce their husbands, yet they do bring on divorce by deserting them. They then forfeit the animals promised as dower (*mār*), but retain their right to the animals they eventually received as dowry plus their offspring, for "all these are a woman's to take". After divorce women never remain unmarried for long. A woman's position is rather ambiguous in the practice of divorce and polygyny, and I think it may be wrong to generalise; while some women are treated entirely as pawns, others do manage to assert themselves, although in a limited manner. Rebañ expressed herself in her usual matter-of-fact way and apparently thought that if a woman did not get along with her husband a fairly reasonable step for her to take would be to leave him:

> Divorce is common among us. A woman goes if *mijāj* of her husband is too different [from hers], if she doesn't like the food she gets, or for so many other reasons. She can go to her parents, or she can go with another man.... The bridewealth is repaid only if the ex-husband is powerful – but in that case she wouldn't go in the first place!

In other words, a powerful man is less likely to lose his wife in a divorce than a weaker man; on the other hand the former is more likely than the latter to get a second wife. Unlike, for instance, in Kumaon (Sax 1991: 114–5) but somewhat as in Garhwal (Berreman 1962: 526), here a woman who leaves her husband due to alleged ill-treatment is not sent back to him by her parents. On the contrary, in the cases I encountered the women were encouraged by their mothers to stay in the parental home till matters were sorted out; though in a few cases the fathers grumbled, they gave in. Bushi, the mother of two happily married daughters, was thinking about marrying her next two children in an exchange marriage. She told me: "If one of my daughters is maltreated for say, up to three years, we'll bring her back and return the entire bridewealth ... and here the problems can arise when there is an exchange marriage...." Returning the entire bridewealth is known as *khulla* and symbolises the general recognition of a woman having been freed from a previous marriage. Through this act of repayment the ambivalent divorcée – the liminal sent-away-one (*bhēj chuṛiyā*) – becomes a woman fit to be given away once again in marriage. Usually the new husband is supposed to pay this sum and thus compensate the former husband, but sometimes fathers can, or have to do so, as in the case of Bashki.

> Bashki was Nizama's eldest and only surviving child; when she was about thirteen her mother fell sick and died. As her father did not remarry then, the entire burden of the household fell on her shoulders. When she was sixteen her father married her to a young man who lived and ate with them and worked for them as a hired shepherd. He was fairly poor and an orphan, but had a rich and influential uncle. Bashki gave birth to her first child when she was twenty. When this boy was about four she fell in love with a man she had met at a wedding and went off with him. To "get her *khulla*", her father had to pay Rs. 5000/- and four goats to her first husband, who went back to his uncle with the little boy. This amount was much more, Nizama claimed, than the bridewealth he had received for Bashki, but he wanted to avoid further problems with the influential uncle of the jilted husband.

Not all Bakkarwal, however, feel that a woman has any right to leave her husband. Once when I asked Pari, whose sister was having problems with her husband, about divorce, she said, "Yes, divorce is quite common – the man divorces naturally: he takes the woman, he leaves the woman, the woman doesn't take the man, so how can she leave him?" – [general laughter] – "of course there are prostitute (*kanjaṛ*) women too …" Bibo (cf. Ch. 4) was one such "*kanjaṛ* woman". "She had three husbands one after another! She was dissatisfied with the treatment she got and ran off and ran off. Then she came back to the first one and said, 'I've cooked for you, and washed your clothes and kept house. Where are my wages (*tankhā*)?' The police were here the other day looking for her." But, as so often, there were other versions of Bibo's story.

> This X (a *zāt* name) woman was married for over twenty years to another X. Then this chap married their eldest daughter to a fellow and in exchange himself married this fellow's sister and divorced this woman – who was his first wife and the mother of all his eight children. She has no parents and her two brothers are very poor. She has got her two youngest children with her and doesn't have anywhere to go. She's now fighting for her dower rights.

There was this X-family here with eight children. The couple never got on and the wife ran away thrice – twice with a Kashmiri and once with a Banihara [buffalo breeding mobile pastoralists]. Thrice her husband persuaded her to come back and she did, but then again she left with a Banihara from R. The husband then divorced her, gave her some animals and did not remarry. I was looking for a bride for my son and we decided to make it an exchange marriage with these people. We gave our daughter for their son and took their daughter for our son. When we arranged all this, our *birādari* and their *birādari* got together and we were assured on the Qor'an that the mother had been divorced and that everything was settled. The weddings took place in winter and then during the spring migration this year, this woman and her friends attacked the caravan of her ex-husband, stole some animals and mildly injured our daughter. Then yesterday she turned up here with the one ten-year-old son she has with her and brought the police along and said I borrowed Rs. 3000/- from her. I hardly know her! But I didn't want any quarrels, so I borrowed money from a shopkeeper and settled with her for Rs. 300/- and with the police for another 200/.

When a man divorces his wife, their children usually remain with him; if they are very young their mother can bring them up, but strictly speaking "regardless of whether they're boys or girls, they must be returned to their father when they're a little older". Not all such cases run smoothly, however, as Soṇe and her baby girl's case illustrates.

In summer 1985 Soṇe who is seventeen, is separated from her husband, Dulla. "She's with her father", says her mother-in-law and FZ, and "has taken her child". No money has as yet changed hands, "but we still expect to get the child". "Soṇe was bad, lazy, selfish, and her mother was even worse and always poked her nose into our affairs...." Soṇe's brother works as a shepherd for Dulla, to whose eldest daughter he has also been married. This marriage has, however, not yet been consummated. This daughter is Dulla's eldest child by his deceased first wife; Soṇe was his second, and recently he has taken a fourth wife.

Not surprisingly, Soṇe's mother had another story to tell:

Dulla is bewitched – his first wife died mysteriously; then his third one [in polygyny with Soṇe] got weak and coughed and coughed and ultimately all her blood came out and she died [of tuberculosis]. Then he asked for her younger sister and paid thirty thousand for her. She was a big, strong girl and she produced twins. Then she was still so strong, she became pregnant and delivered when her baby was hardly

Figure 5.3 Kinship relations which provided the background to a case of divorce. For details see text.

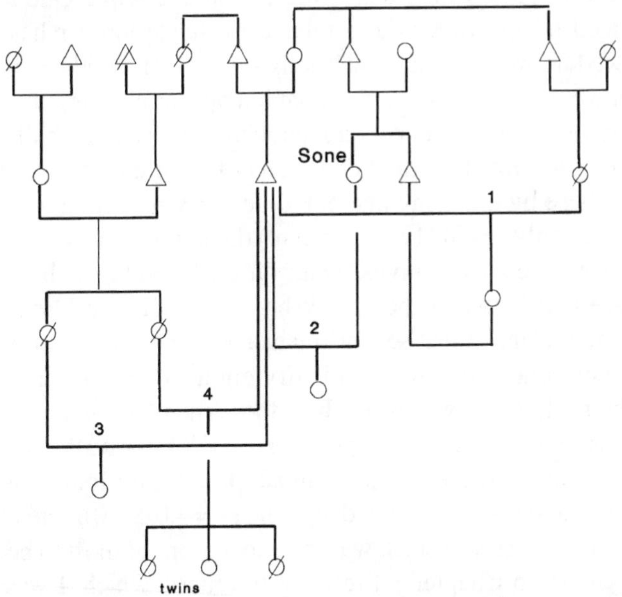

Note: The numbers indicate the sequences of the marriages.

one year old. Now see, she too is dead – and the baby too. My daughter is young and pretty – thanks be to God and His Prophet. The marriage took place years ago, but he didn't come to take her. Now it's dangerous to be with him. God knows what all he has done. He is always only full of thoughts of himself (*apaṇ*) – his *nafas* knows no limits, and one day or the other one has to pay for this. No, I won't send my daughter back to them. And the old woman [i.e. Soṇe's HM] rants and raves and always blames the girl. Knowingly (*jān pūčhie*) why should I send her? And her baby will also remain here. Look, we've given them a man to work [her son, the shepherd]; they get all the work out of him and then some when they'll give him the girl. Who knows what'll happen till then …

Figure 5.3 illustrates the kinship relations mentioned above. Bashki and Bibo, and to a certain extent even Soṇe left their husbands voluntarily and so do some others, but many women are said to do so to give into pressure exerted on them by their fathers or brothers, who in their turn may be pressurised by men of influence.

But why does a man marry more than one wife? One reason advanced by informants and related to innate temper has been reviewed above. Let me now briefly discuss a few other reasons, which were not mentioned by them but appear plausible to me. It may be reasonable to expect a man who has few or no children – and in a patriarchally orientated society few or no sons – to try to obtain these by marrying again. Of the thirty-nine men who married twice only seven (17.95 per cent) did not have surviving children from their first wives. Data on thirty-eight of these men indicate that between them they had 137 living children when they entered into their second marriages; of these seventy-nine (57.6 per cent) were sons and fifty-eight (42.3 per cent) were daughters. In other words, each of these men had on an average 2.1 sons (± 2.4) and 1.5 daughters (± 1.3). Similarly, the nineteen men who married a third time already had eighty-four sons ($\bar{x}$ = 4.4 ± 3.3) and seventy-seven daughters ($\bar{x}$ = 4.0 ± 2.0). The lack of surviving children, or sons, was thus no reason for most to become polygynous. In Chapter 3 I referred to criteria which, I was told, parents try and keep in mind while arranging a match for their children; two of these relate to the age of the prospective partners at the time of marriage and to their difference in age. Early marriages were said to be largely unsuccessful, while the ideal was for the wife to be four or five years younger than her husband. Table 5.4 sets out comparative data on ages of husbands and wives in monogamous and polygynous marriages. These data show that, as compared to marriages which remained monogamous (cf. Ch. 3), in the marriages which were to become polygynous, the husbands were considerably younger when they were first married (16.8 as compared to 21.3 years); so were their first wives (13.3 as against 16.2 years). This could indicate what people meant when they said that early marriages tend to go wrong. A similar indication is found in the age difference between the partners (H1-W1, etc.), which is on an average 5.70 years in monogamous marriages and 2.73 years in those which turned polygynous.

Finally, my data on marriages which remained monogamous at least till the end of my fieldwork show that fifty-eight of 103 women (56.31 per cent as opposed to 100 per cent whose husbands

Table 5.4 Age at marriage of husbands and wives who were partners in a polygynous marriage

Age at Marriage of Partners in Polygyny																	
H1			**W1**			**H1-W1**			**H2**			**W2**			**H2-W2**		
N	$\bar{x}$	sd	N	$\bar{x}$	sd	N	$\bar{x}$	sd	N	$\bar{x}$	sd	N	$\bar{x}$	sd	N	$\bar{x}$	sd
24	16.8	3.1	21	13.3	3.4	22	2.7	4.5	26	28.9	7.4	21	17.3	3.5	21	11.9	6.5
H3			**W3**			**H3-W3**			**H4**			**W4**			**H4-W4**		
N	$\bar{x}$	sd	N	$\bar{x}$	sd	N	$\bar{x}$	sd	N	$\bar{x}$	sd	N	$\bar{x}$	sd	N	$\bar{x}$	sd
15	44.9	8.5	11	19.7	2.0	10	23.2	7.6	4	60.7	11.6	3	18.6	1.5	3	36.6	5.9

Note: H = husband, W = wife; the numbers 1, 2, 3 and 4 denote respectively the first, second, third and fourth marriages of a man.

became polygynous) married "relatives". There thus appears to be a basic difference in the nature of first marriages contracted by those men who became polygynous, and those who remained monogamous. This difference could be explained by considering the *zāt* the men belong to. The men in the monogamous marriages investigated are members of various types of *zāt*. In striking contrast, twenty-six (66.66 per cent) of the polygynous men belong to *zāt* estimated as large, while twelve (30.76 per cent) and only one belong to *zāt* estimated as medium or small respectively. The only example of a polygynous man from a small *zāt* is the son of Babaji Larvi, the primary *pīr* of the Bakkarwal community (Rao 1988b; 1990). Now, not only is *zāt* endogamy highest among the large *zāt* (cf. Table 3.6), the ideal of the consolidation of solidarity through *zāt* and *birādari* networks is also greatest among them. The frequency of large *zāt* in the polygynous sample can in its turn be explained not only through pure numbers, but also by taking a look at the current social status of the polygynous husbands. Of the thirty-nine men, thirty-one (79.48 per cent) are or were men of influence (sixteen *lambardār*, eleven *khaṛpẽñč*, four *sirgardā*: see below for details), as opposed to only eight men, who had no special status (Casimir and Rao 1995). Now large *zāt* count more male members who are influential in the community than do smaller *zāt*; these are often the men who can afford to become polygynous – which is a sign of and for well-being, agency and autonomy.

Knowing to Choose

We have considered certain reasons why a man may decide to take a new wife, why he may choose between remaining monogamous and becoming polygynous. To take a decision means choosing between two or more possibilities (*rāsto*, lit. "ways"); but to be able to choose, one must have information and (social) knowledge (*khabar*). It is on the basis of this *khabar* that informed and morally sound opinions (*rāe*) can be formed and eventually expressed through the choices made, the decisions taken and implemented. *Khabar*, or rather the access to it, may, I suggest, be conceived of as a kind of reward which accrues to a person according to his/her status and reinforces this. As in most high-risk contexts (here because pastoral, high-altitude), the "… rapid acquisition of adaptive information is crucial …" (Spencer 1993: 47) to survival. Those who acquire information more rapidly than others can also consolidate and eventually enhance their well-being more rapidly, and perhaps for a longer period of time, than those who are slower at doing so. Both information and the access to it are in most cases intergenerationally transmitted, so that the son of a man who had access to a great deal of information is likely to have more access than the son of a man who had little access. In other words, there exists an intergenerational hierarchisation of information processing which leads to a social hierarchy in the capacity to make choices.

Just as the importance of a reward can vary both synchronically and with time, so also does the precise nature and content of information vary greatly both in quantity and quality. *Khabar* can be classified for purposes of analysis according to three spheres to which it pertains: the private, the public and the alien (i.e. beyond that of the group or community), whereby partial overlapping between two or more spheres is inevitable. He/she who has access to all three obviously has qualitatively the maximum information, even though someone else may have quantitatively more access to information within only one sphere. The Bakkarwal conceive of these spheres in a hierarchical fashion, the alien (*pablik*, or *ukumati* when relating more specifically to government matters) increasingly being accorded the greatest formal value. This is largely because access to information in the alien sphere can imply – and in its turn lead to – becoming known as the representative of a group of families. This in turn can lead to obtaining more information in the public sphere (of one's own community), and this again to more options. But to gain access to the alien sphere one must first have access to and enough information about the other two (*kareḷu*: private, household, domestic, and *birādari/kaumi*: public at two different levels within the community). This hierarchy – perhaps comparable to that obtaining among the Tallensi (Fortes 1987) – was brought home to me again and again in the early days of fieldwork, when women I questioned about certain matters almost invariably told me they knew only about domestic matters ("*miṇa koi khabar na rakhiā, miṇa kareḷu gal puč̌h*" – I don't have any knowledge, ask me things about the household) and that I should put my questions about the world at large to men who had more experience and knowledge ("*meṇo ke pato, e marad ki gal e, duniya ki gal e sārī*" – what do I know, these are men's questions, all questions about the world). When I then put these questions to certain poorer men, they too said that I should question persons with *khabar*, those who mixed with (*uṭhan beṭhan*) different types of people; they themselves had little *sulūk*, and did not feel competent to give the right information (*sai khabar*).

To mix with a large variety of persons, to visit them and eventually extend them hospitality means expanding one's acquaintances (*tālukāt*), one's social network which is conceived of as equivalent to what we can call economic and political networks. Obtaining information depends on one's access to and position within such networks. The more frequent one's access to and the higher one's position within these networks, the greater the likelihood that the information will also be correct. This in turn will help one take the right decisions and make the optimal choices. Getting information tantamounts to learning, becoming wise and being able to discriminate in order to choose properly. As a corollary, a person who is relatively secluded can not be wise, can not say the right things and can not make the right choices. Women are much more secluded than men even in this nomad society; they never go visiting long distances on their own and even during migration have very little contact beyond their community. Whereas men away from home do spend a night or two with Kashmiri village friends, women do so only if they are accompanying their husbands or close agnates. Only at weddings do women from other communities eventually come visiting. Thus women have only indirect access to most information beyond their kin-group. Yet they have equal if not more access to information within this group, and do help men obtain crucial information in the private sphere. However, as in the case of decision making, here too women's agency is by and large denied. To obtain information is to listen to the "important" and "right" things, so that one is able to say the right things. "Listening to others" does not here automatically "... bring a man down to the common level" (Marriott 1976: 132); according to local etymology it was listening to the Qor'an or God's word in general that made the Bakkarwal Muslim, and "hence we are called *sunnā*" (from the verb for "to listen"), and so it all depends on whom and what one listens to. This pervasive ideology is the basis for surrogate decision making by those perceived to have well-being and information; it is further reinforced by bureaucratic structures, as we shall shortly see.

The objective veracity of information may or may not be important. I was often advised to "ask so-and-so for the right information (*sai khabar*)", whereby the degree of exactitude is related not only to information but also to propriety. As Khana put it, "a man like X. knows about everything, he knows your value, he knows the value of your questions which people like me don't fully realise. I just say what I think – he says what should be said". Whether relating to the *ukumati*, community, or private spheres, veracity of information is of course of great importance, since it can afford or suppress access to crucial resources. It is essential to be aware in time of the availability of medicines for goats and sheep, of weather conditions in particular areas, of the current rates for silver jewellery, of wages for shepherds or going rates of interest within the community. When relating to the *pablik* sphere, however, objective veracity is fairly unimportant, since the information is rarely verifiable for most. While the importance of objective veracity is contextual, the manner in which it is displayed is always of significance, since once can impress others, obtain their following and through them create still larger networks – as a kind of mediator or patron – to then improve one's situation further. To be acknowledged as a chooser one must thus have access to what is perceived of as information. The following statement is, I believe, a good example of the interrelationship of meaning and context, of power and discourse, emotion and historicity. Made in early 1984 by a *Kunhāri* man of influence in the presence of several other Bakkarwal, some non-Bakkarwal villagers and myself, its objective veracity was nearly nil; what was important was the manner in which the bits of information were used to create – for me and for the rest of the audience – social and political identities, which could turn out to be transient or more lasting, depending on the further course of local events.

> Indira [Gandhi, then Indian prime minister] is a great friend of the Muslims. Her husband, Feroze Khan, was a Muslim* – the son of Padsha [the Pashtunistan leader in Pakistan, Khan Abdul Ghafur Khan] – a real Pathan. He's fighting the Russians in Afghanistan, like all the other Pathan. You know [turning to me], don't you, that we are Pathans.
>
> *Feroze Khan is a well-known Bombay movie star; I.G.'s husband was Feroze Gandhi, a Parsi; neither of the Ferozes are related to Khan Abdul Ghafur Khan, and none of these three again had any part in fighting the Soviets. Finally, the image of I.G. being pro-Muslim was part of her party's (Congress) propaganda to wean Muslims away from voting for other parties.

In all other conversations I heard the *Kunhāri* claim Gujar, rather than Pashtun origin, but this particular man had to legitimise to most of his audience his change of plans: he had recently decided to dabble in local party politics, and had told everyone how he would be received with open arms by the National Conference, the then regionally dominant party, whose chairman was half-Gujar. He had however been snubbed for a variety of reasons which can not be discussed here, and now planned to turn to the rival, national party. The Gujar disclaimer, or rather the claim to "Pathan" identity, combined with the display of information was this man's way of establishing his credentials as someone who, contrary to Bakkarwal ideals of authenticity and maturity, no doubt changed his opinion rather suddenly, but did so for the right moral reasons, which would benefit his community and help bring it into the larger Muslim fold.

Information, Status and Identity

The relations among the members of a group are no doubt expressed in a variety of ways, but can be summed up for the observer's empirical purposes in the concept of status, defined here as the "differential allocation of rewards to the incumbents of [the] roles" (Eisenstadt 1968: 63) of which every social system is composed. Information, I suggest, is one such major reward, and obtaining and having information of any kind, in any sphere, is both a measure of and for one's status in society. In Bakkarwal society this is at a minimum for infants of the poor, and at a maximum for a well-to-do male adult who has attained and demonstrated a large measure of well-being. He has raised large herds and many children, especially sons; the former have multiplied and the latter have in their turn become parents. He is no longer a potentially impetuous youth, nor yet an old man frail in mind and body. He is ripe in age, prosperous and the head of a large number of nuclear and eventually extended families. He is "*baṛo-baṛo, moṭo-moṭo*" (lit. "big-big, fat-fat"), portliness here as in traditional Middle Eastern and Mediterranean societies being an obvious sign of success, "… be[ing] thin usually mean[ing] low social status" (Bromberger 1994: 201) and diminished well-being. Such a man defines his extended household and is an important member of his community. Only as an enormously successful householder, and from within this context, can a Bakkarwal thus demonstrate his maximal autonomy, not only as "l'agent empirique …", but also as "l'être de raison, le sujet normatif …" (Dumont 1966: 22). Figure 5.4 illustrates the intermeshing of the factors of gender and age with status, seen as a dynamic element, and their roles in the processes of decision making.

To form and above all express opinions, make choices and take decisions one must, however, also have confidence (*immat*), or what is known in the West as "self-esteem". Someone who is not expressing humility or shyness, or is simply trying to put one off by saying "I know very little about anything … you will benefit by asking those who know …" is, I dare say, in all cultures a person sorely lacking in such culturally sanctioned esteem and confidence. The greater the projection of culturally constructed and represented self-esteem, the more likely one is to be able to influence the behaviour of others and also be autonomous. The idea of "self" as a construction is in keeping with Bakkarwal concepts discussed in the early chapters of this book; we may then suggest that the self can be "… an object of cognition similar to other

Figure 5.4 Intermeshing of gender, age, status and access to information in the processes of decision making and implementation

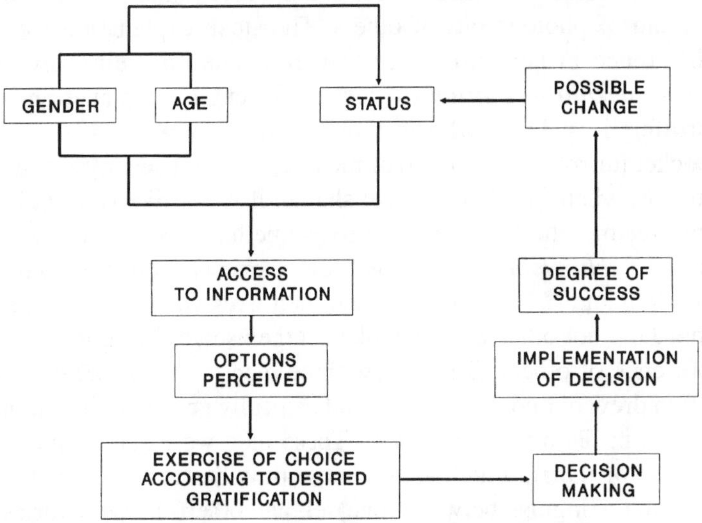

social objects" (Leahy 1991: 856). Identity is created through confrontation with the "other", which can be another person, or alternatively one's own person as a reflection or picture (as in a mirror or photo), premised on the concept of self-reference (e.g. Kauffman 1987). If then we consider both these possible but often ignored aspects (e.g. Schull and Smith 1992: 167) of the "other", we recognise that self-awareness and other-awareness must be mutually dependent. The result of the interaction between these mutually dependent "others" are the "I's" and the "Me's" Mead (1934: 142, 175) wrote about. In Bakkarwali terms one could expect both these aspects to be termed *bandā*; but this is not so. There is a basic differentiation made between seeing one's own reflection in a mirror or photograph and seeing those of others; reflections in water or shadows are not, however, imbued with the same value as those in a mirror. When I first showed Malia two photographs I had taken of him some months earlier, he glanced at them hesitatingly, and then put them away. But he scrutinised the photographs of friends and neighbours quite carefully. This experience was repeated often with both women and men. Embarrassment and general discomfiture marked most occasions on which I showed or gave various men and, more so, women their own photographs, or photographs in which they figured prominently; lengthy comments were equally sure to mark the handing around of photographs of others. The stock explanation for the difference in behaviour was "I feel shame on seeing myself" (*apaṇ dekhio te sharam āyo*). A more lengthy explanation was proffered by Janti, who was one of the few women to own a pocket mirror: "Your photo of me is like when I see myself in the mirror; when I look at it I feel shame. It is not like you think … you see me, the *bandā* Janti; I see something else. I see my own *nafas – tobā, tobā*!" As far as I know, except on the festivals of *Besākhi* and *'Id*, when they lined their eyes with collyrium, neither Janti nor other women looked at themselves in a mirror in the presence of others. But I knew three men – all *kharpēñč* – who often drew out pocket mirrors and carefully groomed their moustaches in plain view of others. These men were said to have an excess of *nafas*, which as we know provides the basis of being able to distinguish between (one)self and other(s). *Nafas* varies in quantity, and as Sherio put it, "in some persons there's so much *nafas*, some of it must be visible". Since an excess of *nafas* is disapproved of, being confronted with it is obviously unpleasant, and can emotionally speaking be a moral problem. As old Ājra commented: "One sees others in photos. You see old Ājra. How can I see Ājra? No, I see Ājra's *nafas* … it is a sin (*gunā*)." Excessive *nafas* is in a way self-generative, as we saw in Chapter 2, and can, if one does not take heed, lead to self-destruction as illustrated in Figure 5.5.

It would, however, be wrong to conclude that women and men do not look at their own photographs; from several conversations it was amply clear that they had inspected their images rather carefully – only stealthily, and not in the presence of others. The cognition behind Janti and Ājra's explanations are thus complex. The only occasion on which a man or woman may be confronted with his/her own *nafas* is when faced with his/her own photograph or mirror reflection. While conversation ranges freely on the excessive or diminutive *nafas* of others, I never heard anyone mention his/her own *nafas*. From Janti's point of view, each of her neighbours and relatives, friends and enemies is a specific *bandā*, who emerges as one unique unit. She is of course aware that each of these units also has a *nafas*, but then she does not need to look at someone's picture to see his/her *nafas*; there are plenty of other occasions on which this manifests itself in one way or another. The composite unit that she recognises in the picture has in her mind a specific and unique identity – which she may or may not be in a position to split into its component parts – which has been created in confrontation with other comparable units of identity – other *bandā*. But when Janti looks at her own picture or mirrored reflection there is no confrontation and hence no conscious creation of personal identities. It is thus very hard to comment in this cultural context on the applicability of the theory of the multiplicity of self schemas, according to which "… an individual can have a repertoire of systematic views of self" (Horowitz 1991: 2). Here, efforts to subdue "self-views" of all kinds constitute the dominant discourse. In practice, however, those who have a solid self-view and can project it properly are identified with this self-view and credited with well-being and the capacity to choose and decide at various levels and within various spheres.

Figure 5.5 The interrelationship between excessive *nafas*, vanity and ruin

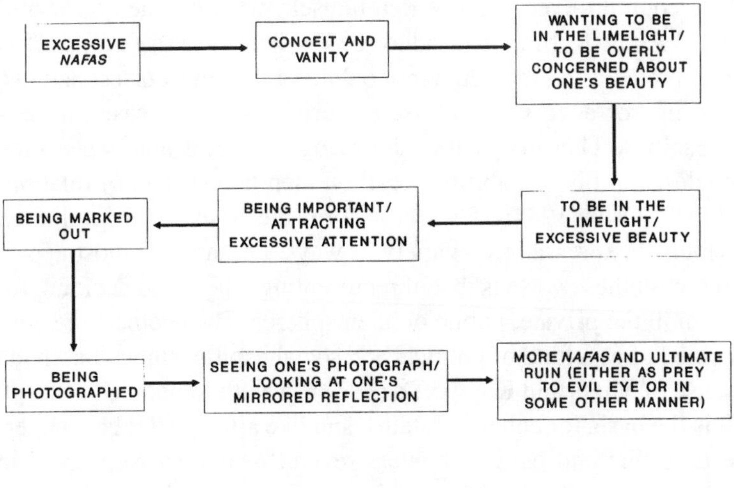

Well-being, Surrogate Agency and Cooperation

> *... Many properties of individuals, such as "powerful", are irreducibly relational, so that accurate description of one individual may requirereferences to other individuals.*
> — Elster, "Marxism, Functionalism and Game Theory"

Identity, as we know from the abundant literature on the subject, can be either ascribed, achieved or both, whereby the boundaries between ascription and achievement are often fluid. I have so far considered how a man can, through the interplay of ascription and achievement, attain the identity of a person who can choose and decide not only for himself, but also for others. Identity when both ascribed and achieved has been referred to as "social category" (Goodenough 1965: 2), and this is precisely what men empowered with surrogate agency constitute. In many parts of South Asia honour (*izzat*) is linked to control over wealth, women and land (*zar, zan, zamin*); the more the better. The Bakkarwal do not use the term *izzat* in this context, nor do they speak of land; but in a similar fashion they speak of *bal ōṇā* being linked to the control over wealth, women and livestock (cf. Table 5.1). As with Hindus in Karimpur (Wadley 1977: 152), in this society also "material prosperity is closely tied to people's perceptions of someone's powers". As Gama commented on a certain non-Bakkarwal politician: "He couldn't even become rich himself, what can he do for others?" As in Karimpur (Wadley 1977), here wealth (*sarmāyā*) is interpreted as an indication not only of a person's correct actions, but also of access to and use of certain – in this case innate – capacities. These capacities are recognised in a man when they coalesce in his "... ability to call on men in a system of relationships" (Östör 1984: 155); these form the basis of his authority, which is expressed in a variety of ways. Perhaps the most apparent of all these ways is that of representing others and deciding for them in the private, public or alien spheres. These others are conceived of as a kind of political and social capital, somewhat in the sense of Miers and Kopytoff's (1977) "wealth in people" concept. It is the basis for enhanced status, and like all capital it bears interest. In this and earlier chapters several examples were cited in which surrogate decision making was observed in the domestic and community spheres. A common manifestation in the alien sphere is through the system of vote banks known throughout India, in which men of influence usurp (from my perspective) the right of specific persons under their power to exercise electoral choice and thus impose their political decisions on them. "The only one to vote here was *Hāji*, since the names of the others do not figure in the [voters'] lists ... but then he voted for us too ...", said Karim, a distant relative of the *Hājji* who voted. Whereas in this rather extreme case this *Hājji* voted for several men and women of several households belonging to his *kumbā* (see below), usually only the heads of households exercise franchise for themselves and all the adult members of their respective households. As Makhṇi explained: "The other men – the sons, shepherds and others – are with the animals and we women are busy at home or fetching firewood ... so Sifo's father went and put his mark [thumb impression as a voter] for us all."

Alien structures further reinforce these intracommunity relations of dependence and surrogate decision making, since for almost every action in the *ukumati* sphere – be it the rare opening of a bank account, the periodic process of getting oneself registered as a voter, or even the basic question of obtaining a ration card – an average Bakkarwal must request some man of substance to testify to the veracity of his/her identity. Such a man "will always want some money", and so "it all becomes very expensive". In this alien sphere the capacity of those with relatively little well-being to exercise choice is even more reduced than it is within the community. But this is apparently rarely resented, since the man deciding for others is credited with capacities denied to and by others. It is indeed his duty to express in this manner that he is different from those under his care – that "the longest finger of a hand reaches the farthest to get something for the whole hand", as old Adeo put it. Ideally, in surrogate decision making the dichotomy postulated by much of social science between society and the individual dissolves. Evidence for individual agency is thrown up only through society, and without the social there is no individual. But also without some individual agency social institutions do not function, nor is the idealised Muslim community conceivable.

The expression of surrogate agency – and its continuation – depends on those who acquiesce and form a sodality. The authorised agency to choose for others is, at least ideally, conditional to the needs of this we-group, which must cooperate. The aim of cooperating is to reach goals which may not be contradictory, though they must not necessarily be identical. A man of influence generally has a different aim from a dependent man, but each aids the other in realising his respective aims. There is thus a certain reciprocity at work here, which is ideally based on mutual trust. From this perspective "… individuality and sociality seem to dissolve into one another" (Callan 1984: 417). As opposed to Hindu Tamil society (Mines 1992: 134) where "… success and altruism are … contradictory", here only a successful man can eventually be "altruistic", since only a man with well-being has something to give; such a man can also eventually be emulated. What is important is not the negation of autonomy and individuality but the prevention of its eventu al clash with the interests of the corporate group. A balance must thus be achieved between individual forces and group elements. Such a system can function as long as there is little or no external intervention favouring either the former or the latter. With external pressure the individual leader can retain power even though he may no longer be perceived of by community members as representing their interests; this has increasingly been true of Bakkarwal men of influence, especially those affiliated to political parties.

The birādari

Traditionally, cooperation and mutual help are symbolised by the term *birādari*; when referring to mutual acts of help the Bakkarwal speak of *birādari karāñ* (Rao 1988a), somewhat as Afghan Durrani nomads speak of "doing *qaumi*" (Tapper 1991: 51). As mentioned in Chapter 3, the terms *birādari* and *zāt* are sometimes used synonymously, and often enough the head of a *zāt* is also the head of the *birādari* patrilineage. *Birādari* members often live close to one another, especially in winter. But region and territory are not limiting factors, and the concept of *birādari* is a highly flexible one. This flexible structure is illustrated by the imputation by Makhṇi, a *Kāḷo-Khēl* woman, of my husband and myself to the *birādari* of the then Chief Minister of Jammu and Kashmir, Farooq Abdullah, and his mother, Begum Abdullah. Makhṇi's argument ran as follows. Since Abdullah's wife and the Begum's father hailed from Europe, they were grouped together with my German husband. So then, was I: "She [referring to me] is of Farooq's *birādari*, as we're of Y's – not related – just of the *birādari*", she explained to a visitor. Sometimes persons can, therefore, be recruited into a *birādari*, irrespective of where they reside. This aspect of the concept of *birādari* is in keeping with observations made for South Asia as a whole and whereby,

> … membership in a polity … is not primarily defined by residence in a specific well-defined territory, but rather … certain differential rights in a territory are from personal ties of kinship and dependency. (Heesterman 1979: 67; cf. also Dumont 1970a: 152ff.)

The various implications of the single term *birādari* are summed up below (cf. also Rao 1988a; Alavi 1995):

1. the genealogical level of the patrilineage at which no fission or fusion may take place; i.e. a solidarity group as opposed to the egocentric individual;
2. the levels of production and consumption at which fission can take place;
3. the reproductive level at which fission can also take place;
4. the political level, which too is fissive and at which the representatives of the community or segments thereof function. This is the highest level and the largest possible community unit within which mediation is attempted in cases of conflict and dispute.
5. A fifth and new implication of the term *birādari* can occasionally be observed among literate Bakkarwal while speaking to non-Bakkarwal. They may refer to "our Gujar *birādari*"; this is to be understood in the context of growing mobilisation of ethnic feelings on broader platforms (Rao 1988b). Here the taxons *birādari* and *kaum* (see below for details) are interchangeable, and the phenomenon is comparable to what Weiner (1978: 557) called "the discovery of *varna* identities" among Hindus. In its exclusion of non-Gujar (especially Kashmiri) it is also comparable to the concept of the "Hindu *birādari*" (as opposed to Muslims) in pre-1947 Punjab (Tandon 1961: 82). However, no Bakkarwal felt that a Gujar could be a member of any

Bakkarwal *birādari* at any of the other levels of functioning. Like the term *mahal* in sedentary rural North India (Neale 1969: 13), *birādari* here thus represents a knot of individual interests at various, interdependent levels of social, economic and political interaction. But each *birādari* is simultaneously a largely endogamous and more or less small group of persons. Taking responsibility (*bār lenāñ*, lit. "taking the load") for fellow *birādari* members, caring for them (*parvash karāñ*) by choosing for them can at times find expression in selective acts of generosity, which – like hospitality – can of course also be construed as a form of cooperation, of binding together a particular we-group. These also legitimise the exercise of authority, since both hospitality and generosity are positive expressions of *nafas* in the form of large-heartedness, which again is related to wealth, since "a poor man can't be large-hearted".

In a context of increased commoditisation generosity and patronage have become rare. "Till some years ago within the *birādari* no interest was taken – only help was given" was a commonly heard statement. But even now when the common rate of private interest in the region ranges between 16 to 20 per cent, loans of up to Rs. 500/ are given free of interest within the *birādari*. Such rules do not apply beyond this group, and it is said that formerly the annual interest demanded by rich men for loans of up to Rs. 2000/ from outside the *birādari* was the labour of a man, preferably the borrower's son. Within the *birādari*, however, help was largely mutual and took many forms.

When the ancestors of contemporary Bakkarwal migrated into Jammu and Kashmir from the valleys of Allai and Kunhar, they came as individuals or in small groups of nuclear and extended families (Rao 1988b). These individuals and families came to form several sodalities which were economically far from homogenous. Within each such corporate group (*birādari*) the richer supported the poor, partly due to kinship obligations and partly out of feelings of Islamic piety. In both ideological contexts *ōsh* played its part, for it enabled "wealthy men to help and support the poor … it was the capacity for empathy and sympathy (*amdardi*) – created through enough *ōsh* – which helped them overcome their desire for self-enrichment". Partly in exchange for this help many of the poorer men helped tend the flocks of their benefactors. Their wives and children "helped in the households of the wealthier to kindle the fire, fetch wood, fodder and water. When they grew too old or sick to help, their grown sons and sometimes even their daughters took on these tasks". These relationships were "a mutual thing – if I do this for you, you will also help me". However, at a later stage of Bakkarwal history, with the growing importance of "wealth in people", it also became important to maximise the number of herd owners over whom one had control, thereby gaining direct or indirect access to their animals. This control and access enhanced power and wealth as explained above.

"Those days a man could not be employed as a shepherd if he were a cousin, or nephew or younger brother-in-law"; and yet there were many such poor and even indigent relatives who did work de facto as shepherds, without being considered employees. There was also a growing need for men and muscles to obtain and retain pastures and power (Casimir and Rao 1995), for as discussed elsewhere (Rao 1988b: 58ff.) in this period (between about 1910 and 1925) there was intense competition for pasture. Here as among the Kababish, "clients [were] expected to support their patron both morally and physically" (Asad 1986: 191). Since heavy taxes were now also being levied on livestock it was to no one's advantage to officially multiply stock much. On the contrary, it was much more rational to distribute taxable stock and minimise the tax burden of each household. All this led to the emergence of the system of *sakāwat*, which became the principal manner in which a reasonably wealthy and politically ambitious and pious man could now retain wealth and acquire power. *Sakāwat* is remembered today by elderly wealthy Bakkarwal and projected by their children as representing Islamic charity (cf. Ar. *zakāt*, plur: *zakāwat*). Former beneficiaries and their children speak of it as a mixture of charity and bondsmanship, the proportion between the two depending on the individual donor's nature (*mijāj*), and the degree of kinship relations between donor and recipient. Indeed, most donors and recipients had long been bound by reciprocal relations; these were now institutionalised, and the status of each side more clearly defined. Within each *birādari* there now arose localised sets of donors and recipients, who as members of the same corporate group were ideologically speaking "equal as brothers are"; additionally, most were agnates or affines. By binding themselves to poorer men with little or no stock in relationships of at least apparent socio-economic mutuality, men with great well-being gifted surplus, taxable stock, and sometimes food and clothing to poor families who helped in herding. Distribution of livestock created social reciprocity and also tended to minimise the socio-economic risk of each individual through dependence on others within each *sakāwat* network. The notions of morality and help underlying this system closely resemble that of "patronage", which has been defined as a set of "political relationships in which inferiority is accepted and then defended by moral suasion" (Davis 1974 in Silverman 1977: 18).

Receiving Recognition

"By forty, one should be able to sit back and let the children and grandchildren do the work" is a wish commonly expressed by Bakkarwal women and men. The figure forty echoes ritual rhetoric and for most the wish remains an idle one, but by the time most men and women are about forty they do have sons and daughters who in their turn have become parents. As shown in Figure 4.8, in an extended household where the parents are between forty-one to fifty-four years (N = 14) the number of working hands (5.0) far exceeds the number of children and aged (2.8). Such a household belongs by definition to a man of well-being, and is in a transitory phase of relative leisure. In this vicious socio-economic circle, those with little well-being rarely manage to establish extended households, since the sons have to leave to work as hired hands for others. Such households are small and have few grandchildren.

Having grandchildren is, however, also a sign of having reached a certain phase in the life cycle in which semen and blood gradually begin to lose their viscosity and hence also cool down. This process should, ideally, find expression in an unspoken reduction in the frequency of sexual intercourse, and many women told me that "it's a shame to bear children when one's own daughters are bearing babies". The idea that it is improper to indulge in sex when one's children are having sexual relations is not restricted to the

Bakkarwal (e.g. Vatuk 1985; Patel 1994: 165–6), or even South Asia (e.g. Caldwell and Caldwell 1977; Firth 1957: 492; Héritier 1984: 145–7; Wilson 1957: 102). Data on thirty-one women past menopause show that on average they were last pregnant at the age of 41.16 (±6.60) years, and yet I met enough greying grandmothers who were proud that they were still "strong enough" to become pregnant. In fact when women are among themselves they do joke on the subject: "get her the right man and she'll get hot enough again to get a son", or "you can see well enough old woman, so may be you can get a child!".

Grandmothers may or may not continue to bear children and the load of domestic chores, but usually a well-to-do man with adult sons and young grandsons no longer does much real herding; he supervises, inspects and counts. Thus while seven-year-old Jilo, ten-year-old Miro and their father in his late twenties took care each of a mixed herd of goats and sheep, their grandfather went around now and then inspecting, between stints of sunning himself. His presence was nevertheless very much felt by both his son and grandsons, for he would be the one to count the stock every morning and evening. Following Asad (1986: 51–52) for the Kababish, one should distinguish here between "herding control" (guarding, watering, obtaining additional fodder, giving salt, etc.) and "management control" (directing and taking decisions on herding, as well as on the sale of culled animals and animal products, migration, eventual recruitment and labour input, etc.). In the above example, while Jilo, his brother and their father guarded, watered and executed most of the major daily tasks, it was the grandfather who delegated precise responsibility to each of them; it was he who decided to cull certain animals, keep others and negotiate with a shepherd for the following season. Only when we differentiate between these two spheres of control do we realise how subtly a man with some well-being begins to gradually "trespass" into his father's domain and take first minor, and then major decisions together with his father and then gradually on his own, till he is ready to form an independent household and take charge of both herding and management control – till he too in his turn has sons and grandsons.

A man of well-being in his forties thus often undergoes the experience of seeing his (usually eldest) son move out of the joint paternal *ḍēṛā*-household to form his own *ṭabbar*-household. The decision to separate is taken by the young couple and agreed to, if not openly encouraged, by the man's parents. If open conflict is not frequent the new household remains nearby and the family members see each other every day. For the son, it marks the beginning of a partially independent identity; for the father it signals the breakup of his extended family. Around this time, the elder daughters also marry and leave the paternal home, and for the parents structures they have been used to slowly break or fall apart. But the emotions involved are not undilutedly negative – they are ambivalent. The ambivalence stems from this very breakup: the setting up of the son's *ṭabbar* represents the first step towards the eventual evolution of the father's existing *ḍēṛā* into a *kumbā*. *Ṭabbar*, *ḍēṛā* and *kumbā* are types of family which (can) come into being at different stages of a man's life cycle, and correspond among others to different types and degrees of what Pasternak et al. (1976) termed "incompatible activity requirements".

When the Bakkarwal speak of a man's *kumbā* – a *kumbā* is never associated with a woman – they imply that he is alive and wealthy, that he has a large number of living, married progeny, and finally that his own fairly numerous male siblings recognise his authority over themselves because he is much richer than they are, and perhaps also because he is much older. If this last requirement is not met, one continues to speak of the man's *ḍēṛā* rather than of his *kumbā*, and this applies to all except those with great well-being. After their father's death brothers with little well-being, who have long separated from each other economically, also tend to do so at the social and perhaps emotional levels. The binding power of the *rag* appears much greater when it combines with general well-being. In other words, if at least one of many brothers has great well-being, there is a likelihood that they will all stick together in the morally legitimate expectation that they will receive resources through or from him, in order to enhance and consolidate their own well-being. This brother will be the *kumbā* leader. Hence a *kumbā* is always linked to – though not necessarily named after – a specific man of some substance, both economically and biologically. The term *kumbā* is used to designate part of a *zāt*, or alternatively, a collection of nuclear or extended families considered as descended from one living man (and his wife/ves); it is thus a specific type of descent group. Additionally, the term *kumbā* also has the connotation of clique and faction. Elsewhere it has been shown (Casimir and Rao 1992; 1995) that the numbers of especially male offspring and siblings are crucial to a Bakkarwal man's position in society. This is particularly striking for men holding positions of political importance, and apparently holds true for large parts of South Asia. Oldenburg (1992: 2658–9) has postulated that in contemporary northern India, for example, there exists

> … the perception of a need for sons to uphold, with violence, a family's power vis-à-vis neighbours (not infrequently including kinsfolk) … additional sons enhance their capacity literally to defend themselves or to exercise their power …

He further cites a study in which

> Mahadevan and Jayashree (1989: 128), surveying 6,500 respondents in U.P., Andhra Pradesh, and Kerala, report that parents who thought sons were important "for physical force to dominate in the family and village" had more children born than those who thought it unimportant.

The principle of the Bakkarwal *kumbā* is one of segmentation; hence it is said that "there are no new *birādari* [here, patrilineages], but one *kumbā* [of old] has now become twenty *kumbā*". While several *ḍēṛā* compose a *kumbā*, these in turn make up a *ṭōlā*, which is a loose migrating unit (rather than a "household" as in Kangra – Parry 1979: 157). There is great seasonal flux in the number of men, women and children in a *ṭōlā*, which at its maximum generally consists of several *kumbā*, represented by the migrating subunits of humans and herds. While the members of each subunit move and camp very close together during migration, all these subunits do not actually move and camp in a contiguous fashion. They converge at short intervals towards specific locations and keep contact with one another throughout the migration periods, which can last from two-and-a-half to five months, depending on the distance between summer and winter pastures. Migration begins at dawn, with the healthy animals first being taken by the men and boys over about sixteen years of age, while most of the sick ones are left to follow somewhat later with the women carrying head loads, the elderly and the children, who take the household belongings as pack luggage (*bār*) on horses or

Table 5.5 Seasonal flux in two migration units in 1983 and 1984

Age at Marriage									
	Beginning			Middle			End		
Season	N	Adults	Children	N	Adults	Children	N	Adults	Children
Spring 1983	130	60	70	390	182	208	31	13	18
Autumn 1984	38	22	16	288	136	152	6	4	2

mules. Table 5.5 sets out data collected in 1983 and 1984 on fission and fusion during migration; for further details see Khatana (1976a, b; 1992), FAIR (1980), Kango and Dhar (1981).

The terms *ṭōlā* and *zāt* are sometimes also used synonymously, since each *ṭōlā* is usually dominated by one *zāt*. Except when used in this manner a *ṭōlā* at its maximum is, like a *kumbā*, usually directly linked with a living adult male. But not every man has a *ṭōlā* linked to him. *Ṭola* are linked to – and often named after – specific older men with extreme well-being, i.e. high economic and social status and large consanguineal kin-groups.

Obtaining Influence

> *... good qualities attest the (potential) existence of ... authority in a person who possesses group feeling.*
>
> — Ibn Khaldun, *The Muqaddimah*

By now it should be clear that subjected to the empirical reality of Bakkarwal society, the analytical concept of household must be redefined according to season and to the gender, age and status of its various members. Yet the term is used, for example, by the Census of India, which also tries to identify "heads of household". An analysis of 202 Bakkarwal domestic units, irrespective of the phase in the development cycle, shows that only 5.4 per cent of them were said to be "headed" by women, a figure (7.6 per cent) lower than that given by the Census of India (1961) for rural

Jammu and Kashmir as a whole. These eleven women-headed domestic units were on average smaller than those headed by men (3.5 ± 1.9 as against 5.6 ± 2.9 for all 180 units analysed), and except in one case of an orphan all these women were widows aged between about fifty and seventy years. This suggests that unlike among certain other Islamic pastoralists (e.g. Tapper 1991: 212ff.) a Bakkarwal woman can become the acknowledged head of a domestic unit only when she does not have a living spouse, or any other adult affine or agnate who can be considered responsible for her. The eleven women had to become household heads because their poor agnates and affines could not afford to take them in. I should recall that a *ḍēṛā* is a patrilineal unit of socio-economic organisation, and even an elderly woman can achieve a reasonably high status only through a high-status husband or son. The husband – *kārāḷo*, for which there is no female equivalent in Bakkarwali – is both the worker and the one who gets work done. Without a *kārāḷo* a *ḍēṛā* shrinks symbolically to a unit without work or workers – simply to a unit of "eaters" and dependants. A woman becoming its head is an indication of poverty and helplessness. The status of even a "household-head" thus depends on gender and other intrinsic criteria of well-being. By simply becoming heads of *ḍēṛā*, those not authorised by ideology to hold such positions fail to attain the social benefits that accrue from the latter.

The major social benefit is that of exercising choice and taking decisions for and on behalf of the members of the household. This authority in the domestic sphere of the *ḍēṛā* is acknowledged for every adult married male sound of body and mind. I have already discussed how authority at the wider levels of *kumbā* and *ṭōlā* is acknowledged, how surrogate agency functions. Beyond these genealogical domains there are no permanent positions of authority. But there are several men to whom specific *kumbā* or *ṭōlā* are linked and who, by common consent, are "the cleverest and most capable among all the rich and important men (*safedpōshi*)" of the community. Not only have these men all achieved the status of "big men" (*baṛo ādmi*), they have gone further to be acknowledged as *lambardār*, or recognised as *mukaddam, kharpēñč* or *sirgardā*. Figure 5.6 illustrates the relative status of these various types of men of influence in relation to one another and in relation to other men. Thanks to their *mijāj* these specific men, "like certain

Figure 5.6 The relative positions of power and esteem enjoyed by three types of men of well-being as compared to "others"

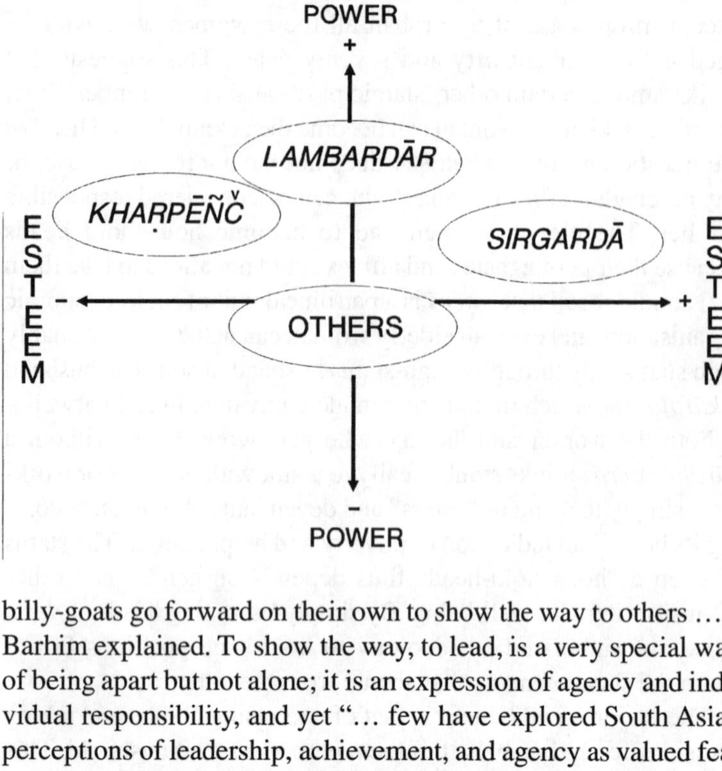

billy-goats go forward on their own to show the way to others ...", Barhim explained. To show the way, to lead, is a very special way of being apart but not alone; it is an expression of agency and individual responsibility, and yet "... few have explored South Asian perceptions of leadership, achievement, and agency as valued features of individuality ..." (Mines and Gourishankar 1990: 761).

The mukaddam

The emergence of the Bakkarwal in Jammu and Kashmir as a distinct community in its present form can be traced back to the early years of this century (Rao 1988b). The ancestors are said to have originally belonged to diverse decentrally organised ethnic groups, and to have come together to form the community as we now know it. Within each of these groups there were elderly men widely respected for their personal qualities and generally considered exemplary (*rehnuma baṛā*, cf. Ur. *rahnuma* = guide). Known as *mukaddam* (<Ar./Pers. *muqaddam*), they were old enough to be *kumbā* leaders; they were, however, not "too old" and "in good

[enough] health" to often also function as migration leaders (i.e. as *ṭōlā* leaders). They were wealthy (*moṭo*), though not necessarily always the wealthiest; had physical strength (*jismāni tākat*); were brave (*dilāwar*), intelligent and smart (*čālāk*) and of good character (*akhlāki*); and finally as men of understanding (*samajdār*) they acted as middlemen between their respective groups and other groups. They are also said to have best understood the needs of their groups and helped generously in times of need. Because of all these characteristics, it is said that these men "could control and protect the best"; they were not only men of influence, they were also men of authority. Like other ideal leaders in South Asia, the *mukaddam* was therefore "… defined by a public recognition of individuality and instrumentality that is circumscribed by values that subordinate his liberty to the common good" (Mines and Gourishankar 1990: 763). Although there was no formal system of elections, a *mukaddam* was chosen "because he told the truth, wasn't corrupt, was the most fair-minded".

It would be beyond the scope of the present work to discuss the controversial relationship between saintly and secular authority in South Asian Islam, but it should be mentioned that even now when Bakkarwal speak of having chosen a man as *mukaddam*, they use a religious analogy – that of following ("*takyā pakṛāñ*", lit. "holding onto the seat of") a saintly man. Indeed, a member of the former regional assembly comes from a family of *pīr*, and while one of his sons has joined state politics, another son is designated to follow his father, grandfather and great-grandfather as *pīr*. But the position of *mukaddam* was in no way permanent. Men have been declared unfit by a *birādari* and removed from their positions, and Gama threatened: "If X. does to others what he's doing to me, we may ultimately declare him unfit and ask him to go." The position of *mukaddam* was also not necessarily hereditary, but if it was felt that a *mukaddam*'s son had the requisites, he was likely to be recognised as his father's successor when he died or grew too old to fulfil his duties. A *mukaddam*'s qualities, like all others, are intergenerationally transmitted, and there are cases in which *mukaddam*-ship has been handed down in the paternal line for several generations. Among the *Bijāṛ zāt*, for example, *mukaddam* have been recruited from one single family for four generations (see Fig. 5.7), and Alia recounted that:

Figure 5.7 Kinship diagram of a part of the *Bijāṛ zāt*, showing the succession of *mukaddam*

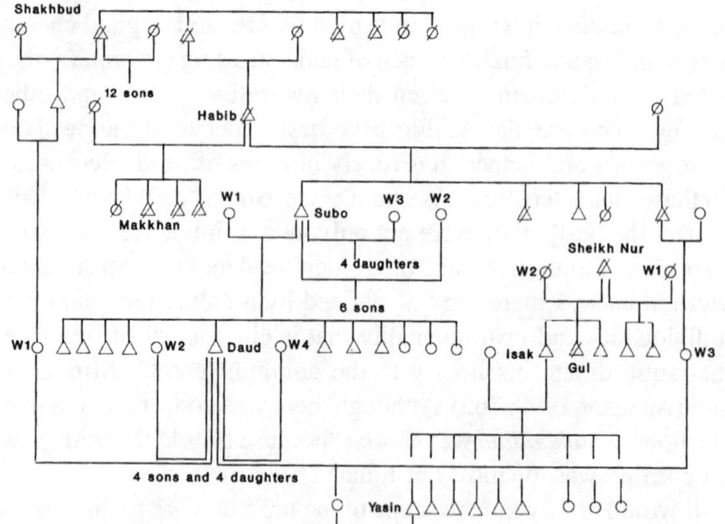

Figure 5.8 Kinship diagram of a part of the *Ḍōi zāt*, showing the succession of *mukaddam*

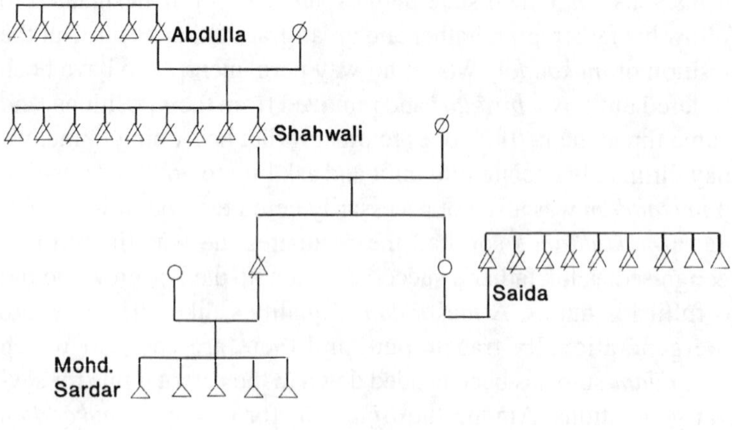

> Among the *Bijāṛ* formerly Shakhbud was *mukaddam*. He had thirteen sons…. But all these thirteen sons were known to be very cruel (*ḍaḍḍā*). The eldest was Gulsaid; my father, Salar, was the third. So when my father's grandfather (*dādā*) grew old, he decided that Habib should become *mukaddam* – he was his younger brother's son. Habib became *mukaddam* and then briefly *lambardār* [see below]. Then came Makkhaṇ, Habib's eldest son. He was removed by the Government and replaced by his younger brother Subo. After Subo, it's his son Daud, who as you know is our *mukaddam*; and now we also have Daud *lambardār*'s daughter's husband Yasin, who's actually not *Bijāṛ*, but *Mandaṛ*.

This example, as well as that illustrated in Figure 5.8, indicates that the qualities appropriate for a *mukaddam* – and *lambardār* – can at times also be transmitted through marriage. The following apocryphal anecdote also pertaining to the *Bijāṛ* highlights that a *mukaddam*'s affines are also expected to live up to the ideals expected of him personally.

> Before 1947 there was Subo Bijāṛ – with three wives – father of Daud. He had an elder brother, Makkhaṇ, who was *mukaddam*. One day a policeman was sent to arrest a culprit. When he reached Makkhaṇ's home he was very hungry. Daud's stepmother gave him something to eat. Unable to catch the culprit, the policeman went back. On his way back, he met the *rājā*, Hari Singh, and his *rāṇi*. He went to them and said, that though he had gone to Makkhaṇ, his wife was so miserly, "she didn't give me anything to eat or a place to rest, but Suba's wife did; make him *lambardār* instead of Makkhaṇ". The *rājā* then made Suba *lambardār*, and after him Daud, his son, followed. This is how it all happened.

Even a cursory look at the genealogies of the *mukaddam* of various *zāt* shows, however, that not just qualities such as bravery, hospitality and wisdom, but also the number of siblings appears to play a role in their attaining this position. Like all *kumbā* leaders, all *mukaddam* had and have large sibling groups, and are often the eldest. Thus, for example, among the *Bokṛā and the Khaṭāṇā zāt*,

> … formerly Halim [Bokṛā] was *mukaddam*. He had five real brothers and six brothers from another mother. But he had only one son, so Israel [Khaṭāṇā] … took it away. Then … Alamdin [Bokṛā] … got it. Before Halim his ancestors were not *mukaddam*, because they were only sons; who'll listen to a man who's alone? How will he sit apart? How will he get things done? …

Data on twenty-seven men who were or had been *mukaddam/ lambardār* also show that they had an average of 6.1 brothers, while thirty-nine men of similar age with little well-being had only 3.4 brothers on average (cf. Table 5.1). Figure 5.9 illustrates these findings (for further details see Casimir and Rao 1995). "Who listens to an only son …?" is a commonly heard expression of helplessness. No Nietzschean "outsider", but only a man recognised as socially bound in a large, preferably male, kin network can aspire to become *mukaddam*.

The lambardār

Towards the early years of this century there were thus several *mukaddam*, who were all men of influence and authority within the community, but whose relative influence is said to have been of little consequence. This was to change as a response to the system of indirect rule that the area was soon subjected to. The colonial administration had experience in collecting land taxes in North India through the institution of the *lambardār* – literally a man, representing several smaller landholders, with a number (*nambardār*), which was entered in the tax records. Following this model, each larger grouping of Bakkarwal was now assigned a *lambardār* from among the existing *mukaddam*. Most of these larger groupings corresponded with *zāt/khēl* boundaries. Thus the number of more or less informal leaders was officially reduced to a few formal ones, and from among the *mukaddam*, whose relative importance had until now been negligible, a select few were elevated to higher positions of authority. While some of the *lambardār* were chosen by the Bakkarwal themselves and then recognised by the Government, others, such as Suba Bijāṛ mentioned above, were simply designated by the administration. They were paid a small salary and made accountable for law and order within their respective groupings. They were also responsible for procuring animals on the hoof which were destined to be compulsorily sold for meat to the British Indian army. Their primary task was, however, to collect grazing taxes (in kind or in the regionally standard silver *rupees*) from the herdsmen of their groups and submit these to the Government. Hence, the larger a grouping, and the greater the revenue forthcoming, the more important it became. The *lambardār* of the largest

Figure 5.9 Data concerning the number of sons and brothers of twenty-seven *lambardār* compared with similar data for sixty-nine other men

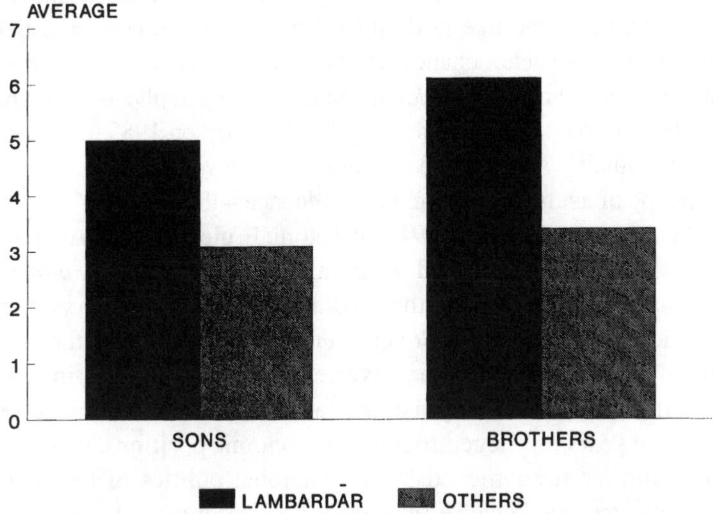

groupings thus also automatically became – or at least were confirmed officially in their roles as – the most important representatives of the community. Since for every unit of tax collected, a *lambardār* got a certain share in cash (Rs. 5/- for every Rs. 100/- collected and given to the Government), and since the entire economy was monetarising, it was also in his interest to expand the size of the group he represented. Thus, perhaps more than before, political power and economic status became inseparable.

Competition also emerged among *lambardār*, and among *mukaddam* who aspired to become *lambardār*. To become *lambardār* a *mukaddam* had to effectively coordinate old internal, factional roles with the new external, extrafactional ones (cf. Sahlins 1963: 290ff.). This often led to the system of preferential primogeniture being replaced by new criteria and hence, as Abdulla, Nura's brother, explained, "Though Nura was not the eldest, he was literate, so he became *lambardār*". The former criteria of wisdom and helpfulness were now less in demand, and older Bakkarwal remember that "most of the *lambardār* were cruel". As old Jima recounted: "Those days the Government (*ukumat*) was very cruel to the Bakkarwal.... In addition the *lambardār*'s job was to tyrannise (*julum*) over the rest. He was supposed to act as a go-between, but most of us never got any help...." Muscle power, which had always been an important component of *mukaddam*-ship, now became indispensable, and, for example, men who like "Adarji [Bargaṭ] used to be great wrestlers (*pahlwān*)" had better chances than ever before. It was this competition between various *mukaddam* and the ensuing application of what has been termed indirect bias (Boyd and Richerson 1985 in Spencer 1993), which is said to have encouraged the development of the second type of acknowledged man of influence – the *kharpẽñč*.

With the cessation in 1947 of colonial rule in South Asia and feudal rule in Jammu and Kashmir, the position of *lambardār* gradually changed among the Bakkarwal. They stopped receiving salaries, and in 1983 the Government decided to abolish the post; this decision was, however, reversed following protests in 1984 (Sharma 1984). Not only had the families of these men acquired over the years privileged social and economic positions, these had been further strengthened by the factional politics of the wider society. Perhaps because they no longer received salaries, these men are said to have become increasingly corrupt (*rishwatkhor*). Although they are known to take their cut in Government deals, they are also thought to help those "of their own *birādari*", and as such they, like South Indian "leaders", are perceived of as "self-interested patrons" (Mines 1992: 133).

Even after 1947 the terms *lambardār* and *mukaddam* continue to be used, with the *mukaddam* from the ex-*lambardār* families still being known as *lambardār*. There is no difference in their formally recognised duties, each of these men now being considered primarily responsible for settling disputes (*tanāzā*) within his respective faction: "When one was involved in a quarrel within or without the *birādari* one went to the *mukaddam* for help, unless one knew that he's closely related to the opponent." With time even this role is said to have changed somewhat, and I was often told that "these days within the community there's no real justice done". I would now like to briefly mention two cases as examples of dispute settlement and jural decision making.

In 1982 a *Bijāṛ* "lost" two of his goats on the autumn migration. On 25 July 1983 the thief – or rather thieves, two *Bijāṛ* brothers – were caught. In November the brothers fell out with each other and each accused the other of being a thief. Neighbours heard this and went to the man who had lost his goats. He in turn complained to Daud *lambardār*, who sent for the two brothers and then took one goat from each of them, of the same age and sex as the stolen ones. Both were given to the wronged man, who offered them [in gratitude, as he said] to Daud, who did not accept. [Most men and women who heard about the case said that Daud refused only because I was present.]

Mioñ Bokṛā saw Gogra with a goat and had a feeling it was stolen. Gogra said: "Take Rs. 150/- from me, but please don't tell anyone." Mioñ replied: "I won't take any money, but if I find that the goat belongs to someone in our *birādari*, I'll report you; otherwise I'll keep quiet." After about fifteen days it was generally known that Leñtha had lost one of his very best goats. When Mioñ heard this, he told him about the goat he had seen with Gogra. The case went up to Alamdin *mukaddam*, who it was rumoured was bribed by Gogra to side with him. Alamdin then told Mioñ, "Go to Delhi. There the bull (*dāñ*) which detects the truth will decide which of you is the liar". [The rest of this story was narrated to me by Jijo, whose sister is married to Gogra's brother.] "Mioñ, Gogra and two of Alamdin's men – including … [one of his sons] – went to Delhi, and there they located one of these bulls. The bull was first asked, 'Who's the thief?' The bull went and stood in front of Gogra. Then … [Alamdin's son] asked the bull, 'Is Mioñ telling the truth or a lie?' This time the bull went and stood in front of Mioñ, and this was interpreted by … [Alamdin's son] as proof that Mioñ was lying. So Mioñ was made to pay all the travel expenses [Rs. 1500/-], and he'll also have to give a goat to Alamdin for having settled the dispute." [Incidentally, Alamdin's son had been planning to go to Delhi anyway to buy goods which he sold on his return.]

With increasing police intervention in case of disputes, even these jural responsibilities have been reduced, and a Phāmṛā *mukaddam*'s son commented:

My father has little work these days. My grandfather was *lambardār* and collected taxes from the people. These days even the main job of settling disputes is done by the police. I think in the next ten or twenty years there will be no work at all left for a *mukaddam*.

But in many other respects these men have become "even more important than before, because we have more and more problems, and new ones too, and we can't cope with them". It was generally felt that "there is no comparison in the degree of Government interference now and formerly"; "those days only the money was collected and put directly in the treasury (*khajānā*), and no officer (*afsar*) had any connection with us". Indeed the perceived "problems" can be traced primarily to the direct or indirect intrusion of the *ukumati* sphere in the lives of every family, through Government restrictions on grazing, the official allotment of browsing areas, the need for ration cards, census operations, veterinary services and the like. Whereas short-term daily or seasonal negotiations with officers of various kinds are carried out by all "big men" on the behalf of "their people", negotiations with long-lasting implications with administrators and politicians are left to men of influence, and especially to the *mukaddam/lambardār*, who are considered personally accountable for families within their sphere of influence.

The *lambardār/mukaddam* are not formally elected, but in contrast to what was reported of earlier times, the wishes of the previous *lambardār/mukaddam* are now taken into account, and are said to ensure that "what prevails is either might or money" ("*yā čale ḍanḍā yā paiñsā*"). In the 1980s in certain areas given *lambardār* were recognised as heads of a number of *mukaddam*, in others *mukkadam* and *lambardār* competed for recognition, and "now for every fifteen to twenty *ḍēṛā* there is a *lambardār* or *mukaddam*". There is also a certain hierarchy among the *mukaddam*, and this has led to a hierarchy of patron-client structures in every grazing and browsing locality. Each of these structures forms a subfaction, with patrons at every level often being related by birth or marriage to the patrons of the structures above them. Old *sakāwat* networks are also part of these structures. Thus in the Kathua area:

> In my father's time our *mukaddam* was Sher Mohammad, then Hāji Mir. Our big man now is Abdul Hamid; he's still young but has studied up to Class X. Hāji Mir also does some work for us, but he's now too old. Hāji Mehndi is that way more useful and helps a lot. My great-grandfather used to get *sakāwat* from Hāji Mehndi's grandfather. Abdul Ghani Khaṭāṇā – Chaudhri Shafi's brother – is also our *mukaddam*, but he's far and we need someone nearby.

Many such patrons are older *khaṛpēñč* rather than *mukaddam* or *lambardār*, but they too are the heads of *ṭōlā* or *kumbā*, and in this society also "patrons … value as many males as possible in their dependent clients" (Oldenburg 1992: 2659). Since each client is also a member of a particular *zāt* and *birādari* his freedom to choose between patrons, his decision to affiliate with one rather than with another set of patrons, is de facto extremely limited, though theoretically possible. Since both *zāt* and *birādari* are territorially distributed, so are the influence spheres of the *lambardār/mukaddam*. Thus Daud's sphere, for example, covers the areas of Lidderwat, Sekwas, Kolhoi, Rakh Dachigam, and he exercises authority over most *Bijāṛ* and some *Bargaṭ*. Choice is yet more circumscribed if one's father or grandfather were part of a *sakāwat* structure. At the lowest factional level however, political allegiance is perceived by some as a matter of individual choice.

> "Why did you choose K. as your *mukaddam*", I asked Saiñfo one day, after he had complained a lot against him. "You see, it's like this", he explained, "you've seen Pahalgam, you've seen Islamabad, you've seen all these places, haven't you? Now there are so many shops in Islamabad – many more than in Pahalgam. There are also a few houses in Pahalagam, and I know many of the people there. But whenever I take a loan – last week I took one for Rs. 1500/- – I take it from one particular shop in Pahalgam. I don't go to Islamabad, or to any other place; I don't go to any and every shop in Pahalgam – I go only there, like when I'm in A. I go to only one house there – that of our common friend. I never go elsewhere, but I can go there and stay for days. It's all a question of mutual trust. That's all. We all trusted K. in the beginning, we all went to him; each time we went to him, and then again and again, and in the beginning he was trustworthy. Then it all changed ... Only God can see into a man's heart."

There are thus numerous vertical chains of loyalty based primarily on the patron-client tradition of *sakāwat* and factionalism. But increasingly solidarity is also based on wealth which runs horizontally, cutting across factions. I was often told that even while settling disputes between members of different factions "all these men always take money from all the parties concerned and usually reach some sort of *status quo*". It is generally felt that "most *lambardār* care not a bit for the poor, but rather eat and eat, and share only with other rich men of their kind". This tendency can be observed not only among the *mukaddam/lambardār*, but among all men of influence who tend to stick together and intermarry (Rao 1997). "For the rich I may die like a dog – they don't care", said old Makhṇi, who had come all the way from Trehat to Jammu to request a *mukaddam* to sign a petition on her behalf. She waited in vain for over a week, and slept on the pavement in winter, but this man "simply didn't find the time"; "there are so many who want something or the other, I can't see them all!", he told me later.

The kharpēñč

A second type of man of influence is known as *kharpēñč* (<*pēñč denāñ* = to screw; the term did not seem to be known among non-Bakkarwal in their winter area, but has been apparently borrowed, along with its connotations, by rural Kashmiri Hindus and Muslims who use it in the context of politics and power relations – Madan, per. comm., 1996). Often in their thirties when starting off on their careers, most *kharpēñč* are known to outsiders who have more frequent contact with the Bakkarwal – other pastoralists or villagers living near pasture areas, forest guards, veterinary surgeons, etc. – since they tend to know their way in and out of centres of power (both *pablik* and *ukumati*) in the alien sphere. Many opine that "it is the *kharpēñč* who are the first to get the merino sheep for breeding", and "In the name of helping, the *kharpēñč* take money and animals. When some big Government officer comes they feed and feast him – not with their own animals, but with those they take from us poor people". Their image is one of wealthy, well-dressed men who tend to be innovative, efficient, and generally "get things done". In his desire to "come up" and assert himself, a potential *kharpēñč* will try to experiment. Such a man symbolises lack of scruples and intense competitiveness; in his attempt to assert autonomy he lets no opportunity slip even if this entails running risks or refuting certain norms. If he fails he will be condemned as a rash fool; if he succeeds he will be feared and admired by many, and will become known as a *kharpēñč*.

All Bakkarwal I came across agreed that physical strength (*jismāni tākat*), wealth (*sarmāyā*), coupled with intelligence (*čālāki*) and an excess of *nafas* are the ingredients that go into the making of a *kharpēñč*. These characteristics form the basis of his unique *mijāj*, his special blend of authenticity, and lead to "many automatically listening" to him. A would-be *kharpēñč* is thus a wealthy, perhaps overly ambitious, impetuous and unscrupulous (youngish) man who uses both his muscles and his brains to obtain influence and attain power as rapidly as possible, or as Mawali expressed it, "to take money and women". The following incident illustrates the kind of tactics employed by a *kharpēñč* to retain power and extend hold over an even greater number of persons.

On 20 August 1983 in Pahalgam, Sadia, who had two horses but was badly in need of cash, offered to sell one of them to a Kashmiri villager for Rs. 800. A policeman happened to be standing nearby and overheard the conversation; not surprisingly, he found the sale price extraordinarily low and assumed that the horse must be stolen. So he marched Sadia and the villager off to the police station; both men protested in vain. Finally, as the charge of dealing with stolen horses was being recorded, Sadia requested that M. be asked to testify to his innocence. The policemen all knew of M., a few even knew him personally, and they agreed to Sadia's request. M., who at that stage did not know Sadia, came and testified that the two horses genuinely belonged to the latter, and that he was selling one of them so cheaply because he was very hard up. He offered to testify in writing, and requested the release of both men. The police agreed. It is not known what exactly transpired between M. and the police after this. By late evening the villager was released, but Sadia was told that since it was raining quite hard and it was too late for him to walk all the way back to his mountain camp, he could spend the night at the lock-up with them and go back the following morning. Sadia agreed. Next morning, however, he was not released. Instead M. sent a man to inform him that the police had decided to keep him in detention and impound both his horses till the Hindu pilgrimage (*yātrā*) to Amarnath was over. [Pahalgam is used as a base by pilgrims visiting a particular holy cave above the eastern Lidder Valley.] After this he and his horses would be released and he was free to sell his horse – on condition that M. would be responsible for producing his other horse whenever required. M. had of course agreed, in order to help his "own men". But from now on Sadia, who had had practically no contact with M. previously, was bound to him in more ways than one.

Although physically strong and often brutal, *kharpēñč* are imputed with inherently female characteristics such as faithlessness and vanity. While he can not logically be considered as "a volume in perpetual disintegration" in the Foucaultian sense, a *kharpēñč* is said to be unstable (liable to change, *tabdili*) and, unlike other adult men of well-being, forever immature, pubertal (*jawāni*) and *shoñki*; hence he is considered faithless, unreliable and untrustworthy (*bewafā*). His agency is seen as that of egoism and intense personal ambition, regardless of the welfare of even his close kin. "A *kharpēñč* doesn't help even his own brothers and sisters; he only gets himself rich with masses of [herd] animals, horses, money." Selfishness can ignore even the bonds of blood. The characteristics ascribed to a *kharpēñč* are hence negative, and yet it is this ascription which is his purpose. As Kuba and Farid expressed it, "we ourselves make them, anyone, of any age, who can talk and represent well and get things done". "We ourselves create our problems, we make someone big, someone who can talk – nowadays, often someone who can read and write. We make him and then he deceives (*pēñč denāñ*, lit. "screws") us." It is perhaps this very creation and deception which, however, keep the *kharpēñč* orientated towards their own community, and not beyond it. In this sense they may not, in spite of their ambition, innovativeness and selfishness, qualify for classification as truly "cosmopolitan individuals", who are by definition "… orientated to the world outside of [their] social system" (Merton 1968 in Valente 1996: 74).

A *kharpēñč* is a man of influence and one who could provide links to information from both within and beyond the community; yet he is not a man of authority, and is never respected as much as a *mukaddam* or *lambardār* is. A *mukkadam*'s son can, but must not, become a *kharpēñč;* every *kharpēñč* aspires, however, to become a *mukaddam.* Some are successful, while others remain *kharpēñč* till they are too old to instill enough fear in others, and retain their status only as *kumbā* or *ṭōlā* leaders. To become a *mukaddam* a *kharpēñč* must over the years tone down his rashness considerably and transform his behaviour so that his supposedly female characteristics are replaced by manly qualities; he must convince others that they benefit enough from his surrogate agency to become his steady clients. Were one to draw a continuum between rashness and heedfulness, the *kharpēñč* would be located at the rash end. Ideally, the *mukaddam* would be at just the right point, somewhere in the middle, with the *sirgardā*, the third type of men of influence, more heedful still. As among the Ilongot, here too

> … the central issues of social thought are not only the conventional ones of cohesion and the normative order, but also the emergent ones of discussion and the politics of persuasion, both artful and forceful. (Rosaldo 1989: 21)

While a *kharpēñč* is forceful, a *mukaddam,* and especially a *sirgardā*, is artful. But there is yet another criterion which is important for a *kharpēñč* to become a *mukaddam* – the number of close agnates, and especially sons and brothers, he has. Those who fail to become *mukaddam* usually have much smaller and poorer kin-groups, and fewer brothers. As Bājā commented:

> A man who's poor but has many kin can't achieve anything – who listens to him? A man who has [herd] animals (*māḷ*) and no kin can be a *kharpēñč* if he has the *mijāj* for it – many will listen to him. To become *kharpēñč* animals and wealth (*sarmāyā*) are better than kin-group. To become *mukaddam* you need *māḷ* and many kin and the right *mijāj*. A rich man with many kin is the most powerful.

The sirgardā

To achieve the status of *sirgardā* (cf. Pers. *sar-gord* = a major) a man must be perceived to have well-being, and must be somewhere between about forty-five and fifty years old. While a *kharpēñč* starts off fairly young, in the generally gerontocratic authority structure of northern India to be recognised as either *mukaddam* or considered *sirgardā* one must be older, the image of a man of authority being *per se* that of an elderly man, a man with experience. To be *sirgardā* a man must in addition consistently demonstrate certain qualities over a period of time: he must be seen as God-fearing (*khōf*), impartial and honest (*insāf*); sincere and truthful (*sadākati*); "large-hearted", as looking after the interests of both poor and rich equally and taking decisions even-handedly. Some of the *sirgardā* I came across supported indigent and aged widows, whose husbands or fathers had once been dependants within the *sakāwat* network, living in their camps. A *sirgardā*'s son rarely achieves this status, and it is conceivable for him to become a *kharpēñč*:

> Jimio had two twin sons, about thirty-five years old. Of one of them it was generally said that he was well on his way to becoming a *kharpēñč*. The other son had a very good reputation as an honest, helpful man. But he was much too young to be considered a *sirgardā*. To explain the difference between the two, neighbours and relatives again referred to the analogy of the five unequal fingers of a hand or

> the different branches of a tree. Both sons were men of well-being, both were said to have drunk the same mother's milk – and yet their respective *mijāj* were different.

Unlike *mukaddam* who can be de-recognised, and unlike *kharpēñč* who may become *mukaddam* or cease to have influence when too old, a *sirgardā* remains so all his life. The term is not familiar beyond the community, but individual *sirgardā* are known even outside as wealthy and good men, worthy of respect.

Unlike the *kharpēñč* who epitomise a maximum of *nafas* in an evil way, the *sirgardā* have the right amount of it; they embody the ideals of Bakkarwal society and represent the moral order. A *sirgardā* is highly respected – perhaps more so than a *mukaddam* is – because his agency is seen as that of solidarity and ultimate good; he also stands for male virtues and characteristics. The Weberian distinction between *Herrschaft* and *Macht* could well be applied to the dichotomy between *kharpēñč* and *sirgardā*: while a *sirgardā* would represent the nearly pure concept of domination, a *kharpēñč* would stand for power. The *sirgardā* exemplify the concept of agency through individuality, of autonomy through action, without, however, precluding holistic goals. To achieve something for oneself but also care for others is the surest sign of wisdom. In this respect the *sirgardā* also seem to represent orthodoxy in Bourdieu's (1977: 168) sense, his concept of heterodoxy appearing to fit the *kharpēñč*.

The Comparative Status of Men of Influence

In the precolonial period men of influence achieved their respective status by demonstrating that they possessed certain characteristics. While a *mukaddam* derived his framework of legitimacy partly from tradition and partly from charisma, a *sirgardā* seems to have derived it almost entirely from the latter. These two types of men of influence formed a sequential hierarchy (cf. Johnson 1982: 396–409), with the as yet only aspiring *kharpēñč* butting in now and then. With the growth of the market economy and the formation of coalitions, a *mukaddam*'s domination, in the Weberian sense, became subject to notions of exchange and negotiable relations. Only a *sirgardā* remained beyond such negotiability – and hence also beyond economic and political flexibility. With the emergence of *lambardār* and the superimposition of bureaucratic organisation, the sequential system slowly modified into one of simultaneous hierarchies covering several subfactions. The early colonial period corresponded with new forms of ethnic awareness (Rao 1988b) and with an overall context of rapid cultural change. The entire community was thus confronted with a fairly high-risk situation, in which it has been postulated that the authority of a man will be accepted when he

> … has demonstrated success in an activity that is critical to group survival. Other expressions of his authority would then tend to be accepted as part of the leadership package through the mechanism of indirect bias. (Spencer 1993: 48)

It was, I submit, this new kind of acceptance of authority which ultimately led to the transformation from sequential to simultaneous hierarchies, and to the emergence of *lambardār/mukaddam* as the most important of all the various men of influence. That the *sirgardā* lost out to them in the final count of power – though not respect – is clear from the fact that rarely could people remember the status of a *sirgardā*'s father – unless he had been a *lambardār/mukaddam*.

The increasing acceptance of a "leadership package" apparently also led to the greater importance of the principle of inheritance for the *mukaddam/lambardār*. While among all three types of men of influence the respective relative socio-economic advantages do tend to be handed down to the following generation, only among the *lambardār/mukaddam* is the retention of high status combined with recognition as a group representative largely achieved. As discussed in earlier chapters, all characteristics are in principle inheritable and 57 per cent of the fathers of the twenty-seven *lambardār/mukaddam* considered had also held this position, but the father of only one of nine *kharpēñč* was reported to also have been a *kharpēñč*. The principle of inheritance and of transmission over at least two generations of the status of *kharpēñč* and *sirgardā* is rare. For them, unlike for the *mukaddam/lambardār*, the principle of individual achievement, eventually through the exercise of personal choice, is ultimately more crucial than that of inheritance, although the two principles combine to form all men of influence, and the latter plays an important role in the creation of the former.

For all men of influence patterns of socialisation and the inculcation of status-specific norms and values are of importance. Information – and access to it – is also intergenerationally transmitted, so that the son of a man who had access to a great deal of information is likely to have more access than the son of a man who had little access. There thus exists an at least informal system of intergenerational hierarchisation of information processing, and based thereon the capacity to make choices and take and formulate decisions, both individual and surrogate. The access to information can also imply – and in its turn lead to – becoming known as a knowledgeable man. This can lead to obtaining still more information, and this again both to more options to choose from and actual occasions in which decisions are to be taken. All this adds up to greater authority or power, which again can be transmitted over generations. This intergenerational transmission of information and decision-making capacity has led to the emergence of a certain pool of families, all of whose male heads are, or were in the recent past, men of influence of one kind or the other. Other members of these families also enjoy considerably higher status than do members of families of less influence. Children from these high-status families also largely intermarry, and the combined practice of bridewealth and dowry among them (Rao 1997) has helped raise both their economic and demographic status. These families, who were in any case wealthier than most others, have by and large become wealthier, and their fairly large number of offspring has proportionally increased more than that of other families (Casimir and Rao 1995). Thus their already great well-being has increased further.

Controlling Persons through the Alien Sphere

I have already used the term "leader" for Bakkarwal *mukkadam*, *lambardār* and *kharpēñč,* and have compared the former to "leaders" in India. This could be misleading and hence I should add that although the English term "*līḍar*" is used by the Bakkarwal themselves it does not denote men who occupy these positions, or play these roles. The term *līḍar* is used by them only to denote men who are openly affiliated with any political party (*siyāsi pālṭi*), or try to canvas for a party's candidate. As Hājji Suba Phāmṛā, who married thrice and now has roughly one hundred descendants, told me: "My father was *lambardār*, and after him I was *lambardār* … I was not a *līḍar* as you now have – as Iqbal is – those days were different …" Iqbal, Hājji Suba's son, is well known as a *kharpēñč,* and at the time this conversation took place he was going around trying to persuade people to attend a rally of the Congress Party. Other men such as Chaudhri Mohammad Shafi Khaṭāṇā have entered party politics; Hājji Zubair Khaṭāṇā stood as a Janata Party candidate in 1977, and Mohammad Yasin Mandaṛ tried to get nominated in 1981 for the National Conference Party. *Līḍar* are, however, recruited exclusively from among the existing men of influence, since political parties are also interested in using the power or authority bases of their members. There is thus a clear nexus of power between *līḍar*, *mukaddam*/*lambardār* and even *kharpēñč,* and it is widely reported that increasingly Chaudhri Mohammad Shafi Khaṭāṇā imposes *mukaddam* on various sub-factions of the *Kunhāri*. The interplay of these various power bases is illustrated by what Dina, a Mandaṛ told me:

> Since Daud Bijāṛ is getting too old, now Yasin is *lambardār* of almost all *Allaiāḷ*, and calls himself Yasin Allaiāḷ, rather than Mandaṛ. The *Mandaṛ* are very few in number, so what's the point in calling himself Mandaṛ. Yasin's mother is *Bijāṛ*, so is his wife, so he can be their *mukkadam* too.… The *Bijāṛ* are also *Allaiaḷ*, like the *Bargaṭ*.… Before Yasin his father Isak was the *mukaddam* of the *Mandaṛ*, before him his elder brother Gul, and before him their father Sheikh Nur. When Sheikh Sāb [Sheikh Abdullah] came back to power [as Chief Minister of Jammu and Kashmir], Yasin decided to give a great feast. From each *Allaiāḷ* he took a *lēlu* (sheep) and he also managed to get eight *kharwār* [wheat]. He promised to help all *Allaiāḷ* in future, and we swore on the Qor'an in the presence of Nanga Bāji Pīr* to follow him.
>
> *Yasin's opponents contend that the present incumbent of this Chishti shrine in Bandipore, northern Kashmir, accompanied Yasin to various *Allaiwāḷ* camps for about ten days prior to the feast and used his religious authority to persuade people to "accept Yasin as *lambardār* of all the *Allaiwāḷ* and to say they will vote for him in the elections".

However, the political affiliations of these *līḍar* are often temporary, and this lack of loyalty is morally disapproved of, since it is in blatant contradiction of the idea of authenticity discussed in earlier chapters. Such men are thus considered as untrustworthy as the

Figure 5.10 The major differences in economic, social and political status between various types of men with great well-being

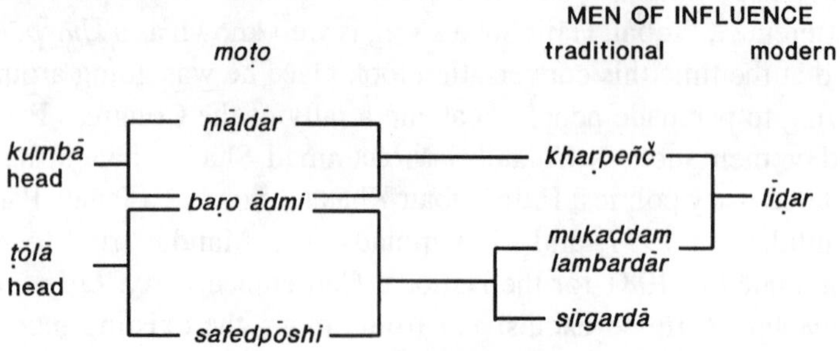

kharpēñč, and yet they have followers and their agency is recognised because the benefits they can bestow are clear. Figure 5.10 illustrates the basic classificatory differences between various types of men with great well-being, influence and eventually authority.

Since the late 1980s, however, the influence and authority of many of these men appears to have been badly affected. During the spring migration of 1987 there were severe hailstorms, very heavy rain and landslides. Thousands of animals perished while crossing the steep and narrow passes. Fairly rapidly, the central Indian government at Delhi sanctioned a very large amount of compensatory money for the affected families. While the rich received compensation immediately, it was widely held among the less well-to-do that almost all wealthy men – except the *sirgardā* – had pocketed the shares of those allegedly under their care (Rao 1995). This was not considered surprising, since it was equally widely opined that "anyway these murderous and deadly (*murdār*) people have been eating our money for years". Nearly two and one-half years later, shortly before the autumn migration in 1989, several of these wealthy men, and especially *mukaddam/lambardār* and *kharpēñč,* were asked by Kashmiri militants for large sums of money as contribution towards their campaign to fight the Indian State; most, including Hājji Suba Phāmṛā, refused to pay and were beaten up. Those who demanded the money mentioned explicitly the compensatory amounts issued in 1987, and felt that "since that was anyway not their own money, they should now hand it over". On the face of it at least, these demands for money were thus being made – perhaps by new would-be patrons – on behalf of the poor who felt cheated of their dues. In spring 1990 and summer 1991 again some men of influence were beaten up – this time both by Kashmiri militants and by Indian army or paramilitary forces. The latter suspected them of aiding the militants by accepting them as part of their migrating units (*ṭōlā*). Hence identity and migration permits were made compulsory for each household in a *ṭōlā*; to obtain a permit each *ḍēṛā* head had to request (and often bribe) his *kumbā* leader, and these men in turn had to bribe local officials (e.g. *tehsildār*); those who failed to obtain permits had to bribe their way through the military check-posts either with cash or livestock. The wealthier the herd-owner, the larger the bribe, and the greater the humiliation *vis-à-vis* his traditional clients and followers. Large bribes also had to be paid to the Indian forces posted in and near some of the choicest summer pasture areas of Talel, Gurez and Bandipora, close to the Indo-Pakistan cease-fire line and used primarily by the rich. Grazing was now curtailed in many of these areas; flocks straying over army lines of control were confiscated, and their owners penalised. The wealthier the owner identified, the heavier the penalty. The richer the herd-owner, the greater his chances of being blackmailed and the more he had at stake.

For a variety of reasons, therefore, the wealthiest ceased to migrate as they had before, and gradually even those slightly below them in the socio-economic hierarchy kept to their respective winter areas. Since to survive their flocks must, however, migrate, these men of wealth and influence grew more dependent than ever on the labour of those with less well-being. This dependency led to a gradual de-recognition of the surrogate agency of men of influence; as Chāñdi expressed it in 1992: "Now that these men – who were imposed on us just as the ministers were imposed on the whole state – have been beaten up, they've no more power over us...." Others gave vent to their pent-up feelings of submission by openly refusing for the first time to pay their traditional patrons dues of various kinds, which (they now said) they had always found excessive, if not illegitimate. For the first time resentment was expressed; for the first time the status of *sirgardā* has apparently yielded more sustained well-being than those of other men of influence.

The Two Sides of a Coin

Data presented in this chapter suggest that according to concepts prevailing locally it would be logically incorrect to contrast holism with individualism. They indicate that it would be more meaningful to conceive of them as two sides of the same coin, to think of individual agency as "grounded in the social totality" (Ingold 1986: 223). In most cultures

> … socialization consists of constantly renewed attempts on the part of society to encompass the social actor as agent in its purposes, attempts that are repeatedly contravened … On the level of interactive systems, culture consists not so much in clear-cut "effects" as in topics of negotiation and dispute. However, even these disputes are culturally orchestrated. (Mageo 1991: 406)

In a society with differential access to resources even the ideology of social organisation must, however, be based simultaneously on competition, individual achievement and generalised help. Social practice consists, then, of constant negotiation between competition and cooperation, between coercion and help.

To compete or cooperate, to coerce or help successfully, one must have both the capacity and the desire to do so. The basis of the capacity to compete, coerce and help is constituted by personal well-being and self-esteem; the ability to cooperate is perceived to lie in a certain amount of agency. In other words, all these call for the right amount of *nafas*. The desire to help, to "do good to others" (*pare*) as opposed only to oneself (*apaṇ*) is generated by unselfishness. This in turn presupposes empathy and sympathy (*amdardi*), the capacity to put oneself in someone else's place, which in the local view in its turn presupposes a great amount of *ōsh*. It is *ōsh* which, however, enables one to distinguish between oneself and others, to compete and coerce, but also cooperate.

Chapter 6

WAITING FOR THE LIFE BEYOND

... We bring you forth as infants; then We make you attain your full vigour; and some of you die (young); and among you is he who is reduced to the most contemptible stage of life, so that after knowing something he may know nothing ...

— Qor'an (CIX/22; cf. also XL/67)

This is going to be a brief chapter, largely because I had relatively little intimate access to the elderly. My own age probably came in the way (cf. Cohen 1994: 154 for a reference to this problem), and I often felt that most of the aged were resentful of my spending time with those younger. This weakness in my study is all the graver since I have chosen the life-course perspective, but it is also typical perhaps of studies on South Asia, where though those above sixty years of age form an increasingly large percentage of the total population (in India over 38 per cent; cf. Joshi 1996), "... little detailed attention seems to have been given to [the study of]s the later years of life" (Vatuk 1995: 289). But first I must clarify what I mean by the "elderly", or the "aged". It has been debated whether "old age" as a stage in life is universally recognised. Even in societies in which this phase is explicitly mentioned, the criteria of definition, as well as the chronological age at which it begins, vary considerably (cf. Cowgill 1986: 6–7 for a brief overview). Though biological, chronological ages are sometimes mentioned by the Bakkarwal as stereotyped, "heaped" markers for the onset of old age ("above forty", "fifty", "sixty") in both women and men, it appeared to me that these have as little cognitive relevance here as they do in neighbouring societies (Vatuk 1990: 69).

It has been mentioned time and again in earlier chapters that following a basically Hellenistic principle (Onians 1951: 215) the Bakkarwal conceive of the process of life as a gradual increase and then decrease of bodily strength. This in turn is based on the gradual rise and fall of body substances (cf. Fig. 1.5) which rise in youth to reach a certain plateau in maturity and fall slowly thereafter. Symptoms of this decrease are numerous – greying hair, pain in the joints, weak vision, loss of teeth, failing memory, general slowness, bad temper, etc. Menopause (there is no specific word in Bakkarwali for this) is not considered a symptom of old age but rather its consequence, and a woman is considered old when she reaches this stage. In Western medicine the final cessation of menstruation is related to a variety of physiological phenomena (cf. Wise et al. 1996); here it is explicitly connected to weakening vision and lack of strength which themselves are the result of the decrease in the level of blood in the body. No particular chronological age appears to be attached to climacterium, but it is widely held that among men the level of blood (manifested in semen) sinks later than it does in women. This sex-based differentiation did not, however, appear to be biased in the sense Pierce (1981: 3 in Cowgill 1986: 8) suggested, when he stated that in most cultures, "women 'age', while men 'mature'". For both women and men in this society growing old – *buḍo/buḍi ōṇāñ* – is understood as being well on the way to becoming decrepit, and hence dependent and helpless in much the same ways as described by Vatuk (1990: 67ff.) for other North Indians. Biologically aged persons of either sex in full possession of their mental and physical faculties are not categorised thus. On the other hand, frail and elderly women and men are often said to be "ninety or even one hundred years old", even when their biological ages, established through careful questioning and sifting of chronology, did not exceed fifty or sixty years. As discussed below, the Bakkarwal also distinguish terminologically between being *buḍo/buḍi* (cf. Hd. *buḍḍhā* = old, aged) and being *bujurg* (cf. Pers./Ur. *buzurg* = old, venerable, great), a distinction which, I submit, is closely related to perceptions of power and well-being. Indeed, in practice old age itself appears here as in certain other societies (cf. Wilkes 1992) to be less a matter of chronology than of perception by oneself and by others.

Biological Age

Ideologically, however, one is considered *buḍo*/*buḍi* at the latest when one's eldest grandchildren have married and reproduced. Taking the average age at marriage as 16.2 (±3.4) years for women and 18 (±3.2) years for men respectively (Ch. 3) and age at first pregnancy at 21.3 (±6.0) years (Ch. 4), this comes to around sixty years for both men and women. By this time a man must have long distributed his property among his inheritors; whether he still retains control over them symbolically or not depends on his social status – on whether he is considered *buḍo* or *bujurg*. For analytical purposes I now turn, then, to the question of biological age. Figure I.2 indicates that Bakkarwal women and men spontaneously tended to give their ages in "heaps", and that according to this no one mentioned her/his own age as greater than seventy-five years – though others may well have referred to them as "over one hundred" years old. Figure 6.1 now shows, however, that of 710 women and men, five and three respectively were found to be greater than seventy-five years; these ages were established after much counter-checking and sieving of data, as described in the introductory chapter. In most Third World societies, with high mortality rates, men outlive women; this is true for India as well, and in Jammu and Kashmir the proportion of aged women to men was 646/1,000 (National Sample Survey 1986/87 in Dandekar 1993: 1189). The very small sample at hand can not, however, be compared meaningfully with such general data on sex-specific longevity. In my small sample available for the age-group above sixty years, we find almost equal proportions of women (thirteen 3.5 per cent) and men (twelve, 3.4 per cent), but here again, much larger samples would be required to make any conclusive statements. Nevertheless, all these figures appear to compare favourably with the all-India figure for life expectancy (in 1986), which is fifty-six for men and 56.5 for women (Ahooja-Patel 1993).

Figure 6.1 Distribution of a sample of 347 men and 363 women according to age classes

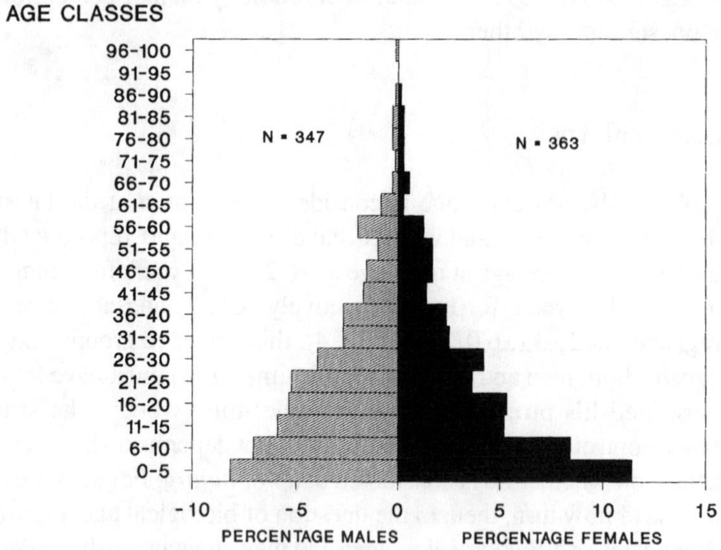

"One Does Not Argue with the Young"

The title of this chapter is taken from a conversation I had with blind Kāḷu, who was in his late eighties and who, when I once asked him how he spent the days sai: "What can I do? I sit and wait for the life beyond." Kāḷu's was certainly an extreme case of aged "disengagement", but indeed all persons categorised by themselves and others as *buḍo/buḍi* are also considered physically as "eaters" rather than as "workers" (cf. Ch. 4 for a discussion of this classification). Their activities are no doubt played down by the younger, but many a time did I observe elderly men, and more so women, withdrawing physically from even minor tasks. A few elderly women I came to know better grumbled that they were still expected by their daughters-in-law to look after small children. "I have served all my life, now it is for me to be served", Janti complained (cf. Vatuk 1990: 68 for similar observations). One could generalise and say that ideally at least one youngish woman is required in a household to take care of the elderly, and Imama's case below exemplifies this. An examination of actual residential

Table 6.1 Residential patterns of thirty-eight elderly women and men aged sixty and above

Ego	Alone	+ Son	+ S & Fam	+ D & Fam	+ Other Rel	+ Non-Rel	+ Much Younger W & Ch
Man	0	0	2	1	0	0	5
Woman	0	3	2	3	2	0	—
Couple	7	3	10	0	0	0	—

Note: + = with; Fam = family; S= son; D = daughter; Rel = relatives; W = wife; Ch = children.

patterns (Table 6.1) indicates that of thirty-eight households which included members of either sex aged sixty years (thirteen cases) and above (twenty-five cases), in ten instances elderly parents lived together with a married son and his family; in seven cases elderly couples lived alone, although they had both sons and daughter; and four households consisted of an old man or woman living with a married daughter and her family. At no stage in the domestic cycle was an old man or woman found to live entirely alone, and no elderly man lived only with his son; thus in practice one woman of any age is required in every domestic group to care for the elderly (also see Fig. 4.8).

Yet the title of the present chapter may mislead – not all elderly Bakkarwal withdraw from involvement in community or domestic life, nor are they expected to: those classified as *buḍo/buḍi* do, those categorised as *bujurg* do not. One speaks of the *bujurg* of the community to denote elderly men known for their (former) well-being; women and men without well-being never qualify for this epithet. The *bujurg* are expected to know, to be wise, the *buḍo* to be silly and foolish. Whereas the terms *buḍo/buḍi* connote (respectively male and female) helplessness and uselessness stemming from age, the term *bujurg* connotes the power and authority of experience. While the *buḍo/buḍi* may be worth pitying, the *bujurg* are considered worthy of respect. The latter continue to be consulted at least formally, and hence at least partly feel that they are of use to others; the former are more than ever before made to feel as burdens. Since elderly men do not participate in any domestic work, the *buḍo* tend to lose their former status as *kārāḷo*, whereas somewhat like the "*korwala*" among Durrani pastoralists the *bujurg* retain theirs, as "the senior or big man of the house" (Tapper 1991: 119). But even a partial retention of high status is painful for those elderly men who were especially used to exercising authority and indulging in surrogate decision making. This is especially true of men who were known as *kharpẽñč* and who with loss of physical strength also tend to lose power. Dulla, now crippled with pain in the joints and extremely hard of hearing, wept as he recalled how strong he had once been, and recounted the days when bare-handed he had fought off bears attacking his huge herds; now he was entirely dependent on his sons and grandsons. Indeed, in spite of the ideals of filial piety and duty, aged Bakkarwal men who once had considerable well-being and were accustomed to exercising choice find it difficult to accept such dependence and increasing loss of autonomy (cf. Riesman 1992: 102ff. for similar observations among the Fulani). Yet they know better than to altercate with those younger. "If one has enough *ōsh*, one does not argue (*tarak karāñ*) with the young", Jima once told me, and in only an apparent reversal of what Vatuk (1990: 72–73) noted, Sāiñ echoed a similar sentiment when he said: "The young make many mistakes, they should be corrected with love; argument is only among equals – what will I argue about with one twenty or thirty years younger than myself?"

Care and Well-being

The older one becomes the fewer "equals" one is left with; the death of peers, of siblings and even of a spouse accompany the process of aging. Hence old women and men have only their children to turn to for care and company. "If a man does not care for his old father he can be disinherited", I was told a few times by disapproving neighbours, but I never actually came across any such case, and since inheritance is primarily if not wholly premortem, the value of this statement must be largely theoretical. The question of care is, not surprisingly, closely related to economic ability and hence to that of status, and among the wealthy fathers may well be given special care. In 1981 Gama, for example, bought a cow for Rs. 5,000/- from a Gujar because his father had been advised by a doctor to drink a lot of milk every day. The poor can not afford to take such specific care of the aged, or for that matter of any other category; in these families no one has the time or wherewithal to cater to specific needs or demands. The elderly in these families are often seen sitting by themselves, huddled up; taken little notice of, they have practically no one to keep them company, and even when they are almost toothless they are given the same maize bread, relish and tea as everyone else. Unlike among several Hindu communities where dietary restrictions on the aged – and especially on the widowed – can be severe, here no specific prohibitions are placed on the elderly. I got the general impression that here the helplessness, loneliness (through loss of peers, eventually also of spouses and children) and resulting sorrow of old age are considered slightly funny; pity may be briefly expressed, but the general attitude is matter-of-fact. On the other hand, cases were noted of families who stopped going to their regular summer pastures because it was too cold there for the aged parents; the terrain was also not suitable for riding all the way up and they were too infirm to climb the steep paths on foot. There was also the case of Imama and his wife.

> When I first met them they had been spending the summers at lower altitudes with their youngest son Shadi. They were much too old to climb all the way up to their own mountain pastures then being used by their eldest son Ghafura. Then Shadi's wife died and Imama's wife was not in a position to take care of the household, which also included Ghafura's three small children. Imama and his wife had to shift to higher pastures where Shadi's son and daughter-in-law were. So in summer 1983 and 1984 Ghafura and Shadi's eldest son carried Imama and his wife all the steep way up on their backs.

While almost all Bakkarwal derive their income mainly from animal husbandry, there are a few poor widows and aged couples who supplement their income, especially in summer, largely through begging or even subsist on it. Their patrons are a few tourists, but mostly other pastoralists (Bakkarwal, Gujar, Pathan, etc.) who are charitable in return for what many say are token services rendered. Specific old and indigent women with a reputation for preparing and administering medicine against sterility or menstrual pains are given a handful of rice or maize flour, a little milk, cooking oil, or a few *rupees*; but their medical knowledge earns them no high status, probably since it had not contributed to enhance their own well-being. When hired shepherds grow too old and frail to work (the oldest I knew in 1983 was about sixty-five years old) they too are often reduced to begging; when they die their widows have no where to go. Thus Lal Din, who had worked as a shepherd all his life, survived by begging, along with his wife; their only son tended their ten goats and worked as a shepherd cum live-in son-in-law for his wealthy father-in-law.

It appears, then, that both the activity theory (e.g. Lemon et al. 1972) and the theory of disengagement (e.g. Henry 1964) can be applied in context-specific situations to different elderly Bakkarwal depending on their gender and socio-economic status. My limited information suggests that those having worked very hard all their lives and had little autonomy feel they have a right to retire and do nothing; those who worked comparatively less and were in positions of greater authority, however, continue to want to be useful to others. The former are primarily women and men of little well-being, the latter are men who took and implemented decisions for themselves and others. Unlike, for instance, among the Fulani where "being useful for a woman is the major source of being valuable … and a man's sense of being valuable … comes … from being capable and powerful …" (Riesman 1992: 101), in this pastoral society one can not generalise about the status of "the aged"; once again, one must consider gender and economic status as well. It may also be pertinent to compare my data with those from traditional peasant societies, where high status has been largely reported for the aged and explained by the four following interrelated clusters (Cowgill 1972, Press and McKool 1972 in Sokolovsky 1990: 16); almost all of these criteria are basically lacking in Bakkarwal society.

Peasant Society	**Bakkarwal Society**
Role set emphasising continuity in community organisation	Organisation is and must be fluid and flexible.
Integration into a residentially viable extended family	Such integration exists only for a short period in the development cycle (Figs. 4.7, 4.8).
Control of important material and informational resources	Such control exists only for those with well-being.

A value system praising a group-oriented ideology while de-emphasising individual ego development	Although the ideal exists, it it can not be seen in opposition to the individual, and, as discussed in earlier chapters, its practice is gender and status specific.

Indeed, the lack of the stable joint family, the specific pastoral imperative to take quick and new decisions and the spatially mobile lifestyle which necessitates considerable sturdiness and good health contribute largely to the diminished power of most of the aged. The very fact that only those men who have had large *kumbā* associated with themselves retain some of their former power and authority underlines the intimate relation between residence patterns obtaining in a society and the status of the aged within it : "Some degree of gerontocracy is characteristic of all societies displaying the joint-household formation pattern. The process of aging thus entails … the accumulation of power and prestige" (Cain 1985: 150). As shown in an earlier chapter, men of well-being also tend to come from families with a large measure of endogamy (cf. also Rao 1997), so that the kinship networks not only of their generation but also of those succeeding them are fairly dense. This appears to help in reinforcing feelings of obligation towards seniors, much as it does among the Berti of Sudan (Holy 1990).

In Bakkarwal society there is accumulation of prestige with age (and only with age) *provided* in earlier years one has performed well socially and culturally. In other words, high status is achieved not simply through the process of aging, but with the earlier demonstration (in terms of large herds, numerous progeny, eventually many wives, cf. Ch. 5; also Casimir and Rao 1995) of cultural and social success measured on the basis of reputation for well-being. Such a man's sons will also gain in symbolic capital by taking care of one in old age. That age *per se* does not bring prestige – because it augurs the reduction of physical power – is also apparent from the fact that, as in many neighbouring areas of South Asia, here too henna (*basma*) is applied to cover greying hair, by women and men, and by men on their beards; indeed an euphemism for an aging man is "*ratti dāṛī*" (red beard). It is the generally strengthening effect of henna which is invoked. "It strengthens the white (*čiṭṭa*) hair, and prevents it from growing whiter and falling", explained Makhṇi, while Nawaba was of the view that henna had a much needed healing effect on the scalp and skin, since hair greyed with the decrease of blood in the whole body, pulling out its force and heat from the skin. While the preventive and healing characteristics of henna are appreciated, any attempt at masking the process of ageing and greying by, for example, using black dye is considered sinful for it transgresses the basic principle of authenticity. Men (I never came across the case of a woman) known to dye their hair black are disapproved of as both silly and vain, characteristics which indicate an excess of *nafas* over *ōsh*. Old Baādura, who dyed his hair and beard with a black powder he obtained from Gamio, a transhumant Gujar he knew in the upper reaches of the Lolab Valley was criticised by most for his "silly attempt at deceiving God about his real age". But Gamio told me he had numerous Bakkarwal clients, and did fairly brisk business with his product which he made by pouring mustard oil onto the roots of a walnut tree early in the month of *besākh* (mid-April). In October to November (*kattā*) he collected thick black juice from these roots and dried it to form a powder-dye. The powder was mixed to a paste with butter oil (*ki*) or mustard oil and then applied to the hair, which was kept bound up for two or three hours and then washed. The colour was said to keep for up to two weeks.

The Dimming of Light

In Chapter 5, I referred to the ideal following which mothers-in-law, and certainly grandmothers, are not expected to have sex. Since levels of body fluids are held to decline with age, sexual desire is also thought to decrease (cf. Vatuk 1985: 144 for similar views). But these notions are not as rigid and censure not comparable with that mentioned by Patel (1994: 165ff.) for a Rajasthani community, or by Vatuk (1985: 148) for other parts of South Asia. Unlike the Hindus Patel and Vatuk worked among, here the sleeping arrangements are not adjusted to meet such requirements. Monogamous couples continue to sleep in their own tents or huts, which are rarely shared on a regular basis by other family members, and even young grandchildren usually do not regularly sleep close to their grandparents, as they do in many other societies of rural South Asia. Elderly women whose husbands are polygynous tend to move out of the conjugal household and live with one of their sons.

As discussed in earlier chapters a direct link is seen not only between coitus and pregnancy, but between the latter and the cessation of menstrual flow. Since menstrual discharge is related to strength, its increasing absence is logically enough ascribed to a decrease in the latter. Infertility, infecundity and menopause are, however, not conceptually related, and even older women like Quresha (see below) who wanted more children, but could not have any, never mentioned menopause as the reason for their being unable to conceive. Infertility is related to general weakness; in elderly women it is connected to the weakness brought about by old age, a major indication of which is the lack of (rather than excess of) blood – manifested in the phenomenon medically termed menopause. The low level of blood in the body excludes the possibility of its "wreak(ing) havoc in the brain", a fear reported by Formanek (1990: 4) from some contemporary Western societies. Another important symptom of weakness is failing eyesight (*lō*, lit. light), and this is directly connected to lack of blood and hence to menopause. In many societies weak vision and ultimately blindness are connected to failing strength and even death; as a corollary the eye and eyesight are equated to life.

Quresha, who I reckoned was fifty-two in 1983, had never been pregnant and did not know whether it was her "fault" or her husband's (she had asked him to go see a doctor, but he had not). She had stopped menstruating completely in 1981, but still wanted a child. She explained that she probably never had "too much blood" and that now, with age, she certainly did not have enough, and this is why she could not conceive. In 1984 she asked for my help in taking her to a doctor, who could eventually help her to conceive. "But the doctor can give me pills and injections to make more blood, can't he? Even if it's a girl it'll be good", she insisted. "We can get a boy down for her and bring them up like son and daughter." Since the level of body fluids determines physiological change, menopause is conceivably reversible; this argument is given all the more credence by the fact that some elderly men are known to be potent enough to beget children – so why can not a woman (once again) have enough blood to conceive. Besides some old women are known to be able to breast-feed (*čuča denāñ*) a little, and I tle, and I myself occasionally witnessed old women pacify whimpering babies by giving them the breast. Perhaps because menopause *per se* is not considered as necessarily irreversible, and the cessation of menstrual discharge does not mark the end of sexuality (this should ideally happen much earlier, cf. Chs. 4 and 5), a woman in the climacteric does not consider this transition as transforming her gender or sex, of turning her "into (a) man inside" (Skultans 1970: 648). Perhaps this is why this transition – which takes place between the ages of about forty and fifty (Fig. 4.7), in other words, when their respective husbands are roughly between forty-five and fifty years old – is also not considered problematic in itself, and insofar as I could gather is not related to any physical or psychological problems a woman may have at the time. Among women of all ages it is referred to in a perfectly matter-of-fact manner as a phenomenon known to all and unfortunate only for those few who, like Quresha, want (more) children. Those who felt they had enough children appeared to welcome it as a release from monthly pains and discomfort (cf. Datan 1990: 118 for similar findings among traditional women in the Middle East).

But Quresha's case was different. To have lived through life without a child was bad enough, she said; but the worst was perhaps yet to come, she felt, since for a woman to die childless could mean – she was not sure about this – that even in death she would find no peace, that she would roam the hills as a *čarel*, a woman who died childless and hence unfulfilled. Like the *čurel*, feared in large parts of northern India as the spirit of a woman who dies in childbirth (e.g. Crooke 1896: I, 269–74; Pocock 1973: 34), the *čarel* are dangerous to adolescent and adult men and to horses. With reversed feet, a crooked, skeleton back and a beautiful face they may well be a mixture of the *čudel* as pictured in Gujarat (Enthoven 1914: 107) and certain other beings such as the *mādar-e āl* or *shishak* encountered in Afghan and Central Asian belief systems (Johansen 1959). The *čarel* can take the form of either an extraordinarily beautiful young woman or an old hag, with enormous, sharp teeth, wide eyelids and feet turned backwards; it is interesting here to note the similarities between these images and those applied to Hindu widows, both young and old, in neighbouring areas (cf. Chowdhry 1995: 49). The *čarel* are said to fear only fire and water, and are commonly known to "turn men into sheep or goats, or anything else they please and make them obey their wishes" (also in sexual matters). "They take complete possession of their victims", I was often told, and sometimes also teach old women magic spells (*jādu, mantar*), and then use them to get what they want. According to Baso: "They attack by counting each hair one has on head and body and are successful when they've managed to count all the hair. With horses they succeed less, since sooner or later a horse says 'prrr', and this interrupts their counting and they forget the count." No wonder then, that Quresha was afraid of becoming a *čarel.*

The Loss of a Spouse

Bakkarwal women and men – whether old or middle-aged, whether married or widowed – wear basically the same kind of caps and clothes; there are no formal restrictions on colour, but elderly women and men tend to wear less bright colours. Older men tend not to trim their beards, and while there is no formal age or status-wise restriction on wearing jewellery, older women and even young widows generally wear less jewellery than young married women. In old age a woman is free to gift her jewellery to whomsoever she pleases; usually she distributes it among her daughters.

As mentioned in Chapter 3 there is a certain ambivalence about widow (*ranḍi*) remarriage, and I believe this is growing (cf. Chen and Drèze 1995: 281; but also Chowdhry 1995: 41, 65). This increase can be explained by greater contact with other communities, more schooling and general upward social mobility, for in the wider society in which the Bakkarwal live, those to be emulated (no longer) practice widow remarriage (cf. Chakravarti 1995 for a recent and more general discussion of this topic). "Formerly", said Phata, "people did not know any better, and so there were more such marriages, but now in good families we don't do such things." Though there is no sanction on bachelors marrying widows as there is for example in rural Haryana (Chowdhry 1995: 46) or western Rajasthan (Rao, ongoing research), the wedding of a Bakkarwal widow is not an occasion for much celebration (cf. Ch. 3), and she is brought home in silence. It is possible that there is an attempt to play down the sexuality of the widow who is still "*garam*" (hot), but whose heat (sexual) has at least temporarily lost its legitimate controller. Normatively, a young widow may marry beyond the kin-group of her former husband only if she has no young children to be cared for, but if the deceased had offspring, and especially sons, junior levirate (*dēvar lenāñ*), though not compulsory, is said to be preferred by his family; this is however not corroborated by data given below. The preference is explained in terms of directly protecting the economic rights of the "orphaned" children. Unfortunately I have no information on the perspective of the women who entered into levirate unions, but from the remarks of other women I could gather that the institution of *dēvar lenāñ* is considered with scepticism. This may in part be related to the reversal of roles such a marriage involves: while in a "normal" marriage "a woman is taken" (cf. Ch. 3), *dēvar lenāñ* entails "a woman taking a man" (her HyB) – who may well be much younger than herself. Bakkarwal society imposes no similar restrictions or preferences on a widower, and the two cases of junior sororate noted did not fall into any general pattern.

Of my sample of fifteen widows (*Allaiwāḷ* = eight, *Kunhāri* = seven) who remarried once (none married more often), I had access to recollection data on age and status at marriage of the spouses in fourteen cases. Of these, three contracted junior levirate marriages, while in six cases their second spouses were not related; the frequency of levirate did not seem to be related either to the relation to first husband or to the number of surviving offspring (no offspring in one case, and three daughters and one son respectively in the other two cases). While five widows took unmarried men as their second husbands (of these two were levirate unions), seven women entered polygynous unions (three became second wives, one each became a third and fifth wife, and two became fourth wives). Only one widow married a widower, and another a divorced man. In contrast to this, in an official Census sample (unpublished, 1981) of thirteen widow remarriages, nine married widowers, while two each married divorced or unmarried men; these data do not specify whether any of these women entered into polygynous unions, nor do they mention kinship. The widows with children in the Census sample remarried irrespective of the number of children they had (seven without children, and six with); the men they married themselves had a range of zero to five children. The difference between these two small samples (cf. also Chen and Drèze 1995: 263 for rural Indian Hindus), and especially the high proportion of women in my sample marrying unmarried men, may result from the average age of widows reported on; in my sample their average age was 21.8 (± 2.8) years, while in the Census sample it was 33.5 (±7.9) years. The average age difference between these widows and their second spouses at the time of marriage was 10.5 (± 4.8) years in eleven instances in the Census sample, while in two cases the wife was older (by five and twenty years) and the husband was previously unmarried. In my sample, too, there were two such cases (the wife was older by four and five years), both of which involved junior levirate.

For women, primary access to resources is through marriage, and it would appear that with the death of her husband a woman's economic status declines fairly rapidly. Table 6.1 shows that old women never live alone, but even when they join others' households (e.g. those of their married sons or daughters) their economic status is low, since the legitimate *kārāḷo* (cf. Chs. 4, 5) here is no longer officially responsible for her as her husband once was. When a widow is considered too old to remarry she must face many problems unless her husband and her father or brothers were or are men of well-being. "Ideally even a poor widow with a son or only with daughters inherits the entire herd. In reality the husband's family sells her and her daughters and takes away whatever animals she may have", was Bibo's bitter comment. With no sons and two teenaged daughters, she lived as a poor relative in a fairly wealthy household, and her situation reflected the general rural pattern in North India, where 20 per cent of 262 widows "reported serious conflicts with their in-laws" over land and property rights (Chen and Drèze 1995: 261). The following two cases are further illustrative of the impact of economic status on the situation of aged widows.

Makhṇi was a widow in her mid-sixties; her husband had been lame and very poor, and had had to supplement the family income by working as a seasonal road labourer. After his death his wealthy FyBS Kima offered to take care of her few animals and help her arrange the marriages of her two beautiful daughters. Kima pocketed the bridewealth of the two girls and grazed her animals in his pastures, but she never got to see any of the milk. In return for Kima's help and a little grain Makhṇi's son worked for him as a shepherd; Makhṇi lived in Kima's camp, but was too old and sick to do any work (Kima's grandchildren were sent off to be in her charge when they grew too naughty). From what I could gather Makhṇi survived mainly by begging on the roads and in the nearest bazaar.

Janti's case was entirely different. She too was a widow in her late seventies and half-blind. But Janti's husband had been very rich; her sons and brothers were men of well-being and great influence. Janti was left with a large herd but no labour. So she adopted the thirty-year-old Daud, her own eldest son's eldest son as her heir (*wāris*); she lived with him and his wife (her ZDD) and children, who took great care of her.

But not all adoptions runs so smoothly, as the following example shows.

B.J. had become a young widow around 1970; her husband had died, leaving her with an only daughter aged nine, with ninety goats, fifteen sheep, two horses and his pasture. Two years later, B.J. married her husband's FFBSS, a childless widower with twelve goats; he had lost his own pasture many years earlier to his own younger brother. This second marriage remained issueless. In 1974 she adopted as her heir the seventeen-year-old Q.P., who was her sister's son and was already engaged to her daughter. In the eyes of the community, Q.P. slowly became the owner of the herd and of the pasture which B.J. had inherited from her deceased husband. The marriage between Q.P. and B.J.'s daughter in 1976 made this inheritance doubly legitimate. After this, however, relations between Q.P. and B.J.'s second husband steadily worsened. Things came to a head in 1981, when Q.P. started bringing part of his own brother's herd along to B.J.'s pasture to graze. B.J. objected, but was told by Q.P. in no uncertain terms that that pasture was now his. In summer 1982 he and his wife moved up to the pasture with all their animals, leaving B.J. and her husband to fend for themselves with two milch goats at a lower altitude, where no pasture rights were to be had (cf. Rao 1992a: 125–6).

Drying Up

Studies in South Asia have shown (e.g. Fernandes 1982: 4) that religion plays an increased role in the daily life of the aged, and that the idea of death preoccupies elderly women and men (Kakar 1978: 36). Neither of these statements appears to apply to the Bakkarwal, either conceptually or in practice. The comparatively little preoccupation with religion could perhaps be related to the decisive roles the concepts of *nafas* and *ōsh* play in Bakkarwal ideas about life and death. At death both *nafas* and *ōsh* "dry up"; what remains is *rū* (cf. Fig. 1.5). In most humans *rū* remains more or less dormant throughout life, but at death, shed of the social trappings of the person, the *rū* now enters into an eternal and unique relationship with God. With death, the *bandā* turns into *ādam*, the complete and pure individual, and *ādam*'s only characteristic is *rū* – his individualhood. It may be of interest to note that Adam was not only the first human, but also that, according to Sufi concepts, the essence of Muhammad was manifested in *'adam* (cf. EI: *'Adam*). Since in their lifetime most men and women, however, do not or can not activate their *rū*, after death, too, it remains passive and can not be used by anyone for good or evil, and can not be communicated with. An active *rū* in death is premised on an active *rū* in life; this happens in the case of the witch (*ḍākini*), just as much as in that of the saint (*pīr* or *azrat*).

Those the dead leave behind must now bathe the corpse on the special wooden board (*paččh*); they must wave an earthen fire pot (*kāngṛi*) containing the glowing seeds of the wild rue (*Peganum harmala*, cf. Ch. 3) and daub the body with camphor (*pārā*) to keep away the *jin* who are in love with its odour (*āshuk e bair ko mushak nāḷ*). They must conduct the funeral prayers (*junāzā*) at the last of the three ritual washings of the life cycle and at the grave, and finally follow the correct burial procedure. Most important here is that during their burial the deceased of both sexes (from the age of about two or three years onwards) must be concealed from the "glance of the sky" (*āsmān ka najar*). Were they not, they would not only never have a chance of entering Paradise (*bahista*), where, among others, God and His Prophet (*paigambar*) and Yārmiallā (the saint, Pīr Ghulam Dastagir widely venerated in Kashmir) and Khuda Khizr (the legendary figure who appeared before Wali Jamal, cf. Ch. 1) dwell, but they could in the intervening liminal period roam the world as spirits who find no rest. For the physically dead are still accountable – they are not *be-esāb* – a point which can not be expanded upon here since it is an accountability that stretches beyond the life-course (cf. Casimir and Rao forthcoming).

As a woman, in other words, as someone who is *per se* imperfect (*aibdār*), I was not in a position to attend Bakkarwal burials; for women to be present at open graves would be bad (*mandish e*) for both the dead and the living. While the men and older boys take the corpse to bury, women stay at home. Those who occasionally follow a corpse, do so at a great distance, clearly separated from the pallbearers. While the men dig the pit, lower the body into it and close the grave, these women may look on, but from a distance, more or less hidden behind bushes. For one day and night following burial ideally no fire may be lit in a home, and neighbours should help out with food and drink. But often enough this is simply not possible, especially in the summer area, due to the widely dispersed campsites. No elaborate concepts of pollution, however, accompany even this ideal.

Bakkarwal graves are almost always fenced off and marked by beautifully carved wooden posts. In the Lidder Valley these are made by a Kashmiri carpenter who learned it from a Gujar now dead; but the Kashmiri in this area do not use them. Later iris (*lātar*) are planted on the graves as a marker (*nishānā*) of the deceased; these flowers are considered most suitable since they are said to grow quickly and are perennials.

The dead are remembered each year at the festival of *'Id*, when men go and pray together at the graveyards, while women mourn their personal losses – especially of husbands and older children – at home through songs of mourning. If an adult has died within the last year, men go and visit the bereaved – so, ideally, do women; if a woman has lost a child she may be visited by close female relatives. But there is a difference in the way most men and women mourn; the former never speak of their own grief, or of how the loss affects them – they only praise the deceased. Women, however, speak openly of their grief and loudly lament the deceased and call out to them in their misery. Yet death, on the whole, is accepted by both men and women as an inevitable consequence of life, and the event itself is spoken of in what appeared to me a reasonably matter-of-fact manner. Consequently, the bereaved are not treated with special consideration, though older women are especially expected to grieve.

A Concluding Note

One question I asked many while attempting to obtain information on life histories was: "Do you regret anything in your life", or "Is there anything you would have done differently?" Apart from gender- and status-specific differences in style of narration (e.g. women tended to talk about others, while men spoke about themselves in the "I" form), it seemed that most women and men did not regret anything. This can be interpreted in many ways. Following Thurner (1974 in Cross and Markus 1991: 234), one could suggest that this indicates a revision of aspirations in such a manner that life is "… not experienced as personal failure or loss". But for this society I would tend to interpret it as the result of the combination of three factors: the attitude common to Islamic societies whereby an "… individual is not responsible for the larger events in his life" (Sandler 1991: 137), the lack of perception of choice among those not ideologically authorised to exercise any, and the low level of articulated personal aspirations.

If choice is considered minimal in life for all except a handful of high-ranking men, it is considered entirely lacking at the time of death. Unlike elsewhere in the region (Madan 1992: 428ff.), "the good death" here is not – and should not – be the result of choice and preparation. This suggests no "arbitrariness of the biological occurrence" (Bloch and Parry 1982: 15), but sheer surrender to God. The hour, the place and the contingencies of death are known to one's Maker alone.

AFTERWORD

As this ethnography goes to press, political events in Jammu and Kashmir continue to serve as stark reminders of the practical importance of terms such as "self" and "autonomy" – and of the urgency of defining them. While hundreds of men and women still lay down their lives to attain self-determination for their nation, the Indian Government courts international censure for its massive and brutal repression of the entire population and spends millions to deny them self-determination but deliberates on granting them autonomy. The issues of surrogate decision making, of negating agency have always been at the core of politics in South Asia. Kashmir is no exception. With hegemonic logic the Indian State has denied the people of Kashmir their rights to a plebiscite and to self-determination, claiming that such practice and assertion of agency would in effect be a result of surrogate decision making by and through Pakistani agents.

But this book is not about autonomy or the role of the self *vis-à-vis* the State, nor did this issue surface during most of my conversations with the Bakkarwal, whose stands and views on the issue of the self-determination of Jammu and Kashmir were complex and at times ambivalent. This was partly perhaps because of the tensions that had been created over the decades between them – (and with them the Gujar) – and the Kashmiri by a series of "divide and rule" measures first adopted by the feudal-colonial government of the despotic Dogra dynasty and continued thereafter by the sovereign Indian State. In 1987 and then again in 1992, when I raised the topic, a few young men responded with "We want independence/ freedom (*āzādī*) or "Who doesn't want independence [from India]?" Further conversations revealed that independence was being equated here with automatic liberation from several existing partly community-specific, political and socio-economic structures, many of which have been discussed in Chapter 5.

In the preceding chapters an attempt has been made to describe and analyse the day-to-day absence and/or presence of personal autonomy and agency among women and men, primarily as reflected in decision making, at different stages in their lives, in a framework of social and religious concepts and authority and power structures. Some of these concepts will probably modify to adapt to changing political and economic circumstances. The concomitant changes in power structures – hence in gender, age, status and, perhaps increasingly, class – and specific practices of decision making (and the acknowledgement thereof) will, perhaps, be studied by others. In such studies, culture and cultural concepts will hopefully not be conceived of as autonomous agents.

Something which, for example, Markus and Kitayama (1991) tend to do in a recent and influential, though controversial (cf. Spiro 1993, Lindholm 1997) study of self and the individual, comparing the "interdependent" and "independent" selves of Asians and Americans, of pre-industrial and capitalist contexts. Unfortunately, this study too is plagued by conceptual and terminological confusion and logical contradictions, and the outcome is largely restricted to a repetition of clichés and stereotypes. To mention just one shortcoming in the argument: several features which the authors ascribe to the "interdependent self" – public, with contextual cognition and flexibility, shaped by and adaptive to others, in other words "unbounded" – are essential criteria for any anthropologist in the "field". Does this mean that the Western (preferably white American male, to fit Markus and Kitayama's model) anthropologist takes on a non-Western self during fieldwork, abandoning this when he returns home to his own society which thrives on the "independent self"? If so, he must be endowed with a readily discardable self and must spring back and forth between a "bounded" and an "unbounded" self – a contradiction in itself.

Aside from these problems, it is specially regrettable that Markus and Kitayama leave the links between economic processes

(Japan, US), concepts of self and the practice of agency within specific historically evolved structures of subordination and power unexplored. Treating cultural concepts as monolithic, consistent structures, negating intra-cultural difference and considering culture in a kind of political and economic vacuum runs the risk of a dangerous determinism, whose most recent and extreme form is represented by the work of Samuel Huntington.

Questions of agency, self and person are of increasingly ideological importance and political relevance in a world that is rapidly commoditising and globalising and where conflicts are surfacing as perhaps never before. This is evident in individual cases such as those of Shamim (cf. Ewing 1990) whose perception of choices, however theoretical, confront her with dilemmas of decision making based on eventually irreconcilable representations of the self. But it is perhaps even more evident in broader contexts of identity, where multiple perceptions of self which have always co-existed are increasingly suppressed and reduced to so-called coherence, where sentiments of embeddedness are abused to construct situations of monolithic consistency in order to deny individual agency, legitimise surrogate agency and serve the political ends and economic interests of the deciding few.

Appendices

Appendix A: Frequency of endogamy and exogamy in the first-ever marriages contracted by 187 Bakkarwal women of 29 *zāt/khēl* in relation to the estimated size of their respective paternal *zāt/khēl*. These estimates, which showed remarkable consistency, were made on different occasions by 44 Bakkarwal women and 79 Bakkarwal men of 29 *zāt/khēl* for their own and each of the 28 other *zāt/khēl*.

N_i = total number of informants; n = number of informants per *zāt/khēl*. NA = no answer; L = large; M = medium; S = small; N_m = total number of marriages recorded; En = endogamous; Ex = exogamous.

Informants *Zāt/Khēl*		**Estimated Size of 29 *Zāt/Khēl* (N_i = 123)**								**Marriages Recorded**		
	n	NA	%	S	%	M	%	L	%	N_m	En	Ex
Āwāṇ	4	16	13.0	3	2.4	97	79.0	7	5.7	4	2	2
Bargaṭ	8	22	17.9	9	7.3	92	74.8	0	0.0	11	8	3
Baṛwāḷ	2	15	12.2	82	66.6	14	11.3	12	9.8	1	0	1
Bijāṛ	7	9	7.3	0	0.0	0	0.0	114	93.5	41	28	13
Bijrān	4	48	39.0	65	52.8	0	0.0	10	8.1	1	0	1
Bokṛā	9	7	5.7	11	8.9	89	72.3	16	13.0	19	10	9
Čārā	6	10	8.1	8	6.5	105	85.3	0	0.0	2	0	2
Čauhāṇ	3	18	14.6	59	50.0	27	22.0	19	15.4	2	0	2
Čēči	4	9	7.3	0	0.0	114	93.0	0	0.0	1	1	0
Dedaṛ	2	12	9.8	90	73.0	20	16.2	1	0.8	6	1	5
Ḍōi	2	13	10.6	0	0.0	110	89.4	0	0.0	2	1	1
Gakkaṛ	3	55	44.7	68	55.3	0	0.0	0	0.0	3	0	3

Appendix A: Frequency of endogamy and exogamy in first-ever marriages *(continued)*

Informants *Zāt/Khēl*		**Estimated Size of 29** ***Zāt/Khēl*** **(N$_i$ = 123)**								**Marriages Recorded**		
	n	NA	%	S	%	M	%	L	%	N$_m$	En	Ex
Jangal	3	24	19.5	60	48.7	39	31.7	0	0.0	4	1	3
Jātal	3	25	20.3	60	48.7	33	26.8	5	4.0	6	2	4
Jīndaṛ	2	69	56.0	54	44.0	0	0.0	0	0.0	2	0	2
Kāḷo Khēl	8	4	3.2	9	7.3	10	8.1	100	100.0	12	7	5
Kānḍal	5	6	4.9	3	2.4	114	93.0	0	0.0	5	1	4
Kasāṇā	4	2	1.6	0	0.0	102	82.9	19	15.4	1	1	0
Kaṭāriā	3	11	8.9	3	2.4	98	79.6	11	8.9	5	3	2
Khāri	3	8	6.5	10	8.1	98	79.6	7	5.7	21	12	9
Khaṭāṇā	3	0	0.0	0	0.0	0	0.0	100	100.0	7	6	1
Mandaṛ	3	10	8.1	30	24.3	82	66.6	1	0.8	7	3	4
Paswāl	5	3	2.4	0	0.0	10	8.1	110	89.4	4	4	0
Phāmṛā	7	7	5.7	72	58.5	43	35.0	4	3.2	3	1	2
Pōṛ	8	4	3.2	0	0.0	0	0.0	119	96.7	11	9	3
Pujwālā	4	15	12.2	89	72.3	6	4.9	10	8.1	1	0	1
Teruā	2	45	36.6	60	48.7	18	14.6	0	0.0	2	1	1
Tīñḍā	3	47	38.2	63	51.2	16	13.0	0	0.0	1	0	1
Wāṇā	3	34	27.6	80	65.0	9	7.3	0	0.0	2	0	2
29	123									187	101	86

Appendix B: Recollected or reported age at engagement for 55 women and 48 of their spouses now aged between 14 and 75 years and 16 and 80 years respectively at the time of data collection

Women		**Men**	
Age Now	Age at Engagement	Age Now	Age at Engagement
75	1	80	5
17	1	29	13
20	14	22	16
17	14	29	27
14	12	20	18
40	14	45	19
35	16	45	26
60	12	?	?
22	16	25	19
18	14	26	22
27	12	31	16
50	15	62	27

Appendix B: Recollected or reported age at engagement *(continued)*

Women		Men	
Age Now	Age at Engagement	Age Now	Age at Engagement
30	16	31	17
23	14	25	16
25	13	30	18
15	13	16	14
37	11	50	24
22	14	25	17
28	16	35	23
26	15	30	19
23	18	28	23
60	10	65	15
22	14	28	20
55	13	60	18
30	10	38	18
50	11	63	24
60	12	65	17
25	13	30	18
19	16	22	19
28	16	30	18
30	15	35	20
17	15	20	18
45	17	50	22
50	13	55	18
22	15	25	18
26	11	28	13
16	7	27	18
28	17	?	?
70	15	?	?
18	13	20	15
30	14	?	?
27	14	30	17
18	13	24	19
24	13	28	17
25	15	30	20
22	12	25	15
18	12	23	17
70	15	?	?
23	8	25	11
55	4	59	8
20	17	25	23
28	10	55	37
55	29	50	24
25	14	50	39
23	16	45	38

Appendix C: Bakkarwal Wedding/Menarche/Coresidence/ Cohabitation

All data refer to age of women in years; N (53) = total number of women questioned. WD = wedding; CR = coresidence; CH = cohabitation; PR = 1st. period; Kn = Kinship between wife and husband prior to marriage and reckoned from the woman's perspective; Dif = age difference (husband-wife); nr = no relation. The code numbers refer to entries in my field notebooks.

Code No.	WD	CR	CR-WD	CH	CH-CR	CH-WD	PR	CH-PR	Kn	Dif
14,2	8	9	1	0	0	—	14	—	?	4
14,3	3	3	0	12	9	9	12	0	FZS	12
16,2	16	16	0	16	0	0	16	0	MZS	2
59,4	15	15	0	15	0	0	14	1	eZH	13
59,6	13	13	0	0	—	—	0	—	FWB	6
86,2	15	15	0	15	0	0	16	-1	MFBS	5
90,2	16	17	1	17	0	1	17	0	?	10
90,3	13	15	2	16	1	3	15	1	?	?
180,5	17	17	0	17	0	0	16	1	MBS	3
128,11	16	16	0	16	0	0	16	0	?	8
128,4	17	17	0	17	0	0	17	0	FZS	4
128,2	16	18	2	18	0	2	16	2	MBWS	10
129,2	18	18	0	18	0	0	16	2	BWB	1
130,2	16	17	1	17	0	1	15	2	FBS	2
132,2	14	14	0	14	0	0	14	0	?	5
137,4	14	14	0	0	—	—	12	—	FBS	1
139,2	11	18	7	18	0	7	16	2	nr	13
141,2	14	16	2	16	0	2	14	2	nr	3
192,2	18	18	0	18	0	0	16	2	nr	7
194,2	16	16	0	16	0	0	14	2	nr	4
195,2	20	20	0	20	0	0	17	3	nr	5
189,2	11	16	5	16	0	5	16	0	nr	5
190,2	15	15	0	15	0	0	14	1	nr	6
+191,2	14	14	0	14	0	0	14	0	nr	5
173,2	11	15	4	17	2	6	14	3	nr	8
166,2	13	13	0	15	2	2	13	2	?	?
164,2	13	15	2	15	0	2	17	-2	BWB	5
106,2	14	14	0	14	0	0	14	0	FBS	5
104,2	17	17	0	17	0	0	16	1	?	3
103,2	17	17	0	17	0	0	16	1	?	2
99,2	16	16	0	16	0	0	14	2	?	5
98,2	17	17	0	17	0	0	15	2	?	3
93,2	18	18	0	18	0	0	17	1	MFBDS	5
92,2	14	15	1	15	0	1	13	2	?	5
81,2	16	17	1	17	0	1	17	0	?	3
79,2	12	14	2	14	0	2	13	1	?	2
68,2	11	14	3	14	0	3	14	0	FFBSS	11
65,3	18	18	0	18	0	0	16	2	MZS	6

Appendix C: Bakkarwal Wedding/Menarche/Coresidence/ Cohabitation *(continued)*

Code No.	WD	CR	CR-WD	CH	CH-CR	CH-WD	PR	CH-PR	Kn	Dif
65,1	16	17	1	17	0	1	14	3	?	?
57,2	14	14	0	14	0	0	13	1	?	2
52,2	19	19	0	19	0	0	12	7	?	?
47,2	15	16	1	16	0	1	14	2	?	3
49,2	14	17	3	17	0	3	15	2	?	6
38,2	13	14	1	14	0	1	13	1	?	4
24,9	20	20	0	20	0	0	17	3	FFFBSS	5
29,2	13	13	0	13	0	0	12	1	?	3
17,7	12	16	4	16	0	4	12	4	FZS	5
9,1	20	20	0	20	0	0	15	5	FBS	?
12,2	11	15	4	15	0	4	15	0	FZS	3
1,2	16	16	0	16	0	0	15	1	FZS	4
2,2	18	18	0	18	0	0	16	2	?	6
5,2	12	14	2	14	0	2	13	1	MFZDS	10
6,2	30	30	0	30	0	0	16	14	FFBS	5

		Min	Max	x̄	sd
CH-WD	N = 50	0	9	1.46	2.02
CR-WD	N = 53	0	7	0.94	1.54
CH-CR	N = 51	0	9	0.27	1.31
CH-PR	N = 50	-2	7	1.46	1.58

Note: The last case (Code No. 6,2) was not taken into account in calculating CH-PR. The two exceptional cases are Nos. 86,2 and 164,2.

Appendix D: The Bakkarwal calendar

Month	English Equivalent	Season
besākh	mid-April – mid-May	*bāñdh*
jēṭh	mid-May – mid-June	no specific name
hāṛ	mid-June – mid-July	
sāoñ	mid-July – mid-August	*bareya*
pādru	mid-August – mid-September	
asu	mid-September – mid-October	*shard*
kattā	mid-October – mid-November	
mangar	mid-November – mid-December	
pō	mid-December – mid-January	*siyāḷ*
mā	mid-January – mid-February	
phagaṇ	mid-February – mid-March	
čait	mid-March – mid-April	*bāñdh*

Bibliography

Aggarwal, P. 1976. Kinship and Marriage among the Meos of Rajasthan. In, I. Ahmad (ed.) *Family, Kinship and Marriage among Muslims in India*: 265–296. Delhi: Manohar.

Ahmad, A. 1986. *The Concept of Self and Self-Identity in Contemporary Philosophy. An affirmation of Iqbal's doctrine*. Lahore: Iqbal Academy.

Ahmad, I. 1978. (ed.) *Caste and Social Stratification among Muslims in India.* Delhi: Manohar.

Ahmed, A.S. 1976. *Millenium and Charisma among Pathans. A Critical Essay in Social Anthropology.* London: Routledge & Kegan Paul.

——. 1984. Religious Presence and Symbolism in Pukhtun Society. In, A.S. Ahmed and D.M. Hart (eds.) *Islam in Tribal Societies. From the Atlas to the Indus*: 310–330. London: Routledge & Kegan Paul.

Ahooja-Patel, K. 1993. Gender Distance among Countries, *Economic and Political Weekly* XXVIII(7): 295–305.

Al-Khayyat, S. 1990. *Honour and Shame. Women in Modern Iraq*. London: Saqi Books.

Alavi, H. 1995. The Two Biraderies: Kinship in Rural West Punjab. In, T.N. Madan (ed.) *Muslim Communities of South Asia. Culture, Society, and Power*: 1–62. Delhi: Manohar.

Alford, R.D. 1988. *Naming and Identity. A Cross-Cultural Study of Personal Naming Practices*. New Haven: HRAF Press.

Ali, H. 1978. Elements of Caste among the Muslims in a District in Southern Bihar. In, I. Ahmad (ed.) *Caste and Social Stratification among Muslims in India*: 19–39. Delhi: Manohar.

Altman, I. 1979. Privacy As an Interpersonal Boundary Process. In, M. von Cranach, K. Foppa, W. Lepenies and D. Ploog (eds.) *Human Ethology. Claims and Limits of a New Discipline*: 95–132. Cambridge: Cambridge University Press.

Altorki, S. 1977. Family Organization and Women's Power in Urban Saudi Arabian Society, *Journal of Anthropological Research* 33: 277–287.

——. 1980. Milk-kinship in Arab Society: an Unexplored problem in the Ethnography of Marriage, *Ethnology* 19: 233–244.

Anderson, J.W. 1982. Cousin Marriage in Context: Constructing Social Relations in Afghanistan, *Folk* 24: 7–28.

——. 1985. Sentimental Ambivalence and the Exegesis of "Self" in Afghanistan, *Anthropological Quarterly* 58(4): 203–211.

Ansari, G. 1960. *Muslim Caste in Uttar Pradesh.* Lucknow: Ethnographic and Folk Culture Society.

Antony, M.V. 1993. Social Relations and the Individuation of Thought, *Mind* 102(406): 110–129.

Anzenberger, G. 1991. Kooperation und Altruismus: ihre stammesgeschichtlichen Wurzeln. In, R. Wunderer (ed.) *Kooperation. Gestaltungsprinzipien und Steuerung der Zusammenarbeit zwischen Organisationseinheiten*: 3–19. Stuttgart: C.E. Poeschel Verlag.

Apffel Marglin, F. and P.C. Mishra. 1992 Women's Blood. Challenging the Discourse of Development, *The Ecologist* 22(1): 22–31.

Ariès, P. 1960. *Centuries of Childhood.* New York: Vintage Books.

Awasty, I. 1982. *Rural Women of India: a Socio-Economic Profile of Jammu Women.* Delhi: B.R. Publ. Corp.

Asad, T. 1986 [1970]. *The Kababish Arabs. Power, Authority and Consent in a Nomadic Tribe.* London: C. Hurst & Co.

Bacon, F. 1597. [reed. 1906]. *Essays.* London: Dent.

Ballard, R. 1990. Migration and Kinship: the Differential Effect of Marriage Rules on the Processes of Punjabi Migration to Britain. In, C. Clarke, C. Peach and S. Vertovec (eds.) *South Asians Overseas*: 219–248. Cambridge: Cambridge University Press.

Banaji, M.R. 1994. The Self in Social Contexts, *Annual Review of Psychology* 45: 297–332.

Bandura, A. and R.H. Walters. 1969. *Social Learning and Personality Development.* London: Holt, Rinehart & Winston.

Barth, F. 1959. *Political Leadership among Swat Pathans.* London: London School of Economics, Monographs on Social Anthropology, 19.

Basu, A.M. 1996. Girls' Schooling, Autonomy and Fertility Change: what do these Words Mean in South Asia? In, R. Jeffery and A.M. Basu (eds.) *Girls' Schooling, Women's Autonomy and Fertility Change in South Asia*: 48–67. Delhi: Sage.

Basu, S. and S. Roy. 1972. Change in the Frequency of Consanguineous Marriages among the Delhi Muslims, *The Eastern Anthropologist* XXV(1): 21–28.

Bauer, J.L. 1985. Sexuality and the Moral "Construction" of Women in an Islamic Society, *Anthropological Quarterly* 58: 120–129.

Beck, K. and G. Klute 1991. Hirtenarbeit in der Ethnologie, *Zeitschrift für Ethnologie* 116: 91–124.

Beck, L. 1991. *Nomad. A Year in the Life of a Qashqa'i Tribesman in Iran.* London: I.B. Tauris & Co.

Bellah, R.N., R. Madsen, W.M. Sullivan, A. Swidler, and S.M. Tipton 1989 [1st ed. 1985]. *Habits of the Heart. Individualism and Commitment in American Life.* Delhi: Tata McGraw Hill Publ. & Co.

Benthall, J. 1991. The Middle East. Fantasies and Realities, *Anthropology Today* 7(3): 16–18.

Berger, M. 1964. *The Arab World Today.* New York.

Berland, J.C. 1982. *No Five Fingers are Alike. Cognitive Amplifiers in Social Context.* Cambridge (Mass.): Harvard University Press.

Berreman, G. 1962. Sib and Clan among the Pahari of North India, *Ethnology* 1: 524–528.

Béteille, A. 1986. Individualism and Equality. *Current Anthropology* 27(2): 121–134.

——. 1987. Individualism and the Persistence of Collective Identities. In, André Béteille (ed.) *The Idea of Natural Equality and Other Essays.* Delhi: Oxford University Press.

——. 1991. Distributive Justice and Institutional Well-Being, *Economic and Political Weekly* XXVI(11/12): 591–610.

Bhargava, R. 1992. *Individualism in Social Science. Forms and Limits of a Methodology*. Oxford: Clarendon Press.

Bhasin, V. 1988. *Himalayan Ecology, Transhumance and Social Organisation. Gaddis of Himachal Pradesh*. Delhi: Kamla-Raj Enterprises.

Bhatt, E. 1989. *Grind of Work*. Ahmedabad: SEWA.

Biersack, A. 1984. Paiela "Women-men": the Reflexive Foundations of Gender Ideology, *American Ethnologist* 11: 118–138.

Bisaria, S.D. 1971. *The Gujjars of Kashmir*. Agra: University of Agra, PhD. Thesis.

Black-Michaud, J. 1986. *Sheep and Land. The Economics of Power in a Tribal Society*. Cambridge: Cambridge University Press.

Blanchet, T. 1987/1984. *Meanings and Rituals of Birth in Rural Bangladesh. Women, Pollution and Marginality*. Dhaka: University Press Ltd.

Bloch, M. and J.P. Parry 1982. Introduction: Death and the Regeneration of Life. In, M. Bloch and J.P. Parry (eds.) *Death and the Regeneration of Life*: 1–44. Cambridge: Cambridge University Press.

Boddy, J. 1988. Spirits and Selves in Northern Sudan: the Cultural Therapeutics of Possession and Trance, *American Ethnologist* 15(1): 4–27.

Bonfiglioli, A.M. 1988. *Dudal. Histoire de famille et histoire de troupeau chez un groupe de Wodaabe du Niger*. Paris: Eds. de la Maison des Sciences de l'Homme.

Bourdieu, P. 1977. *Outline of a Theory of Practice*. Cambridge: Cambridge University Press.

Boyd, R. and P. Richerson 1985. *Culture and the Evolutionary Process*. Chicago: University of Chicago Press.

Brittain, A.W. 1991. Can Women Remember How Many Children they Have Borne? Data from the East Caribbean, *Social Biology* 38(3–4): 219–232.

Bromberger, Ch. 1994. Eating Habits and Cultural Boundaries in Northern Iran. In, S. Zubaida and R. Tapper (eds.) *Culinary Cultures of the Middle East*: 185–201. London: I.B. Tauris Publs.

Buchanan, A.E. and D.W. Brock 1989. *Deciding for Others. The Ethics of Surrogate Decision Making*. Cambridge: Cambridge University Press.

Burgoyne, J. 1987. Change, Gender and the Life Course. In, G. Cohen (ed.) *Social Change and the Life Course*: 33–66. Cambridge: Cambridge University Press.

Cain, M. 1985. Fertility As an Adjustment to Risk. In, A. Rossi (ed.) *Gender and the Life Course*: 145–159. New York: Aldine.

Caldwell, J. and P. Caldwell 1977. The Role of Marital Abstinence in Determining Fertility: a Study of the Yoruba in Nigeria, *Population Studies* 31: 193–217.

Callan, H. 1984. The Imagery of Choice in Sociobiology, *Man* 19: 404–420.

Campbell, J. 1949. *The Hero with a Thousand Faces*. New York: Pantheon Books (Bollington Ser. XVII).

Canfield, R.L. 1973. *Faction and Conversion in a Plural Society: Religious Alignments in the Hindu Kush*. Ann Arbor: University of Michigan, Anthropological Papers 50.

Carrier, N.H. and J. Hobcraft 1973. *Demographic Estimation for Developing Societies*. London.

Casimir, M.J. 1991. *Flocks and Food: a Biocultural Approach to the Study of Pastoral Foodways*. Cologne: Böhlau Verlag.

____ and A. Rao 1985. Vertical Control in the Western Himalayas. Some Notes on the Pastoral Ecology of the Nomadic Bakkarwal of Jammu and Kashmir, *Mountain Research and Development* 5(3): 221–232.

——. 1992. Kulturziele und Fortpflanzungsunterschiede: Aspekte der Beziehung zwischen Macht, Besitz und Reproduktion bei den nomadischen Bakkarwal im westlichen Himalaya. In, E. Voland (ed.) *Fortpflanzung: Natur und Kultur im Wechselspiel*.

Versuch eines Dialogs zwischen Biologen und Sozialwissenschaftlern: 270–289. Frankfurt: Suhrkamp Verlag.

——. 1995. Prestige, Possessions and Progeny. Cultural Goals and Reproductive Success among the Bakkarwal, *Human Nature* 6(3): 241–272.

——. 1998. Sustainable Herd Management and the Tragedy of No Man's Land: An Analysis of West Himalayan Pastures Using Remote Sensing Techniques, *Human Ecology*.

——, forthcoming. *Of Dangers, Dogs, and Darkness. The Terrors of Transition*. (Ms.).

Census of India 1941. *Kashmir. Vol. XXII, Part II. Important Elements*. 1942.

——. 1961. *Jammu and Kashmir. Vol. VI, Part IIC, Cultural and Migration Tables*. 1962.

——. 1971a. The Incidence of Polygynous Marriages in India. *Census of India, 1971*. Delhi: Government of India.

——. 1971b. Members of Household by Relationship to Household Head, Classified by Age Group of Household Head. *Census of India, 1971. Pt. IIC(iii) Vol. I. Series 1. Social and Cultural Tables*. Delhi: Government of India.

Centlivres-Dumont, M. 1981. Rites de mariage en Afghanistan: le dit et le vécu. In, *Naître, vivre et mourir*: 119–134. Neuchâtel: Musée d'Ethnographie.

Chakravarti, U. 1995. Wifehood, Widowhood and Adultery. Female Sexuality, Surveillance, and the State in 18th Century Maharashtra, *Contributions to Indian Sociology* 29(1/2): 3–21.

Chaudhuri, B. 1981. *The Bakreshwar Temple. A Study on Continuity and Change*. Delhi: Inter-India Publs.

Chen, M.A. and J. Drèze 1995. Widowhood and Well-Being in Rural North India. In, M. Das Gupta, L.C. Chen, and T.N. Krishnan (eds.) *Women's Health in India: Risk and Vulnerability*: 245–287. Delhi: Oxford University Press.

Chodorow, N. 1974. Family Structure and Feminine Personality. In, M.Z. Rosaldo and L. Lamphere (eds.) *Woman, Culture, and Society*: 43–66. Stanford: Stanford University Press.

Choksy, J.K. 1989. *Purity and Pollution in Zoroastrianism. Triumph over Evil*. Austin: University of Texas Press.

Chowdhry, P. 1995. Popular Perceptions of Widow-Remarriage in Haryana: Past and Present. In, B. Roy (ed.) *From the Seams of History. Essays on Indian Women*: 37–66. Delhi: Oxford University Press.

Christianat, J-L. 1989. *Des parrains pour la vie: parenté rituelle dans une communauté des Andes péruviennes*. Paris: Eds. de la Maison des Sciences de l'Homme (Recherches et Travaux 9, Université de Neuchâtel).

Cohen, A. 1977. Symbolic Action and the Structure of the Self. In, I. Lewis (ed.) *Symbols and Sentiments. Cross-Cultural Studies in Symbolism*: 117–128. London: Academic Press.

Cohen, L. 1994. Old Age. Cultural and Critical Perspectives, *Annual Review of Anthropology* 23: 137–158.

Cort, J.E. 1991. The Svetambar Murtipujak Jain Mendicant, *Man* 26(4): 651–671.

Crapanzano, V. 1990. On Self-Characterization. In, J.W. Stigler, R.A. Shweder and G. Herdt (eds.) *Cultural Psychology: essays on Comparative Human Development*: 401–423. Cambridge: Cambridge University Press.

Cribb, R. 1991. *Nomads in Archaeology*. Cambridge: Cambridge University Press.

Crooke, W. 1896. *The Popular Religion and Folklore of Northern India*. 2 Vols. London: Archibald Constable & Co.

Cross, S. and H. Markus 1991. Possible Selves Across the Life Span, *Human Development* 34: 230–255.

Cowgill, D.O. 1986. *Aging Around the World*. Belmont: Wadsworth Publ. Co.
Crawford, J., S. Kippax, J. Onyx, U. Gault and P. Benton 1992. *Emotion and Gender. Constructing Meaning from Memory*. London: Sage.
Dandekar, K. 1993. The Aged, their Problems and Social Intervention in Maharashtra, *Economic and Political Weekly* XXVIII(23): 1188–1194.
Daniel, E.V. 1984. *Fluid Signs. Being a Person the Tamil Way*. Berkeley: University of California Press.
Das, V. 1973. The Structure of Marriage Preferences: An Account from Pakistani Fiction, *Man* 8(1): 30–45.
——. 1976. Masks and Faces: An Essay on Punjabi Kinship, *Contributions to Indian Sociology* 10(1): 1–30.
Das Gupta, M. 1987. Selective Discrimination Against Female Children in Rural Punjab, India, *Population and Development Review* 13(1): 77–100.
Datan, N. 1990. Aging into Transitions. Cross-cultural Perspectives on Women at Midlife. In, R. Formanek (ed.) *The Meanings of Menopause. Historical, Medial, and Clinical Perspectives*: 117–153. London: The Analytic Press.
Davies, M.W. 1988. *Knowing one another. Shaping an Islamic Anthropology*. London: Mansell Publ. Ltd.
Davis, M. 1983. The Individual in Holistic India. In, G.R. Gupta (ed.) *Religion in Modern India*: 49–77. New Delhi: Vikas.
Delaney, C.1991. *The Seed and the Soil. Gender and Ccosmology in Turkish Village Society*. Berkeley: University of California Press.
——. 1994. Untangling the Meanings of Hair in Turkish Society, *Anthropological Quarterly* 67(4): 159–172.
Derné, S. 1992. Hindu Men's "Languages" of Social Pressure and Individualism: the Diversity of South Asian Ethnopsychologies, *International Journal of Indian Studies* 2(2): 40–71.
Desai, N. and M. Krishnaraj 1987. *Women and Society in India*. Delhi: Ajanta Publs.
Desjarlais, R. 1989. *Self, Space and Healing among the Yolmo Sherpa*. Unpublished conference paper.
Diemberger, H. 1993. Blood, Sperm, Soul and the Mountain. Gender Relations, Kinship and Cosmovision among the Khumbo (N.E. Nepal). In, T. del Valle (ed.) *Gendered Anthropology*: 88–127. London: Routledge.
Diener, Ed. 1984. Subjective Well-Being, *Psychological Bulletin* 95(3): 542–575.
Djurfeldt, G. and S. Lindberg 1976. *Pills Against Poverty*. Delhi: Oxford University Press.
Donaldson, B.A. 1938. *The Wild Rue. A Study of Muhammadan Magic and Folklore in Iran*. London: Luzac & Co.
Donnan, H. 1988. *Marriage among Muslims. Preference and Choice in northern Pakistan*. Delhi: Hindustan Publ. Corp.
Dua, H. 1984. Personal Names in Panjabi: an Ethnographic Study, *Man in India* 64(3): 243–262.
Dube, L. 1986. Seed and Earth: the Symbolism of Biological Reproduction and Sexual Relations of Production. In, L. Dube, E. Leacock, and S. Ardener (eds.) *Visibility and Power. Essays on Women in Society and Development*: 22–53. Delhi: Oxford University Press.
Dumont, L. 1966. *Homo hierarchicus. Essai sur le système des castes*. Paris: Editions Gallimard.
——. 1970a. *Homo Hierarchicus. The Caste System and its Implications*. Chicago: University of Chicago Press.
——. 1970b. *Religion/Politics and History in India*. Paris: Mouton.

——. 1987. On Individualism and Equality, *Current Anthropology* 28(5): 669–672.

Durkheim, E. 1914. Le dualisme de la nature humaine et ses conditions sociales, *Scientia* XV: 206–221.

——. 1976 [1st ed. 1915]. *The Elementary Forms of Religious Life*. London: Allen & Unwin.

Dyson, T. & M. Moore 1983. On Kinship Structure, Female Autonomy and Demographic Behaviour in India, *Population and Development Review* 9(1): 35–60.

Dyson-Hudson, R. and N. Dyson-Hudson 1980. Nomadic Pastoralism, *Annual Review of Anthropology* 9: 15–61.

Edwards, D.B. 1990. Frontiers, Boundaries and Frames. The Marginal Identity of Afghan Refugees. In, A.S. Ahmed (ed.) *Pakistan: the Social Sciences' Perspective*: 61–99. Karachi: Oxford University Press.

Eglar, Z. 1960. *A Punjabi Village in Pakistan*. New York: Columbia University Press.

Eickelman, C. 1984. *Women and Community in Oman*. New York: New York University Press.

Eisenstadt, S.N. 1968. Prestige, Participation and Strata Formation. In, J.A. Jackson (ed.) *Social Stratification*: 62–103. Cambridge: Cambridge University Press.

Elster, J. 1982. Marxism, Functionalism and Game Theory, *Theory and Society* 11: 453–482.

E.I. Encyclopaedia of Islam [New/old editions]. Leiden: E.J. Brill.

Enthoven, R.E. 1914. *Folklore Notes Vol. I. Gujarat*. Bombay: British-India Press.

Erikson, E. 1975. *Life History and the Historical Moment*. New York.

Ewing, K. P. 1990. The Illusion of Wholeness: Culture, Self, and the Experience of Inconsistency, *Ethos* 18: 251–278.

——. 1991. Can Psychoanalytic Theories Explain the Pakistani Woman? Intrapsychic Autonomy and Interpersonal Engagement in the Extended Family, *Ethos* 19(2): 131–160.

FAIR 1980. *A Study of Migratory Shepherds*. Delhi: Ministry of Commerce. (Foundation to Aid Industrial Recovery).

Fajan, J.1985. The Person in Social Context: the Social Character of Baining 'Psychology'. In, G.M. White and J. Kirkpatrick (eds.) *Person, Self and Experience. Exploring Pacific Ethnopsychologies*: 367–397. Berkeley: University of California Press.

Ferdinand, K. 1978. Marriage among Pakhtun Nomads of the Kabul-Laghman Area and Matrimonial Songs with an Analysis of Case Material Concerning Marriage Ties. *Pasto Quarterly* II(2): 126–133.

Fernandes, W. 1982. Aging in South Asia As Marginalisation in a Neo-Colonial Economy: an Introduction. In, A. de Souza and W. Fernandes (eds.) *Aging in South Asia*: 1–23. Delhi: Indian Social Institute (Monograph Series 6).

Firth, R. 1957. *We, the Tikopia. A Sociological Study of Kinship in Primitive Polynesia*. London: George Allen & Unwin.

Fogelson, R.D. 1979. Person, Self, and Identity. In, B. Lee (ed.) *Psychological Theories of the Self*: 67–109. New York: Plenum Press.

Forchheimer, P. 1953. *The Category of Person in Language*. Berlin: W. de Gruyter & Co.

Formanek, R. 1990. Continuity and Change and "The Change of Life". Premodern Views of the Menopause. In, R. Formanek (ed.) *The Meanings of Menopause. Historical, Medical and Clinical Perspectives*: 3–41. London: The Analytic Press.

Fortes, M. 1987. *Religion, Morality and the Person. Essays on Tallensi Religion*. Cambridge: Cambridge University Press.

Fricke, T., W.G. Axinn, and A. Thornton. 1993. Marriage, Social Inequality, and Women's Contact with their Natal Families in Alliance Societies: Two Tamang Examples, *American Anthropologist* 95(2): 395–419.

Fruzzetti, L.M. 1981. Muslim Rituals: The Household Rites versus the Public Festivals in Rural India. In, I. Ahmad (ed.) *Ritual and Religion among Muslims in India*: 91–112. Delhi: Manohar.

Fruzzetti, L.M., A. Östör, S. Barnett. 1976. The Cultural Construction of the Person in Bengal and Tamil Nadu, *Contributions to Indian Sociology* 10(1): 157–182.

Fry, C. 1980 (ed.) *Aging in Culture and Society*. New York: Praeger.

Gaborieau, M. 1989. Pouvoirs et autorité des soufis dans l'Himalaya. In, V. Bouillier and G. Toffin (eds.) *Prêtrise, pouvoirs et autorité en Himalaya*: 215–238. Paris: Eds. de l'EHESS (Colls. Purusartha 12).

Gardner, P.M. 1991. Foragers' Pursuit of Individual Autonomy, *Current Anthropology* 32(5): 543–572.

Geertz, C. 1993 [1st. ed. 1973]. *The Interpretation of Cultures*. London: Fontana Press.

Ghosh, B.R. 1975. An Analysis of the Patterns of Personal Naming among a Few Communities of Delhi, *The Anthropologist* XIX(1–2): 44–48.

Gideon, H. 1962. A Baby is born in the Punjab, *American Anthropologist* 64: 1220–1234.

Gil'adi, A. 1992. *Children of Islam. Concepts of Childhood in Medieval Muslim Society*. Oxford: Macmillan.

Glatzer, B. 1977. *Nomaden von Ghārjistan*. Wiesbaden: F. Steiner Verlag.

—— and M.J. Casimir 1983. Herds and Households among Pashtun Pastoral Nomads: Limits of Growth, *Ethnology* XXII(4): 307– 325.

Gnoli, G. 1966/67. Lichtsymbolik in Alt-Iran. Haoma-Ritus und Erlöser-Mythos, *Antaios* 8: 528–549.

Goffmann, E. 1972. *Encounters. Two Studies in the Sociology of Interaction*. London: Allen Lane.

Gold, A.G. 1989. Stories of Shakti: Interpreting Female Traditions in some Rajasthani Traditions. *Paper presented at the Panel, Paragons, Paradigms and Paradoxes: South Asian Women in Varying Contexts. Assoc. for Asian Studies Ann. Meeting*, March 1989. Washington, D.C.

Goldschmidt, W. 1979. A General Model for Pastoral Social Systems. In, *Production pastorale et société*: 15–27. Paris: Eds. M.S.H.

Good, A. 1991. *The Female Bridegroom. A Comparative Study of Life-Crisis Rituals in South India and Sri Lanka*. Oxford: Clarendon Press.

Goodenough, W.H. 1965. Rethinking 'Status'and 'Role'. Towards a General Model of the Cultural Organization of Social Relationships. In, *The Relevance of Models for Anthropology*: 1–24. London: Tavistock.

Goodfriend, D.E. 1983. Changing Concepts of Caste and Status among Old Delhi Muslims. In, I. Ahmad (ed.) *Modernization and Social Change among Muslims in India*: 119–152. Delhi: Manohar.

Goodwin Raheja, G. 1988. *The Poison in the Gift. Ritual, Prestation, and the Dominant Caste in a North Indian Village*. Chicago: Chicago University Press.

Grima, B. 1992. *The Performance of Emotion among Paxtun Women*. Austin: University of Texas Press.

Grob, A. 1995. Subjective Well-Being and Significant Life-Events across the Life Span, *Swiss Journal of Psychology* 54(1): 3–18.

Hallowell, A.I. 1955. *Culture and Experience*. Philadelphia: University of Pennsylvania Press.

——. 1959. Behavioral Evolution and the Emergence of the Self. In, B.J. Meggars (ed.) *Evolution and Anthropology. A Centennial Appraisal*: 36–60. Washington, D.C.: Anthropological Society of Washington.

Hallpike, C.R. 1969. Social Hair, *Man* 4: 254–264.

Hanna, N.S. 1982. *Ghagar of Sett Guiranha. A Study of a Gypsy Community in Egypt.* Cairo: The American University (Cairo Papers in Social Science, Vol. 5, Monograph 1).

Hardman, C. forthcoming. We, Brothers of Tiger and Bamboo: or the Notions of Person and Kin in the Eastern Hills of Nepal. In, M. Böck, A. Rao (eds.) *Culture, Creation, and Procreation: Concepts of Kinship in South Asian Practice.* Oxford/New York: Berghahn Publishers.

Harris, G.G. 1989. Concepts of Individual, Self, and Person in Description and Analysis, *American Anthropologist* 91(3): 599–612.

Hathurani, M.A.M. nd. *Names for Muslim Children.* Delhi: Adam Publs. & Distributors.

Heelas, P.L.F. and A.J. Lock. 1981. (eds.) *Indigenous Psychologies. The Anthropology of Self.* New York: Academic Press.

Heesterman, J.C. 1979. Power and Authority in Indian Tradition. In, R.J. Moore (ed.) Tradition and Politics in South Asia: 91–110. Delhi: Oxford University Press.

Hendricks, J. and C.B. Peters. 1986. The Times of Our Lives, *American Behavioral Scientist* 29(6): 662–678.

Henry, W.E. 1964. The Theory of Intrinsic Disengagement. In, P. Hansen (ed.) *Age with a future*: 419–424. Copenhagen.

Héritier, F. 1984. Sterilité, aridité, sècheresse: quelques invariants de la pensée symbolique. In, M. Augé et C. Herzlich (dirs.) *Le sens du mal. Anthropologie, histoire, sociologie de la maladie*: 123–154. Paris: Eds. des archives contemporaines.

Hermansen, M.K. 1988. Shah Wali Allah's Theory of the Subtle Spiritual Centers (Lata'if): A Sufi Model of Personhood and Self-Transformation, *Journal of Near East Studies* 47(1): 1–25.

Hershman, P. 1981. *Punjabi Kinship and Marriage.* Delhi: Hindustan Publ. Corp.

Hewlett, B.S. 1991. Demography and Childcare in Preindustrial Societies, *Journal of Anthropological Research* 47(1): 1–37.

Hollan, D. 1992. Cross-Cultural Differences in the Self, *Journal of Anthropological Research* 48(4): 283–300.

Holy, L. 1989. *Kinship, Honour and Solidarity. Cousin Marriage in the Middle East.* Manchester: Manchester University Press.

——. 1990. Strategies for Old Age among the Berti of Sudan. In, Paul Spencer (ed.) *Anthropology and the Riddle of the Sphinx. Paradoxes of Change in the Life Course*: 167–182. London: Routledge.

Honigman, J.H. 1960. Education and Career Specialization in a West Pakistan Village of Renown, *Anthropos* 55: 825–840.

Horowitz, M.J. 1991. Introduction. In, M.J. Horowitz (ed.) *Person Schemas and Maladaptive Interpersonal Patterns*: 1–8. Chicago: University of Chicago Press.

Howard, A. 1985. Ethnopsychology and the Prospects for a Cultural Psychology. In, G.M. White and J. Kirkpatrick (eds.) *Person, Self, and Experience*: 401–420. Berkeley: University of California Press.

Howell, S. and M. Melhuus. 1993. The Study of Kinship; the Study of Person; a Study of Gender? In, T. del Valle (ed.) *Gendered Anthropology*: 38–53. London: Routledge.

Humphrey, C. 1992. Women and Ideology in Hierarchical Societies in East Asia. In, S. Ardener (ed.) *Persons and Powers of Women in Diverse Cultures*: 173–209. Oxford: Berg.

Hussain, M.Y. 1990. The Concept of Human Capacity in Relation to the Problem of Free Will and Predestination: the Mu'azilite and the Ash'arite Theology, *Islam and the Modern Age* XXI(2): 101–118.

Ibn Khaldun 1967. *The Muqaddimah.* London: Routledge & Kegan Paul (Abridged Translation).

Inden, R.B. 1985. Hindu Evil As Unconquered Lower Self. In, D. Parkin (ed.) *The Anthropology of Evil*: 142–164. Oxford: Basil Blackwell.

—— and R.W. Nicholas. 1977. *Kinship in Bengali Culture*. Chicago: University of Chicago Press.

Ingold, T. 1986. *The Appropriation of Nature. Essays on Human Ecology and Social Relations*. Manchester: Manchester University Press.

——. 1990. An Anthropologist Looks at Biology, *Man* 25(2): 208–229.

——. 1991. Becoming Persons: Consciousness and Sociality in Human Evolution, *Cultural Dynamics* IV(3): 355–378.

James, W. 1981. *The Principles of Psychology*. Cambridge (Mass.): Harvard University Press. (1. ed. 1890).

Janata, A. 1962/63. Verlobung und Hochzeit in Kabul, *Archiv f. Völkerkunde* XVII/XVIII: 59–72.

Jeffery, P. 1979. *Frogs in a Well: Indian Women in Purdah*. London: Zed Press.

Jeffery, P., R. Jeffery and A. Lyon. 1985. *Contaminating States and Women's Status*. Delhi: Indian Social Institute, Monograph 22.

——. 1989. *Labour Pains and Labour Power. Women and Childbearing in India*. London: Zed Books Ltd.

Jettmar, K. 1961. Ethnological Research in Dardistan 1958. Preliminary Report. *Proceedings of the American Philosophical Society* 105(1): 79–97.0

Johansen, U. 1959. Die Alpfrau: eine Dämonengestalt der türkischen Völker, *Zeitschrift der Deutschen Morgenländischen Gesellschaft* 109(2/n.s.34): 303–316.

Johnson, G. 1982. Organizational Structure and Scalar Stress. In, C. Renfrew, M. Rowlands, B. Seagraves (eds.) *Theory and Explanation in Archaeology*: 389–421. New York: Academic Press.

Joseph, R. 1974. Choice or Force: a Study in Social Manipulation, *Human Organization* 33(4): 398–401.

Joshi, R. 1996. Politics of Old Age, *Business India* Feb. 26–Mar. 10: 45.

Kaare, B. 1995. Field Research among the Akie, *Anthropology Today* 11(5): 18–19.

Kakar, S. 1978. *The Inner World. A Psycho-analytic Study of Childhood and Society in India*. Delhi: Oxford University Press.

——. 1979. *Indian Childhood. Cultural Ideals and Social Reality*. Delhi: Oxford University Press.

Kango, G.H. and B. Dhar. 1981. N*omadic Routes in Jammu and Kashmir (Part I)*. Srinagar: Directorate of Soil Conservation.

Kauffman, L.H. 1987. Self-Reference and Recursive Forms, *Journal of Social and Biological Structure* 10: 53–72.

Keddie, N. and L. Beck. 1978. Introduction. In, L. Beck and N. Keddie (eds.) *Women in the Muslim World*: 1–34. Cambridge (Mass.): Harvard University Press.

Kessinger, T.G. 1979. *Vilayatpur: 1848–1968*. Delhi: Young Asia Publishers.

Khan, M.E. 1979. *Family Planning among Muslims in India. A Study of the Reproductive Behaviour of Muslims in an Urban Setting*. Delhi: Manohar.

Khare, R.S. 1970. On Hypergamy and Progeny Rank Determination in Northern India, *Man in India* 50(4): 350–378.

——. 1984. *The Untouchable As Himself: Ideology, Identity, and Pragmatism among the Lucknow Chamars*. Cambridge: Cambridge University Press.

Khatana, R.P. 1976a. Marriage and Kinship among the Gujar Bakarwals of Jammu and Kashmir. In, I. Ahmad (ed.) *Family, Kinship and Marriage among Muslims in India*: 83–126. Delhi: Manohar

——. 1976b. *Some Aspects of Transhumance in Mountainous Tracts – A Case Study of the Gujar Bakarwals of Jammu and Kashmir*. M.Phil Dissertation. New Delhi: Jawaharlal Nehru University.

——. 1992. *Tribal Migration in Himalayan Frontiers. Study of Gujjar Bakkarwal Transhumance Economy*. Gurgaon: Vintage Books.

——. 1993. Development and the Process of Sedentarization among the Gujjar Bakarwals of Jammu and Kashmir. In, A. Ahmad (ed.) *Social Structure and Regional Development. A Social Geography Perspective*: 283–307. Jaipur: Rawat Publs.

Khatib-Chahidi, J. 1992. Milk Kinship in Shi'ite Islamic Iran. In, V. Maher (ed.) *The Anthropology of Breast-Feeding. Natural Law or Social Construct*: 109–132. Oxford: Berg.

Kluckhohn, C. and H.A. Murray. 1948. Introduction: A Conception of Personality. In, C. Kluckhohn and H.A. Murray (eds.) *Personality in Nature, Society, and Culture*. New York: A. Knopf.

Kohistani, B.L. 1990 [Reprinted in Hari Om 1992]. Forgotten Facts of Kashmir Scenario. *Debacle in Kashmir*: 252–259 (Appendix XIV). Jammu: Jay Kay Book House.

Kolenda, P. 1984. Woman As Tribute, Woman As Flower: Images of "Woman" in Weddings in North and South India, *American Ethnologist* 11(1): 98–110.

Krengel, M. 1989. *Sozialstrukturen im Kumaon. Bergbauern im Himalaya*. Wiesbaden: F. Steiner Verlag.

Kurin, R. 1990. Turbans, Skirts and Spirits: Folk Models of a Punjabi Muslim Brotherhood, *Social Analysis* 28: 11–25. (Special Issue: P. Werbner (ed.) Person, Myth and Society in South Asian Islam).

—— and C. Morrow 1985. Patterns of Solidarity in a Punjabi Muslim Village, *Contributions to Indian Sociology* 19(2): 235–249.

Lakoff, G. 1987. *Women, Fire, and Dangerous Things: what Categories Reveal about the Mind*. Chicago: Chicago University Press.

Lambert, H. forthcoming. Village Bodies? Reflections on Locality, Constitution, and Affect in Rajasthani Kinship. In, M. Böck, A. Rao (eds.) *Culture, Creation, and Procreation: Concepts of Kinship in South Asian Practice*. Oxford/New York: Berghahn Publishers.

Lapoint, E.C. 1981. Solar Contagion: Eclipse Ritual in a North Indian Village, *Man in India* 61(4): 327–345.

Leahy, R.L. 1991. Development of the Self. In, R. Dulbeco (ed.) *Encyclopedia of Human Biology*, Vol. 2: 853–859. New York: Academic Press.

Leaman, O. 1978. Power and Women in Saudi Arabia: A Note, *Journal of Anthropological Research* 34: 589–590.

Lecomte-Tilouine, M. 1993. The Proof of the Bone: Lineage and Devali in Central Nepal, *Contributions to Indian Sociology* 27(1): 1–23.

Lemon, B.W. et al. 1972. An Exploration of the Activity Theory of Aging: Activity Types and Life Satisfaction among In-Movers to a Retirement Community, *Journal of Gerontology* 27: 511–523.

Leslie, I.J. 1986. Strisvabhava: The Inherent Nature of Women. In, N.J. Allen, R.F. Gombrich, T. Raychaudhuri and G. Rizvi (eds.) *Oxford University Papers on India*. Vol. I, Part 1: 28–58. Delhi: Oxford University Press.

Levine, N.E. 1987. Differential Child Care in Three Tibetan Communities: Beyond Son Preference, *Population and Development Review* 13(2): 281–304.

Lewis, O. 1958. *Village Life in Northern India. Studies in a Delhi Village*. New York: Random House Inc.

Lienhardt, G. 1985. Self, Public, Private: Some African Representations. In, M. Carrithers, S. Collins and S. Lukes (eds.) *The Category of the Person*: 141–155. Cambridge: Cambridge University Press.

Lienhardt, M.1947. *DoKamo. La personne et le mythe dans le monde melanésien*. Paris: Gallimard.

Lifton, R.J. 1993. *The Protean Self: Human Resilience in the Age of Fragmentation*. New York: Harper & Row.

Lindholm, C. 1997. Does the Sociocentric Self Exist? Reflections on Markus and Kitayama's "Culture and the Self", *Journal of Anthropological Research* 53(4): 405–422.

Linton, R. 1942. Age and Sex Categories, *American Sociological Review* 7: 589–603.

Littmann, E. 1956. *Eigennamen der heutigen Ägypter*. Roma: Istituto per L'Oriente.

Madan, T.N. 1989a [1. ed. 1965]. *Family and Kinship. A Study of the Pandits of Rural Kashmir*. Delhi: Oxford University Press.

——. 1972. Religious Ideology in a Plural Society: The Muslims and Hindus of Kashmir, *Contributions to Indian Sociology* (n.s.) 6: 106–141.

——. 1975. Structural Implications of Marriage in North India: Wife-Givers and Wife-Takers among the Pandits of Kashmir, *Contributions to Indian Sociology* (ns) 9(2): 217–243.

——. 1989b. Religion in India, *Daedalus. J. of the American Academy of Arts and Sciences* 118(4): 115–146. (Special Issue: Another India)

——. 1992. Dying with Dignity, *Social Science Medicine* 35(4): 425–432.

——. 1994. The Social Construction of Cultural Identities in Rural Kashmir. In, T.N. Madan *Pathways. Approaches to the Study of Society in India*: 167–201. Delhi: Oxford University Press.

Mageo, J.M. 1991. Samoan Moral Discourse and the *Loto*, *American Anthropologist* 93(2): 405–420.

Malhotra, S.P. and H.S. Trivedi 1981. Child Population and Attitudes towards Children in an Arid Village, *Man in India* 61(4): 357–367.

Mamdani, M. 1972. *The Myth of Population Control. Family, Caste and Class in an Indian Village*. New York: Monthly Review Press.

Mani, S.B. 1981. From Marriage to Child Conception: An Ethnomedical Study in Rural Tamil Nadu. In, G.R. Gupta (ed.) *The Social and Cultural Context of Medicine in India*: 194–220. Delhi: Vikas Publ. House.

Markus, H. and S. Kitayama. 1991. Culture and the Self: Implications for Cognition, Emotion and Motivation, *Psychological Review* 98: 224–253.

Marriott, M. 1976. Hindu Transactions: Diversity without Dualism. In, B. Kapferer (ed.) *Transactions and Meaning. Directions in the Anthropology of Exchange and Symbolic Behavior*: 109–142. Philadelphia: Institute for the Study of Human Issues.

——. 1989. Constructing an Indian Ethnosociology, *Contributions to Indian Sociology* 23(1): 1–39.

Marsella, A.J., G. DeVos, and F.L.K. Hsu 1985. (eds.) *Culture and Self: Asian and Western Perspectives*. New York: Tavistock Publications.

Marx, E. 1967. *The Bedouin of the Negev*. Manchester University Press.

Massé, H. 1938. *Croyances et coutumes persanes*. Paris: Eds. G.-P. Maisonneuve.

Mauss, M. 1938. Une catégorie de l'esprit humain: la notion de Personne, celle de Moi, *Journal of the Royal Anthropological Institute* 68: 263–282.

Mawet, F. 1980. "Light" in Ancient Iranian, *Journal of Indo-European Studies* 8: 283–299.

Maya Singh, B. 1972 [1st ed. 1895]. *Punjabi-English Dictionary*. Patiala: Language Department, Panjab University.

McHugh, E. 1989. Concepts of the Person among the Gurungs of Nepal, *American Ethnologist* 16(1): 75–86.

Mead, G.H. 1934. *Mind, Self, and Society: from the Standpoint of a Social Behaviorist*. (ed. by C.W. Morris) Chicago: University of Chicago Press.

Miers, S. and I. Kopytoff. 1977. *Slavery in Africa. Historical and Anthropological Perspectives*. Madison: University of Wisconsin Press.

Mill, J.S. 1927 [1st. ed. 1859]. *On Liberty*. Oxford: Oxford University Press.

Milner, M.Jr. 1994. *Status and Sacredness. A General Theory of Status Relations and an Analysis of Indian Culture*. New York: Oxford University Press.

Mines, M. 1992. Individuality and Achievement in South Indian Social History, *Modern Asian Studies* 26(1): 129–156.

—— and V. Gourishankar. 1990. Leadership and Individuality in South Asia: The Case of the South Indian Big-Man, *The Journal of Asian Studies* 49(4): 761–786.

Misri, U. 1991. *The Child and Society: A Study of Pandit Children in a Kashmiri Village*. University of Delhi: PhD Thesis.

Monier-Williams, M. 1951 [1st. ed. 1877]. *Hinduism*. Calcutta: Susil Gupta & Co.

——. 1976. [1st. ed. 1899]. *Sanskrit-English Dictionary*. Delhi: Munshiram Manoharlal.

Morris, B. 1978. Are there any Individuals in India? A Critique of Dumont's Theory of the Indvidual, *The Eastern Anthropologist* 31(4): 365–377.

——. 1994. *Anthropology of the Self. The Individual in Cultural Perspective*. London: Pluto Press.

Murdock, G.P. 1949. *Social Structure*. New York: Macmillan.

Myers, D.G. and E. Diener 1996. The Pursuit of Happiness, *Scientific American* 274(5): 54–56.

Nandy, A. and S. Visvanathan. 1990. Modern Medicine and its Non-Modern Critics: A Study in Discourse. In, F.A. Marglin and S.A. Marglin (eds.) *Dominating Knowledge. Development, Culture, and Resistance*: 145–184. Oxford: Clarendon Press.

Narayan, K. 1993. How Native is a "Native" Anthropologist? *American Anthropologist* 95(3): 671–686.

NCERT. 1989 [1st ed. 1988]. *Hamara Nagarik Jivan*. (A textbook for Class VI) Delhi: NCERT.

Neale, W.C. 1969. Land is to Rule. In, R.E. Frykenberg (ed.) *Land Control and Social Structure in Indian History*: 3–15. Madison: University of Wisconsin Press.

Nicolas, M. 1972. *Traditions populaires turques concernant les naissances*. Paris: Publications orientalistes de France.

Obeyesekere, G. 1981. *Medusa's Hair. An Essay on Personal Symbols and Religious Experience*. Chicago: The University of Chicago Press.

——. 1990a. *The Work of Culture. Symbolic Transformation in Psychoanalysis and Anthropology*. Chicago: University of Chicago Press.

——. 1990b. The Illusory Pursuit of Self – a Review of Culture and Self: Asian and Western Perspectives (eds. A.J. Marsella et al.), *Philosophy East and West* XL(2): 239–250.

O'Flaherty, W. 1980. *Women, Androgynes and other Mythical Beasts*. Chicago: University of Chicago Press.

Ohnuki-Tierney, E. 1991. Embedding and Transforming Polytrope. The Monkey As Self in Japanese Culture. In, J.W. Fernandez (ed.) *Beyond Metaphor. The Theory of Tropes in Anthropology*: 159–189. Stanford: Stanford University Press.

Oldenburg, P. 1992. Sex Ratio, Son Preference and Violence in India: a Research Note, *Economic and Political Weekly* XXVII(49–50): 2657–2662.

Onians, R.B. 1951. *The Origins of European Thought about the Body, the Mind, the Soul, the World, Time, and Fate*. Cambridge: Cambridge University Press.

Orywal, E. 1986. (ed.) *Die ethnischen Gruppen Afghanistans: Fallstudien zu Gruppenidentität und Intergruppenbeziehungen*. Wiesbaden: L. Reichert Verlag.

O'Shaughnessy, T.J. 1991. The Qur'anic View of Youth and Old Age, *Zeitschrift der Deutschen Morgenländischen Gesellschaft* 141(1): 33–51.

Östör, Á. 1980. *The Play of the Gods. Locality, Ideology, Structure, and Time in the Festivals of a Bengali Town.* Chicago: University of Chicago Press.

——. 1984. *Culture and Power. Legend, Ritual, Bazar and Rebellion in a Bengali Society.* Delhi: SAGE Publs.

Östör, Á., L.M. Fruzzetti, and S. Barnett. 1982. (eds.) *Concepts of Person. Kinship, Caste, and Marriage in India.* Cambridge (Mass.): Harvard University Press.

Ott, S. 1981. *The Circle of Mountains. A Basque Shepherding Community.* Oxford: Clarendon Press.

Ovesen, J. 1981. The Continuity of Pashai Society, *Folk* 23: 221–234.

Oxfeld, E. 1992. Individualism, Holism, and the Market Mentality: Notes on the Recollections of a Chinese Entrepreneur, *Cultural Anthropology* 7(3): 267–300.

PAK DBGR. 1982. The Dowry and Bridal Gifts (Restriction) Act 1976, *Islamic and Comparative Law Quarterly* II(1): 70–78.

Pandit, T.N. 1990. A Note on the Gujar of North-west India (Kashmir). In, L. Icke-Schwalbe and G. Meier (eds.) *Wissenschaftsgeschichte und gegenwärtige Forschungen in NordwestIndien*: 107–112. Dresden: Staatliches Museum für Völkerkunde (International Colloquium, 9–13. March, 1987, Herrnhut).

Paques, V. 1991. *La religion des esclaves. Recherches sur la confrérie marocaine des Gnawa.* Bergamo: Moretti et Vitali Editori.

Parish, S. 1987. *Hierarchy and Person in the Moral World of the Newars.* PhD. Diss. University of California, San Diego.

Parkes, Peter. 1987. Livestock Symbolism and Pastoral Ideology among the Kafirs of the Hindu Kush, *Man* 22: 637–660.

Parry, J.P. 1979. *Caste and Kinship in Kangra.* Delhi: Vikas.

Pasternak, B., C.R. Ember, and M. Ember. 1976. On the Conditions Favoring Extended Family Households, *Journal of Anthropological Research* 32(2): 109–123.

Patel, T. 1994. *Fertility Behaviour. Population and Society in a Rajasthan Village.* Delhi: Oxford University Press.

Perrett, R.W. 1989. The Rationality of Asceticism. In, Shlome Biderman and Ben-Ami Scharfstein (eds.) *Rationality in Question. On Eastern and Western Views of Rationality*: 57–76. Leiden: Brill.

Peters, E.L. 1990. *The Bedouin of Cyrenaica. Studies in Personal and Corporate Power.* Cambridge: Cambridge University Press.

Phillimore, P. 1991. Unmarried Women of the Dhaula Dhar: Celibacy and Social Control in Northwest India. *Journal of Anthropological Research* 47(3): 331–350.

Pocock, D.F. 1973. *Mind, Body and Wealth. A Study of Belief and Practice in an Indian Village.* Oxford: B. Blackwell.

Poirier, S. 1992. 'Nomadic' Rituals: Networks of Ritual Exchange between Women of the Australian Western Desert, *Man* (ns) 27(4): 757–776.

Prater, S.H. 1971 [1st. ed. 1948]. *The Book of Indian Animals.* Bombay: Natural History Society.

Pugh, J. 1983. Astrology and Fate: The Hindu and Muslim Experiences. In, C.F. Keyes and E.V. Daniel (eds.) *Karma. An Anthropological Enquiry*: 131–146. Berkeley: University of California.

Radcliffe-Brown, A.R. 1952. *Structure and Function in Primitive Society.* London: Cohen & West Ltd.

——. 1977. On Social Structure. In, S. Lienhardt (ed.) *Social Networks A Developing Paradigm*: 221–232. New York: Academic Press (repr.).

Rao, A. 1982. *Les Ġorbat d'Afghanistan. Aspects économiques d'un groupe itinérant 'J̌at'*. Paris: Eds. ADPF/Institut français d'Iranologie de Téhéran.

——. 1986. Roles, Status and Niches: a Comparison of Peripatetic and Pastoral Women in Afghanistan, *Nomadic Peoples* 21/22: 153–177. (Special Issue: J.C. Berland and M. Salo eds. Peripatetic Peoples).

——. 1988a. Levels and Boundaries in Native Models: Social Groupings among the Bakkarwal of the Western Himalayas, *Contributions to Indian Sociology* 22(2): 195–227. (Repr. 1995, in T.N. Madan ed. *Muslim Communities of South Asia*: 289–332. Delhi: Manohar.)

——. 1988b. *Entstehung und Entwicklung ethnischer Identität bei einer islamischen Minderheit in Südasien: Bemerkungen zur Geschichte der Bakkarwal im westlichen Himalaya.* Berlin: Das arabische Buch (Freie Universität Berlin, Occasional Papers No. 18).

——. 1990. Reflections on Self and Person in a Pastoral Community in Kashmir, *Social Analysis* 28: 11–25. (Special Issue: P. Werbner ed. Person, Myth and Society in South Asian Islam).

——. 1992a. The Constraints of Nature or of Culture? Pastoral Resources and Territorial Behaviour in the Western Himalayas. In, M.J. Casimir and A. Rao (eds.) *Mobility and Territoriality. Social and Spatial Boundaries among Foragers, Fishers, Pastoralists and Peripatetics*: 91–134. Oxford: Berg.

——. 1992b. Die Stellung der Frau und die Ehre der Gruppe: Einige Bemerkungen zur Situation islamischer Frauen in Nordindien, *Sociologus* 42(2): 157–179.

——. 1995. From Bondsmen to Middlemen: Hired Shepherds and Pastoral Politics, *Anthropos* 90(1/3): 149–167.

——. 1996. Die Konstruktion von Schande: Gedanken zur Eskalation eines Konflikts. In, E. Orywal, A. Rao, M. Bollig (eds.) *Krieg und Kampf: Die Gewalt in unseren Köpfen*: 91–105. Berlin: Reimer Verlag.

——. 1997. Prestations and Progeny: the Consolidation of Well-being among the Bakkarwal of Jammu and Kashmir (Western Himalayas). In, T. Schweizer, D. White (eds.) *Kinship, Networks and Exchange*: 210–233. Cambridge: Cambridge University Press.

——, forthcoming. Blood, Milk, and Mountains: Marriage Practice and Concepts of Predictability among the Bakkarwal of Jammu and Kashmir. In, M. Böck, A. Rao (eds.) *Culture, Creation, and Procreation: Concepts of Kinship in South Asian Practice*. Oxford/New York: Berghahn Publishers.

—— and M.J. Casimir. 1985. Pastoral Niches in the Western Himalayas (Jammu and Kashmir). *Himalaya Research Bulletin* 5(1): 28–42.

——. 1990. Perspectives on Pastoral Economy and Ecology in the Western Himalayas. In, N.K. Sah, S.D. Bhatt, R.K. Pande (eds.) *Himalaya: Environment, Resources and Development*: 386–402. Almora: University of Kumaon.

Riesman, P. 1992. *First Find Your Child a Good Mother. The Construction of Self in Two African Communities*. New Brunswick: Rutgers University Press.

Roland, A. 1985. Psychoanalysis in India. In, P. Gaeffke and D.A. Utz (eds.) *Science and Technology in South Asia*: 95–117. Philadelphia: Department of South Asia Regional Studies.

——. 1988. *In Search of Self in India and Japan: Toward a Cross-Cultural Psychology.* Princeton: Princeton University Press.

Rosaldo, M.Z. 1986 [1st ed. 1984]. Toward an Anthropology of Self and Feeling. In, R.A. Shweder and R.A. LeVine (eds.) *Culture Theory. Essays on Mind, Self and Emotion*: 137–157. Cambridge: Cambridge University Press.

Rosaldo, R. 1989 [1st ed. 1980]. *Ilongot Headhunting 1883–1974. A Study in Society and History*. Stanford: Stanford University Press.

Roy, S. 1979. *Status of Muslim Women in North India*. Delhi: B.R. Publ. Corp.

——. 1984. Concept of *Zar, Zan* and *Zamin* – a Cultural Analysis of Indian Islamic Traditions of Inheritance and Kinship, *Man in India* 64(4): 388–396.
Rudolph, L.I. 1997. Self As Other: Amar Singh's Diary As Reflexive "Native" Ethnography, *Modern Asian Studies* 31(1): 143–175.
Sacks, O. 1987. *The Man who Mistook his Wife for a Hat*. New York: Harper Perennial.
Sahlins, M. 1963. Poor Man, Rich Man, Big Man, Chief: Political Types in Melanesia and Polynesia. *Comparative Studies in Society and History* 5: 285–303.
Salam, Z. 1996. The Winds of Change among Muslims, *The Indian Express*, Feb. 20: 8.
Salzman, P.C. 1992. *Kin and Contract in Baluchi Herding Camps*. Naples: Istituto Universitario Orientale.
Sandler, R. 1991. The Changing Concept of the Individual. In, R.M. Savory (ed.) *Islamic Civilization*: 137–145. Cambridge: Cambridge University Press.
Sant Cassia, P. 1986. "Bloodmoney and Brideprice have no Merit": Marriage, Manipulation, and the Transmission of Resources in a South Tuinisian Village, *Cambridge Anthropology* 11(3): 35–60.
Sax, W.S. 1991. *Mountain Goddess. Gender and Politics in a Himalayan Pilgrimage*. New York: Oxford University Press.
Scheper-Hughes, N. 1989. Death without Weeping. Has Poverty Ravaged Mother Love in the Shantytowns of Brazil?, *Natural History* 10: 8–16.
Schlegel, A. and H. Barry III. 1991. *Adolescence. An Anthropological Inquiry*. New York: The Free Press.
Schull, J. and J. D. Smith. 1992. Knowing Thyself, Knowing The Other: They're Not the Same, *Behavioral and Brain Sciences* 15: 166–167.
Schweizer, T. 1978. *Methodenprobleme des interkulturellen Vergleichs*. Cologne: Böhlau-Verlag.
Scott, J.C. 1990. *Weapons of the Weak. Everyday Forms of Peasant Resistance*. Delhi: Oxford University Press.
Scrase, T.J. 1990. Cultural Hegemony and the Dialectics of Educational Reform in India, *International Journal of Indian Studies* 1: 23–40.
Sen, A. 1985. Well-Being, Agency, and Freedom: the Dewey Lectures, 1984, *Journal of Philosophy* 82: 169–221.
——. 1990. *On Ethics and Economics*. Delhi: Oxford University Press.
Shafiq, M. 1984. The Meaning of *Ra'y* and Nature of its Usage in Islamic Law, *Islamic Studies* 23: 21–32.
Shahshahani, S. 1986. Women Whisper, Men Kill: A Case Study of the Mamasani Pastoral Nomads of Iran. In, L. Dube, E. Leacock and S. Ardener (eds.) *Visibility and Power. Essays on Women in Society and Development*: 85–97. Delhi: Oxford University Press.
Sharif, J. 1975 [1st. ed. 1921]. *Islam in India or the Qanun-i-Islam*. (Trans. and edited). London: Curzon Press.
Sharma, B. and P.S. Jamwal. 1988. *Flora of Upper Liddar Valleys of Kashmir Himalaya*, Vol. I. Jodhpur: Scientific Publishers.
Sharma, N.D. 1984. Unsigned "Ordinance" irks Jagmohan, *The Indian Express*, 1.10.1984.
Sharp, H. 1916. *A Note on Education in the State of Jammu and Kashmir*. Calcutta: Government of India.
Shweder, R.A. and E.J. Bourne. 1984. Does the Concept of the Person Vary Cross-culturally? In, R.A. Shweder and R.A. LeVine (eds.) *Culture Theory*: 158–199. Cambridge: Cambridge University Press.
Siegel, J.T. 1969. *The Rope of God*. Berkeley: University of California Press.

Silverman, S. 1977. Patronage As Myth. In, Ernest Gellner and John Waterbury (eds.) *Patrons and Clients in Mediterranean Societies*: 7–19. London: Duckworth.

Singelis, T.M., H.C. Triandis, D.P.S. Bhawuk, and M.J. Gelfand 1995. Horizontal and Vertical Dimensions of Individualism and Collectivism: a Theoretical and Measurement Refinement, *Cross-Cultural Research* 29(3): 240–275.

Skinner, D. 1990. Nepalese Children's Construction of Identities in and around Formal Schooling, *Himalayan Research Bulletin* X(2/3): 8–17.

Skultans, V. 1970. The Symbolic Significance of Menstruation and the Menopause, *Man* 5: 639–651.

Snoy, P. 1962. *Die Kafiren. Formen der Wirtschaft und geistigen Kultur*. University of Frankfurt/Main: PhD. Diss.

SOC. WELF. 1969. *Report of Socio-Economic Survey of Gujjars and Bakerwals in Jammu and Kashmir State.* Delhi: Government of India, Department of Social Welfare.

Sokolovsky, J. 1990. Culture, Aging, and Context. In, J. Sokolovsky (ed.) *The Culture Context of Aging. Worldwide Perspectives*: 13–18. New York: Bergin & Garvey Publs.

Spencer, C. 1993. Human Agency, Biased Transmission, and the Cultural Evolution of Chiefly Authority, *Journal of Anthropological Archaeology* 12: 41–74.

Spencer, P. 1984. Pastoralists and the Ghost of Capitalsim, *Production pastorale et Société* 15: 61–76.

——. 1990. The Riddled Course: Theories of Age and its Transformations. In, P. Spencer (ed.) *Anthropology and the Riddle of the Sphinx. Paradoxes of Change in the Life Course*: 1–34. London: Routledge.

Spielmann, K.A. 1989. A Review: Dietary Restrictions on Hunter-gatherer Women and the Implications for Fertility and Infant Mortality, *Human Ecology* 17(3): 321–345.

Spiro, M. 1993. Is the Western Conception of the "Self" Peculiar within the Context of the World Cultures? *Ethos* 21: 107–153.

Steingass, F. 1973. *A Comprehensive Persian-English Dictionary*. Delhi: Munshiram Manoharlal (repr.)

Stellrecht, I. 1992. Umweltwahrnehmung und vertikale Klassifikation im Hunza-Tal (Karakorum), *Geographische Rundschau* 44: 426–434.

Strathern, M. 1981. Self-Interest and the Social Good: Some Implications of Hagen Gender Imagery. In, S.B. Ortner and H. Whitehead (eds.) *Sexual Meanings. The Cultural Construction of Gender and Sexuality*: 166–191. Cambridge: Cambridge University Press.

Sublet, J. 1991. *Le voile du nom. Essai sur le nom propre arabe*. Paris: PUF.

Sutherland, G.H. 1990. *Bija* (seed) and *Ksetra* (field): Male Surrogacy or *Niyoga* in the Mahabharata, *Contributions to Indian Sociology (ns)* 24(1): 77–103.

Tagore, R. 1925. The Cult of the *Charkha*, *The Modern Review*, September: 263–270.

Tandon, P. 1961. *Punjabi Century 1857–1947*. Delhi: Orient.

Tapper, N. 1980. Matrons and Mistresses: Women and Boundaries in Two Middle Eastern Tribal Societies, *Archives Européennes de Sociologie* XXI(1): 59–79.

——. 1981. Direct Exchange and Brideprice: Alternative Forms in a Complex Marriage System, *Man* (ns) 16: 387–407.

——. 1991. *Bartered Brides. Politics, Gender and Marriage in an Afghan Tribal Society*. Cambridge: Cambridge University Press.

Tiemann, G. 1970. The Four-*got*-Rule among the Jat of Haryana in Northern India, *Anthropos* 65(1/2): 166–178.

Tod, J. 1983 [1st. ed. 1829]. *Annals and Antiquities of Rajasthan, or the Central and Western Rajpoot States of India.* Delhi: M.N. Publishers.

Unbescheid, G. 1985. Blood and Milk, or the Manifestation of the Goddess Manakamana, *Journal of the Nepal Research Centre* VII: 9–135.

Valente, T.W. 1996. Social Network Thresholds in the Diffusion of Innovations, *Social Networks* 18: 69–89.

Van der Veer, P. 1987. Taming the Ascetic: Devotionalism in a Hindu Monastic Order, *Man* 22: 680–695.

Vasavi, A.R. 1994. "Hybrid Times, Hybrid People": Culture and Agriculture in South India, *Man* 29(2): 283–300.

Vatuk, S. 1985. South Asian Cultural Conceptions of Sexuality. In, J. K. Brown and V. Kerns (eds.) *In her Prime. A New View of Middle-Aged Women*: 137–152. Mass: Bergin & Garvey.

——. 1990. "To be a burden on others". Dependency Anxiety among the Elderly in India. In, O.M. Lynch (ed.) *Divine Passions. The Social Construction of Emotion in India*: 64–88. Berkeley: University of California Press.

——. 1995. The Indian Woman in Later Life: Some Social and Cultural Considerations. In, M. Das Gupta, L.C. Chen, and T.N. Krishnan (eds.) *Women's Health in India: Risk and Vulnerability*: 289–306. Delhi: Oxford University Press.

Vaudeville, C. 1993. *A Weaver Named Kabir*. Delhi: Oxford University Press.

Vergati, A. 1982. Social Consequences of Marrying Visnu Narayana: Primary Marriage among the Newars of Kathmandu Valley, *Contributions to Indian Sociology* 16(2): 271–287.

Vetscher, T. 1973. Betrothal and Marriage among the Minas of South Rajasthan, *Man in India* 53(4): 387–413.

Visaria, L. 1988. Level, Trends, and Determinants of Infant Mortality in India. In, A.K. Jain and P. Visaria (eds.) *Infant Mortality in India. Differentials and Determinants*: 67–126. Delhi: Sage Publs.

Vieille, P. 1967. Birth and Death in an Islamic Society, *Diogènes* 57: 101–127.

Vogel, C. 1985. Helping, Cooperation, and Altruism in Primate Societies. In, B. Höll-dobler and M. Lindauer (eds.) Experimental Behavioral Ecology: 375–389. Stuttgart: G. Fischer Verlag.

Wadley, S.S. 1975. *Shakti. Power in the Conceptual Structure of Karimpur Religion*. Chicago: Department of Anthropology.

——. 1977. Power in Hindu Ideology and Practice. In, K. David (ed.) *The New Wind. Changing Identities in South Asia*: 133–155. The Hague: Mouton.

——. 1994. *Struggling with Destiny in Karimpur, 1925–1984*. Berkeley: University of California Press.

Wakil, P.A. 1972. *Zat* and *Qoum* in Punjabi Society: A Contribution to the Problem of Caste, *Sociologus* 22(1/2): 38–48.

Weiner, M. 1978. *Sons of the Soil. Migration and Ethnic Conflict in India*. Princeton: Princeton University Press.

Werbner, P. 1986. The Virgin and the Clown. Ritual Elaboration in Pakistani Migrants' Weddings, *Man* 21: 227–250.

Westphal-Hellbusch, S. and H. Westphal. 1964. *The Jat of Pakistan*. Berlin: Duncker & Humblot.

Whiting, B.B. & J.W.M. Whiting. 1975. *Children of Six Cultures: A Psycho-Cultural Analysis*. Cambridge (Mass.): Harvard University Press.

Wikan, U. 1982. *Behind the Veil in Arabia. Women in Oman*. Baltimore: John Hopkins University Press.

Wikeley, J.M. 1991 [1st ed. 1915]. *Punjabi Musalmans*. Delhi: Manohar.

Wilkes, R.E. 1992. A Structural Modelling Approach to the Measurement and Meaning of Cognitive Age, *Journal of Consumer Research* 19(2): 292–301.

Wilson, M. 1957. *Rituals of Kinship among the Nyakusa*. Oxford: Oxford University Press.

Wise, P.M., K.M. Krajnak, M.L. Kashon 1996. Menopause: The Aging of Multiple Pacemakers, *Science* 273: 67–70.

Wolff, H.W. 1974 [1st. ed. 1973]. *Anthropologie des Alten Testaments*. München: Christian Kaiser Verlag.

Wu, F.C.W. 1988. The Biology of Puberty. In, P. Diggory, M. Potts, and S. Teper (eds.) *Natural Human Fertility. Social and Biological Determinants*: 89–101. Houndmills: The Macmillan Press Ltd.

Zimmermann, F. 1987. *The Jungle and the Aroma of Meats. An Ecological Theme in Hindu Medicine*. Berkeley: University of California Press.

Zonabend, F. 1980 [1. French ed. 1980]. Namen – wozu? (Die Personennamen in einem französischen Dorf: Minot-en-Châtillonais). In, J-M. Benoist (ed.) *Identität. Ein interdisziplinäres Seminar unter Leitung von Claude Lévi-Strauss*: 222–249. Stuttgart: Klett-Cotta.

Zutshi, J.N. 1974. *Jammu and Kashmir. A Portrait of Population*. Srinagar: Government of India (Census of India 1971).

Index

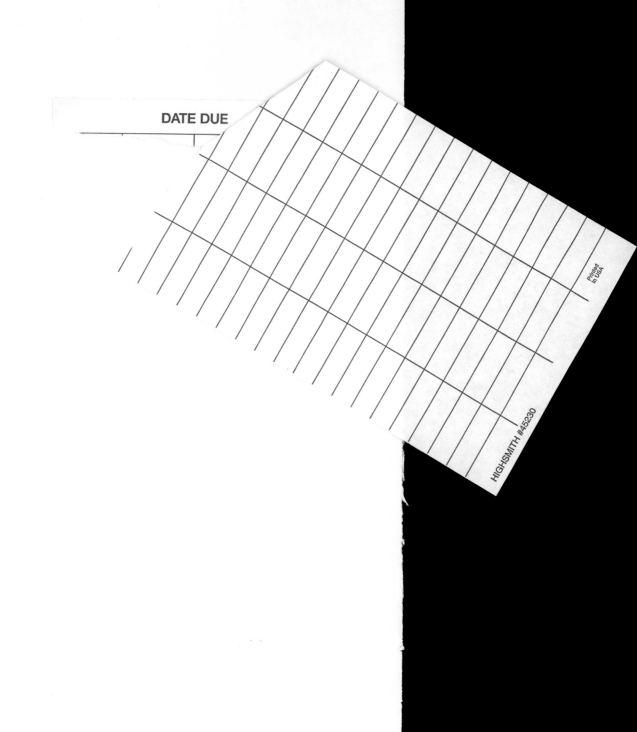